THE HOLOCAUST
AND MASCULINITIES

THE HOLOCAUST AND MASCULINITIES

CRITICAL INQUIRIES INTO THE PRESENCE AND ABSENCE OF MEN

Edited by

Björn Krondorfer and Ovidiu Creangă

Cover image: Adam Zivner, Chimneys of collapsed buildings in Auschwitz II Birkenau. (2009). Wikimedia Commons.

Support for this publication was provided by the Martin-Springer Institute, Northern Arizona University

Published by State University of New York Press, Albany

© 2020 State University of New York

All rights reserved

No part of this book may be used or reproduced in any manner whatsoever without written permission. No part of this book may be stored in a retrieval system or transmitted in any form or by any means including electronic, electrostatic, magnetic tape, mechanical, photocopying, recording, or otherwise without the prior permission in writing of the publisher.

For information, contact State University of New York Press, Albany, NY
www.sunypress.edu

Library of Congress Cataloging-in-Publication Data

Names: Krondorfer, Björn, 1959- editor. | Creangă, Ovidiu, 1976- editor. Title: The Holocaust and masculinities : critical inquiries into the
   presence and absence of men / Björn Krondorfer and Ovidiu Creangă.
  Description: Albany : State University of New York Press, [2020] | Includes
  bibliographical references and index.
Identifiers: LCCN 2019028960 | ISBN 9781438477794 (hardcover : alk. paper) |
   ISBN 9781438477787 (pbk. : alk. paper) | ISBN 9781438477800 (ebook)
  Subjects: LCSH: Masculinity—Congresses. | Holocaust, Jewish (1939-1945)—
   Psychological aspects—Congresses. | World War, 1939-1945—Psychological
   aspects—Congresses.
Classification: LCC BF692.5 .H646 2020 | DDC 940.53/180811—dc23
LC record available at https://lccn.loc.gov/2019028960

10 9 8 7 6 5 4 3 2 1

Contents

Acknowledgments   vii

Introduction   1
   Björn Krondorfer and Ovidiu Creangă

Part I: Genocide

1. Hiding in Plain View: Bringing Critical Men's Studies and Holocaust Studies into Conversation   17
   Björn Krondorfer

2. Masculinity and Death: De- and Resexualization in Nazi Concentration Camps   53
   Robert Sommer

3. The Experiences and Behavior of Male Holocaust Victims at Auschwitz   77
   Lisa Pine

4. "Higher Reasons for Sending People to Death?" Male Narrativity and Moral Dilemmas in Memoirs and Diaries of Jewish Doctors   99
   Monika Rice

5. *Muselmänner* in Nazi Concentration Camps: Thinking Masculinity at the Extremes   129
   Michael Becker and Dennis Bock

6. Tests of Manhood: Alcohol, Sexual Violence, and Killing
   in the Holocaust   147
   Edward B. Westermann

7. Catholic Seminarians and *Vernichtungskrieg*: How Nationalism,
   Religion, and Masculinity Mattered   171
   Lauren Faulkner Rossi

Part II: Aftermath

8. Contested Manhood: Autobiographical Reflections of
   German Protestant Theologians after World War II   203
   Benedikt Brunner

9. Post-Holocaust Conceptualizations of Masculinity in Austria   221
   Carson Phillips

10. Multiple Masculinities among German Jewish Refugees:
    A Transnational Comparison between Canada and
    Palestine/Israel   245
    Patrick Farges

11. Redemptive Masculinity: American Images of Jewish Men
    from the Holocaust to the Six-Day War   267
    Sarah Imhoff

Epilogue: The Holocaust and Masculinities   285
   Thomas Kühne

Contributors   305

Author Index   311

Subject Index   319

Acknowledgments

This volume, like many books, has multiple sources of inspiration. It started with an accidental meeting between Ovidiu Creangă and Björn Krondorfer at the archives of the United States Holocaust Memorial Museum, when Björn noticed someone else's pages on "masculinity in biblical studies" left at a photocopy machine. This "someone" turned out to be Ovidiu, and this is where and when our conversation started about the lack of awareness of masculinity studies in Holocaust history and historiography. In 2014, Björn presented this issue on a panel on gender at the international Holocaust conference Lessons and Legacies, after which we started in more serious ways to conceptualize the contours for this volume. In 2015, the Martin-Springer Institute, under Björn's directorship at Northern Arizona University, organized a three-day, international symposium on "Colonial Conquest in the Nazi East and the American West: Value and Limits of Comparative Approaches." This symposium included a panel on gender, and Ovidiu was one of the presenters. In 2016, the Martin-Springer Institute together with Misericordia University organized another three-day symposium, this time in Oxford, United Kingdom, on the theme "Thinking Critically about Masculinities in Mass Atrocity Crimes," which broadened the scope of inquiry. The contributions written for this volume will, we hope, deepen our understanding and widen the conversation on gender and the Holocaust. We thank the Martin-Springer Institute for its generous support for the printing of this volume, which made possible the simultaneous paperback and hardcover publication of *The Holocaust and Masculinities: Critical Inquiries into the Presence and Absence of Men*.

Introduction

BJÖRN KRONDORFER AND OVIDIU CREANGĂ

Masculinities are everywhere in history, but rarely does scholarship investigate critically the experiences of men as gendered beings in relation to the Holocaust. Beyond the more obvious observation that it is mostly men who were engaged as perpetrators in the killing fields, issues of masculinities—understood broadly to relate to male identity, identifications, roles, and relations—are consistently assumed rather than interrogated. Men were perpetrators, for sure, but they were also victims, survivors, bystanders, beneficiaries, accomplices, and enablers; they often negotiated multiple roles as fathers, spouses, community leaders, prisoners, soldiers, professionals, lovers, authority figures, resisters, chroniclers, or ideologues. This volume seeks to critically investigate men's variegated roles, behaviors, attitudes, conduct, and choices during the Holocaust. It will probe assumptions about masculinities and articulate the "male experience" as something obvious (the "everywhere" of masculinities) and yet invisible (the "nowhere" of masculinities).

The contributions to *The Holocaust and Masculinities: Critical Inquires into the Presence and Absence of Men* approach the history and legacy of the Holocaust through the varied experiences of men as gendered experiences. They aim to make visible experiences that pertain to the gendered character of male agency. Victimization, privilege, choice, accountability, authority, power, complicity, or culpability, when seen through the lens of gender, are some of the more obvious elements that help to explain and contextualize particular men's words, narratives, habits, deeds, behaviors, and conduct under conditions of extremity. We thus seek to reveal and engage conceptual links between the fields of Holocaust studies and critical masculinity studies, and we hope that the case studies presented here can fruitfully be applied to other genocidal situations.

Three Areas of Gender Investigations

In a 2017 forum, five historians of gender and the Holocaust discussed the current state of affairs of integrating the study of sexuality and gender into the history of Nazism and the Holocaust. Among the many important issues they raised, the panelists voiced their concerns that a gendered perspective on the Holocaust often implicitly refers to women and that masculinity still constitutes a "significant lacuna" in this field—and this despite an increased student interest on "including masculinity(ies) and men's experiences as well as more fluid and intersectional notions of identity in examinations of gender" (Forum 2017, 85, 92).[1] The observed scarcity of a critical men's studies inquiry regarding the history and legacy of the Holocaust might be all the more surprising when we consider briefly three areas of scholarship: first, research on women and the Holocaust; second, research on perpetrators of the Holocaust; and third, research on Jewish pre- and post-Holocaust masculinities.

First, regarding the scholarship on women and the Holocaust, after an embattled and difficult start in the mid-1980s and pioneered by scholars like Joan Ringelheim (on the Holocaust) and Claudia Koonz (on Nazism), it has grown exponentially over the last twenty-five years. It now includes the groundbreaking works by Dalia Ofer, Lenore Weitzman, Marion Kaplan, Atina Grossmann, Lilian Kremer, Zoë Waxman, Carol Rittner, Rochelle Saidel, Elisabeth Baer, Myrna Goldenberg, and Marlene Heinemann, to name but a few.[2] Despite the fact that book or chapter titles often reference "gender and the Holocaust," and despite the fact that gender historians understand, in principle, that gender necessitates the inclusion of the male gender, in almost all cases the focus in these works remains on women, with only a "perfunctory" and "limited" investigation of masculinity, as Maddy Carey argues in her recent book (2017, 5). As a result, the rich and productive research trajectory that prioritized women produced few studies of masculinity during the Holocaust.

This is understandable. Having to battle against an overwhelmingly male-dominated field and a scholarship that largely overlooked women's experiences, feminist historians needed to keep their focus on women, not men. Questions of men and masculinities were often dealt with under the rubric of power and privilege, which, of course, fittingly described Holocaust perpetrators as well as gender relations in Nazi Germany and beyond (as it also alerted the academic community to the disciplinary blindness regarding gender among male historians). As Jane Caplan points out, there is a "troubling relationship between power and masculinity, between absolute power and hypermasculinity" (2012, 86). Yet, the equation of Nazi masculinity and power cannot be projected onto all men (German or not). The study of the masculinities of Jews and other persecuted groups challenges the union of power/privilege with masculinity writ large. Furthermore, the linkage between masculinity and power that Caplan speaks about is in need of continued investigations within a broad geographical spectrum of social, institutional, and political practices. Recently, this research has been augmented with the theoretical insights of intersectionality and the analysis of asymmetrical power relations. Those tools allow scholars to understand gender relations within a web of overlapping and mutually reinforcing constituents (such as race, class, age, and disability); they also make visible other power relations, such as ordinary German women's power over East European laborers (Usborne 2017), LGBT and "queer interactions," or the (limited) range of agency of men in "subordinate or marginal" positions.[3] Such intersections are now essential to the study of Nazi masculinity and its assumed power.

Second, there is abundant scholarship on male perpetrators of the Holocaust, though the degree to which it proceeds with a critical and deliberate lens on masculinity studies varies widely. Klaus Theweleit's *Male Fantasies* (1989) and George Mosse's *The Image of Man* (1996) were pathbreaking in their time, but they focused less on the Holocaust and more on the interwar period with respect to national and *völkisch* ideologies, male eros, male bonding, and male respectability. Stephen Haynes asked in his article, "Ordinary Masculinity: Gender Analysis and Holocaust Scholarship," why the study of masculinity achieved so little "scholarly recognition in the interdiscipline of Holocaust studies" (2015, 167); he then proceeded with a select analysis of German male perpetrators. Lisa Pine (2017) traces the attributes of masculinity instilled by the Nazis in the *Wehrmacht* and the disciplinary mechanisms by which these behaviors were carefully enforced among combatants. The English translation of Thomas Kühne's work on World War II comradeship of German soldiers (2017) sheds important light on the emotional power of male bonding as an enabling factor in genocide. The linkage between masculinity and homosocial/homosexual bonding has also been applied to analyze Nazi paramilitary units such as the Stormtroopers (Wackerfuss 2015). These bonds may have constituted a kind of *Ersatzfamilie* (substitute family), as the title of Wackerfuss's book *Stormtrooper Families* implies. With the renewed focus on family history in Holocaust studies (both with regard to victims and perpetrators),[4] it is possible to reveal gender relations on the micro-level of everyday life, but this approach can also obfuscate issues of hegemonic masculinity, such as studies on fatherhood among the Nazi elites (Carney 2018).

The range of what it means to be a perpetrator has widened over time by looking beyond criminal culpability to various levels of complicity. The term "enablers," for example, is being evoked with more frequency, bringing into view (male) occupations—such as clergymen—that traditionally do not fall into the category of active perpetrators (or neutral bystander, for that matter).[5] Furthermore, feminist scholars have begun to pay attention to female perpetrators (Mailänder 2015; Lower 2013; Bock 2005; Harvey 2003; Schwarz 1997); and research is conducted on the impact of Nazism, fascism, and genocidal culpability on German men in the decades following the war and on changing conceptions of masculinity in postwar Germany (though the degree of integrating masculinity theory differs in these works; see, e.g., Linke 1999; Jerome 2001; Herzog 2005; Kellenbach 2013). In sum, research on perpetrator history continues to benefit from a sustained application of gender theory.

Third, when looking at scholarship on Jewish masculinities, we would assume that the topic of the Holocaust plays a significant role. Strikingly, though, it is absent or severely understudied in the relevant literature (e.g., Nur 2014; Schüler-Springorum 2014; Hakak 2012, 2016; Brod and Zevit 2010; Boyarin 1997; Peskowitz and Levitt 1997; Breines 1990). In these books, a similar pattern can be observed: Jewish masculinities are traced through the centuries, all the way up to the *maskilim*, Jewish Enlightenment, the *Wissenschaft des Judentums*, Nordaus's turn-of-the-century *Muskeljudentum*, World War I, early Zionist ideals, and the pre-Holocaust antisemitic race and medical sciences targeting the Jewish body.[6] Yet, the years of the Holocaust are skipped. Studies take up again the thread of Jewish masculinities as they developed in fresh ways after 1945 in places like Israel, Europe, and America, or in film and popular culture. Jewish masculinities during the Holocaust, however, remain largely uninterrogated, and the term "Holocaust" is often missing in the index of these works. Even the important volume *Jewish Masculinities: German Jews, Gender, and History* (Baader, Gillerman, and Lerner 2012) fails to tackle the Holocaust period. Instead, this volume, as it progresses chronologically, jumps from the "Jewish strongman" Sigmund Breitbart in the 1920s in Poland to its last chapter on German Jewish masculinities among postwar refugees.

Similarly, books on the Jewish body, which include reflections on the Jewish male body, by and large skip the Holocaust (e.g., Gilman 1991; Biale 1992). Biale's book, which follows a chronological order, repeats the familiar pattern mentioned earlier: the second to last chapter addresses "Zionism as an Erotic Revolution" followed by the concluding chapter on American Jewish culture. The Holocaust period is absent. Jay Geller's *The Other Jewish Question* (2011) also ends just before the Holocaust. Geller traces anti-Jewish tropes of European discourse on the Jews and, in response, the Jewish counterdiscourses in the period between Rahel Levin Varnhagen's birth in 1771 and Walter Benjamin's death in 1940, exploring how fictitious discourses on Jews entangled them in the impossibility of freeing themselves from such misrepresentation. Geller's book concludes with Benjamin's suicide, just at the moment when antisemitic ideology reached its pinnacle of genocidal destructiveness during the Holocaust. Maddy Carey's *Jewish Masculinity in the Holocaust: Between Destruction and Construction* (2017) addresses this lacuna head on. Following an excellent theoretical survey on how masculinity theories can be applied to understanding the experiences of Jewish men in the Holocaust, Carey focuses her study on two periods: the collapse of civil life for Jews in Nazi occupied countries (deconstruction) and their subsequent ghettoization (enclosure).[7] Her careful research comes to the counterintuitive conclusion that Jewish men went through a devastating crisis of their masculine identity in the early years but recovered their masculine identities in the enclosure period—in the ghettos—despite the objectively harsher and deadlier environment.

Given these three areas, it is evident that more work needs to be done at the interstices of Holocaust studies and critical masculinity studies.[8] Such work must accomplish more than merely mentioning a man, or men, as the topic of study. To do so without investigating masculinity would reinforce a normative presence that, at times, actually renders men—and the power structures in which they are embedded—invisible. As coeditors of this volume, we received a number of contributions that fell into this category: men were the topic of research (e.g., letters written by German soldiers from the front), but no attempt was made to think conceptually or theoretically of what the materials actually tell about masculinities. Would they shed light, for example, on the dynamics of male bonding, on patterns of male-male conduct, on narrative erasures, on instances of emasculation, on conflicting "masculine" expectations, or on power relations? When we asked those levels of analysis to be added, several authors withdrew their chapters.

Rather than treating maleness as a "powerful normalizer," to paraphrase Doris Bergen (Forum 2017, 80), a critical approach tries to reveal—rather than "re-veil"—the many ways male agency operates and functions under extreme conditions.

What to Expect from This Book

The articulations of masculinity explored in this volume are those of Jewish victims of National Socialism, Nazi soldiers, Catholic priests enlisted in the *Wehrmacht*, Jewish doctors in the ghettos, men from the *Sonderkommando* in Auschwitz, and *Muselmänner* in the camps. Also included in the present study on masculinities are men in the postwar context: German Protestant theologians, Jewish refugees, representations and self-presentations of non-Jewish Austrian men, and Jewish masculinities in the United States. By necessity, this volume is more exemplary than comprehensive. It signals pathways that we deem helpful for continued research in this area.

The volume follows roughly a chronological trajectory, interweaving variegated experiences of men during and after the Holocaust, taking us from the narrow confines of the camps and ghettos (part 1, Genocide) to the wider perspectives of new postwar realities, where conceptions of masculinities were shaped by those years of genocidal madness (part 2, Aftermath). The geography of these gendered expressions and interactions includes death and labor camps, ghettos, and the killing fields, but also Allied internment centers for Jews emigrating from Germany, settlements (*kibbutzim*) in Palestine/Israel, and *Burschenschaften* in Austria. The constructs of male gender are gleaned from a variety of sources: textual documents (such as archival materials and memoirs), oral testimonies and interviews, and visual documentation.

The volume opens with Krondorfer's chapter, in which he builds a case for why attention must be paid to the experiences of men as "gendered" experiences with regard to the Holocaust, and how to proceed critically when gender norms render men *as* men invisible. After illustrating the accomplishments of earlier scholarship with the help of select case studies, his chapter introduces two mechanisms of analysis: the concepts of "non-absence" as a way to deconstruct forms of hegemonic masculinity of perpetrators, and of "double non-absence" as a way to approach the subordinate and marginal masculinities of Jewish men in the Holocaust.

Robert Sommer's chapter on masculinity, sexuality, and death in the Nazi camps provides a gendered reading of the sexual encounters taking place between prisoners entrapped in a world of death and despair. Though the denial of the right to sexual activity was part of the individual's destruction in the camps, available documentation also shows that prisoners resisted their dehumanization and emasculation in this way. They actually engaged in sex, even if mostly through "situational homosexual sex" and occasionally "situational heterosexuality." Sexual activity in the camps was instrumentalized and economized, but on a rare occasion mutual love complemented sexual relations among prisoners. Sommer's focus on the gendered experiences and implications of male sexuality includes the camp brothels.

Lisa Pine's chapter on male Holocaust victims in Auschwitz tackles the ways in which male gender norms and expectations (as well as deviations from such norms) colored the behavior and emotions of Auschwitz prisoners, including those of the *Sonderkommando*. While some of the features she identifies as "male" are found also among women survivors, Pine argues that Jewish camp inmates faced challenges particular to their male identities to which they responded with a desire to remain strong (or at least project strength), to seek survival at all cost, and to suppress feelings of fear, sadness, and abandonment. Though their narratives comport to traditional gender norms by routinely stressing the work these men had to do in order to survive while downplaying companionship outside of familial ties, anguish over the fading of their masculinity observed in the deterioration of their body and mind is also present in their recollections.

Monika Rice analyzes self-writings by Jewish doctors in ghettos that reveal aspects of male gender identities. Drawing insights from the field of autobiography studies, she illustrates differences between men's and women's writings. Male doctors, for example, tended to emphasize an autonomous individual who strives to overcome difficulties, while female doctors were more concerned with forming relationships with their patients.

For all discernible differences, Rice is aware that written testimonies and memories are, like gender, fluid and, at times, can undercut established literary markers of gender identity.

Michael Becker and Dennis Bock's chapter on *Muselmänner* shows that gendering is part of the prisoners' internal camp society. Inmates in Nazi concentration camps—even as they themselves underwent a process of emasculation at the hands of their captors—established the parameters of their restrictive environment with the help of the most vulnerable: the *Muselmänner*. They came to represent all that the rest of the male prisoners resented for fear of becoming—physically and mentally too weak to wish to survive—and hence to maintain a trace of manliness. If the *Muselmann* was perceived as the most unmanly of men, the camp functionaries occupied the other end of the gender hierarchy within the camp: as privileged prisoners they embodied a subform of hegemonic masculinity among the prisoners. Becker and Bock argue that the role of *Muselmänner* contributed to the maintenance of the social and economic gender hierarchy within the camp.

Shifting to Nazi perpetrators, Edward Westermann delves into the little-studied relationship between masculinity, alcohol, and violence during the Holocaust. He shows how the Nazi glorification of martial masculinity was tied to alcohol consumption, and how alcohol played an important role not only in cementing intricate homosocial relations among perpetrators but also in lubricating the Nazis' genocidal machinery. Alcohol made those men feel invincible; it also caused actions that contravened Nazi ideology, such as having sex with or sexually assaulting non-Aryan women, particularly during operations in the East. Underneath the façade of camaraderie, alcohol (ab)use also indicates that these men needed alcohol to enhance their sense of a militarized masculine identity and to assist in their performance of an "ideal" Nazi soldier.

Lauren Faulkner Rossi addresses another form of German masculinity, namely, that of German Catholic seminarians in the *Wehrmacht* (German army). She argues that the priests' masculinity, in conjunction with their Catholic faith and German nationalism, explains their presence in the armed forces. Fear of being shamed and dishonored was likely a factor in the overwhelming acceptance of going to war. Other factors had to do with their strong conviction that, as soldiers, they could defeat the "satanic forces" of Bolshevism. Rossi argues that Catholic seminarians in uniform were not simply mouthpieces of Nazi propaganda; because they harvested the benefits of Nazi ideology, which invested Aryan men with the creation of a new history, their sense of masculine identity became complicit in the hegemonic and criminal ideals of their time.

German Protestant theologians are the subjects of Benedikt Brunner's chapter, which opens part 2. He samples postwar autobiographies written by Protestant theologians that were published between 1959 and 1977. Far from being innocent recollections of the past, these autobiographies are shaped by the war and its aftermath while also mirroring fundamental changes that occurred in postwar Germany. Examining the language with which these theologians described the troubled relationships between church and state during the Nazi regime, Brunner observes a decidedly martial vocabulary that harks back to the militaristic attitude prevalent among Protestant churches and theologians in the 1930s. Traditional gender roles remained intact in their postwar autobiographies, with men positioned at the helm of history and women appearing in supportive roles.

How representations of masculinity intersect with national identity is the question that Carson Phillips pursues in his chapter on post-Holocaust Austrian masculinities. The nation's mythologized retelling of Austria as "the first victim of Nazism" (despite Austria's widespread welcome of the 1938 *Anschluss* with Germany) shaped some of the emerging post-1945 ideals of masculinity. Phillips focuses on five versions of masculinity and their loci of expression: the "cultured gentleman," the subcultural strand of male student fraternities (*Burschenschaften*), the new ideal of social inclusiveness represented by Austria's soccer players; and a novel masculinity emerging in the late 1980s and 1990s in the form of introspective memory workers. The latter were young men choosing to do their service years not in the military but to assist Holocaust survivors and become active Holocaust educators.

With Patrick Farges's contribution, the volume returns to Jewish masculinities in the form of German Jewish refugees in Canada and Palestine/Israel after 1933. With the rise of Nazism, waves of Jews were forced to migrate from Germany and its immediate neighbors, scattering around the world where they became known as *Yekkes* (German-speaking Jews). These refugee men had to negotiate new and challenging social and economic circumstances, which affected their perceptions of male identity and male gender norms. Farges shows how in two different national settings, Canada and Israel, the gender expectations of these German Jewish men were deeply upset, inhibiting the ways in which these middle-class, educated men (*Bildungsbürger*) performed their masculinity. In Canada, they felt marginalized, partly because they were unable to recreate a safe space of "little Jewish Germanies"; in Israel, they encountered the new Zionist ideal of a disciplined, agile, and muscular masculinity, which many of the urban German-Jewish *Bildungsbürger* were unwilling or unable to accept.

Sarah Imhoff's chapter on redemptive masculinity looks at how images of Jewish men were absorbed by the American public between the end of the Holocaust and the Six-Day War in 1967. What started with the perception of "a tragic Jewish masculinity" (the image of Jewish men emaciated by hunger, dressed in rags, and huddled together in an undifferentiated mass), flipped to its opposite twenty-two years later during the Six-Day War. Jewish men were now seen as strong, confident, armed, and ready to defend the land of Israel. Imhoff excavates the literary articulations that brought about this transformation. "Redemptive masculinity," she argues, explains why the post-1967 image of strong Jewish men resonated so powerfully in America, because it reflected America's own story of overcoming adversity through hard work, sacrifice, courage, and optimism.

The volume concludes with Thomas Kühne's epilogue, in which he deepens the conceptual and theoretical framing that a critical masculinity studies approach offers to our understanding of the Holocaust. Emphasizing the notion of gender as a relational category of power, he affirms the importance of investigating the "unmarked" maleness within gender dynamics and recommends utilizing sociological and poststructural thinking about masculinity. He illustrates the advantages of such an inclusive approach with regard to German soldiers and perpetrators as well as Jewish victims of the Holocaust. Subsequently, he discusses the contested and changing nature of masculine norms and ideals.

Developing cogent frameworks for inserting critical masculinity approaches into the study of the Holocaust and its aftermath is crucial if we want to go deeper into the mechanisms of genocide (e.g., Pergher and Roseman 2013) and men's resilience when faced with extreme conditions. The present volume moves us forward in this direction.

Notes

1. The forum was held at the 2016 German Studies Association, and proceedings were subsequently published in *German History* (Forum 2017). The panelists were Anna Hájková, Elissa Mailänder, Doris Bergen, Atina Grossman, and Patrick Farges (the latter also represented in this volume).

2. Ringelheim (1990); Koonz (1987); Bridenthal, Grossmann, and Kaplan (1984); Heinemann (1986); Ofer and Weitzman (1998); Kremer (1999); Baer and Goldenberg (2003); Hedgepeth and Saidel (2010); Rittner and Roth (2012); Waxman (2017).

3. These points were raised by Mailänder and Farges (Forum 2017, 97, 92, 82).

4. For example, Gilbert (2017); for an article that registers gendered communication patterns in family archives, see Saraga (2014).

5. Doris Bergen, for example, frequently uses the term "enablers" to describe clergy, military chaplains, German Christians, and other religious groups connected to Nazism and the Holocaust. The "enablers," she writes, "invoke and perform gender to navigate extreme circumstances, justify and cover up violence, and shift blame" (Forum 2017, 80). See also her 2018 public presentation, "Neighbors, Killers, Enablers, Witnesses: The Many Roles of Mennonites in the Holocaust" (https://anabaptisthistorians.org/2018/03/17/mennonites-and-the-holocaust-neighbors-killers-enablers-witnesses), accessed August 14, 2018. In her earlier work on the German Christian Movement (1996) and her textbook *War and Genocide* (2013), Bergen uses the term "enablers" rather sparingly. On the complicity of male clergy, see also Rossi's and Brunner's contributions to this volume.

6. On Jewish masculinity in Germany, see Zwicker (2011, esp. chapter 5) and Swartout (2003), who researched Jewish men in dueling fraternities, and Caplan's work (2003) on Jews in the German military from Imperial Germany to the First World War.

7. Her study deliberately does not include the concentration camps.

8. When this volume was completed and under review by State University of New York Press, the journal *Central European History* came out with a special issue on masculinity and the Third Reich (Kühne 2018); it can be consulted as an additional resource on the themes addressed in our volume.

References

Baader, Benjamin Maria, Sharon Gillerman, and Paul Lerner, eds. 2012. *Jewish Masculinities: German Jews, Gender, and History*. Bloomington: Indiana University Press.

Baer, Elisabeth, and Myrna Goldenberg, eds. 2003. *Experience and Expression: Women, the Nazis and the Holocaust*. Detroit: Wayne State University Press.

Bergen, Doris. 1996. *Twisted Cross: The German Christian Movement in the Third Reich*. Chapel Hill: University of North Carolina Press.

———. 2013. *War and Genocide: A Concise History of the Holocaust*. Lanham: Rowman & Littlefield.

Biale, David. 1992. *Eros and the Jews: From Biblical Israel to Contemporary America*. New York: Basic Books.
Bock, Gisela, ed. 2005. *Genozid und Geschlecht: Jüdische Frauen im nationalsozialistischen Lagersystem*. Frankfurt: Campus.
Boyarin, Daniel. 1997. *Unheroic Conduct: The Rise of Heterosexuality and the Invention of the Jewish Man*. Berkeley: University of California Press.
Breines, Paul. 1990. *Tough Jews: Political Fantasies and the Moral Dilemma of American Jewry*. New York: Basic Books.
Bridenthal, Renate, Atina Grossmann, and Marian Kaplan, eds. 1984. *When Biology Became Destiny: Women in Weimar and Nazi Germany*. New York: Monthly Review Press.
Brod, Harry, and R. Shawn Israel Zevit, eds. 2010. *Brother Keepers: New Perspectives on Jewish Masculinity*. Harriman, TN: Men's Studies Press.
Caplan, Gregory. 2003. "Germanising the Jewish Male: Military Masculinity as the Last Stage of Acculturation." In *Towards Normality? Acculturation and Modern German Jewry*, ed. Rainer Liedtke and David Rechter, 159–184. Tübingen: Mohr Siebeck.
Caplan, Jane. 2012. "Gender and the Concentration Camps." In *Concentration Camps in Nazi Germany: The New Histories*, ed. Jane Caplan and Nikolaus Wachsmann, 82–107. New York: Routledge.
Carey, Maddy. 2017. *Jewish Masculinities in the Holocaust: Between Destruction and Construction*. London: Bloomsbury Academic.
Carney, Amy. 2018. *Marriage and Fatherhood in the Nazi SS*. Toronto: University of Toronto Press.
Koonz, Claudia. 1987. *Mothers in the Fatherland: Women, the Family, and Nazi Politics*. New York: St. Martin's Press.
Forum: Holocaust and the History of Gender and Sexuality. 2017. With panelists Anna Hájková, Elissa Mailänder, Doris Bergen, Atina Grossman, and Patrick Farges. *German History* 36, no. 1: 78–100.
Geller, Jay. 2011. *The Other Jewish Question: Identifying the Jew and Making Sense of Modernity*. New York: Fordham University Press.
Gilbert, Shirli. 2017. *From Things Lost: Forgotten Letters and the Legacy of the Holocaust*. Detroit: Wayne State University Press.
Gilman, Sander. 1991. *The Jew's Body*. New York: Routledge.
Hakak, Yohai. 2012. *Young Men in Israeli Haredi Education: The Scholars' Enclave in Unrest*. Leiden: Brill.
———. 2016. *Haredi Masculinities between the Yeshiva, the Army, Work, and Politics*. Leiden: Brill.
Harvey, Elizabeth. 2003. *Women and the Nazi East: Agents and Witnesses of Germanization*. New Haven: Yale University Press.
Haynes, Stephen R. 2015. "Ordinary Masculinity: Gender Analysis and Holocaust Scholarship." In *Genocide and Gender in the Twentieth Century: A Com-*

parative Survey, edited by Amy E. Randall, 165–188. London: Bloomsbury Academic.

Hedgepeth, Sonja, and Rochelle Saidel, eds. 2010. *Sexual Violence against Jewish Women during the Holocaust*. Hanover: University Press of New England.

Heinemann, Marlene E. 1986. *Gender and Destiny: Women Writers and the Holocaust*. Westport, CT: Greenwood Press.

Herzog, Dagmar. 2005. *Sex after Fascism: Memory and Morality in Twentieth-Century Germany*. Princeton: Princeton University Press.

Jerome, Roy, ed. 2001. *Conceptions of Postwar German Masculinity*. Albany: State University of New York Press.

Kellenbach, Katharina von. 2013. *The Mark of Cain: Guilt and Denial in the Post-War Lives of Nazi Perpetrators*. Oxford: Oxford University Press.

Kremer, Lillian S. 1999. *Women's Holocaust Writing: Memory and Imagination*. Lincoln: University of Nebraska Press.

Kühne, Thomas. 2017. *The Rise and Fall of Comradeship: Hitler's Soldiers, Male Bonding and Mass Violence in the Twentieth Century*. Cambridge: Cambridge University Press.

———, ed. 2018. "Special Issue: Masculinity and the Third Reich." *Central European History* 51, no. 3: 335–522.

Linke, Uli. 1999. *German Bodies: Race and Representation after Hitler*. New York: Routledge.

Lower, Wendy. 2013. *Hitler's Furies: German Women in the Nazi Killing Fields*. Boston: Houghton Mifflin.

Mailänder, Elissa. 2015. *Female SS Guards and Workaday Violence: The Majdanek Concentration Camp, 1942–1944*. East Lansing: Michigan State University Press.

Mosse, George. 1996. *The Image of Man: The Creation of Modern Masculinity*. New York: Oxford University Press.

Nur, Ofer Nordheimer. 2014. *Eros and Tragedy: Jewish Male Fantasies and the Masculine Revolution of Zionism*. Boston: Academic Studies Press.

Ofer, Dalia, and Lenore Weitzman, eds. 1998. *Women in the Holocaust*. New Haven: Yale University Press.

Pergher, Roberta, and Mark Roseman. 2013. "The Holocaust—an Imperial Genocide?" *Dapim: Studies on the Holocaust* 27, no. 1: 42–49.

Peskowitz, Miriam, and Laura Levitt, eds. 1997. *Judaism since Gender*. New York: Routledge.

Pine, Lisa. 2017. *Hitler's "National Community": Society and Culture in Nazi Germany*, 2nd ed. London: Bloomsbury Academic.

Ringelheim, Joan. 1990. "Thoughts about Women and the Holocaust." In *Thinking the Unthinkable: Meanings of the Holocaust*, edited by Roger Gottlieb, 141–149. New York: Paulist Press.

Rittner, Carol, and John Roth, eds. 2012. *Rape: Weapon of War and Genocide*. St. Paul: Paragon House.

Saraga, Esther. 2014. "Personal Letters—to Keep: Managing the Emotions of Forced Migration." *Jewish Culture and History* 15, nos. 1–2: 27–42.
Schüler-Springorum, Stefanie. 2014. *Geschlecht und Differenz*. Paderborn: Ferdinand Schöningh.
Schwarz, Gudrun. 1997. *Eine Frau an seiner Seite: Ehefrauen in der "SS-Sippengemeinschaft."* Hamburg: Hamburger Edition.
Swartout, Lisa. 2003. "Segregation or Integration? Honour and Manliness in Jewish Duelling Fraternities." In *Towards Normality? Acculturation and Modern German Jewry*, edited by Rainer Liedtke and David Rechter, 185–200. Tübingen: Mohr Siebeck.
Theweleit, Klaus. 1989. *Male Fantasies*, 2 vols. Minneapolis: University of Minnesota Press.
Usborne, Cornelie. 2017. "Female Sexual Desire and Male Honor: German Women's Illicit Love Affairs with Prisoners of War during the Second World War." *Journal of the History of Sexuality* 26, no. 3 (September): 454–488.
Wackerfuss, Andrew. 2015. *Stormtrooper Families: Homosexuality and Community in the Early Nazi Movement*. New York: Harrington Park Press.
Waxman, Zoë. 2017. *Women in the Holocaust: A Feminist History*. Oxford: Oxford University Press.
Zwicker, Lisa Fetheringill. 2011. *Dueling Students: Conflict, Masculinity, and Politics in German Universities, 1890–1914*. Ann Arbor: University of Michigan Press.

PART I
GENOCIDE

Chapter 1

Hiding in Plain View
Bringing Critical Men's Studies and
Holocaust Studies into Conversation

Björn Krondorfer

"I don't understand: what is specifically male about these testimonies?" a colleague with a research expertise in women and the Holocaust asked when I presented two textual excerpts for Arizona teachers during an advanced Holocaust education seminar. "I just don't see how they say anything particular about men," she insisted. "It could very well be a general human reaction." Her skepticism augmented the uncertainty among the attending educators who were unaccustomed to a critical reading of Holocaust testimonies through the lens of gender. Yet they were willing to explore the gendered implications in the select excerpts from a Jewish ghetto policeman and a Nazi German perpetrator.[1] In our discussion we oscillated between perceiving these excerpts as just "normal" texts with no gender implications and our not so clearly articulated presumptions about men and masculinity.

The sincere and persistent questioning of my colleague, wondering aloud how these male-authored testimonies would tell us anything about men, their experiences, or their narrative strategies, led to a kind of litmus test: Could we have predicted the authors' gender accurately in a blind review? Since the two testimonial excerpts lacked more obvious "essentially masculine" features (such as hardness, stoicism, bravery, violent behavior), what made them gender-specific? Missing ostentatious male markers, there was, perhaps, not much to discover, and attempting to analyze them through a consciously male-gendered lens would be a curiosity at best—but ultimately irrelevant. What the Jewish ghetto policeman and the German perpetrator wrote about the Holocaust—and how they wrote about it—did not seem to say much about their identities, behavior, identifications, or roles as *men*.

But what if it was not the absence of male markers that puzzled my colleague but our inability to recognize the omnipresence of maleness? Normative operations of maleness might be so present in the testimonies that they render their gendered character structurally invisible. If maleness is hiding in plain view, "a gendered study of men," as Maddy Carey aptly put it, "requires more skilful gymnastics of reason" (2017, 2). How then could we find a path toward greater visibility? For the Arizona educators in this seminar, the case I made was only half-convincing, and I too began wondering whether we were chasing shadows. Were we looking for something ephemeral, thus absconding the stable ground of studying the political, ideological, and genocidal core of the Holocaust? Were we just frolicking in the shadows of the Shoah?

The image of "chasing shadows" invites another take. Could we, perhaps, compare the study of masculinities during the Holocaust to the chasing of shadows insofar as the object of inquiry disappears the moment we shine light on it? Does masculinity escape our firm grasp like a shadow that bends, grows, shrinks, and vanishes depending on the direction and source of light? Is masculinity a slippery category because we cannot get hold of it apart from contrasting it with something else? Can we advance beyond the statement that "men are what women are not"?[2]

This chapter is, in some ways, a response to my colleague's skepticism about the usefulness of studying the Holocaust through a male-gendered lens. The omnipresence of a male reality might blind us to the tangible presence of "maleness" in history and its documentation—for the weight of history and historiography confirms a skeptic's doubt about the validity of a men's studies approach. This chapter explores what seems to be "hiding in plain view," namely, that which we have accepted as regulative male norms, habits, practices, narratives, and interpretations.

Arguing with the Critics

The reticence I encountered among the educators is not an uncommon response. The self-set task of telescoping on men in their gendered subjectivity as our object of scholarly inquiry in the context of the Holocaust raises concerns regarding the validity of such an undertaking. At the core of these concerns is the question of what, if anything, can be learned when applying a consciously gendered approach to the historical, social, and political realities of genocide.

Is the purpose of such a venture to contribute to a better understanding of the Holocaust? In this case, a specific male-gendered lens might compartmentalize and trivialize the murderous Nazi policies that engulfed whole populations, because, so a critic might say, history has been subjected to narrow disciplinary interests. The study of genocidal antisemitism might thus fall prey to an ideological agenda. Critics of gender studies have claimed that the lens of gender distorts the historical realities that led to the full-scale annihilation of a people declared undesirable regardless of their gender—men, women, and children.[3]

What, however, if the purpose of this study is not so much about improving our knowledge of the Holocaust as getting a good grasp on the nature of masculinity? In this case, we might end up stereotyping male behavior by zooming in on a political and behavioral context of extreme circumstances, merely reconfirming what we already believe to be true about men: that they are prone to aggression and (sexualized) violence. Masculinity scholars might wonder if the extreme circumstances of genocide would not reduce the realities of men to facile assumptions.

Then there is the concern whether a focus on masculinity studies would remasculinize an already male-dominated field plowed by Holocaust historians, thus undermining the achievements of feminist scholarship. In this case, gender scholars might judge the blending of masculinity and Holocaust studies a politically precarious project because it would reassert, through the backdoor, a domineering male perspective.

Passionate flare-ups over the study of gender in relation to the Holocaust have, in the past, primarily focused on women and the Holocaust. An oft-quoted example regarding a general critique of gender studies is Gabriel Schoenfeld's polemic attack against feminist Holocaust scholarship. "Between the Scylla of an academicized 'Holocaustology' and the Charybdis of a universalized victimology," Schoenfeld wrote in 1998 in the neoconservative Jewish magazine *Commentary*, "the worst excesses of all on today's campuses are being committed . . . by the voguish hybrid known as gender studies." The magazine's senior editor lamented the "ideological" agenda of "consciousness-raising" that "target[s] the male sex."[4] Joan Ringelheim, a pioneer in the study of women's experiences during the Holocaust, also recalls harsh criticism launched against her research, in her case by Jewish American novelist Cynthia Ozick. "You are asking a *morally* wrong question," Ozick charged, for it would lead "down the road of eradicating Jews from history." For Ozick, to differentiate between Jewish men and women meant an erasure of their Jewishness. "Your project is, in my view, an ambitious falsehood," Ozick argued. "The Holocaust happened to victims who were not seen as men, women, or children, but as Jews" (qtd. in Ringelheim 1990, 144). In such equations, studying the nexus of genocide and gender is seen as unproductive, and a gender-differentiated analysis is perceived as a threat to the interpretation of the Holocaust as a unifying experience of a people. More recently, historian Annette Timm recalls a conversation she had with her male adviser when working on her PhD in Berlin in the 1990s. At that time, the adviser dismissed any research on "the rape of German women by invading Soviet soldiers" as a marginal topic "unworthy of serious historical investigation" (Timm 2017, 351). Those critics, no doubt, would express similar consternation today if they encountered a critical men's studies perspective on the Holocaust.

Though feminist scholarship has received the brunt of criticism, caustic remarks and sweeping claims regarding the study of masculinities in the Holocaust can be found, perhaps ironically, among gender and feminist studies scholars, where a men's studies perspective has not always received an easy welcome. Rather than being considered an enrichment to the research on women in the Holocaust, anecdotal evidence points to the puzzlement that such an approach elicits. Haynes, for example, recalls the reactions of a panel on women's voices in the Holocaust at a 1997 academic conference when he asked whether their work might open "the way for a consideration of men's experiences in the Holocaust." Not intending his question to be polemic, the responses he received "indicated that they regarded my question as a threat, as one more in a series of male attempts to silence or marginalize their voices" (2015, 166). At other times, scholars who have advanced our understanding of women's experiences in the Holocaust have made sweeping claims about masculinity, stating, for example, that the Nazi camps were the "ultimate expression of the extreme masculinity and misogyny that undergirded Nazi ideology," which was ruled by "the perverted patriarchal bureaucracy" of "one of the most women-hating regimes of the modern world."[5] Though it is beyond dispute that the violence in the camps was extreme, the administration of genocidal practices perverted, and the regime's misogynist policies controlling women's bodies and lives repulsive, to lay blame mono-causally—at least on a rhetorical level—on masculinity leaves little room to explore men's lived experiences. It explains little, for example, about layers of complicity; it cannot account for the discrepancies between ideals of militarized masculinity and the lives of real men who became accomplices and beneficiaries; it does not distinguish between ideologically trained, elite Nazi units who, by and large, truly believed in their genocidal mission and ordinary men undergoing the "soldiering" process by which they became "what military institutions desire and in which they acquire certain martial characteristics through exposure to and repetition of particular practices and skills" (Krondorfer and Westermann 2017, 19).

Objections raised against a gender studies approach are often more subtle than blatant. As regards women's experiences, Holocaust historians have vacillated on the validity of investigating gender differences. While, for example, some have argued that experiences were frequently based on "situational accident" rather than a "gender-driven choice" (Langer 1998, 362), others, like Raul Hilberg and Yehuda Bauer, have recognized the importance of gendered approaches even when they themselves did not pursue them forcefully and consistently.[6] Likewise, though with inverse focus, feminist scholarship has recognized the importance of an inclusive understanding of gender but frequently consigns the subject of masculinity to marginal comments and footnotes; or it carries "gender" in the title of publications but proceeds exclusively with women's history without further explanation.[7] Other scholars have developed a fine sensitivity to men's experiences while their work remains concentrated on women. Lenore Weitzman and Dalia Ofer, for example, are concerned about too narrow a view on women's experiences (such as sexuality and motherhood), because it "marginalizes women and, ironically reinforces the male experience as the 'master narrative.'" It is important, they continue, "to pay attention to the particularity of gendered wounding that both sexes experienced" (Weitzman and Ofer 1998, 16).

A purposeful critical men's studies approach (e.g., Connell and Messerschmidt 2005; Krondorfer 2009; Hearn 1997; Hearn and Collinson 1994) provides incentives to investigate the ways in which men negotiate their various roles or the choices they make during times of pressure, scarcity, threats, and opportunities. While, on the one hand, a critical men's studies approach exposes the violent nature of hardened male perpetrators, it equally invites a more nuanced analysis of male agency in the gray zone, whether it pertains to degrees of culpable wrongdoing or compromised options of survival in ghettos, hiding places, and the camps. With a few exceptions, the majority of scholars, whether in the male-dominated field of Holocaust history or feminist scholarship, has sidestepped the analysis of men as gendered beings. As Carey put it in the context of Jewish men (though her analysis can be applied more widely), previous research resulted in a "highly problematic, minimal history of Jewish masculinity during the Holocaust" (2017, 5).

As the scholarly landscape is gradually changing, gender is now often understood in relational and intersectional terms in which it is investigated as an experience of women *and* men across levels of complicity, age, class, location, sexualities, and racialized identities. What needs to be carried forward is the importance of addressing power and privilege of men in modern nation-states that operate within a more or less enduring patriarchal social order; at the same time, it is important to enrich such analysis with the granularity of male experiences on micro- and meso-social levels as well as with an awareness of the conceptual obstacles that leave normative assumptions untouched. I believe that we are at a place well poised to probe further and more deeply the implications of a critical men's studies approach to the Holocaust and—insofar as it intersects with Nazi ideology and the German war effort—to Nazism and the Second World War.

Select Examples

A few examples from earlier publications will illustrate the kind of insights related to men and masculinities that can be teased out of available materials and documents. Those examples show what scholarship has accomplished so far, and how and why it will benefit from widening its scope and refining its conceptual and theoretical frames.

The Myth of the Solitary Male Fighter

For a while, it was assumed that male Holocaust survivors fought mostly for themselves in the camps while women formed relational bonds in order to survive. Given a social context that valorized independence as a manly virtue, it is not surprising that many male testimonies credit a solitary struggle and independent decision-making as their reasons for survival. Ironically, external expectations and self-perceptions of male independence might have affected men adversely in the camps: in a situation where all subjectivity was destroyed, not to let go of the ego was a death sentence (Goldenberg 1990; also Van Alphen 1997, 49–50). Regarding male testimonies, we could thus content ourselves with Lillian Kremer's observation that "in male Holocaust writing, interdependence is exceptional rather than commonplace" (1999, 18). Alternatively, we can adopt Lisa Pine's interpretive suggestion that "male [survivor] memoirs tend to underplay bonds and relationships" (2008, 132). In the latter case, the lack of recounting instances of male bonding in the homosocial environment of labor and death camps is not taken as factual evidence of men's emotional reality. Rather, it is seen as a result of employing certain narrative strategies and "discursive construction[s]" of the past (Pine 2008, 123). Because male survivors rarely talk about close male companionships in their testimonies does not mean that these relations did not exist. The concept of "narrative erasure" can serve here as a helpful reminder that testimonies are not only valuable for the factual information they contain but also for what is not being said and for the less obvious elements of "emotionality, stress and omissions, and narrativity" (Hájková 2017, 79).

Instances of male friendship are actually reported in male testimonies, most famously in Primo Levi's 1947 *If This Is Man*.[8] Levi credits his friendships with the Italian civilian worker Lorenzo and French prisoners Charles and Arthur for surviving the camp. "Lorenzo was a man; his humanity was pure and uncontaminated. . . . Thanks to Lorenzo, I managed not to forget that I myself was a man" (Levi 1993, 122). Anna Reading comments on the "relational sense of masculinity" that is visible in Levi's friendship with Lorenzo, and how this contributed to his "return to a sense of manhood [that] began with acts of kindness, not revenge" (2002, 72); Valerio Ferme suggests that the "actual warmth" among Charles, Arthur, and Levi led to a "pervasive thawing of human relationships among them" (2001, 68); and Lisa Pine concludes that examples like this show that "social bonding [also] applied to male relationships" (2008, 132).

To form male friendships or, to the contrary, remain apprehensive of male companionship may have been individual choices. Similarly, to reflect on these friendships or to disavow such companionship in later writings are also individual choices. Such individual multiplicity does not leave us, however, stuck in the morass of useless subjectivity. Rather, as Carey helpfully suggests, we need to look at the "gender that [men] practised [as] a product of the interplay between normative masculinities and the individual elements of gender identity that each man sustained" (2017, 48). Normative masculinity informs but does not predetermine individual men's choices. The example of male bonding among victims, then, illustrates two things: first, a critical men's studies approach must be alert to instances that confirm *and* contradict assumptions about masculinity; second, it must be willing to suggest interpretive possibilities that can shed light on what is being said and what is not said in male testimonies, memoirs, and other documents.

Bodily Markers

A second example illustrating the gender specificity of male victims concerns their outward appearance and bodily markers, such as hair and traditional clothing. Though such external features were less a concern for assimilated Jewish men in Western Europe, they were a matter of life and death in the Nazi occupied East. "Beards, sidelocks, and traditional garb made orthodox Jewish men identifiable as such, and they were subjected to abuse because of them" (Pine 2008, 123). Circumcision, which differentiated almost all Jewish men from their non-Jewish male peers in Europe, rendered them particularly vulnerable if they were suspected of hiding their Jewish identity. In memoirs and scholarship, observations about outward appearances are often taken matter-of-factly without further investigating the impact they had on individual men and male social collectives such as the *Judenräte* (Jewish Councils). Carey reports on Jewish men in the ghettos losing interest in their "physical appearance, hygiene and dress" (2017, 115) and how the men themselves addressed this issue. Although women mention men's lack of self-care more frequently (and also disapprovingly), when men talk about it, they describe the crumbling of their masculinity with an air of self-deprecating sadness and a touch of tragic irony. "Hesitant, almost fearful, the hand feels the restless body, finds bones, ribs, finds limbs," writes Oskar Rosenfeld from within the Łódź Ghetto, "and discovers the self, suddenly becoming aware that not so long ago one was fatter, meatier . . ." (qtd. in Carey 2017, 114).

It is difficult to second-guess how men internally processed the decline of their external appearance; hence, a critical men's studies approach is tasked to find innovative, multidisciplinary approaches that enable entry into the interiority of men's lives in response to external threats. Moving beyond the surface of textual testimonies, a critical men's studies approach can seek to integrate studies of psychology and of visual and material culture. It can also consult more richly documented cases of men acting and surviving in other situations of extreme duress in order to shed light, in a comparative fashion, on the Holocaust (e.g., Ferrales, Brehm, and Mcelrath 2016).

Everyday Routines

A third example illustrates the problem of how to make sense of the everyday routine under conditions of extremity. Natalia Aleksiun has provided a fine-tuned gender analysis of Jewish men and women in hiding in Eastern Galicia. The granularity of everyday life in crowded bunkers speaks through the men's and women's voices. Far from upending the gender order, these conditions frequently kept people within traditional gender roles and divisions of labor. "Daily life in hiding," Aleksiun writes, "reveals continuity with prewar patterns . . . with Jewish men and women exercising traditional social and familiar roles." The problem for scholars reporting on "familiar practices of food preparation and personal hygiene" is that one might inadvertently end up "'normaliz[ing]' lives in hiding during the Holocaust," thus effacing the larger genocidal context with its constant lethal threats (Aleksiun 2014, 53). For a critical men's studies approach, however, the seeming mundaneness of everyday life under duress might be a welcome antidote to the unintended yet more popular tragic and (anti)heroic tropes of male survival stories. Many men enduring the hardship of merciless persecution did not or could not escape their habits, leaning on learned behaviors and roles into which they had been socialized.

Dismantling Historiographic Assumptions

A fourth example concerns historiography. Carey provides a compelling example of how scholars can fall into the trap of repeating certain gender assumptions that, over time, take on an air of facticity and unquestioned truth. Her example is of historians citing the story of fathers in the ghettos who stole food from their children while mothers purportedly gave up their portions for the children. This story is then used as evidence for arguing that victimized men lost their masculine identity as traditional providers under the dire circumstances of the Holocaust. Carey identifies two problems with this case: First, on the interpretive level, hungry fathers taking food from their starving children might actually not prove the "erosion of a man's gender identity" but reconfirm an "active display of masculinity"—in accordance with a tradition where it was understood that the head of a household would get more and better food (Carey 2017, 5). Second, on the level of sources, scholars using this example for assessing gender differences rely mostly on the testimony of one prominent text, *The Diary of Dawid Sierakowiak* (1996). In this diary written in the Łódź Ghetto, seventeen-year-old Dawid had some harsh words to say about his father. On one occasion he accused him of stealing food from him and his sibling. Carey comments disapprovingly that "this and other similar quotations have been used by historians to support their representation of Jewish fathers and men in the Holocaust" (2017, 130). Ignored are other parts of the diary where Dawid, for example, acknowledges sympathetically his father's role as protector of and provider for the family, portraying the father-son relation in more nuanced and complex ways. A critical men's studies approach, in line with Carey's observation, must examine the historiographic representation of men in the Holocaust and examine previous scholarly views on gender differences on the grounds of their own gendered blind spots that drive those judgments.

Sexual(ized) Violence

A fifth example moves the discussion to male perpetrators. There is an abundance of literature on male perpetrators simply because most perpetrators during the Holocaust were men. Studying perpetrators, one could argue, is a study of men;[9] yet, the gender of those men is in most cases assumed rather than interrogated.[10] Though serious historical and social studies shy away from concluding that because most perpetrators are men, most men are perpetrators, the linkage of violence and masculinity is commonly examined through the impact it has on victims, particularly as it concerns the grave issue of sexual(ized) violence against women.[11] From the perspective of a victim of sexual(ized) violence, it might matter little to learn why men commit these crimes; and in light of the persistent insufficiency of resources to assist with the physical, mental, and moral repair of victims of sexual assault, it can be a reasonable ethical stance to demur at comprehending these male behaviors.[12] A critical men's studies perspective, however, cannot shy away from the gendered implications *for men* regarding the perpetration of sexual violence.

Binary Constructions

Another example concerns binary constructions of masculinity and femininity. Klaus Theweleit (1989), a German literary scholar, was an early pioneer in applying the study of masculinity to fascist dynamics preceding the Holocaust. He analyzed both the writings of German *Freikorps* soldiers returning from World War I and the visual culture in the interwar period. Arguing that ideals of a hard, steely, and tough masculinity were promulgated and intensified during this period, he juxtaposed them to the supposed feminine values of tenderness, compassion, and domesticity. Although the *Freikorps* predate the Holocaust, their masculinity was seen as preparing "the way in Germany to a misogynist brutalization of politics and the rise of the Nazi state and eventually the Holocaust" (Kühne 2017, 22).[13] That Germany was not alone in shaping fascist and militarized ideals of masculinity during the interwar period has been pointed out, for example, in comparative studies with Italy (Ponzio 2015; Salvante 2015) and the United States (Jarvis 2010).

Theweleit's binary construction of gender (hard men / soft women), with its concomitant assumption about men's suppressed emotionality, has been adopted as an explanatory guide for reading documents pertaining to perpetrators.[14] Indeed, such binary language can easily be identified in ego documents by perpetrators during the war as well as during their postwar trials and other postwar writings: "We were Germany's best and hardest" (SS veteran and former camp guard); "We men of the new Germany have to be very tough with ourselves" (police unit leader); "Gentlemen, if there is ever a generation after us so cowardly, so soft, that it would not understand our work as good and necessary, then, gentlemen, National Socialism will have been for nothing" (Nazi guard from Belzec at his trial). All three statements are quoted as epigraphs in Haynes's chapter on "Ordinary Masculinity" (2015), where he traces the paradigm of hardness and toughness in the accounts of the Auschwitz commandant Rudolph Höss and select midlevel perpetrators from the SS and mobile killing units (on hardness, see also Werner 2008; Klee et al. 1991). Haynes also points out that perpetrators, despite their ubiquitous rhetoric of hardness, do employ emotional language, though mostly reserved for ingroup identification with their own family, *Volk*, and nation.

A critical men's studies approach cannot remain arrested on the level of binary constructions but must probe the affective dimension buried within self-representations by male perpetrators—for it is there that we might find clues to whether certain emotions serve as lubricants for a genocidal mind-set and machinery.

Homosocial Bonding

Another example shifts the focus from individual motivations to the power of social bonding among men. Here we can point, for instance, to comradeship and alcohol consumption as two forms of social lubricants that kept men in line with the killing operations. Kühne's detailed study on comradeship shows how close emotional ties among fighting men—in this case German soldiers during World War II—relieved individual men from feeling guilt and moral responsibility. "Comradeship as the solidarity of a community of fate," Kühne writes, relied on a certain "moral grammar." Within a homosocial group, "anything was allowed that enriched and intensified social life" (2017, 291, 293), for these men had to cooperate with each other and depend on each other with their lives, regardless of personal likes and dislikes. Such dependency in an all-male social group, Kühne contends, could not have functioned if it had entirely renounced all feminine and emotional traits (contrary to Theweleit's binary model of masculinity). For comradeship to function, daily social interactions relied on "the display of femininely coded affection" among men, such as "tenderness, empathy, caring [and] periods of weakness" (Kühne 2017, 292).

Part of such comradely bonding was shared alcohol consumption, in regular army units and even more so among those directly involved in the killings such as camp guards, *Einsatzgruppen* (mobile killings units), and police battalions. Though it is generally known that intoxication and acts of violence (including sexual violence and mass atrocities) are connected, the role of alcohol in the Holocaust has only recently been studied. In his article "Stone-Cold Killers or Drunk with Murder?," Edward Westermann writes that "for Himmler, alcohol . . . was to be used not as an inebriant, but rather as a means for social bonding . . . as a place for camaraderie rather than debauchery" (2016, 3). If comradeship and alcohol facilitated processes by which male perpetrators could proceed with their killing operations, it is prudent not to mistake them as explanations in and of themselves. "Was alcohol used as a facilitator, creating a psychological disinhibition so that their perpetrators could pull their triggers?" Westermann wonders. "Or, was alcohol an incentive to kill? [Or did it] serve as a mechanism for relief of stress, or a means of social bonding among the killers?" A critical men's studies approach asks these kinds of questions as it tries to make sense of the violent practices of men and changing ideals of masculinities.

Gender Consciousness

A last example returns to historiographic concerns. In his study of ordinary masculinity, Haynes points to a lack of gender analysis in Holocaust scholarship.[15] Looking at two seminal texts on German perpetrators that were widely debated in the 1990s, he asks whether Daniel Goldhagen's work on *Ordinary Germans* (1996) and Christopher Browning's work on *Ordinary Men* (1992) have taken gender seriously when trying to understand German perpetrators. Although Browning's phrase "ordinary men," which he applied to the men of the Reserve Police Battalion 101 that committed mass atrocities in the East, suggests awareness of gender as a factor that influenced these men's moral decision-making (or lack thereof), Haynes contends that both Browning and Goldhagen fail to take gender sufficiently into account. Both scholars prefer situational and environmental factors over gender as "key[s] to understanding these ordinary perpetrators." By doing so, they tacitly assume that "the dynamics of masculinity possess no explanatory value for interpreting the behavior of Holocaust perpetrators" (Haynes 2015, 182–183). Haynes concludes his critical survey with an additional challenge. To recognize the "gendered character of male experience[s]," he writes, is not merely a matter of gender theory but of "gender consciousness." Gender consciousness is more than a question of "style, methodology, or advocacy"; rather, it is "a kind of vision developed by interpreters of history" and "a way of seeing that emerges as men and women engage in conversation" (183).

Non-Absence

Haynes's plea for adopting a conscious male-gendered approach as a new "way of seeing" aligns well with the observation that men and masculinities are so omnipresent in the history of the Holocaust and in our scholarship about the Holocaust that we remain in the thralls of a normative perspective that resists to be read as "male." The disinclination to read documents, testimonies, texts, material evidence, court trials, or previous historical interpretations as products of male expressions and experiences is also a reluctance to think critically about the significance such materials may hold for men. By extension, it is also a reluctance to ask how deeply we are invested in describing reality in gender-neutral terms when, in fact, this reality is shaped on micro-, meso-, and macro-levels by male agency. Developing some "kind of vision" (Haynes 2015, 183) or "skilful gymnastics of reason" (Carey 2017, 2) is important if we want to break with an interpretive tradition that posits male perpetrators, accomplices, bystanders, enablers, survivors, or victims as *accidentally* male. In its stead, we need to create new pathways that grasp men's genderedness more exhaustively.

One such conceptual pathway is to think about masculinity as a "non-absence." It is a concept that assists in the task of rendering visible an unmarked experience of what is considered normative. Part of the difficulty of making men's experiences intelligible as gendered experiences is related to the linkage of dominance and normativity that regulates privileges of social groups. Like all privileged positions, dominant masculinity in a given cultural and historical moment is so overwhelmingly present as a normative force that it becomes invisible and unproblematic to those who inhabit such a position. Normative masculinity is ubiquitous (i.e., it is present and visible everywhere) and, at the same time, is taken for granted and not subject to inquiry, and thus absent and invisible. The unsettled dynamic of presence/absence can, for example, explain why scholars are able to acknowledge that most Holocaust perpetrators were men while nevertheless proceeding as if this fact does not matter much. We see the men, but then forget to see them *as* men. If this sounds like a paradox, it is. It points to the difficulty of grasping and rendering intelligible the genderedness of men's activities, motivations, choices, behaviors, agency, bodies, roles, and feelings without essentializing any of these attributes.

Todd Reeser states in his introduction to *Masculinities in Theory* that masculinity is unmarked (2010, 8–9); precisely because it is unmarked men do not see themselves *as* men, and scholarship also neglects to see men *as* men. Borrowing a phrase by Roland Barthes, we can call this "a significant absence" (1967, 77). Holocaust historian Jane Caplan notes in a study on Nazi concentration camps that "the unmarked male ostensibly escapes gender altogether" (2010, 84). In a slightly different context, Elizabeth Heineman (2002) refers to "the doubly unspeakable" when trying to analyze the impact of sex and sexuality with regard to mostly male perpetrators. Haynes put the issue of invisibility in the following terms: "if women have been obscured from scholarly view by being relegated to the background of the Western imagination, men have been distorted by being thrust into the foreground" (2015, 167). The unmarkedness of dominant men in the context of the Holocaust is similar to what critical whiteness studies have identified as the privilege of white masculinity. It is the privilege of inhabiting unmarked bodies, as Donna Haraway points out, and this, in turn, maintains the fiction of a disembodied, coherent, and "rational self of universal species of man" (1991, 210). "As long as white people are not racially seen and named," Richard Dyer adds, "they/we function as a human norm" (2017, 1). The very notion of invisibility thus becomes "a necessary condition for the perpetuation of white and male dominance, both in representation and in the realm of the social" (Robinson 2000, 1).[16] Applied to dominant forms of masculinity in the Holocaust—especially with respect to perpetrators—the unmarked gender is an absence that needs our attention.

Elsewhere I have called this normativity-induced invisibility—in both the source materials and the scholarship—the *non-absence* of men (Krondorfer 2010a, 74–99). Non-absence refers to the observation that male-gendered experiences are hegemonic and yet remain unmarked. Male agency and the male body (the body as the most intimate site of inscriptions of masculinity) are always *in* our sources and texts about or from men, but they are *not present* as a consciously gendered experience. The concept of non-absence, then, signals that there is no awareness of that which is present—and so that which is omnipresent does not get articulated with deliberate intent. With respect to the body, a non-absent male body is man's obliviousness toward his gendered body's materiality; with respect to agency, a non-absent agency is a man's obliviousness of his position of power and of his ability to assert a "self" in the public sphere.[17] The concept of non-absence also accounts for the blindness toward the textual and social transformations of the male self and body into law, social institutions, normative discourse, cultural customs, personal habits, artistic expressions, and so forth.

The difficulty with the concept of non-absence, or the "unmarked," is that the sources will not explicitly mention men *as* men and do not reflect in any deliberate and obvious ways on masculinity. The documentary materials, testimonies, and self-writing that we possess do not, with a few exceptions, explicitly mention masculinity or account for their gender bias—because their gender is assumed to be standard and normative. Since men, as Sarah Imhoff writes in a different context, "likely never thought of themselves as writing about gender" (2013, 157), the interpreter needs to apply an imaginative (though not imaginary) reading. It is a reading behind and between the lines, a discursive analysis that makes sense of the silences and omissions that, if left unrecognized, continue to maintain and enforce the unmarked disposition of masculinity.[18]

In ego documents written by Nazi perpetrators, non-absence can play out in different ways. It is frequently at work when shirking responsibility for culpable wrongdoing. A telltale sign of such operations is the use of passive voice constructions. For example Rudolph Höss, the commandant of Auschwitz, writes in a last letter to his wife in April 1947, shortly before he is executed:

> Without realizing it, I had become a cog in the terrible German extermination machine. My activities in performing my task were out in the open. Since I was the Kommandant of the extermination camp Auschwitz, I was totally responsible for everything that happened there, whether I knew about it or not. . . . My dear good Mutz [his wife], I beg you, don't become hardened . . . [and] start the proceedings to change your name. Take back your maiden name again. . . . And so my actions in the service of this ideology were completely wrong, even though I faithfully believed the idea was correct. . . . I have found again my faith in my God. . . . And so there is only a pile of rubble left from our world from which the survivors have to build a new and better world with great difficulty. (Höss 1996, 190–192)

This passage, filled with contradictions and allusions, is a good example of how a perpetrator vacillates between presence and absence in order to assert his former male authority while dampening his culpability and moral responsibility at the moment his former dominance had vanished. "I was totally responsible," Höss writes, but he may not have "known about it." When pleading with his wife for changing her last name, he takes on the role of protector while inadvertently revealing his fear of retribution (thus implicitly acknowledging guilt). The ideology he served, Höss admits, was "completely wrong," yet he "faithfully believed the idea." As someone who had turned his back to Catholicism during his Nazi career, he found new "faith in God" while lingering in prison. He envisions a future in which "the survivors" would build a "new world"; but the survivors he has in mind are not the surviving Jews but postwar Germans who must rise from the "rubble left of our world."

Similar ambiguity is contained in several passages in Höss's autobiographical recollection written while awaiting his trial in a Polish prison. Recounting times when he was present at the gas chambers, he writes: "I had to appear cold and heartless during these events which tear the heart apart in anyone who had any kind of human feelings. I couldn't even turn away when deep human emotion rose within me. Coldly I had to stand and watch as the mothers went into the gas chambers with their laughing or crying children" (1996, 162). Passages like these raise the question of sincerity. Does Höss admit those feelings only retrospectively in the hope for clemency?[19] They also raise questions for the interpreter regarding binary theories of masculinity that fixate on the external ideals of an anti-emotional male hardness with no room for the complexity of men's interior emotional life. Whatever we think of the juxtaposition of Höss's external coldness and his internal heart torn apart, the concept of non-absence alerts us to these discrepancies. Here is a man who knows enough about himself and enough about the situation into which he speaks that he allows some cracks to appear in the soldierly masculinity he once performed. Did he rediscover in prison what he had always felt but had to repress (a heart torn apart)? Or is he an outright liar (because he has always been heartless)? Is the psyche of a male perpetrator just hopelessly self-delusional? A critical men's studies approach navigates between dissecting narrative strategies used by perpetrators for ulterior motives and examining the emotionality hidden in narrative structures that might tell us about their drives and motivations.

In Oswald Pohl's writing we can detect similar dynamics. As the head of the Main Office for Economic Administration, Pohl was in charge of handling all economic aspects of the Nazi concentration camp system. While in Allied prisons, he writes a personal account in the form of a religious confession. Like Höss, he testifies to his newfound love of God (both men wrote their accounts while receiving pastoral care in prison).[20] Like Höss, Pohl admits partial responsibility while simultaneously eschewing culpability. "Many things did not remain hidden from me, even if I personally did not take part in them. . . . I had never beaten anyone to death, nor did I encourage others to do so . . . I energetically opposed [any] inhumanities, provided I learned about them" (Pohl 1950, 40, 43). Pohl thickly applies religious language in his writing, explicitly hoping for clemency (he is executed by the Americans in 1951). "The moment of transformation filled me with an ardent love," he writes. "It is love that counts. Indeed, love is the essence and main objective of Christianity: the true love for God and our neighbors" (57–58). During his steep Nazi career a few years earlier, such a statement would have been ridiculed by his peers and judged as (male) weakness. Now in prison and robbed of his dominant masculinity, Pohl wants clemency but is afraid of being seen as dwelling in "feminine" religious sentimentality. Hence, he casts his newfound masculinity in martial language. It was the "totalitarian claim" of Christ's teaching (19) and the "authoritative leadership of the Catholic Church" (60), he writes, that moved him to reconvert to Christianity. Pohl has not become a soft man. Only the paradigms for what he considered strong masculinity changed—from a nationalist to a religious-clerical framework. Pohl thus continues to assert normative masculinity, even after having lost the virulent masculinity of a Nazi leader.

That Pohl's proclaimed love of God and neighbors is disingenuous rhetoric is revealed in documents outside his published confessional writing. In a 1948 letter to a friend, he writes:

> I was fifty-four years old, had served unimpeachably my fatherland for thirty-three years, and was [regarding my person] not aware of any crimes. . . . [The American prosecution] lacked any objectivity. . . . Driven by blind hate and plain vindictiveness, the goal of the prosecution, which was dominated by Jewish representatives, was not to determine truth but to annihilate as many adversaries as possible. (Qtd. in Koch 1988, 156, 158)

This is a different postwar side of Pohl: positioning himself in the role of a subordinate masculinity in hope of clemency, he takes recourse to the antisemitic stereotype of Jewish world domination.

The examples of Pohl and Höss demonstrate the fluid nature of tropes of masculinity that men in positions of dominance use in describing themselves during times of political transition. Their texts are devoid neither of emotionality nor of narrative manipulation. Their writings also tell us about the malleability of hegemonic masculinity as it tries to reassert itself in an environment that forced these men to abdicate power. The discursive pattern is one of vacillation: expressions of self-exculpation (the passive voice construction suggests absence of male agency) mixed with claims to political or moral authority (the re-assertive voice suggests presence of male agency). Similar dynamics of making complicit male agency disappear (non-absent) can be observed in other postwar writings by men who associated with, benefited from, or enabled aspects of the Nazi regime. These currents remained alive well into the 1970s of German society until they were eventually replaced by new ideals of masculinity due to cultural changes and generational transitions.[21]

Doubly Non-Absent

The concept of non-absence—which indicates the ubiquitous presence of men and, simultaneously, their escape from our epistemological grasp—

applies to dominant and normative masculinities. In the context of the Holocaust this helps us to analyze those groups of men that were positioned somewhere on the spectrum of hegemonic and complicit masculinities, such as perpetrators, accomplices, collaborators, beneficiaries, enablers, or bystanders. A non-absent male agency, however, does not apply in the same way to subordinate and marginal masculinities. Men who live under oppression, exploitation, or the threat of annihilation are denied a subjectivity that dominant men can claim without having to "mark" it. Men in subordinate and marginal positions are to a great extent denied the presence of agency and self-representation when compared to men in power. Yet, with regard to gender relations in their own subjugated communities, they can claim positions of relative power and privilege. In other words, men in positions of a subordinate or marginal masculinity are still operating under the mechanism of non-absence vis-à-vis their own intracommunal relations (toward women, children, and other stratifications along the lines of gender, age, prosperity, sexualities, and disability), but are denied more assertive forms of manliness vis-à-vis dominant masculinity.

In order to account for this necessary differentiation, I suggest speaking of these men as "doubly non-absent." They are denied a presence and forced into absence in the public sphere by dominant power structures outside their communities, yet they retain certain male privileges within their own community along traditional norms that render them non-absent. In the context of the Holocaust, this differentiation helps us to analyze those groups of men that were positioned somewhere on the spectrum of marginal, subordinate, and resistant masculinities such as victims, *Muselmänner*, men in the gray zone, selfless caretakers, men attracted to or forced into compromised positions (like *Judenräte*), partisans, or resistance fighters.

Jewish masculinities in Europe during the pre-stages to the Holocaust can be, to some extent, analyzed with the concept of *non-absence* as long as the Jewish communities remained somewhat intact. Because Jews never occupied the status of hegemony in Europe, Jewish men in their respective countries struggled for visibility, respectability, and acceptance over against a normative and dominant masculinity that was often hostile to them. Within the larger sociopolitical environment, Jewish men occupied positions of subordinate masculinities. As such, Jewish men—like all men occupying subordinate masculinities in relations to power—were rendered visible in their "difference," albeit falsely. The difference constructed for and around them misperceived and misconstrued their reality. They inhabited "marked" bodies. In centuries of Christian Europe, Jewish men were seen as other, mostly—though not always—in negative terms. Yet, Jewish men could still assert authority and independence within their own communities and, to some extent, within the larger political environment that granted them (limited) access. Carey suggests speaking of an "independent Jewish masculinity" (2017, 46) to escape the binary model of a dominant versus subordinate masculinity.[22] This conceptual move allows her to analyze gender relations as they played out within the Jewish communities (wherein Jewish men could assume dominant positions), while not ignoring the coerciveness of male-to-male interactions within the hostile environment of Nazism and the Holocaust (wherein Jewish men were relegated to the humiliating positions of marginality and subordination).

With respect to Jewish masculinities during the Holocaust itself, the concept of non-absence needs to be augmented with the idea of becoming *doubly non-absent*. As practices of Jew-hatred shifted from religious anti-Judaism to bioracial antisemitism, perceptions of Jewish men took on threatening contours. Konnor (2009) lists dozen of terms by which Jewish men were described in bodily characteristics: bulging belly, bulbous protruding lips, hooked noses, repulsive, overbearing, lustful, rapacious, shriveled, repugnant, odious, greedy, smelly, and so on. We should not forget that much of Nazi propaganda, including the vicious magazine *Der Stürmer*, targeted mostly Jewish men in their caricatures and hateful depictions. Jewish men responding to these accusations got quickly entangled in defensive postures that did not help them inhabit a masculinity independent of what their antisemitic environment wanted it to be. Jewish men became doubly non-absent. They were "non-absent" in the sense that their maleness remained normative and thus unmarked within intracommunal Jewish gender relations; they were "doubly" non-absent insofar as Jewish men had to defend themselves against impositions of who they were supposed to be, thus having little chance of coming into their own on their own terms. Jewish men could embody and enact normative masculinity within their own community, but this norm would never become dominant in the larger (gentile) environment, which, in turn, not only misrepresented Jewish men but eventually sought to destroy them.

If modernity provided Jewish men some outlets to redefine themselves by assimilating and converting, it always happened within an antagonistic environment. It was a struggle to assert oneself against false images produced by dominant ideologies. Projecting and adopting a strong Jewish masculinity—be it through Nordau's *Muskeljudentum* (muscular

Judaism), Jewish fraternities, Jewish-German conscripts in World War I, or the rise of Zionism as part of the nexus of modern nationalism and masculinity—thus always articulated itself in defensive interaction with and against dominant forms of European masculinity.[23] By the time the Nazis implemented their plans to exterminate all Jews, they put an abrupt and brutal end to the multiple attempts at envisioning what it might mean to be a Jewish man in Europe since the *Haskalah*, the Jewish enlightenment. In the Holocaust, Jewish male agency and the Jewish male body were mercilessly assaulted, from social exclusion to intimate humiliation, from slave labor to murder, thus pushing the double non-absence of Jewish men to its limits. At the end of this road, there was the annihilation of the Jewish body—men and women.

The radical destruction of the Jewish community may elicit some ethical reticence to seeing the value of theorizing a double non-absence of Jewish men. Yet, this concept allows us to fine-tune our analysis. For example, Carey observes that Jewish men had little to say about their bodies during the initial phase of discrimination and social exclusion during Nazism, so much so that "the historian must necessarily write from an *absence of sources*" (2017, 74; emphasis added). This "contrast[s] sharply," Carey writes, "with the period of destruction that followed, in which Jewish men wrote more *openly about their bodies*" (74; emphasis added). The concept of a non-absence/double non-absence may help to interpret this difference. Whereas non-absence can be applied to the early phase of Nazism when Jewish men's adoption to modern masculinity still operated within a general framework of seeming normality (albeit a harsh one), a double non-absence acknowledges the impact of the steadily growing coerciveness and brutality of the Holocaust. In the early phase, Jewish male agency was at stake (but not yet the body) through the loss of professional occupation, fear of social exclusion, and the tarnishing of honor and dignity—all markers of normative masculinities. Since Jewish bodies were not yet collectively assailed, there was little need for men to write about them. In the later period, however, when the Jewish male body came under sustained physical assault and was pushed by external forces into a double non-absence, the men themselves began to render their bodies visible as long as they had an opportunity to do so. They did so—perhaps deliberately, perhaps intuitively—as a kind of existential protest against and resistance to their vanishing.

Carey employs the phrase "doubly damned" to describe the situation of Jewish men before and during the Holocaust. The phrase alludes to men being targeted for reasons of race and gender. Carey follows here in the footsteps of Sander Gilman's observation that in Europe's "gendered imagery of antisemitic rhetoric" (Carey 2017, 6), "the Jew at the fin de siècle is [implicitly] the male Jew" (Gilman 1995, 21). As Jewish men (mostly in the assimilated West)[24] strove to obtain, but were repeatedly denied, modes of dominant masculinity, their bodies were constantly scrutinized and, when the Nazis came to power, physically assaulted. Ayşe Altinay and Andrea Pető, in their feminist theorizing of genocide, use the phrase "studying the silences within silences" in order to "delink gender and women" and render men visible, specifically male victims (2015, 380). When combining these two notions—antisemitic targeting of the Jewish male body / rendering male victims visible—we gain a tool to alert to instances of sexual violation of Jewish men during the Holocaust. Still a widely held taboo in survivor testimonies and scholarly literature, the sexually violated male body is a doubly non-absent body, for this body not only needs to survive the physical assault but is also silenced by communal norms.

Seeing the sexually violated male body as a doubly non-absent body can help to discern forms of resilience and resistance. Melvin Konner, in one of the rare stories of sexual assault on men, cites a case from Ephraim Oshry's *Responsa from the Holocaust* (Konner 2009, 105). A Jewish man's testicles had been deliberately crushed by a German policeman because he had tried to smuggle a crust of bread to his family. As a *kohein*, a descendant of the priestly class following ritual purity laws, this man worried that he could no longer be called to the Torah or have sexual relations with his wife. The consulted rabbi ruled that, indeed, he could no longer have sex with his wife but could still fully participate in the life of Torah. This ruling, made under the duress of extreme circumstances, acknowledged the loss of genital-biological manhood while restoring spiritual manhood. By validating the *kohein*'s Torah connection, a vital part of masculine identity for orthodox men remained safeguarded. Testicular assault, documented from the time of the Bible to the frontiers of modern genocide, always aims at a double target: it brutalizes individual men as it assault the social identity and symbolic potency of one's male enemy.[25] It requires individual repair and communal responses.

Examples like the rabbi's ruling in the case of the *kohein*'s physical and spiritual injury illustrate that the Jewish male body and Jewish male agency did not cease to exist during the years of genocidal persecution. As a Jewish man, one had specific burdens (such as the telltale mark of circumcision) and limited privileges (such as joining the Jewish ghetto police); Jewish men struggled to maintain their place in the traditional gender order of Jewish communities even in times of extreme circumstances by trying to assert their roles as provider and protector in the ghettos; Jewish boys came of age during the Holocaust, leaving their post-1945 gender identities, if they survived, burdened with trauma; Jewish men created temporary *Ersatzfamilien* (adopted families) after the loss of loved ones; Jewish men created caring male bonds as a means of survival in the camps; Jewish men succumbed to sexual pressure and bartering, as in the case of the so-called *pipels* or "toy boys" (Sommer 2014; Wallen 2014; Walter 2009); Jewish men were compromised by taking on privileged positions in the camp hierarchy or being forced into the *Sonderkommando*; Jewish men moved in and out of blemished forms of masculinity, such as hiding in latrines (Gastfriend 2000, 122–123) or becoming a *Muselmann* (Becker and Bock 2015).

The gendered implications of these and many other examples do not yet get the attention in Holocaust studies they deserve. Within limited spheres, constrained male agency could still be inhabited. Yet, we cannot lose sight of the fact that Jewish men suffered mounting restrictions to the point of social suffocation, and that the Jewish male body, like all Jewish bodies, was targeted for destruction. Literally, the male Jewish body was to disappear, making the body physically absent—and thus pushing the idea of the double non-absence of a subordinate masculinity to its ultimate racialized negative apotheosis: the annihilation of the body, and hence of Jewish masculinity.

I will conclude with a haunting story from the writing of Calel Perechodnik, a Jewish ghetto policeman in Poland. This is the story I used when introducing the issue of male gender to the Arizona educators mentioned at the opening of this chapter. The story illustrates how a double non-absence foreshadows Perechodnik's eventual physical disappearance but also how it diverts attention from his (moral) agency (Krondorfer 2010a, 74–99).

The night before the execution of Jews caught in an *Aktion* in the Otwock Ghetto, Perechodnik guards the condemned at the train station. Among them is a little girl who resembles Aluska, Perechodnik's young daughter who had already been deported to Treblinka during an earlier *Aktion*. As a ghetto policeman, he had been present at the train station when his daughter and wife were deported. In his diary, which he calls a deathbed confession, Perechodnik writes about the night with the nameless little girl:

> I took her from her mother . . . sat her on my knee, cuddled her, and thus we passed the night. When I heard that the [German] gendarmes were arriving, I understood that I had to part with her. My charge, whose name I did not know, cried loudly and did not want to be returned to her mother. She sensed that death awaited her on the other side of the screen. She tightened her arms around my neck, and I had to forcefully tear myself away. When I returned her to her mother, I felt as if I killed the child with my own hands.
>
> I hear her voice till today. My own thoughts as well: Is there a God? Is there a higher justice that rules this world? If so, why is it silent? (Perechodnik 1996, 74)

In this heartrending scene, the ghetto policeman comes across as a gentle father figure as well as an accomplice to the child's execution. The story unfolds in a manner that seems fated from the start. It sounds as if there were no choices. The unnamed girl would have to go down the same path as Perechodnik's daughter in the earlier deportation.

Choices, however, were made. Driven by the painful loss of Aluska, Perechodnik reaches out to comfort another young girl the night before her transport to death. Like other parents in the ghettos who lost their children, he "adopts" and cares for another child—if only for one night. It is a deeply emotional gesture of a grieving father in response to a child in need of comfort.

Easily overlooked in this bitter scene are the more ambiguous aspects of Perechodnik's choices. Implicit normative assumptions render him simultaneously present and absent in the narrative flow of his recollection: a non-absent body and a non-absent agency. We have to remind ourselves that Perechodnik presents himself in this passage as physically present when he comforts the child. He actively seeks her out and cuddles her. But his agency disappears the moment he abandons the girl in the morning, and he abruptly switches to a passive voice: "I understood that I had to part with her." When Perechodnik returns the girl to her mother, he leaves his "fatherly" body behind as he reassumes the duty of a policeman. In other words, he actively inhabits his body when portraying himself as protector, but he disavows his agency the moment the German gendarmes arrive. The failure to act as a protector at this very moment produces later a guilt-ridden chronicler of the event. In his retrospectively created narrative, Perechodnik abruptly shifts blame to external forces:

God and justice. He asks: Why is God silent? He does not ask: Why did I remain silent?

This narrative operation veils a discomforting thought: Did Perechodnik ask the mother for permission to comfort the girl? The terse phrase "I took her from her mother" hides layers of possible meanings. Did the mother consent? Did she want to let go of her child on this last night? Was she relieved that someone took care of her daughter? Did Perechodnik (mis)use his authority as a ghetto policeman to take the girl away against the mother's wish? We do not know the answer. But we might wonder how this event would have been narrated if the mother's voice had been preserved. We can imagine a whole other layer of pain and desperation.[26]

All we have is Perechodnik's document. It is told from a perspective in which certain moral ambiguities disappear from sight because male agency and authority—as limited as they had been in the ghetto—remain invisible in their non-absence. Perechodnik neglects to see the child's mother; or, in any case, he neglects to tell us about her. In his own words, he is a grieving father who believes he gives comfort to a deserving child. In the eyes of the mother, however, he is a ghetto policeman who can take a child away for the night. In the eyes of the German police, Perechodnik is dispensable, is vermin, is doubly non-absent. In our readers' response, we might empathize with this Jewish man. We feel his desperation and hopelessness because we already know that he too will eventually disappear in the Holocaust. The seductiveness of his surviving text makes us want to believe him; and with him, we tend to forget the mother.

The double non-absence is a twofold direction. Intracommunally, Perechodnik's male position of authority within his own Jewish environment remains obscured and his normative voice seduces us to overlook certain gender dynamics. Outside of that community (intercommunally), this Jewish man is of no importance in the eyes of the German power-holders, his body already slated for death.

Outlook

Given what we know about the Holocaust, we might feel some reluctance toward theorizing the gendered dimensions and implications of male agency among perpetrators, victims, accomplices, bystanders, enablers, beneficiaries, resisters, soldiers, community leaders, fathers, professionals, and the myriad other roles men inhabited during those years. By not engaging these issues, however, we are missing out on what the Holocaust meant for men *as* men, and by extension, on understanding better the linkages between masculinities and genocide in general.

Notes

1. Two brief passages were selected from Calel Perechodnik's *Am I a Murderer?* (1996) and Rudolph Höss's *Death Dealer* (1996). The educators were given the following five questions to guide them through a gendered analysis: 1. Talk about and mark those places you consider to be male experiences; 2. Talk about and mark those place you consider to signal *implicit* male perspectives; 3. Name the emotional quality of the text excerpts; 4. Mark the text where, in your view, it contains normative gender assumptions; 5. Discuss whether narrative strategies are employed that make it a male-gendered text.

2. Michael Kimmel, for example, states that being a man means above all "not being like a woman" and that male identity is defined in contradistinction to femininity (1994, 130–131).

3. See also Weitzman and Ofer's "Introduction: The Role of Gender in the Holocaust," where they list and discuss reasons why there is "resistance to research gender in the Holocaust" (1998, 12–16).

4. Schoenfeld (1998, 42–46); for a response to Schoenfeld, see Horowitz (2001).

5. This quote by Myrna Goldenberg (1990, 163) does not diminish her otherwise formidable scholarship on women and the Holocaust (2016; Goldenberg and Shapiro 2013; Baer and Goldenberg 2003).

6. "The Final Solution was intended by its creators to ensure the annihilation of Jews," Hilberg writes. "Yet the road to annihilation was marked by events that specifically affected men as men and women as women" (1993, 126). Bauer echoes this sentiment: "The problems facing women as women and men as men," he states, "have a special poignancy in an extreme situation such as the Holocaust" (2001, 167). Sara R. Horowitz recalls a conference on women and the Holocaust where Bauer "conceded that while a study on women would be valid, it would be of 'secondary importance'" (2000, 181). On Hilberg and Bauer, see also Lisa Pine (2008).

7. Nicole Ephgrave's "On Women's Bodies" (2016), for example, laments the indifference to "gender and sexual differences" (13) in Holocaust scholarship but relegates the issue of male gender to a short endnote: "While my focus . . . is on the experience of women, an in-depth study of themes derived from men's testimonies and on the subject of masculinity is also an important, and largely under researched, area of Holocaust study" (28). Joyce Marie Mushaben's "Memory and the Holocaust: Processing the Past through a Gendered Lens," to name

another example, criticizes Holocaust studies for its "theoretical frameworks defined by men," but then continues with biographies of women perpetrators without questioning the unspoken equation of gender and women (2004, 149).

8. Originally published in Italy as *Se questo è un uomo*, it appeared in the United States under the title *Survival in Auschwitz*.

9. More recently, a number of studies appeared on women as perpetrators in the Holocaust. For references, see this volume's introduction.

10. Of the many examples that could be cited here, two articles shall suffice: Wolfgang Seibel, "The Strength of Perpetrators—The Holocaust in Western Europe, 1940–1944" (2002) and Michael Mann's "Were the Perpetrators of Genocide 'Ordinary Men' or 'Real Nazis'?" (2000). Both focus on the strength and characteristics of Holocaust perpetrators (such as class, origin, and numbers), but their male gender is assumed rather than investigated. The 2018 study on *Perpetrators and Perpetration of Mass Violence* by Williams and Buckley-Zistel offers a comprehensive list of micro-level studies on perpetrators, especially also in the field of Holocaust studies (2018, 2–5), but with no gender awareness at all. In the introduction, the editors consistently speaks of the perpetrators as "people," and the index shows only one entry for "masculinity" among the eleven chapters.

11. On the question of how to integrate sexual violence into the history writing of the Holocaust, see the brief overview of Timm (2017). On sexual crimes by German male perpetrators, see Mühlhäuser (2014), which contains an extensive reference list on sexual violence against women in the Holocaust; see also Bos (2014); Goldenberg (2013); Rittner and Roth (2012); Mühlhäuser (2010); Hedgepeth and Saidel (2010); Herzog (2009).

12. For how and why victims and perpetrators perceive sexual crimes and culpable wrongdoing differently, see Claudia Card's feminist-philosophical discussion of the magnitude gap: "Perpetrators are likely to underestimate the harm [they inflicted], whereas victims are likely to exaggerate the reprehensibility of the perpetrators' motives" (2002, 9–10).

13. Kühne, who summarizes here the impact Theweleit had on understanding perpetrator masculinity, does not embrace Theweleit uncritically but joins other historians arguing for a more nuanced analysis of his "general theory of masculinity" (Kühne 2017, 22). Theweleit's description of male resentment festering in German culture during the interwar period can be understood as a particularly vile blending of modern nation-building and the rise of new forms of masculinity. Andersen and Wendt write: "The period between the early nineteenth century and World War II is of particular significance for an analysis of these complexities because it saw the simultaneous emergence of new forms of masculinity as well as the emergence of modern nation-states," a period during which "exclusionary ideologies such as scientific racism, imperialism, and eugenics became part and parcel of the gendered nation-building processes" (2015, 2); see also Mosse (1990, 1996).

14. See, for example, Johann Chapoutot, who writes in his chapter "Fascist Virility": "Fascism and Nazism promise to avert the weakness of flesh of hardening the body.... From 1922 in Italy, then after 1933 in Germany, virility is constructed by a series of sharp, blunt oppositions: man is not woman, the Aryan is not Jew, hard is not soft . . ." (2016, 501, 492). Following a similar binary pattern is Sombart's critique of Carl Schmitt (Sombart 1991).

15. Haynes first published the article "Ordinary Masculinity: Gender Analysis and Holocaust Scholarship" in 2002 in the *Journal of Men's Studies* (10, no. 2 [Winter]); it was republished in Amy Randall's *Genocide and Gender in the Twentieth Century* (2015). All quotes in this chapter refer to the 2015 publication.

16. In this quote, Robinson summarizes what she perceives as the core of theories on masculinity and whiteness. In *Marked Men: White Masculinity in Crisis* (2000), she actually challenges some of these assumptions about invisibility. See also Frankenberg (1993) and Roediger (1994).

17. To assert oneself into the public sphere requires a person to see oneself as a "subject," as a person with subjectivity, entitlement, agency, and power, which traditionally was a position occupied by men. See Krondorfer (2010a, 1–33).

18. Among historians, there might be a discipline-specific reluctance to a more imaginative discursive analysis of normative masculinity. Yet, historians too have realized its value. In the article "Great Men and Postmodern Ruptures," Michael Geyer and Konrad Jarusch, for example, argue that "multiple readings" of sources are necessary for "complicating the presumed transparency" of texts (1995, 255, 269). Their advocacy for multiple readings—although in a different context—is applicable to the study of men and masculinity in the Holocaust.

19. On the question of Höss's credibility, see also Deselaers's moral-theological perspective on the Auschwitz commandant (2013).

20. See my chapter "A Perpetrator and His Hagiographer: Oswald Pohl's Confession" (Krondorfer 2010a, 100–131; also 2010b). Regarding the postwar pastoral care of Nazi perpetrators, see Kellenbach (2013).

21. For a study on generational changes of a particular group of men in postwar Germany, see my work on postwar memoirs of Protestant male theologians and clergy, a professional occupation Doris Bergen called "enablers" (see note 6 in the introduction). My analysis teases out the discrepancies between claims to clerical and moral authority and autobiographical strategies that evade questions about moral failure and compromise. Narratively this is performed by switching back and forth between asserting agency and rendering it invisible (Krondorfer 2014, 2006).

22. For the idea of hegemonic masculinity, see Connell and Messerschmidt (2005). For a wider spectrum of masculinities, such as marginalized, subordinate, resistant, or complicit masculinities, see Hinojosa (2010).

23. For Nordau's muscular Judaism, see Gilman (1991) and Gillerman (2012); for Jewish fraternities and World War I conscripts, see Caplan (2003a, 2003b) and Zwicker (2012); for Zionism and masculinity, see Nur (2014) and Byrne (2011).

24. The tight-knit Jewish communities in the East, which lived more reclusively and resisted assimilation pressures, developed separate ideals of masculinity that often disrespected and mocked the masculinity of gentile men; see Boyarin (1997) and, for the post-1980s context, Hakak (2016). For the possibility of Jewish men carving out a third space that falls "between the antisemitic vision of the effeminate Jew and the normative muscular Christian," see Imhoff's case study of American Jewish religious masculinity in the early 1900s (2013, 145).

25. For testicular assault in the Bible, see Tongue (2014) and Boer (2011); for modernity, see Ganzevoort and Sremac (2016). For a harrowing report on sexual torture and testicular assault of Tamil men in Sri Lanka, see the report *Unsilenced* (Touquet 2018).

26. We do not have the words of this unknown mother, but we do have the words of Genia, Perechodnik's later lover, which reveal stark differences of perspective. Perechodnik curtly mentions Genia in his "deathbed confession" addressed to his dead wife: "As concerns Genia, I don't understand why she gave herself to me that night, particularly since she offered me her virginity." In a 1950 letter, Genia, who survived the Holocaust, describes her former relationship with Perechodnik as a deeply caring bond between them (see Krondorfer 2010a, 162–168).

References

Aleksiun, Natalia. 2014. "Gender and the Daily Lives of Jews in Hiding in Eastern Galicia." *NASHIM: A Journal of Jewish Women's Studies and Gender Issues* 27: 38–61.

Altinay, Ayşe Gül, and Andrea Pető. 2015. "Europe and the Century of Genocides: New Directions in the Feminist Theorizing of Genocide." *European Journal of Women's Studies* 22, no. 4: 379–385.

Andersen, Pablo Dominguez, and Simone Wendt. 2015. "Introduction: Masculinities and the Nation." In *Masculinities and the Nation in the Modern World: Between Hegemony and Marginalization*, edited by Pablo Dominguez Andersen and Simone Wendt, 1–18. New York: Palgrave Macmillan.

Baer, Elisabeth, and Myrna Goldenberg, eds. 2003. *Experience and Expression: Women, the Nazis and the Holocaust*. Detroit: Wayne State University Press.

Barthes, Roland. 1967. *Elements of Semiology*. Translated by A. Lavers and C. Smith. New York: Jonathan Cape.

Bauer, Yehuda. 2001. *Rethinking the Holocaust*. New Haven: Yale University Press.

Becker, Michael, and Dennis Bock. 2015. "'Muselmänner' und Häftlingsgesellschaften: Ein Beitrag zur Sozialgeschichte der nationalsozialistischen Konzentrationslager." *Archiv für Sozialgeschichte* 55: 133–175.

Boer, Roland. 2011. "The Patriarch's Nuts: Concerning the Testicular Logic of Biblical Hebrew." *Journal of Men, Masculinities, and Spirituality* 5: 41–52.

Bos, Pascale. 2003. "Women and the Holocaust: Analysing Gender Difference." In *Experience and Expression: Women, the Nazis and the Holocaust*, edited by Elisabeth Baer and Myrna Goldenberg, 23–50. Detroit: Wayne State University Press.

———. 2014. "'Her Flesh Is Branded: 'For Officers Only': Imagining and Imagined Sexual Violence against Jewish Women during the Holocaust." In *Expanding the Perspectives on the Holocaust in a Changing World* (*Lessons and Legacies*, vol. 11), edited by Hilary Earl and Karl Schleunes, 59–85. Evanston: Northwestern University Press.

Boyarin, Daniel. 1997. *Unheroic Conduct: The Rise of Heterosexuality and the Invention of the Jewish Man*. Berkeley: University of California Press.

Browning, Christopher. 1992. *Ordinary Men: Reserve Police Battalion 101 and the Final Solution in Poland*. New York: Harper Collins.

Byrne, Rachel. 2011. "Re-Masculinizing the Jew: Gender and Zionism until the First World War." *Gnovis Journal: A Journal of Communication, Culture & Technology* (April 4, 2011): http://www.gnovisjournal.org/2011/04/04/re-masculinizing-the-jew-gender-and-zionism-until-the-first-world-war/ (accessed March 6, 2018).

Caplan, Gregory A. 2003a. "Militarism and Masculinity as Keys to the 'Jewish Question' in Germany." In *Military Masculinities: Identity and the State*, edited by Paul R. Higate, 175–190. Westport: Praeger.

———. 2003b. "Germanising the Jewish Male: Military Masculinity as the Last Stage of Acculturation." In *Towards Normality? Acculturation and Modern German Jewry*, edited by Rainer Liedtke and David Rechter, 159–184. Tübingen: Mohr Siebeck.

Caplan, Jane. 2010. "Gender and the Concentration Camps." In *Concentration Camps in Nazi Germany: The New Histories*, edited by Jane Caplan and Nikolaus Wachsmann, 82–107. Oxford: Routledge.

Card, Claudia. 2002. *The Atrocity Paradigm: A Theory of Evil*. Oxford: Oxford University Press.

Carey, Maddy. 2017. *Jewish Masculinities in the Holocaust: Between Destruction and Construction*. London: Bloomsbury Academic.

Chapoutot, Johann. 2016. "Fascist Virility." In *A History of Virility*, edited by Alain Corbin, Jean-Jacques Courtine, and Georges Vigarello; translated by Keith Cohen, 491–514. New York: Columbia University Press.

Connell, R. W., and James W. Messerschmidt. 2005. "Hegemonic Masculinity: Rethinking the Concept." *Gender and Society* 19, no. 6: 829–859.

Deselaers, Manfred. 2013. *"And Your Conscience Never Haunted You?" The Life of Rudolf Höß, Commander of Auschwitz and the Question of His Responsibility before God and Human Beings*. Oswiecim: Auschwitz-Birkenau State Museum.

Dyer, Richard. (1997) 2017. *White: Twentieth Anniversary Edition*. London: Routledge.

Ephgrave, Nicole. 2016. "On Women's Bodies: Experiences of Dehumanization during the Holocaust." *Journal of Women's History* 28, no. 2: 12–32.

Ferme, Valerio. 2001. "Translating the Babel of Horror: Primo Levi's Catharsis through Language in the Holocaust Memoir *Se questo è un uomo*." *Italica* 78, no. 1 (Spring): 53–73.

Ferrales, Gabrielle, Hollie Nyseth Brehm, and Suzy Mcelrath. 2016. "Gender-Based Violence against Men and Boys in Darfur: The Gender-Genocide Nexus." *Gender and Society* 30, no. 4 (August): 565–589.

Frankenberg, Ruth. 1993. *White Women, Race Matters: The Social Construction of Whiteness*. Minneapolis: University of Minnesota Press.

Ganzevoort, Ruard, and Srdjan Sremac. 2016. "Masculinity, Spirituality, and Male Wartime Sexual Trauma." In *Interdisciplinary Handbook of Trauma and Culture*, edited by Y. Ataria et al., 339–351. Cham, CH: Springer International.

Gastfriend, Edward. 2000. *My Father's Testament: Memoir of a Jewish Teenager, 1938–1945*. Edited with an afterword by Björn Krondorfer. Philadelphia: Temple University Press.

Geyer, Michael, and Konrad Jarusch. 1995. "Great Men and Postmodern Ruptures: Overcoming the 'Belatedness' of German Historiography." *German Studies Review* 18, no. 2 (May): 253–273.

Gillerman, Sharon. 2012. "A Kinder Gentler Strongman? Siegmund Breitbart in Eastern Europe." In *Jewish Masculinities: German Jews, Gender, and History*, edited by Benjamin Maria Baader, Sharon Gillerman, and Paul Lerner, 197–209. Bloomington: Indiana University Press.

Gilman, Sander. 1991. *The Jew's Body*. New York: Routledge.

———. 1995. *Franz Kafka: The Jewish Patient*. London: Routledge.

Goldenberg, Myrna. 1990. "Different Horrors, Same Hell: Women Remembering the Holocaust." In *Thinking the Unthinkable: Meanings of the Holocaust*, edited by Roger Gottlieb, 150–165. New York: Paulist Press.

———. 2013. "Sex-Based Violence and the Politics and Ethics of Survival." In *Different Horrors, Same Hell: Gender and the Holocaust*, edited by Myrna Goldenberg and Amy Shapiro, 99–127. Seattle: University of Washington Press.

———, ed. 2016. *Before All Memory Is Lost: Women's Voices from the Holocaust*. Toronto: The Azrieli Foundation.

Goldenberg, Myrna, and Amy Shapiro, eds. 2013. *Different Horrors, Same Hell: Gender and the Holocaust*. Seattle: University of Washington Press.

Goldhagen, Daniel Jonah. 1996. *Hitler's Willing Executioners: Ordinary Germans and the Holocaust*. New York: Knopf.

Hájková, Anna. 2017. Forum: Holocaust and the History of Gender and Sexuality. *German History* 36, no. 1: 78–100.

Hakak, Yohai. 2016. *Haredi Masculinities between the Yeshiva, the Army, Work, and Politics*. Leiden: Brill.

Haraway, Donna. 1991. *Simians, Cyborgs, and Women: The Reinvention of Nature.* New York: Routledge.

Haynes, Stephen R. 2015. "Ordinary Masculinity: Gender Analysis and Holocaust Scholarship." In *Genocide and Gender in the Twentieth Century: A Comparative Survey*, edited by Amy E. Randall, 165–188. London: Bloomsbury Academic.

Hearn, Jeff. 1997. "The Implications of Critical Studies on Men." *NORA: Nordic Journal of Feminist and Gender Research* 1: 48–60.

Hearn, Jeff, and David Collinson. 1994. "Theorizing Unities and Differences between Men and between Masculinities." In *Theorizing Masculinities*, edited by Harry Brod and Michael Kaufman, 97–117. Thousand Oaks: Sage.

Hedgepeth, Sonja, and Rochelle Saidel, eds. 2010. *Sexual Violence against Jewish Women during the Holocaust.* Hanover: University Press of New England.

Heineman, Elizabeth. 2002. "Sexuality and Nazism: The Doubly Unspeakable?" *Journal of the History of Sexuality* 11, nos. 1–2 (January/April): 22–66.

Herzog, Dagmar, ed. 2009. *Brutality and Desire: War and Sexuality in Europe's Twentieth Century.* London: Palgrave Macmillan.

Hilberg, Raul. 1993. *Perpetrators, Victims, Bystanders: The Jewish Catastrophe, 1933–1945.* New York: Harper Perennial.

Hinojosa, Ramon. 2010. "Doing Hegemony: Military, Men, and Constructing a Hegemonic Masculinity." *Journal of Men's Studies* 18, no. 2: 179–194.

Höss, Rudolph. 1996. *Death Dealer: The Memoirs of the SS Kommandant at Auschwitz.* Edited by Steven Paulsky; translated by Andrew Pollinger. New York: Da Capo Press.

Horowitz, Sara R. 2000. "Gender, Genocide, and Jewish Memory." *Prooftexts: A Journal of Jewish Literary History* 20, nos. 1–2 (Winter/Spring): 158–190.

———. 2001. "A Response to Gabriel Schoenfeld." *Prooftexts: A Journal of Jewish Literary History* 21, no. 2 (Spring): 279–283.

Imhoff, Sarah. 2013. "Manly Mission: Jews, Christians, and American Religious Masculinity, 1900–1920." *American Jewish History* 97, no. 2 (April): 139–158.

Jarvis, Christina. 2010. *The Male Body at War: American Masculinity during World War II.* De Kalb: Northern Illinois University Press.

Kellenbach, Katharina von. 2013. *The Mark of Cain: Guilt and Denial in the Post-War Lives of Nazi Perpetrators.* Oxford: Oxford University Press.

Kimmel, Michael. 1994. "Masculinity as Homophobia: Fear, Shame, and Silence in the Construction of Gender Identity." In *Theorizing Masculinities*, edited by Harry Brod and Michael Kaufman, 119–141. Thousand Oaks: Sage.

Klee, Ernst, Willi Dressen, Volker Riess, and Hugh Trevor-Roper, eds. 1991. *The Good Old Days: The Holocaust as Seen through the Eyes of Perpetrators and Bystanders.* New York: Free Press.

Koch, Peter-Ferdinand, ed. 1988. *Himmlers Graue Emminenz: Oswald Pohl und das Wirtschaftsverwaltungshauptamt der SS.* Hamburg: Facta Oblita.

Konner, Melvin. 2009. *The Jewish Body*. New York: Schocken.
Kremer, Lillian S. 1999. *Women's Holocaust Writing: Memory and Imagination*. Lincoln: University of Nebraska Press.
Krondorfer, Björn. 2006. "Nationalsozialismus und Holocaust in Autobiographien protestantischer Theologen." In *Mit Blick auf die Täter: Fragen an die deutsche Theologie nach 1945*, edited by Björn Krondorfer, Katharina von Kellenbach, and Norbert Reck, 23–170. Gütersloh: Gütersloher Verlagshaus.
———, ed. 2009. *Men and Masculinities in Christianity and Judaism: A Critical Reader*. London: SCM Press.
———. 2010a. *Male Confessions: Intimate Revelations and the Religious Imagination*. Stanford: Stanford University Press.
———. 2010b. "Männlichkeit und Selbstmitleid: Religiöse Rhetorik in Selbstzeugnissen von NS-Tätern." In *Scham und Schuld: Geschlechter(sub)texte der Shoah*, edited by Maja Figge, Konstanze Hanitzsch, and Nadine Teuber, 195–221. Bielefeld: Transcript.
———. 2014. "Gender and Post-Conflict Self-Representation: Autobiographical Writings of German Theologians after 1945." *Kirchliche Zeitgeschichte / Contemporary Church History* 27, no. 1: 102–119.
Krondorfer, Björn, and Edward Westermann. 2017. "Soldiering Men." In *Gender: War*, edited by Andrea Pető, 19–35. Macmillan Interdisciplinary Handbooks. Farmington Hills, MI: Macmillan.
Kühne, Thomas. 2017. *The Rise and Fall of Comradeship: Hitler's Soldiers, Male Bonding and Mass Violence in the Twentieth Century*. Cambridge: Cambridge University Press.
Langer, Lawrence. 1998. "Gendered Suffering? Women in Holocaust Testimonies." In *Women in the Holocaust*, ed. Dalia Ofer and Lenore Weitzman, 351–363. New Haven: Yale University Press.
Levi, Primo. 1993. *Survival in Auschwitz: The Nazi Assault on Humanity*. New York: Collier/Macmillan.
Mann, Michael. 2000. "Were the Perpetrators of Genocide 'Ordinary Men' or 'Real Nazis'? Results from Fifteen Hundred Biographies." *Holocaust and Genocide Studies* 14, no. 3 (Winter): 331–366.
Mosse, George. 1990. *Fallen Soldiers: Reshaping the Memory of the World Wars*. New York: Oxford University Press.
———. 1996. *The Image of Man: The Creation of Modern Masculinity*. New York: Oxford University Press.
Mühlhäuser, Regina. 2010. *Eroberungen: Sexuelle Gewalttaten und intime Beziehungen deutscher Soldaten in der Sowjetunion 1941–1945*. Hamburg: Hamburger Edition.
———. 2014. "The Historicity of Denial: Sexual Violence against Jewish Women during the War of Annihilation, 1941–1945." In *Expanding the Perspectives on the Holocaust in a Changing World* (*Lessons and Legacies*, vol. 11),

edited by Hilary Earl and Karl Schleunes, 31–58. Evanston: Northwestern University Press.

Mushaben, Joyce Marie. 2004. "Memory and the Holocaust: Processing the Past through a Gendered Lens." *History of the Human Sciences* 17, nos. 2–3: 147–185.

Nur, Ofer Nordheimer. 2014. *Eros and Tragedy: Jewish Male Fantasies and the Masculine Revolution of Zionism*. Boston: Academic Studies Press.

Perechodnik, Calel. 1996. *Am I a Murderer? Testament of a Jewish Ghetto Policeman*. Boulder: Westview Press.

Pető, Andrea. 2015. "Europe and the Century of Genocides: New Directions in the Feminist Theorizing of Genocide." *European Journal of Women's Studies* 22, no. 4: 379–385.

Pine, Lisa. 2008. "Gender and Holocaust Victims: A Reappraisal." *Journal of Jewish Identities* 1, no. 2 (July): 121–141.

Pohl, Oswald. 1950. *Credo: Mein Weg zu Gott*. Landshus: Alois Girnth.

Ponzio, Alessio. 2015. *Shaping the New Man: Youth Training Regimes in Fascist Italy and Nazi Germany*. Madison: University of Wisconsin Press.

Reading, Anna. 2002. *The Social Inheritance of the Holocaust: Gender, Culture and Memory*. Houndsmill: Palgrave Macmillan.

Reeser, Todd. 2010. *Masculinities in Theory: An Introduction*. Malden: Wiley-Blackwell.

Ringelheim, Joan. 1990. "Thoughts about Women and the Holocaust." In *Thinking the Unthinkable: Meanings of the Holocaust*, edited by Roger Gottlieb, 141–149. New York: Paulist Press.

Rittner, Carol, and John Roth, eds. 2012. *Rape: Weapon of War and Genocide*. St. Paul: Paragon House.

Robinson, Sally. 2000. *Marked Men: White Masculinity in Crisis*. New York: Columbia University Press.

Roediger, David. 1994. *Towards the Abolition of Whiteness*. London: Verso.

Salvante, Martina. 2015. " 'Less than a Boot-Rag': Procreation, Paternity, and the Masculine Ideal in Fascist Italy." In *Masculinities and the Nation in the Modern World: Between Hegemony and Marginalization*, edited by Pablo Dominguez Andersen and Simon Wendt, 93–112. New York: Palgrave Macmillan.

Schoenfeld, Gabriel. 1998. "Auschwitz and the Professor." *Commentary* 105, no. 6 (June): 42–46.

Seibel, Wolfgang. 2002. "The Strength of Perpetrators—The Holocaust in Western Europe, 1940–1944." *Governance: An International Journal of Policy, Administration, and Institutions* 15, no. 2 (April): 211–240.

Sierakowiak, Dawid. 1996. *The Diary of Dawid Sierakowiak*. London: Bloomsbury.

Sombart, Nicolaus. 1991. *Die Deutschen Männer und ihre Feinde: Carl Schmitt—ein deutsches Schicksal zwischen Männerbund und Matriarchatsmythos*. Munich: Karl Hanser Verlag.

Sommer, Robert. 2014. "Pipels: Situational Homosexual Slavery of Young Adolescent Boys in Nazi Concentration Camps." In *Expanding the Perspectives on the Holocaust in a Changing World* (*Lessons and Legacies*, vol. 11), edited by Hilary Earl and Karl Schleunes, 86–103. Evanston: Northwestern University Press.

Theweleit, Klaus. 1989. *Male Fantasies*, 2 vols. Minneapolis: University of Minnesota Press.

Timm, Annette. 2017. "The Challenges of Including Sexual Violence and Transgressive Love in Historical Writing on World War II and the Holocaust." *Journal of the History of Sexuality* 26, no. 3 (September): 351–365.

Tongue, Samuel. 2014. *Between Biblical Criticism and Poetic Rewriting: Interpretative Struggles over Genesis 32: 22–32*. Leiden: Brill.

Touquet, Helen. 2018. *Unsilenced: Male Survivors Speak of Conflict-Related Sexual Violence in Sri Lanka*. Report by the International Truth and Justice Project.

Van Alphen, Ernst. 1997. *Caught by History: Holocaust Effects in Contemporary Art, Literature and Theory*. Stanford: Stanford University Press.

Wallen, Jeffrey. 2014. "Testimony and Taboo: The Perverse Writings of Ka-Tzetnik 135633." *Dapim: Studies on the Holocaust* 28, no. 1: 1–16. DOI: 10.1080/23256249.2014.881592.

Walter, Verena. 2009. "Jüdische Jungen in Auschwitz-Birkenau." *Tribüne: Zeitschrift zum Verständnis des Judentums* 192, no. 4: 186–195.

Weitzman, Lenore, and Dalia Ofer. 1998. "Introduction: The Role of Gender in the Holocaust." In *Women in the Holocaust*, edited by Dalia Ofer and Lenore Weitzman, 1–18. New Haven: Yale University Press.

Werner, Frank. 2008. "'Hart müssen wir hier draussen sein': Soldatische Männlichkeit im Vernichtungskrieg, 1941–1944." *Geschichte und Gesellschaft: Zeitschrift für Historische Sozialwissenschaft* 34, no. 1 (March): 5–40.

Westermann, Edward. 2016. "Stone-Cold Killers or Drunk with Murder? Alcohol and Atrocity during the Holocaust." *Holocaust and Genocide Studies* 30, no. 1 (Spring): 1–19.

Williams, Timothy, and Susanne Buckley-Zistel, eds. 2018. *Perpetrators and Perpetration of Mass Violence: Actions, Motivations and Dynamics*. London: Routledge.

Zwicker, Lisa Fetheringill. 2012. "Performing Masculinities: Jewish Students and the Honor Code at German Universities." In *Jewish Masculinities: German Jews, Gender, and History*, edited by Benjamin Maria Baader, Sharon Gillerman, and Paul Lerner, 114–137. Bloomington: Indiana University Press.

Chapter 2

Masculinity and Death
De- and Resexualization in Nazi Concentration Camps

ROBERT SOMMER

According to Michel Foucault, the history of modern penitentiary institutions is a history of the submission of the human body. The castigation of the sexuality of imprisoned humans is an essential element of imprisonment (Foucault 1995, 170; see also Kunze 2008). In Nazi concentration camps active sexuality violated the claim to absolute power and control by the SS camp authority. Any sexual activity of camp prisoners was classified as disobedience to the camp regime and severely punished.

In this chapter I will talk about men's sexuality in Nazi concentration camps.[1] I will show how the Nazis destroyed the individual by eliminating sexuality and how camp inmates tried to resist this method of destruction by reconstructing a sexual identity. Despite the strict prohibition of sexual activity, it existed in the camps. Since camps were sex-segregated, situational homosexuality became the main way to live out sexuality in the camp system. Heterosexual relationships were possible in camps if male and female sections were near each other. Sexual relationships—situational homosexual or heterosexual—ranged from consensual and rational relationships to sexual slavery and rape. The ability to have sex became not only a strategy of rebuilding one's human identity but also a symbol of male power. Only a few had the chance to live out sexuality. From 1942 onward, the Nazis introduced brothels to the concentration camp system and granted the right for sexual intercourse as a privilege to hard-working male prisoners. Based on testimonies and documents, I will draw a differentiated picture of male sexuality as a gendered act in Nazi concentration camps, which is an important chapter in the history of the Holocaust and one that has not received adequate attention so far.

Dehumanization and Desexualization

In stark contrast to living conditions in regular prisons, imprisonment in Nazi concentration camps forced inmates to radically break with all values and moral beliefs they held dear in the ordinary world. In a very short period, the human psyche had to adapt to the *univers concentrationnaire* and focus on one thing only: survival. The Austrian Auschwitz survivor and psychologist Viktor Frankl published in 1947 his autobiography, in which he analyzed the psychology and strategies of survival in the everyday life of an "average" camp prisoner. Frankl combined his personal experience with those of other prisoners and developed a three-phase model of the mental reactions of inmates to camp life. The *first phase* was admission to the camp, the *second* actual life in the camp, and the *third* life after liberation (Frankl 1947, 7–15).

The *first phase* is characterized by shock, which starts right at the moment of arrest. This shock culminates in the psychological reaction to separating from one's previous life. The camp entry procedure was of special importance because of collective showers, the shaving of all hair, and the disinfection of the inmate's body. This is where the act of *dehumanization* (Shik 2009, 223, 240) began: with a blistering attack on the sexuality and intimacy of the human being. Human beings with their individual ethnic, cultural, linguistic, and religious backgrounds were reduced to a mere mass of naked, shaven bodies jammed together. This experience was devastating, especially to women. But male survivors also mention the humiliating intrusion into one's intimacy. Often, family members saw each other naked for the first time and were ashamed (Mariconti 2004, 1).

The *second phase* was the inner adaptation to the horrors of camp life, which included habituation to angst, violence, and death. Incipient apathy dominated the reasoning of the inmate. Suffering, disease, and the notion of omnipresent death became an integral part of the everyday fight of the camp inmate for survival. The feeling of hunger dominated the human psyche and displaced all other drives. The search for food dominated daily life. As Oszkár Betlen put it: "And the people under me and around me were talking of eating. Eating, eating, and once again eating"

(Betlen 1962, 34). Frankl observed how in Auschwitz, inmates imagined food in the most delicious varieties in order to satisfy the stomach. He later called it *Magenonanie*, stomach masturbation (Frankl 1947, 32–44).

A camp inmate's mental faculties were almost entirely preoccupied with sustainment. Everything that did not support sustainment was devalued. At the same time, the inmate adopted the habitus of vanishing in the mass. Not attracting attention was the prime principle of self-protection. To arouse the attention of the SS or a kapo could be fatal. This created within the inmates the feeling of "radical worthlessness of an individual human life" (Frankl 1947, 73). The number on a list of the SS was more important than a single life. That also meant the loss of consciousness about what it meant to be a human subject. Instead, the dominant perception was that an inmate was only an object of fate. The inmate fell into a state of apathy (Frankl 1947, 42–47, 70–79).

Parallel to such apathy was the gradual death of the body. The rapid and shocking psychological dehumanization was augmented by an unstoppable decay of the human body. It lost its sexual function and became only a reservoir of energy. The maintenance of the body as such became a fundamental strategy of survival. The vanishing of secondary sexual features, such as women's breasts, indicated the degree to which the physical condition of an inmate had deteriorated. Physical integrity determined life and death. The *physical capital* of an inmate shrunk with each new day. The organism first consumed fat reserves, then the subcutaneous cellular tissue, and finally human protein, until musculature was mostly gone. Frankl remembers: "Actually, this body there—my body—is already a carcass" (Frankl 1947, 44).

The disappearance of the body and of secondary sexual features led inmates to understand themselves less and less as sexual beings. The Polish survivor of the Sachsenhausen concentration camp, Aleksander Kulisiewicz, describes the arrival of one thousand women to the roll-call area in Sachsenhausen. After initial joy on his part, he recognized that those women looked very similar to the male inmates. In some kind of recollection of his former masculine identity, he sought female beauty but couldn't find it. "The eye searched for calves, it searched and searched. . . . Legs?—Ugh!—So skinny. Distorted . . . like hackneys. The hips were like a long forgotten violin, with no magic sound anymore" (Kulisiewicz 1997, 58). Masculinity was not only lost in the absence of sexual desires or of one's sexual body: the objects of (heterosexual) desire were lost, too. Female survivors often speak of their loss of their femininity (Schäfer 2002, 53).

Male survivors rarely address that subject, probably because the loss of manliness is still a great taboo (Peer 2001).

Sexual Life in Concentration Camps

The German sociologist Wolfgang Sofsky describes the concentration camp as a system of glaring differences and extreme inequality, in which countless prisoners starved in misery while others led a life of veritable luxury. In order to run a system as complex as a concentration camp, the SS relied on giving some power to a few prisoners who organized the camp in "self-management." That gradation of power was mainly based on the racial and political ideas of the Nazi ideology and was realized though a system of classifications based on taxonomy (Sofsky 1997, 117–144). This system of *extreme inequality* had its effect on the sexual life of inmates. For instance, Benedikt Kautsky estimated that for 90 percent of the male inmates there was no "sexual problem," because they had lost their sexual desires (Langbein 1997, 589). Former Auschwitz inmate Tadeusz Borowski, on the other hand, wrote that young male prisoners desperately wanted to be selected for a work squad inside the Birkenau *Frauenlager* (women's camp) to get in contact with women (Borowski 1963, 146). In 1971, the German psychiatrist Paul Matussek wrote in his study of the psychological effects of concentration camp confinement that the nonexistence of sexual drives, as Frankl had described it, could not be true. One of the survivors he interviewed stated that "despite malnutrition, he missed sexual activity. . . . Many [prisoners of Dachau] had sexual dreams and masturbated" (Matussek 1971, 29). Buchenwald survivor Ernst Federn went so far as to write: "Sexuality played a tremendous role" (Federn 2002, 69).

The subject of sexuality inside concentration camps had already been discussed by scholars in the late 1940s. The psychoanalyst Paul Friedman (1990, 165) talked about it during the annual meeting of the American Psychiatric Association (APA) in 1948. At the end of the 1950s, various studies regarding sexuality in Auschwitz were conducted by Polish psychiatrists, such as medical examinations by the psychiatric hospital of the Medical Academy Krakow. Under the direction of Prof. Dr. E. Brzezicki, seventy-seven former Auschwitz inmates (sixty men and seventeen women) were examined for psychiatric problems in 1959. The results showed that only 18 percent of those interviewed remembered having had sexual drives in the camp. Three interviewees stated that they had masturbated, but only if they were not tormented by hunger. Four men mentioned that they had sex in Auschwitz—two of them for the first time in their lives, both inside of a concentration camp brothel (Lesniak et al. 1962, 42–52).

The most important studies on sexuality in concentration camps were conducted by Jerzy St. Giza und Wiesław Morasiewicz. From 1964 to1967 and 1971 to 1972, the two Polish sexologists from Wroclaw interviewed male survivors who were between sixteen and twenty years old during the time of the deportation about sexual issues. The sexologists built their study on Frankl's three-phase model. In the *first phase* of shock at admission, they saw an absolute absence of the sexual drive, evidenced through the deficiency of erotic dreams, the absence of premature ejaculations, or the lack of sexual topics in conversations and thoughts. To them it proved that the human psyche was entirely focused on the process of survival (Giza and Morasiewicz 1973, 29–41).

In the *second phase*, the phase of inner adaptation to the horror of camp life, Giza and Morasiewicz observed the phenomena of postshock regeneration. Fifty percent of the interviewees were able to perform sexual activities. The most common sexual activity was masturbation, though it was still rarely practiced. According to the study, the inmates who masturbated the most did so once, twice, or three times a month. Masturbation did not focus on satisfying sexual desires; rather, it was an attempt to distract from the ineradicable feeling of angst. Furthermore, young men wanted to feel their physical existence and feel "being alive" through sexual activities. Those results were similar to the sexual behavior of women in concentration camps, as the sexologists found in a later study with twenty female survivors (Giza and Morasiewicz 1974).

Those studies provide a general understanding about sexuality in Nazi concentration camps. As groundbreaking as these studies were, they cannot cover the wide range of cultural backgrounds, religions, age, education, sexual orientation, or living conditions of all camp inmates. All interviewees of Giza and Morasiewicz were Polish and Catholic. Hence I suggest that we look more closely at sexual relationships in Nazi camps.

Heterosexual Relationships in Concentration Camps

As mentioned before, heterosexual relationships in the sex-segregated concentration camps were rather exceptional and happened only when contact with the other sex was possible, such as in Bergen-Belsen and

Auschwitz-Birkenau. Sexual relationships between inmates and civilians were possible, for instance, in spaces where they worked next to each other. Only privileged prisoners from the upper stratum of the camp society—such as kapos and foremen—were able to have such relationships. A very rare example is the account from Arthur Lehmann who worked in a subcamp of Auschwitz-Monowitz, called Laurahütte. There, the inmates worked together with civilians and Eastern European forced workers producing guns at the Oberschlesische Gerätebau GmbH. According to him, about fifty women were the objects of desire of the Aryan kapos and other prisoner functionaries (testimony of Lehmann).

Many male prisoners had not seen any women for years. Wiesław Kielar commented on the opening of a women's section in Auschwitz-Birkenau: "Women in a men's camp. That was simply unbelievable!" (Kielar 1980, 81). Seeing them was one thing, but getting in contact with them was impossible, as Samuel Pisar writes: "Contact with the other sex was unimaginable at Auschwitz. Every day separate columns of marching men and women could cross each other. In the circumstances romance was to them an extinct emotion. Only one thought prevailed: 'For us it's horrendous, but what must it be like for them?'" (Pisar 1980, 76).

The situation was different for male inmates of the upper stratum of the prisoners' hierarchy, especially camp functionaries. They were living under much better conditions. Usually they had sufficient food and access to the black market. They openly showed their sexual interest in female inmates. Sometimes it was possible to have sex in a hidden place. The Kapellmeister of the Auschwitz camp orchestra and other inmate doctors were once caught in a sexual act with women who had come from a satellite work squad of Auschwitz to the main camp's hospital for medical examinations and to get teeth pulled. The SS man, who caught the men by surprise, hit their genitals with a wooden stick (Borowski 1963, 145–146). In contrast to the exhausted majority of the camp, sex was a relevant subject for everyday life for the upper stratum of camp society. The physician and survivor of the Neuengamme concentration camp, Paul Thygesen, stated that inmates from the upper stratum usually were doing work that was less exhaustive and that they received sufficient food rations. This led to a surplus of energy and sexual desires (Thygesen 1982, 97). Testimonies like this show that in order to live out one's (hetero)sexuality, the male inmate first of all needed to be in a somewhat good physical condition; furthermore, he needed to have access to areas of the camp where women lived. These inmates needed to have a certain mobility in the camp, whether as messengers, block chiefs, inmate camp doctors, or members of the camp's fire department.

Heterosexual relationships in concentration camps could be love relationships, consensual trade relationships, sexual exploitation, or rape. Love relationships were rare and a sensation for camp prisoners. Well known among the prisoners of Auschwitz was, for instance, the tragic love relationship between the Belgian Jew of Polish descent Mala Zimetbaum and the Polish political prisoner Edek Galiński. They escaped together from Auschwitz in June 1944 but were caught by the SS. After severe torture, Edek was hung; Mala committed suicide shortly before her execution (Nomberg-Przytyk 1985, 100–104). Often the border between these types of relationships was fluid. Simha Naor listened to a conversation between two female German inmates in Bergen-Belsen. One tells the other that her "lover" had asked her for the first time if she loved him. She was surprised about such a question and commented: "Strange question. He gets what he requests and I have my bread" (Naor 1986, 130).

Sexual relationships in which men would provide women with food and protection and received in exchange sexual services were widespread in mixed camps, such as Auschwitz-Birkenau (Shik 2009, 233–239). These *rational relationships*, as the historian Anna Hájková calls them, were a well-known survival strategy in the ghettos, such as Theresienstadt/Terezin (Hájková 2013, 505). In Auschwitz, women in such relationships were called *kochanas* (*kochanie* is Polish for "darling"). Rational relationships were a common strategy of survival, especially for women who had managed to preserve their feminine sexual identity. Hermann Langbein remembered that in the Auschwitz Stammlager Block 10, where female inmates served as human guinea pigs for the sterilization experiments of Dr. Carl Clauberg, all the women had a male "lover" (Langbein 2004, 592). Male inmates who looked "neat and tidy" were able to move in between the separated parts of the Auschwitz Stammlager and Birkenau; they had access to the *Frauenlager* and were desired by young women. Female inmates could have great benefits from such sexual relationships. The Polish survivor Wiesław Kielar describes in his autobiographic novel the situation when entering the *Frauenlager* of Birkenau: "Suddenly I was in another world. In an instant I was surrounded by a swarm of chattering young women" (Kielar 1980, 131). Some prisoners bragged about their sexual adventures. Kielar remembered a young inmate called Dino "who bragged of his amatory successes with Greek Jewesses"; these women stayed in the camp section *Mexiko* under terrible living conditions (180, 211).

Not uncommonly, sexual services by female inmates were given to male camp functionaries or kapos under death threat. Samuel Pisar describes how the compost heap, a particular site in Auschwitz-Birkenau with the official name Kompostierung II, became a location for sex between inmates since it was possible for inmates from different camp sections to access it and because the SS avoided this place. Pisar, who worked there, describes the coercive character of those sexual relationships:

> The men who pushed the garbage carts to the dump where I worked were for the most part privileged kapos—big, sadistic brutes who enjoyed a certain freedom to satisfy their whims. The women selected to push carts from their camp were the youngest and prettiest girls. They had no notion at first of the fate that awaited them. Close by our compost heap stood a small dilapidated house, its attic filled with straw—Auschwitz's improvised brothel for the prisoner elite.
>
> I witnessed some of the orgies, being charged with keeping the participants supplied with water. After the first moment of panic, the instinct for survival made the young women overcome their revulsion and even pretend to enjoy the privilege of submission to our obsessed little gods: because if not pleased, gods can punish. A girl whose embrace proved unsatisfactory would have a black mark against her, the kapos warned, and would be beaten or executed on her return to camp. (Pisar 1980, 76)

In Auschwitz-Birkenau, camp sections existed where women wore civilian clothing and long hair because they had not gone through the initial process of registering, as for example, in the *Zigeunerlager* (gypsy camp), where more than twenty-two thousand Sinti and Roma lived under terrible conditions. There was very little food in the *Zigeunerlager*. Often, food was traded on the black market for valuable objects or sexual services. The situation was similar in *Mexiko*, the unfinished section of Auschwitz-Birkenau, where the SS temporarily housed Hungarian Jewish women before killing them in the gas chambers. Without water and food, they vegetated while waiting for their death. Dealing in sexual services became one of the only ways to get food and water (Kielar 1980, 180–184, 212).

Situational Homosexual Relationships

The most common and sometimes the only form of sexual relationships occurred between partners, in which a (feminine-looking) boy played the female part in the relationship, while the older, mostly hierarchically superior partner lived out his masculine sexuality. Such situational homosexuality is mentioned in many published testimonies from men who spent time in concentration camps, such as Hermann Langbein (2004, 405) and Roman Frister (2001, 240). The most prominent example is Ka-Tzetnik's novel *Karu lo Piepel*, translated into English as *Atrocity*, later as *Piepel: The Most Terrible Story Ever Told* (Ka-Tzetnik 135633, 1961). The phenomenon has also been analyzed by psychoanalysts, such as the former Buchenwald survivor Ernst Federn, and by physicians who examined the effects of camp internment on human sexuality. Federn explains how the absence of the other sex led to finding a substitute partner of the same sex. According to him, a male situational homosexual exclusively searched "girlish" looking boys and young men (Federn 1998, 57). In women's camps, female inmates who had a situational homosexual relationship mostly preferred masculine-looking partners, whom they often gave male first names (Schoppmann 1997, 244–257).

Situational homosexuality—similar to heterosexual relationships in camps—had different faces. It could be consensual, pragmatic (rational), coercive, or simply rape. Federn describes that in Buchenwald, for example, there were fourteen- and fifteen-year-old boys who "prostituted themselves" for money or valuables; they had relationships with prisoners who belonged to the upper stratum of the camp's hierarchy. Federn himself was imprisoned as a political prisoner in Buchenwald. As the son of Paul Federn, a Viennese psychoanalyst, he analyzed the psychology of prisoners and their sexuality in Buchenwald. Even while in the camp, he spoke with experts on sexuality in detention centers and correctional facilities, such as Karl Plättner, the author of the 1931 study *Eros in a Penitentiary*. Federn, therefore, sharpened his focus on this subject and published a profound analysis after the war. He remembered how he was asked by the inmates Bertl Bruckner and Max Heinmann if he wanted a sexual relationship with them. The son of the assassinated Bavarian socialist prime minister Kurt Eisner had a sexual relationship with a young boy. As a prominent inmate, Eisner Jr. believed the SS would not harm him, but he was ordered to the camp hospital and killed (Federn 2002, 70–71).

Young men or boys who had sexual relationships with other, mostly older inmates were called *Pipel* (Yiddish for "small boy"), or *Bubies* (German colloquial term for boys), *Schwungs* (combination of *schwule Jungs* / gay boys), *Bettmann* (bed man), and *Ponimaimänner* (*ponimaiu*, Russian for "I understand"). *Pipels* were the helpmates of prisoner functionaries and had to assist and perform messenger services during the day (Sommer 2014, 86–103). At nighttime, sexual services were their most common duties.

The German political prisoner and *Lagerälteste* (camp senior, the highest position of an inmate in a concentration camp) of Sachsenhausen, Harry Naujoks, remembers in his autobiography the *Pipel* of the Flossenbürg concentration camp. In 1943, Naujoks was discharged from his position in Sachsenhausen and transferred to Flossenbürg as punishment. In his autobiography, written in October 1945, he remembers the conditions in Flossenbürg. In contrast to what he had experienced in Sachsenhausen, it was "the bon ton in the camp" (Naujoks 1989, 341) for prisoner functionaries such as kapos and block chiefs to have sexual relationships with *Pipels*, who were mostly Russian or Polish. At the block for new arrivals, the block chief Hermann G., a German criminal prisoner, picked out the most handsome boys and gave them their own bed, food, and little dainties. He kept those boys in the barrack during the day, and they did not have to work. After a few days, those boys saw what happened to their comrades who did not have the same protection. These boys, between sixteen and eighteen years old, understood then that their lives would be endangered by hunger, cold, flogging, and exertion if they did not comply with the demands of the block chief. Eventually, the block chief would call one of them to his bed. If the boy refused, he was sent to the quarry the next day where he would die soon after. According to Naujoks, every block chief or foreman in Flossenbürg had a *Pipel*. Survivors often describe *Pipels* negatively. H. G. Adler remembered a fourteen-year-old boy who officially worked in a position as a messenger in Auschwitz-Birkenau. He was protected by the block chief with whom he had a sexual relationship. Adler describes him as a "strong lout who can do whatever he likes, an aggressive, cantankerous creature" (cited in Langbein 2004, 405). There is no doubt that some *Pipels* took advantage of their positions in the camps. Witnesses often neglect to say that *Pipels* were victims of sexual exploitation who had little chance to escape from their situation.

It is difficult to look behind the scenes. Most narratives that depict the phenomenon are secondhand descriptions. Firsthand accounts are rare. An exception is the account of Israeli writer Roman Frister. In his autobiography, he describes how he was raped by Arpad Basci, a privileged prisoner from Ellrichhütte, a subcamp of Auschwitz. One night Basci gave him a piece of bread. While Frister ate the piece of bread, Basci penetrated him from behind (Frister 2001, 241). Another rare account is Ka-Tzetnik's prominent and striking novel *Piepel*. Though he provides behind-the-scenes information on young men who were *Pipels*, we do not know the extent to which his account is fictional.

Unpublished testimonies are an important source for learning about *Pipels*' living conditions. In 1990, Kenneth R. was interviewed by two scholars from the Fortunoff Video Archive of Yale University. He mentioned that he had been a *Bettmann* (bed man) in Flossenbürg. When he had previously given testimony to the Wiener Library in 1955, he did not include this part in his story of survival. Kenneth R., a Polish Jew, was sent to Flossenbürg in 1943 when he was seventeen years old. He was placed in Block 19 where all underage prisoners had to sleep overnight. One day the *Blockälteste* (block chief) of Block 7 came to Block 19 to pick out his new *Bettmann*. He chose Kenneth R. At Block 7, Kenneth R. had to prepare the *Blockälteste*'s bed and keep his private room tidy. One evening, the eldest block chief ordered the young boy to get undressed and get into his bed. Kenneth obeyed and was raped. After that, Kenneth felt terrible physical pain but did not understand what it meant. After that night, the block chief gave Kenneth extra food rations. He also became a "little more civilized" and managed to make the dolorous experience a little less agonizing. After a while, the *Blockälteste* decided to pass Kenneth on to a privileged prisoner called Max, who was an older person and, according to Kenneth, not as sadistic. Kenneth had learned that there was no way to resist because resistance would have meant death. The first night was similar to the experience with the *Blockälteste* from Block 7, but soon the pain became tolerable. The young adolescent understood that the relationship could actually help him survive the concentration camp. "I thought to myself, if this is the price of life, let it be" (Kenneth R., FVA, tape 3, minute 29:05). Kenneth was right: when the Jewish prisoners of Flossenbürg were sent on a death march during the last days of the war, the *Blockälteste* arranged to change Kenneth's personal data on the prisoner record card. The young Jewish boy officially became a Polish political prisoner. He survived Flossenbürg.

In Kenneth R.'s detailed insight into the structure of violence and power in an exploitative homosexual relationship in a concentration camp, the experience of sexual abuse is mostly reduced to the description of physical pain. This can be interpreted as a coping strategy for an incredibly humiliating experience. It also must be seen in relation to the victim's absence of knowledge about sexuality due to his young age. He simply did not know what sex was and how it worked. The experience can also be understood in the context of the general psychology of survival in the camps, as described earlier. According to Frankl, in order to survive in the concentration camp, the human being had to subordinate all his or her actions to the principle of survival. In other words, the first priority of any inmate was the search for food. At the same time, the prisoner fell into a state of apathy, which helped him or her to tolerate the incredible pain and torture experienced on a daily basis. The experience of sexual violence cannot therefore be reduced to physical pain but must also be seen in relation to the possible benefit that a victim received from this situation. In the case of Kenneth R., the victim understood rape and sexual slavery as the cost for possible means of survival.

His testimony also shows an obvious asymmetry of power between two individuals: there is a dominating (and penetrating) person, who has power over the life of the other at all times; and there is the person that can either obey or risk facing death. In reality, however, the power structure was more complex. The perpetrator was not interested in onetime sexual satisfaction but rather in a long-term relationship. Therefore, he gave certain benefits to the victim. He provided food and protection and tied the fate of the victim to his own. The victim himself could become a menace to the life of the perpetrator, since homosexuality was often severely punished by the SS. Had the victim reported such a case to the SS—and such cases are known—the perpetrator most likely would have been killed. At the Natzweiler concentration camp, for instance, a prisoner was punished for "masturbation with other prisoners" with the maximum sentence of twenty-five strokes.[2]

The SS was aware of situational homosexuality in the camps. The former commander of Auschwitz, Rudolf Höß, wrote about it in his autobiography. "Similar to homosexuality in male camps, the pest of lesbian love spread in the FL [Frauenlager Birkenau]" (Höß 1958, 120). Höß had experienced the (situational) homosexual "problem" in Dachau where he had worked as *Blockführer* and *Rapportführer* in 1936. There, "homosexual activities" were reported to the SS camp authority. Höß came up with a solution and placed homosexual inmates of Dachau in a separate barrack (Höß 1958, 80). Such separation, in combination with hard labor (such as pulling a street roller), were successful measures. Höß stated: "All of a sudden the pest was gone" (80).

Like Rudolf Höß, the führer of the SS, Heinrich Himmler, believed that some homosexuals can be changed into heterosexuals through a stay in a concentration camp. Those who proved to the SS that they were "healed" were released. Since that became a common way out of the camps for homosexuals, Himmler wanted evidence that they had really become heterosexuals. Hence, in 1944 he ordered some homosexuals to be sent to the women's concentration camp of Ravensbrück for *Abkehr-Prüfungen* (rejection tests). The men would be brought inconspicuously into contact with women who had been prostitutes before their internment in a concentration camp. Those women would try to get the men aroused; if they "reacted positively," they were considered "healed from homosexuality." The men were then cross-checked by being put together with other men in order to see if they would get sexually excited. If a man passed those tests, he was released from the concentration camp (Höß 1958, 81).

Since the SS was also aware of the sexual abuse of young adolescent boys and *Pipel*-relationships, they isolated young men in special barracks in order to prevent them from being victims of sexual abuse by other prisoners.[3]

Camp Brothels

In October 1941, Heinrich Himmler gave the order to establish the first two brothel barracks in the concentration camps of Mauthausen and Gusen in Austria. Himmler had the idea to increase the efficiency of the production of the two quarries in which camp inmates had to work. Since the end of the 1930s, the labor of prisoners in Nazi concentration camps had become an important issue for the economic system of the SS. Slave labor was the backbone of the commercial enterprises of the SS, which granted Himmler a certain kind of autonomy over the SS and power within the Nazi state. But productivity of camp prisoners was low because of the inhuman conditions, the small food rations, poor hygiene, and daily violence. High productivity was contrary to a survival strategy of prisoners: to work as little as possible. Himmler did not want to accept that the efficiency of the camp prisoners was only 50 percent compared to civilian workers, and so he suggested granting in a most liberal manner (*freiesten Form*) certain privileges to hard-working camp prisoners, which included access to females in brothels (*Weiber in Bordellen*) and a small piecework wage (*Akkordlohn*). In his opinion, the denial of the necessity to "provide" women to satisfy sexual needs of male camp prisoners would be "welt- und lebensfremd," out of touch with the world and life (Letter to Oswald Pohl, April 23, 1942). He also ordered a piecework wage system (*Akkordsystem*) for the entire concentration camp system. This *Akkordsystem* was released in May 1943 and called the *Prämien-Vorschrift* (Bonus Order) that allowed the SS to grant special premiums and privileges to hard-working prisoners. Privileges included the ability to write and receive more letters, (military) haircuts, vouchers for cigarettes, extra food rations, and the right to frequent a *Sonderbau*—as the SS called the brothel. These were thought to be effective incentives for boosting the prisoners' performance. According to the Bonus Order, the prisoners would receive bonus coupons if they fulfilled the work quota. These could be used to buy cigarettes or food at the camp canteen or to pay a visit to the brothel. The brothel visit, a maximum of one time per week, was thought to be only for *Spitzenkräfte* (highly trained employees).

By the end of the war, ten brothels had been opened in most of the major concentration camps: Mauthausen and Gusen (July and October 1942), Flossenbürg and Buchenwald (July 1943), Auschwitz I-Stammlager (October 1943), Auschwitz III-Monowitz (November 1943), Neuengamme (Spring 1944), Dachau (April 1944), Sachsenhausen (August 1944), and Mittelbau-Dora (February 1945) (see Sommer 2009a, 171).

The SS selected female prisoners mainly at the *Frauen-Konzentrationslager* (female concentration camps) of Ravensbrück and in the *Frauenlager* Auschwitz-Birkenau. The SS recruited mostly young German women who were confined in a concentration camp as *asozial* (antisocial persons) and preferably imprisoned former prostitutes. Those women were told they would be released from the camp if they volunteered for a six-month term in a camp brothel. As we know today, no woman was ever released from a brothel on the basis of this promise. Often, the SS recruited women who lived under very poor conditions, so it became a decision of life and death. Since not enough women volunteered, the SS simply selected women who looked healthy and feminine (Sommer 2009a, 168–196).

Until the opening of brothel barracks in 1942, there were no women inside male concentration camps. Especially for political prisoners who had been arrested in 1933 it was the first time they could get in contact with women and have (legally) a sexual relationship with them. Many inmates believed that the reason for the construction of these brothels was the battle of the SS against homosexuality. It simply seemed absurd that brothels in the camp would boost the productivity, as Heinrich Himmler assumed (Sommer 2014, 93).

We can understand this better when we look at the anatomy of the camp brothel visit. Prisoners who wanted to visit a brothel had to undergo a long procedure that began with asking permission from the camp administration. When the camp commander granted permission, the names of the visitors were announced at the evening roll call. After the roll call, the permitted brothel visitors marched, accompanied by SS guards, to the brothel barrack in rows of two. At the brothel barrack they went through a medical examination and had to line up in the building's corridor. The SS allocated the men to line up in front of one of the rooms where the women were inside, waiting for their turn, often with their pants down. Then the door would open. Inside the small room, a woman would be waiting. The time was limited to about fifteen minutes. Only the missionary position was allowed. Through spy holes in the door the SS guards ensured that the prisoners obeyed the rules. After the allotted time, a SS guard opened the door and made the inmate leave the room. If he did not leave the room fast enough, a guard would charge in and beat and chase him out (Sommer 2009a, 176–179).

The brothel visit was like bureaucratized coitus under the eyes of SS guards, where any space for eroticism, romance, or affection was completely eliminated. As survivors from various concentration camps state, the opening of camp brothels did not affect the number of *Pipel* relationships in the camps. Federn writes: "When the brothel opened, it soon became apparent that out of the elite of the *Lagerältesten* many preferred a boy to a prostitute" (Federn 2002, 71).

The number of inmates who visited the camp brothel was very small. First, the SS granted the right to visit the brothels only to Germans, Western Europeans, Scandinavians, and some Eastern Europeans. Jews, Soviet POW's, and Sinti and Roma were excluded from this "privilege" at all times. Second, an inmate needed to be physically able to visit a brothel and have access to vouchers for the brothel. Accounting sheets from Buchenwald show that less than 1 percent of camp inmates visited the brothel. Most of the inmates who visited the brothel were prisoner-functionaries, such as the *Lagerälteste* (senior prisoner), *Blockälteste* (block chiefs), and kapos, but also prisoners from privileged work squads such as *Lagerschutz* (camp police), *Lagerfeuerwehr* (camp fire brigade), *Küche* (kitchen commando), *Frisör* (camp hairdresser), *Krankenbau* (camp infirmary), or *Metzgerei* (butcher). Based on a brothel visitor book (*Bordellbuch*) from Mauthausen, it is possible to get a closer look into the social status of brothel visitors as well as the frequency of their visits (for more details, Sommer 2009b).

Brothel visitors could be subdivided into three groups according to frequency and voluntariness: *frequent visitors, sporadic* or *one-time-only visitors*, and those who were forced by the SS. *Frequent* camp brothel visitors were an extremely small number and mainly members of the camp *Aristokratie*, the social upper class of prisoners. Thanks to the existence of a brothel visitor book (*Bordellbuch*) from Block 3 of Mauthausen, we know names and camp serial numbers of visitors as well as the days of their visits during the period from June to December 1942. Block 3 was the *Prominentenblock*, the barrack where most of the prisoner-functionaries slept. In the first months, 107 prisoners were recorded in the *Bordellbuch*. By looking at the frequency of their visits, it shows that some prisoners regularly attended the brothel, up to twice a week, but those were only thirteen men. Other documents show that those men were kapos of various work squads, a worker in the camp parcel post office, and a *Blockschreiber* (block scribe). Those work positions were highly coveted because they gave prisoners the possibility to have access to valuable trade objects or comestibles; they also involved little physical labor. Those kapos and higher-ranking prisoners were part of the *Lagerprominenz* (camp notables) who had money and valuables (both strictly forbidden to most other prisoners). They owned different pairs of shoes (while the mass of prisoners only had one pair), played card games on Sunday with a few thousand Reichsmark stake, and organized sports contests as well as music evenings. Those were also the inmates who had *Pipels* as lovers. Sexuality did not only signal a "higher lifestyle," it was also a symbol of their power. The willful waste of food in front of prisoners who starved to death went along with a waste of sexual energy that other prisoners could not even entertain since they felt nothing but hunger and fatigue.

The second group of brothel visitors constituted the majority among those men. *Sporadic* and *one-time* brothel visitors belonged mainly to the camp's social middle stratum (on the social hierarchy in concentration camps, see Sofsky 1997, 127–129). Their motivations for a visit seemed to be very different; it can be understood as a result of their proximity to death and their will to feel human again through experiencing male sexuality. As Giza and Morasiewicz wrote in their study on sexuality in Auschwitz, the purpose of masturbation was not to satisfy sexual needs but to feel that they were still alive (Giza and Morasiewicz 1973, 40). The expression of the desire to feel like a (male) human being through sexual activity can be found in motivations to visit the brothel as well. This *remasculinization* became part of regaining one's sexual identity, which had been destroyed in the process of dehumanization.

Many young concentration camp inmates never had any sexual relationships prior to their incarceration. They knew they would never survive the camp and so they wanted to have a sexual relationship once in their lifetime. A former Auschwitz prisoner, Johan F. B., once received a bonus coupon from his friend who told him to visit the brothel since he had never been with a woman. He went but regretted it the moment he entered the brothel. Later he stated that he only talked to the woman.

An eighteen-year-old Czech inmate of the Mauthausen concentration camp was a *Pipel* for a prisoner functionary. Since he never had a sexual relationship with a woman, he wanted to know if he was homosexual. However, it seems that in many cases men were not capable of any sexual action, as sexual slave workers from camp brothels confirmed in interviews (Sommer 2009b, 245ff.; Paul 1994, 47). The reasons were not only the poor physical conditions of the prisoners that led to erectile dysfunction and the longstanding absence of sexual contact with a woman, but also the non-erotic atmosphere of the camp brothel and the knowledge that the women did not work there voluntarily. Many prisoners also visited the *Sonderbau* simply to talk to a woman or have personal contact with a human being (Mattusek 1971, 29).

There were also people the SS forced to visit the brothel. The *Lagerälteste* of Buchenwald, Erich Reschke, who was also one of the heads of the camp resistance movement, was forced by the SS to "open the brothel" in his position as prisoner with the highest rank. He refused but was threatened to be discharged from his position. The SS authority openly exhibited their own absolute power (Niethammer 1994, 48). Another example illustrates the devastating effect of forced brothel attendance, especially for prisoners of the lower social stratum. Jean Michel, a French survivor of the Mittelbau-Dora camp, remembered how his compatriot Delarouche returned together with his work squad one evening from the underground factory, where the V2 missiles were produced. SS officials suddenly stopped the marching prisoners and directed them to the brothel. The men only wanted to sleep after a twelve-hour shift. The men had to wait in front of the brothel rooms with their pants down. The order to enter was given. Delarouche entered and "found himself in front of a woman who was waiting. He was worried and blushing with confusion. How could he manage it? The 'little Frenchies' were about to fail to live up to their reputation. That is how legends are destroyed!" (Michel 1979, 156–157) The exhaustion as well as the brothel atmosphere would have made it impossible for the French men to fulfill their designated task.

Even though the brothel visit was thought by the SS to be a privilege, the male prisoner was forced to become an executive agent in a structure of sexual slavery and was thus forced to become a perpetrator, a rapist. At the same time, the absolute power humiliated him by revealing his own loss of masculinity. In the case of forced brothel visits, sexual violence and humiliation can move in different directions: victims become perpetrators who, in turn, get humiliated themselves.

Summary: Masculinity, Power, and Death

If the submission of the body was essential for modern penitentiary institutions, as Foucault states, Nazi concentration camps served to destroy the body. Absolute power over camp prisoners meant absolute power over the social life and sexuality of individuals. Human identity was eliminated upon entry into the camp. In a radical act of dehumanization, women and men were turned into shaven bodies in striped pajamas, their names reduced to numbers. Part of the destruction of the individual was desexualization. The body lost its sexual function. Both women's and men's bodies turned into skin-covered skeletons. The sexual drive disappeared as the food drive took priority over anything else. This is the core of concentration camp sexuality: sexuality was part of an individual inmate's identity, and therefore had to be destroyed.

On the other hand, the preservation of a sexual identity became an act of self-affirmation and therefore resistance against the life-destroying machinery of the SS. The human body needed to appear intact to the SS, because this could save one's life during the next selection. Furthermore, the recollection of one's sexual identity meant reactivating sexuality. That itself can be seen as an act of resistance, since it undermined the omnipresent power of the SS. However, sexual life in the camps followed the rules of the economy of survival. First of all, we can observe that only a small group of inmates was able to reconstruct their sexual identity—mostly prisoner functionaries or inmates who had managed to adapt to camp life and find ways of "organizing" (i.e., obtaining) extra food on the black market. Only through having enough to eat could the food drive lose its dominating presence. Wasting energy, such as during sexual activities, demonstrated the high degree of an inmate's power. Hence, sexual activity was the privilege of a few. Sexuality became a status symbol among prisoners and a sign of power inside the camp.

Since Nazi concentration camps were single-sex environments, until the opening of camp brothels, the primary possibility for sexual activity was same sex. The body of feminine-looking, young adolescent men in male camps—or masculine-appearing women in female camps—received a new significance, since it became an object of desire and therefore important capital of an inmate. In Auschwitz, the corpulent body was an ideal of beauty since it was a very rare sight. It was a marker of the "wealth" and power of an inmate; corpulent men were desired in the *Frauenlager* of Birkenau. The intact and (re-)sexualized body became essential to an inmate because it not only demonstrated health but also could be traded for food, which was essential for survival. The resexualized body became important capital in the economy of sexual barter in the camp.

Those women who possessed a sexualized body in Auschwitz or Bergen-Belsen were able to have rational relationships, securing food and protection through sex. For a significant number of women, this became an important strategy of survival. Certainly, those relationships were not free of coercion. There were the constraints of the bad living conditions, and sometimes these relations were accompanied by death threats from male prisoners. The resexualized female inmate was therefore in constant danger of becoming a victim of sexual violence.

In concentration camps, where every action is subsumed under the prime principle of survival, hunger is a worse enemy than physical pain from being beaten or penetrated. Being raped could mean receiving a piece of bread from the perpetrator, which helped one to survive. Similarly, feminine-looking boys or adolescents could survive by having been rendered into victims of sexual violence. Sexual services were mostly demanded under a death threat; but it also meant another chance at survival. Kenneth R. spoke of the block chief with whom he had a sexual relationship: "I looked after him, like a precious diamond. I was not going to lose a life-saving exercise like this. He was just, what I call normal, maybe a bit smaller. And he used grease. So it became tolerable. I thought to myself, if this is the price of life, let it be" (Kenneth R, tape 3, minute 29:05). Tolerating sexual abuse thus became a survival strategy. The inner rules of the concentration camp demanded the inmate to abandon moral concepts and overcome self-loathing. Those who were able to do that had a better chance at survival.

Those who were able to live out (masculine) sexuality had power; those who did not, were not considered human beings. As the example of Delarouche demonstrates, men who were not able to live out their masculinity were emasculated. The physical inability to have sex became a sign of the absence of power, while the physical ability to have an erection and to penetrate explicitly marked participation in power. In the camps, one's physical condition defined one's position in the social hierarchy.[4]

The SS wanted total control over sexuality: they could severely suppress it or introduce it in limited ways, as the camp brothels demonstrate. To be able to live out masculine sexuality became officially a privilege granted to hard-working prisoners, though in reality it was accessible only to mostly privileged prisoners, to those who were chosen by the SS to guarantee the functioning of the camp. The SS only allowed exploitative and coercive heterosexual intercourse in the missionary position and under supervision. Social relationships were prohibited and intercourse had to follow a scheme defined by the SS. In that way, the SS enforced their own gender model. Thus, the camp brothel embodied a perfidious combination of sexual exploitation and complicity. Masculinity was a privilege that was defined as dominant, hegemonic, virile, and exploitative. This gender model brought the "dogma of male virility" (Dupont 1996, 29) of the Nazis to an extreme. Male sexuality was regulated and channeled in a controlled space. Female sexuality was in the eyes of the SS passive and subordinated to men, demonstrating to the extreme the SS vision of a fundamental patriarchal right.

There was certainly a discrepancy between theory and reality. For example, forced sex workers in camp brothels resisted surveillance by covering the spy holes with tape. They also tried to build closer relationships with certain prisoners in better social positions in the camp who would visit them frequently and bring them food and grant protection. Furthermore, resexualization was accompanied by a certain re-emotionalization. As inmates tried to suppress negative and painful feelings, they longed for positive emotions. Sexual activities could provide those emotions. Having affection for someone else, or even being in love, meant an escape from omnipresent pain and death. Sometimes, male customers of camp brothels fell in love with a sex slave worker. Some even married them after the war (Tanenbaum 1999, 33–50; Sommer 2009b, 220). Even in an act of sexual violence emotions could emerge. Pisar noticed: "Truly, humanity, even at its cruelest and most depraved, can be softened during the intimate surrender of the sexual act. A kapo who has been violent and cruel suddenly plants a tender kiss on a girl's lips and sinks helplessly and quietly away from her arms" (Pisar 1980, 77). Such emotional experiences show another dimension to the dynamics, contradictions, power structures, and complexities of gendered male sexuality in Nazi concentration camps.

Notes

1. This chapter is based on the research for my PhD thesis on forced sex labor in Nazi concentration camps, which was published in 2006 in Germany as *Das KZ-Bordell: Sexuelle Zwangsarbeit in nationalsozialistischen Konzentrationslagern*. I would like to express my special thanks to Ellen van Benschoten for helping with the English translations and Jeffrey Wallen (Hampshire College, Amherst, MA, USA) for his very helpful remarks. All translations from German sources are mine.

2. List of flogging punishment "P. Strafen" of the Natzweiler concentration camp.

3. Jack Terry's testimony (interview with Sommer 2003-07-19 Terry, 8).

4. In this context it would be interesting to discuss Lacan's concept of the penis and phallus. According to Lacan, there is a difference between the penis as biological organ and the phallus as signifier and symbol of power. In concentration camps that difference vanishes, as those who have the physical strength to have an erection and to have sex are those who have power (Grenz 2005, 119; Lacan 1991, 119–132).

References

Betlen, Oszkár. 1962. *Leben auf dem Acker des Todes*. Berlin (GDR): Dietz.
Borowski, Tadeusz. 1963. *Bei uns in Auschwitz: Erzählungen*. Munich: Piper Verlag.
Dupont, Marc. 1996. *Sexualwissenschaft im "Dritten Reich": Eine Inhaltsanalyse medizinischer Zeitschriften*. Frankfurt a. M.: Med. Diss Universtität Frankfurt/Main.
Federn, Ernst. 1998. "Versuch einer Psychologie des Terrors (1946/1989)." In *Ernst Federn—Versuche zur Psychologie des Terrors*, edited by Roland Kaufbold, 35–75. Giessen: Psychosozial-Verlag.
———. 2002."Eros hinter Stacheldraht: Interview-Auszug." In *Stimmen aus Buchenwald: Ein Lesebuch*, edited by Holm Kirsten and Ulf Kirsten, 69–72. Göttingen: Wallstein Verlag.
Foucault, Michel. 1995. *Discipline and Punish: The Birth of the Prison*. New York: Vintage Books.

Frankl, Viktor E. 1947. *Ein Psychologe erlebt das KZ*. Vienna: Verlag für Jugend und Volk.
Friedman, Paul. 1990. "Aspekte einer Konzentrationslager-Psychologie." *PSYCHE: Zeitschrift für Psychoanalyse und ihre Anwendung* 44, no. 2: 165–172.
Frister, Roman. 2001. *The Cap: The Price of a Life*. New York: Grove/Atlantic.
Giza, Jerzy St., and Wiesław Morasiewicz. 1973. "Z zagadnień popędów w obozach koncentracyjnych. Przyczynek do analiz tzw. KZ-syndromu." *Przegląd Lekarski* 1: 29–41.
———. 1974. "Poobozowe zaburzenia seksualne u kobiet jako elemet tzw. KZ-syndromu." *Przegląd Lekarski* 1: 68–75.
Grau, Günter, ed. 1993. *Homosexualität in der NS-Zeit: Dokumente einer Diskriminierung und Verfolgung*. Frankfurt a. M.: Suhrkamp.
Grenz, Sabine. 2005. *(Un)heimliche Lust: Über den Konsum sexueller Dienstleistung*. Wiesbaden: VS Verlag.
Hájková, Anna. 2013. "Sexual Barter in Times of Genocide: Negotiating the Sexual Economy of the Theresienstadt Ghetto." *Signs: Journal of Women in Culture and Society* 38, no. 3: 503–533.
Höß, Rudolf. 1958. *Kommandant in Auschwitz*. Edited by Martin Broszat. Stuttgart: Deutsche Verlagsanstalt.
Ka-Tzetnik 135633. 1961. *Piepel: The Most Terrible Story Ever Told*. London: Anthony Blond.
Kielar, Wiesław. 1980. *1500 Days in Auschwitz/Birkenau*. New York: Times Books.
Kulisiewicz, Aleksander. 1997. *Adresse Sachsenhausen: Literarische Momentaufnahmen aus dem KZ*. Gerlingen: Bleicher.
Kunze, Regina. 2008. *Criminal Intimacy: Prison and the Uneven History of Modern American Sexuality*. Chicago: University of Chicago Press.
Lacan, Jacques. 1991. "Die Bedeutung des Phallus." In *Schriften II*, edited by Norbert Haas, 192–204. Berlin: Quadriga.
Langbein, Hermann. 2004. *People in Auschwitz*. Chapel Hill: University of North Carolina Press.
Lesniak, Roman, et al. 1962. "Einige psychiatrische Probleme des KZ-Lagers Auschwitz im Lichte eigener Untersuchungen." *Przegląd Lekarski* 1: 42–52.
Matussek, Paul. 1971. *Die Konzentrationslagerhaft und ihre Folgen: Monographien aus dem Gesamtgebiete der Psychiatrie*. Berlin: Springer Verlag.
Michel, Jean. 1979. *Dora: The Nazi Concentration Camp Where Modern Space Technology Was Born and 30,000 Prisoners Died*. London: Holt Rinehart & Winston.
Naor, Simha. 1986. *Krankengymnastin in Auschwitz: Aufzeichnungen des Häftlings Nr. 80574*. Freiburg im Breisgau: Verlag Herder.
Naujoks, Harry. 1989. *Mein Leben im KZ Sachsenhausen 1936–1942: Erinnerungen des ehemaligen Lagerältesten*. Berlin (GDR): Dietz Verlag.
Niethammer, Lutz, ed. 1994. *Der "gesäuberte" Antifaschismus: Die SED und die roten Kapos von Buchenwald*. Berlin: De Gruyter.

Nomberg-Przytyk, Sara. 1985. *Auschwitz: True Tales from a Grotesque Land*. Chapel Hill: University of North Carolina Press.

Paul, Christa. 1994. *Zwangsprostitution: Staatlich errichtete Bordelle im Nationalsozialismus*. Berlin: Edition Hentrich.

Peer, Yvonne. 2001. "Gewalt gegen Männer in heterosexuellen Beziehungen: Ein gesellschaftliches Tabu." Diplomarbeit am Fachbereich Sozialwesen an der Hochschule Zittau/Görlitz (FH), University of Applied Sciences.

Pisar, Samuel. 1980. *Of Blood and Hope*. London: Cassell.

Plättner, Karl. 1931. *Eros im Zuchthaus: Sehnsuchtsschrei gequälter Menschen nach Liebe: Eine Beleuchtung der Geschlechtsnot der Gefangenen, bearbeitet auf der Grundlage von Eigenerlebnissen, Beobachtungen und Mitteilungen in achtjähriger Haft*. Hanover: Paul Witte.

Schäfer, Silke. 2002. "Zum Selbstverständnis von Frauen im Konzentrationslager: Das Lager Ravensbrück." Berlin: Dissertation an der Fakultät I Geisteswissenschaften der Technischen Universität Berlin.

Schoppmann, Claudia. 1997. *Nationalsozialistische Sexualpolitik und weibliche Homosexualität*. Pfaffenweiler: Centaurus.

Shik, Na'ama. 2009."Weibliche Erfahrungen in Auschwitz-Birkenau." In *Brutality and Desire: War and Sexuality in Europe's Twentieth Century*, edited by Dagmar Herzog, 221–246. New York: Palgrave Macmillan.

Sofsky, Wolfgang. 1997. *The Order of Terror: The Concentration Camp*. Princeton: Princeton University Press.

Sommer, Robert. 2009a. "Camp Brothels: Forced Sex Labour in Nazi Concentration Camps." In *Brutality and Desire: War and Sexuality in Europe's Twentieth Century*, edited by Dagmar Herzog, 168–196. New York: Palgrave Macmillan.

———. 2009b. *Das KZ-Bordell: Sexuelle Zwangsarbeit in nationalsozialistischen Konzentrationslagern*. Paderborn: Schöningh.

———. 2014. "Pipels: Situational Homosexual Slavery of Young Adolescent Boys in Nazi Concentration Camps." In *Lessons and Legacies Volume XI: Expanding Perspectives on the Holocaust in a Changing World*, edited by Hilary Earl and Karl Schleunes, 86–103. Evanston: Northwestern University Press.

Tanenbaum, Roy. 1999. *Prisoner 88: The Man in Stripes*. Calgary: University of Calgary Press.

Thygesen, Paul. 1982. "Arzt im Konzentrationslager." *Nordfriesland* 63, no. 64 (November): 79–101.

Testimonies

Naujoks, Harry. October 28, 1945. Bundesarchiv Berlin (BArch), BY5 V279/74.

Lehmann, Arthur. Wiener Library, Section II, Reel 53, Index No. PIII h. No. 415.

Mariconti, Gianfranco. 2004. Private Collection Sommer (PRS), Interview with Sommer 2004-05-12 Mariconti 2.

R., Kenneth. Fortunoff Video Archiv (FVA), HVT-2367.
R., Kenneth. Wiener Library (WL), Reel 56. PIII h /Flossenbürg.
Terry, Jack. PRS, Interview Sommer 2003-07-19 Terry.

Archival Material

B., Johan F. In Library of the International Youth Meeting Center Auschwitz (IYMC), without signature, p. 5.
Bordellbuch Block 3 June–December 1942. In Archiv Mauthausen Memorial, K2-1.
Dienstvorschrift für die Gewährung von Vergünstigungen an Häftlinge. Prämien-Vorschrift May 15, 1943. In BArch, NS 3/426.
Letter Himmler to Pohl, April 23, 1942. In Archiv of the Institut für Zeitgeschichte (Munich), MA 304 / 0812.
Letter Himmler to Pohl, March 23, 1942. In BArch, NS 19/2065.
List of flogging punishment "P. Strafen." In Bundesarchiv Berlin-Lichterfelde (BArch), Film 1575.

Chapter 3

The Experiences and Behavior of Male Holocaust Victims at Auschwitz

LISA PINE

The lens of gender has been applied comparatively recently both to the Holocaust in particular and to genocide studies more widely. Research on gender and genocide has expanded considerably over recent years (Warren 1985; Smith 1994; Fein 1999; Jones 2004; Randall 2015). Gender-based distinctions provide a useful analytical tool in the discussion of genocides. As Adam Jones has noted, the perspective of gender allows us to define how men and women are targeted during episodes of genocidal violence (2004, 264). Much of the writing on gender to date has been on women and their experiences (Rittner and Roth 1993; Ofer and Weitzman 1998; Baer and Goldenberg 2003). Stephen Haynes's work on "ordinary masculinity" underlines how a greater recognition of the gendered character of male experiences can enhance our understanding of the Holocaust (Haynes 2015, 165–188). Haynes's research is concerned with perpetrators, but a discussion of the attributes, behavior, and experiences of male Holocaust victims is also highly significant. Conceptions of maleness or masculinity include traits such as strength, toughness, courage, inner direction, and autonomy. These types of characteristics have been socialized into the dominant gender discourses (Seidler 2006; Boyarin 1997). This chapter examines male experiences, as particular to men's gender rather than as universal experiences. Gender is both about the social construction of particular kinds of identities and behavioral expectations, and this chapter explores how this relates to men during the extreme and extraordinary circumstances of the Holocaust, in particular at the dual-purpose labor and death camp at Auschwitz-Birkenau.

This chapter is based on a variety of primary and secondary sources. In particular, it is centered on an analysis of the survivor testimony of male Holocaust victims. By weaving firsthand accounts into this chapter throughout, the events of the Holocaust are linked with the victims who experienced them in an important way, allowing us a deeper knowledge and comprehension of this difficult subject. This approach has been taken by leading Holocaust historians in definitive works on the Holocaust, which utilize testimonies and survivor narratives in order to allow the voices of the victims of Nazi policy to be heard (Friedländer 1997, 2007; Cesarani 2016). This chapter illuminates the centrality of personal accounts and narratives as primary sources to the historiography of the Holocaust. As Marius Turda notes: "There is now an established critical tradition in representing the Holocaust in all its aspects, but there is still need for a critical evaluation of witness testimony in general and memoirs in particular" (2014, 52). Furthermore, Petra Schweitzer underlines the significance of "the gendered dimension of testimony" and of language and expression (2016, xix). This chapter, by revisiting male survivor memoirs through a gendered lens, allows us to reevaluate and reinterpret them as crucial primary sources. It sheds light on the experiences that pertain to the gendered particularities of male victimization. It interrogates men's words, deeds, and behavior under extreme conditions as well as the choices they made in relation to these circumstances. It considers both male conduct that reflected expected gender norms, such as egotism, strength, and identity through work, and male behavior that deviated from these expectations, such as food talk and social bonding to enhance chances of survival. It uses a small selection of narratives in order to explore specifically gendered aspects of the experiences of male Holocaust survivors in more detail.

Survivor Testimonies as Historical Sources

Holocaust survivor testimonies—both written and oral—are essential historical sources, which provide a unique insight into the unfolding of events precisely because they are reflections of personal and individual experiences (Langer 1982, 1991; Rubin and Greenspan 2006; Wieviorka 2006; Matthäus 2009; Greenspan 2010; Lothe, Suleiman, and Phelan 2012).

Paul Bartrop underlines the significance of testimonial accounts: "Survivor testimonies play the most crucial role in forming our understanding of what life was like in the Nazi concentration camps" (2019, 148). The richness of the narratives in written testimonies allows readers to gain a greater understanding of the Holocaust. Each writer has a different story to narrate, even in the description of intrinsically similar events, because it is the way in which the writers have comprehended and related their experiences that comprises the true core of their work. However, it is important to take into account that such written accounts yield a represented truth and to comprehend the constructed nature of the evidence itself in written testimony. Holocaust survivor narratives have been written in a variety of circumstances—some soon after the event, some after the passing of several decades, some with the help of a ghostwriter. While this does not make them less legitimate or valuable as historical sources, there may be problems such as the accuracy and reliability of recall, of which historians must be aware. Moreover, on the whole, the people writing down their narratives were not practiced authors and survivor testimonies are not always elegant and polished. Furthermore, as they were written for publication, a sifting process took place in the mind of the writer and/or the editor. This means that some memories were omitted and others retained or even enhanced. The writing, as Zoë Waxman notes, "comes from the careful representation of experience, or the perceived 'appropriateness' of experiences for publication" (2006, 128).

Nevertheless, published survivor accounts are certainly "subjectively true" (Bartrop 2000, 47). Their authors chronicle events they witnessed themselves. Elie Wiesel writes that "only those who experienced Auschwitz know what it was. Others will never know" (2006, ix). As Bartrop states, Holocaust survivors, in writing their narratives, "do no attempt to make magic, nor do they attempt to imagine the unimaginable. They simply try to tell the stories from their own individual perspectives" (2000, 47). It is their intention to tell the truth as they comprehend it as clearly as possible in order to convey the essence of their experience to their readers. Holocaust survivors may have different reasons for writing down their narratives, but none of them claim to tell the full or only story of the Holocaust. The historian must keep this in mind and not have unrealistic expectations about the nature of these sources. In Holocaust testimony, "the writer's personal experience is representative and used to provide a perspective on the common plight," not to give full histories of camps or even necessarily to relate major incidents that occurred (Des Pres 1976,

38). None of them can tell the whole story on its own, nor do they intend to do so. Survivor testimonies are intimate accounts of personal experiences, which the writers wish to convey to their readers. The process of testifying then is "not merely to narrate, but to commit oneself, and to commit narrative, to others" (Felman and Laub 1992, 204). Holocaust testimonies are such rich accounts that there are certainly multiple layers to be excavated and uncovered within them. The complexity of memoirs as narrative accounts and testimonies of the Holocaust are of significant intrinsic value. The language they use is also important. As Wiesel notes: "Hunger—thirst—fear—transport—selection—fire—chimney: these words all have intrinsic meaning, but in those times, they meant something else" (2006, ix).

Furthermore, historians may overlook difficult subjects or types of behavior that are not expressed in written memoirs or testimonies, thus excluding them from the historical narrative. For example, testimonies that have homogenized women's experiences and identities can be misleading (Gurewitsch 1998). The tendency in historical writing has been to define Jewish women as mothers, sisters, and nurturers, "with a very particular notion of what constitutes female behavior" (Hardman 2000, 12). We must also revisit male testimonies and narratives to see what is extant in their accounts and consider what might be missing from the historical narrative here too. How did male survivors choose to portray their experiences at Auschwitz? Which aspects of their responses to Nazi persecution or their behavior have they selected to tell? Gendered expectations and norms about male behavior undoubtedly played a part in this. Which different kinds of masculinity have been omitted from the historical narrative? Similar to the almost entirely absent reference to lesbians in female accounts is a lack of reference to homosexuality among male accounts (Wiesel 2006, 48). This is partly because this was a taboo subject for many decades. Unexpected conduct or actions that differed from male norms are also harder to detect. Such aspects have remained outside the written historical narrative and therefore hidden or obscured from view. The literature has tended to overlook the desperate actions undertaken by Holocaust victims in order to survive under the appalling conditions in which they found themselves. But this does not mean that they did not occur. The purpose of such discussion is not to judge, but to offer a more complete picture of Holocaust experiences and to try to establish a greater historical understanding of the subject.

Men at Auschwitz: Experiences and Behavior

The terrible privations and circumstances of internment at Auschwitz included thirst and hunger, extremes of temperature, arduous physical labor, overcrowding, inadequate food and foul water, lengthy roll calls, exhaustion, illness, injury, and the constant fear of "selection" for the gas chambers. In terms of men's behavior, gendered expectations were centered on strength and hardness, toughness and determination (Berger, Wallis, and Watson 1995). Signs of weakness fell short of normative conduct for men. Viktor Frankl states that "it was necessary . . . to keep moments of weakness and furtive tears to a minimum" (2004, 86). Men did not wish to appear cowardly or weak. As a result of different social constructions of gender, men were less likely to discuss emotions, admit to weakness or the need for another person with whom to share their burden. Mary Lagerwey notes that "male survivors framed their narratives in order and coherence, and often de-emphasized emotions" and that they told of "personal isolation, personal survival at any cost, ruthless competition" (1998, 75). It appears that because men had been socialized into being independent and autonomous, these characteristics were the ones most often portrayed in their narratives. Male and female survivor accounts also represent work as a means of survival very differently. Pride in work and its impact on their identities is much more common in male writings. By contrast, female accounts have tended to be much less specific on work and how it was conducted. This suggests that work was more central to men's experiences in line with contemporaneous gendered norms.

While "food talk" among women at Auschwitz has been much written about, Frankl also recounts men engaging in food talk (Goldenberg 2003, 165–179). Frankl states that the majority of prisoners, when they were working near each other and not closely watched by guards, "would immediately start discussing food," asking each other about their favorite dishes. "Then they would exchange recipes and plan the menu for the day when they would have a reunion—the day in a distant future when they would be liberated and return home" (Frankl 2004, 41). Moreover, the conscious act of planning for the future in this way was a coping mechanism and a survival strategy. Another aspect that appears in male accounts is related to prayer and faith. Wiesel recounts a loss of faith. Yet, he shows how for other men faith could be life-affirming, even in the circumstances of Auschwitz. He describes another prisoner, Akiba Drumer, who maintained his faith and kept up his prayers throughout a long internment; however, "as soon as he felt the first chinks in his faith, he lost all incentive to fight and opened the door to death" (Wiesel 2006, 77).

Male memoirs have tended to downplay bonds and relationships and to emphasize instead examples of individual valor, strength, or autonomy. Bruno Bettelheim has explained his view on the subject of survival in the camps as follows:

> Survival in the camps—this cannot be stressed enough—depended foremost on luck. . . . While nothing one could do could assure survival, and while chances for it at best were extremely slim, one could increase them through correctly assessing one's situation and taking advantage of opportunities; in short, through acting independently and with courage, decision, and conviction, all of which depended on the measure of autonomy one had managed to retain. (Bettelheim, 1986, 100–101)

Dutch survivor Louis de Wijze underlined the need for care of the self in his memoirs as well: "Everyone lives for himself. Our one and all-encompassing credo is: Survive! Between the outer limits of life and death, previous values and norms lose their meaning, and our spiritual baggage gradually erodes. The only norm that counts is 'I'" (Wijze 1997, 67).

Wiesel describes his arrival at Auschwitz and his separation from his mother and sisters. He walked on with his father, "with the men," and states that they left behind the objects that they had carried with them, as well as their "illusions" (Wiesel 2006, 29). His main concern was not to lose sight of his father and not to remain alone. He repeats later on that "not to be separated from my father" was most important (35). While he mentions that they stood "stunned" and "petrified," he also states that "a few young tough men" among the new arrivals contemplated attacking the armed guards. As the older men begged their sons not to be foolish, the idea of trying to resist soon died down (31). Furthermore, very quickly after separation from family members, "the absent no longer entered our thoughts . . . and their fate was not on our minds. We no longer clung to anything" (36). Like other survivors, Wiesel notes the impact of the arrival rituals: "in a few seconds, we had ceased to be men. Had the situation not been so tragic, we might have laughed. . . . I too had become a different person" (37).

It is important to note that despite expectations about male independence, references to close relationships do appear in male narratives and there are instances of male writing that show men behaving in ways that differed from expected male gender norms of autonomy and care for the self alone. For example, Wiesel mentions Tibi and Yossi, two brothers from Czechoslovakia, who "lived for each other, body and soul" and who quickly became his friends (2006, 50–51). He describes too how they made plans together to go to Palestine if they survived. This making of plans was also a strategy for survival. Primo Levi provides another example of the impact of interpersonal connection, telling of an Italian civilian worker, Lorenzo, who brought him "a piece of his bread and the remainder of his ration every day for six months" (Levi 2000, 148). Without Lorenzo, Levi believes that he would not have survived Auschwitz.

> [This was] not so much for his material aid, as for his having constantly reminded me by his presence, by his natural and plain manner of being good, that there still existed a just world outside our own, something and someone still pure and whole, not corrupt, not savage. . . . Lorenzo was a man; his humanity was pure and uncontaminated, he was outside this world of negation. Thanks to Lorenzo, I managed not to forget that I myself was a man. (Levi 2000, 148)

Levi later describes a "tight bond of alliance" with Alberto, another prisoner (2000, 168). Wiesel also details early advice from a Polish block supervisor: "Let there be camaraderie among you. We are all brothers and share the same fate. The same smoke hovers over all our heads. Help each other. That is the only way to survive" (2006, 41). Hence, cooperation and social bonding did apply to male experiences, not only to female ones, and has been recounted in some male narratives.

Furthermore, the testimonies of other male survivors underline the importance of the father-son relationship to survival, when fathers and sons had managed to avoid separation and stay together. Henry Wermuth recalls: "The presence of my father was, without a doubt, a major factor in my survival; but it also meant that I did not have, nor was I in need of, any other social contacts" (Wermuth 1993, 139). In this case, the father-son relationship was so strong and significant that it completely replaced the necessity for other bonds. On the death march from Auschwitz, Wiesel recalls his momentary desire to fall out of line, to the edge of the road and die: "My father's presence was the only thing that stopped me.... He was running at my side, out of breath, at the end of his strength, at his wit's end. I had no right to let myself die. What would he do without me? I was his only support" (2006, 86–87). Wiesel shows here the significance of his relationship with his father and their mutual support. Yet later, after he and his father had been transferred to Buchenwald after a long and brutal march, and they had been briefly separated, Wiesel recalls:

> I went to look for him. Yet at the same time the thought crept into my mind: if only I didn't find him! If only I were relieved of this responsibility, I could use all my strength to fight for my own survival, to take care only of myself.... Instantly, I felt ashamed, ashamed of myself forever. (Wiesel 2006, 106)

There is some ambivalence demonstrated here and complex emotions. And finally, when his father was dying and calling out for him, Wiesel says that he

> remained deaf to his cries. Instead of sacrificing my miserable life and rushing to his side, taking his hand, reassuring him, showing him that he was not abandoned, that I was near him, that I felt his sorrow, instead of all that, I remained flat on my back, asking God to make my father stop calling my name, to make him stop crying. So afraid was I to incur the wrath of the SS.... I shall never forgive myself. Nor shall I ever forgive the world for having pushed me against the wall, for having turned me into a stranger, for having awakened in me the basest, most primitive instincts. (Wiesel 2006, xi–xii)

The experiences surrounding the evacuation of Auschwitz and the death marches have been described in many memoirs and testimonies. Ironically, Wiesel notes, on leaving Auschwitz the prisoners were required to clean and mop up the floor so that the liberating army knew that "here lived men and not pigs"—"So we were men after all?" (2006, 84). Once they left, they were starving, frozen, and exhausted. Wiesel states that although he was physically spent, he refused to sleep: "Deep inside, I knew that to sleep meant to die. And something in me rebelled against that death" (89). The circumstances they faced after leaving the camp drove many Holocaust victims to increasingly desperate behavior. Wiesel describes what happened when a passerby threw some bread onto the train convoy in which he was traveling: "In the wagon where the bread had landed, a battle had ensued. Men were hurling themselves against each other, trampling, tearing at and mauling each other. Beasts of prey unleashed, animal hate in their eyes" (101). Hans Winterfeld similarly recalls the death march from Auschwitz:

> Normally, one could talk to the other prisoners, but when food was distributed, they began to look and act like lunatics: their eyes stared rigidly at the ladle or at the arm that distributed the bread. When they received their ration, they constantly watched other prisoners to check that nobody had been given more. It was completely irrelevant what kind of person it was: uneducated and primitive, or educated and intellectually superior. I often wondered how cultivated human beings could behave like animals. (Cited in Kolinsky 2004, 27)

Indeed, Levi comments too on the aim of the Nazi camps to "reduce us to beasts." But, he writes, "we must not become beasts; that even in this place one can survive, and therefore one must want to survive, to tell the story, to bear witness; and that to survive we must force ourselves to save at least the skeleton, the scaffolding, the form of civilization" (Levi 2000, 58). His desire to survive was thus underpinned by his resolution to bear witness. He was determined to defend his strength and dignity for this purpose. As Eva Kolinsky (2004, 14) has noted, many other survivors defined their own personal code of behavior in a bid to maintain a sense of their own self-value.

Sonderkommando Narratives

The accounts of *Sonderkommando* survivors are particularly revealing as expressions of male behavior and choices. The *Sonderkommando* (or "special detachments") were engaged in the extremely gruesome task of working in the crematoria where the victims' bodies were burned (Friedler, Siebert, and Kilian 2002). Much discussion on the *Sonderkommando* has been concerned with the moral ambivalence of their positions, as they were living in more privileged circumstances in the camp and had a chance to survive longer while carrying out this unenviable and grisly job for their captors.

Revisiting their testimonies from the perspective of gender sheds light on the particularities of their experiences, as only male prisoners, selected for their strength, were *Sonderkommando*. A number of salient themes emerge from their testimonies, including their experiences upon arrival at Auschwitz, separation from their families, their attitudes to their work, their association with other workers, their relationship to their overseers, and their use of cigarettes and alcohol. These themes suggest important responses and reactions to their circumstances that were male-gendered.

Arrival at Auschwitz and separation from their family members is a significant theme in *Sonderkommando* narratives. Miklos Nyiszli, a Hungarian Jew, clearly describes his arrival at Auschwitz in April 1944, along with a trainload of his compatriots. The male new arrivals jumped out of the railcars and then "turned to take our wives and children in our arms and help them down, for the level of the cars was over four and a half feet from the ground" (Nyiszli 2012, 2). This represented the normative behavior of men attempting to look after their families. However, once families were torn asunder, as other testimonies have also shown, this was no longer possible. Once they were separated, men worried about the circumstances of their wives and children. Nyiszli describes how later, with his family's departure, he was at times "terribly depressed" and "filled with loneliness" (107). Separation from their families and the worry this caused was distressing to men because they were powerless to protect their families any longer. They were not able to carry out their traditional gender role.

Shlomo Venezia, a Greek Jew who spent eight months working in the *Sonderkommando*, describes the day of his deportation to Auschwitz and the impact of the circumstances upon his behavior: "I managed to find my mother and my three sisters. . . . The fact that we were all together reassured us. . . . We'd have to work hard, of course, but at least we'd be able to stay together. That was the main thing" (Venezia 2009, 25–26). He states that he and his brother were determined to escape during the journey, but when they saw how terrified and upset their mother and sisters were, "we began to feel that it wasn't fair to leave them alone were we to try to save ourselves" (30). Hence, their responsibility and care for their closest female relatives made them rethink their position. While they still had a choice, they could not shirk their traditional gendered role as protectors of their family.

On arrival at Auschwitz, Venezia describes his first feeling as a sense of relief, quickly followed by one of disorientation. However, as he details the selection and the speed with which it was carried out, he notes that he did not have any time to think and that he had lost his bearings. His brothers and cousins ended up on the right side with him, but they were separated swiftly from the rest of their families. He describes his anger and humiliation at his circumstances, but is also frank enough to state that he felt afraid: "of course—we felt fear continually, whatever we did, since the worst could happen at any moment" (Venezia 2009, 38–39). This expression of fear is not commonly found in men's survivor accounts, as it runs counter to expected norms of male behavior. Venezia describes the physical pain associated with the arrival rituals at Auschwitz of shaving and especially the tattooing of identity numbers on the prisoners, which, he writes, was extremely painful. Again, this tends not to be much described in male narratives. Venezia details the haphazard distribution of the prison uniforms, noting that some new inmates received trousers that were either much too large or too small. He notes that "we try to sort it out among ourselves by swapping clothes" (42). This is another subject that does not usually emerge in male accounts, and indeed one that is much discussed in female ones (Pine 2015, 45–46).

Having endured the rituals of arriving, Venezia notes that he and his brother could not recognize one another: "it was a really sad moment, perhaps one of the saddest. To see the state we'd been reduced to. . . . but I didn't cry . . . in spite of the sadness and the pain" (2009, 43–44). Interestingly, his narrative suggests that the circumstances made them turn in on themselves and take refuge in silence rather than recounting their sufferings with others who were experiencing them too. This is significant, as other testimonies—especially but not exclusively those of female survivors—have stated the importance of connections with other prisoners to their survival.

Work is another topic that appears as a matter of overriding significance in the *Sonderkommando* narratives, as in those of other male survivors. Nyiszli's testimony explains his experience as a doctor in Auschwitz, working under Joseph Mengele. He gives an eyewitness account of the *Sonderkommando* at Auschwitz. In terms of his own experiences, he describes his endeavors to retain his self-control in the midst of all the horror that he encountered. His writing balances his moral repugnance at the horror of Auschwitz with his own desire to survive. Similar to other male testimonies, Nyiszli describes the significance of work for him and of doing his job well. On describing his duties for Mengele, he writes, "I planned to carry out his orders to the best of my ability" (2012, 16).

He later describes his dissection of a pair of twins and his report on it, stating, "I did my job well" (36). However, he was always cautious of the response of Mengele: "It was not a good idea to exceed the authorized bounds of knowledge or to relate all one had witnessed. And here still less than anywhere else" (38). Yet he further states that while he was at work in the dissection room or the laboratory, he was "no longer a humble KZ prisoner" and that he even contradicted Mengele on several occasions (97). He claims that his own "firm attitude," "measured sentences," and even his silences at his work could make Mengele forget even for a moment the circumstances of their relationship. At one point, he describes his reprieve from death, which gave him "neither comfort nor joy" as his work was important to Mengele and the SS—"for the moment I was indispensable" (116). Hence he perceived himself, as Turda has noted, as "an accomplished medical specialist," whose work was valued (2014, 47). Indeed, Nyiszli makes many references to his work and that of other doctors from the point of view of their profession. As we have already noted, this is commonplace in male narratives and differentiates them from female ones.

One of the most crucial aspects of life at Auschwitz for the *Sonderkommando* was, of course, the ambivalence of their positions and this emerges strongly in their written accounts. As Nyiszli was assigned to the *Sonderkommando*, he was able to have some special privileges, although he clearly states that despite better clothing, conditions, and food rations, the *Sonderkommando* generally had a very limited life span, as the SS regularly replaced the whole unit. He notes that "death would come to him as surely as it had come to every member of all the preceding *Sonderkommandos*" (Nyiszli 2012, 25). His description of the *Sonderkommando* as "young men, handpicked for their strength and good physical constitution," is unsurprising, as their captors required physical strength from those undertaking the task of removing corpses from the gas chambers to the crematoria (45). However, these younger men had

> a general tendency to nervous disorders, for it was a tremendous strain on them to know that their brothers, their wives, their parents—their entire race—were perishing here. . . . The result was acute nervous depression, and often neurasthenia. Everybody here had a past, which he looked back on with sorrow, and a future he contemplated with despair. . . . To be condemned to death and yet forced to perform jobs such

as we had to perform day after day was enough to break the body and soul of the strongest among us, and to drive many to the brink of insanity. (Nyiszli 2012, 45, 48)

The psychological, physical, and emotional effects of this grisly and physically arduous task upon the *Sonderkommando* men were indeed far-reaching. Nyiszli acknowledges that although he was not timorous by nature, there were times when he was "afraid of going mad" and felt his nerves "stretched to the breaking point" (2012, 41–42). Nyiszli stresses the ambivalence of his situation. The privileges of the *Sonderkommando* did make a difference. He writes that "thanks to my civilian clothes, I had managed to maintain a human appearance" (10). This was not the case for the majority of new arrivals at Auschwitz, as we have seen. And yet, very soon after his arrival, he describes passing in front of Mengele and bowing slightly, before realizing that "one would do well not to play the man of the world" here (6). Although he realized the hopelessness of his predicament, his strong character helped him; even in his own impossible situation he managed to encourage others to persevere. He later describes feeling himself "spinning close to the edge of madness" by the powerlessness of his situation (127). However, because he had two fellow doctors and a laboratory assistant to work with, his burdens were shared, and that, for him, was "an undeniable relief" (74). Hence, there is a sense here that sharing the experience with others made the circumstances a little easier than if he had been working entirely on his own.

Once Venezia was placed in the special detachment of the *Sonderkommando*, like Nyiszli, he realized that there were certain privileges attached to this position that were not afforded to the majority of prisoners. He adapted to camp life fairly quickly, and on his arrival for work he thought that one job was the same as any other. However, once he saw the nature of the work in the crematorium, he was left completely paralyzed. He could not exchange a single word with his coworkers and describes feeling terror-struck. "We had turned into robots, obeying orders while trying not to think, so we could survive for a few hours longer. Birkenau was a real hell; nobody can understand or grasp the logic of that camp" (Venezia 2009, 59). He reflected on what was happening, stating that sometimes, despite "intense exhaustion" from the long and strenuous work, he could not manage to get to sleep, as the images kept on haunting him. As for the portrayals of the gas chambers, he found it difficult to speak of these until much later on. Yet he describes the deaths suffered by the victims as "foul" and "filthy." What took place here was "a forced death, difficult and experienced differently by each of them" (64). He honestly notes that

> at a certain moment, under that pressure, that anguish, you become selfish and there's only one thing you can think of: how to save yourself. That was the effect the gas had. The sight that lay before us when we opened the door was terrible; nobody can even imagine what it was like. During the first days, in spite of the hunger that was tormenting my belly, I found it hard to touch the hunk of bread we were given. The stench stuck to my hands; I felt sullied by those deaths. With time, little by little, we had to get used to everything. It became a kind of routine that we couldn't think about. (Venezia 2009, 65)

Venezia shows how he and the other men in the *Sonderkommando* became accustomed to their circumstances and their work over time. He furthermore describes the difficult, gruesome, and uncomfortable nature of their work with much candidness:

> You see, the men in the *Sonderkommando* were also forced to do that kind of thing. It can't be denied, nor can it be said that it didn't exist or isn't true. And yet, in this case, I acknowledge that I feel a bit complicit, even if I didn't kill them. We had no choice, no other possibility in that hell! (Venezia 2009, 79)

The choiceless choice of keeping on going day by day was impossible in itself. Venezia notes that some of his coworkers wanted "to live by any price." Furthermore, he notes, "We were too close to death, but we carried on, day by day. I think we needed a special strength to get through it all, a psychological and physical strength" (2009, 87–88). Again, he details the terrible decisions faced by the *Sonderkommando* each day: "Those of us in the *Sonderkommando* may have had better conditions of day-to-day survival; we weren't as cold, we had more to eat, suffered less violence—but we had seen the worst, we were in it all day long, at the heart of hell" (103). They also did not talk or think about the future because they knew that there was no way of getting out and that they too would be killed. This reaction of closing off and remaining independent reflects a commonality in male responses to their plight. While this was not always the male response—or at the least the response they chose to describe—it appears to have been the usual one, especially in comparison with behavior described in female narratives.

Another important theme that emerges from the *Sonderkommando* accounts is the desire to survive. The memoir of *Sonderkommando* member Filip Müller, who was deported to Auschwitz in April 1942, notes the importance of the "chance to stay alive." He describes how he carried out all his orders "like a robot" in order to convince his superiors that he could do anything expected from him as a crematorium worker (Müller 1999, 14). He writes of his determination to survive: "the more menacing death grew, the stronger my will to survive. My every thought, every fiber of my being, was concentrated on only one thing: to stay alive, one minute, one hour, one day, one week" (18). Müller describes the distribution of bread rations by the SS: "our hands were filthy with blood and excrement, but we did not care: hunger and starvation had taught us to appreciate a hunk of bread. The mere sight of it was enough to make us forget all else" (20). Venezia, too, frankly describes the experiences he endured. He bravely and truthfully tells of the selfishness that was needed for survival and precisely explains the dilemma he faced every day, that is, the simultaneous preference to die and desire to survive. Once again, this struggle to stay alive and the need to think only of the self is much more commonplace in male survivor narratives than female ones.

Prayer is a subject that appears notably in *Sonderkommando* narratives too, as in those of other male survivors. Müller tells of how his foreman divided extra rations into equal parts and how he prayed, with "tears in his eyes," stating that "man differs from animals in that he believes in God. . . . It's prayer which makes you a human being" (1999, 27–28).

> To me it seemed sheer madness to pray in Auschwitz, and absurd to believe in God in this place. . . . But here, on the borderline between life and death, we obediently followed his example, possibly because we had nothing else left or because we felt strengthened by his faith. (Müller 1999, 29)

He later recounts meeting his father in the camp, who neither knew nor suspected what kind of work he was engaged in. He states how happy his father was to see him again, embracing him and stroking his cheeks. Since Müller was a violinist, his father believed he was a musician in the camp orchestra. Müller could not bear to tell him that he was not a musician, but that he cremated corpses: "My throat was so tight, I could not utter a word. My eyes brimming with tears, I rushed from the dark hut" (1999, 48). Müller describes how he met his father a few more times and tried to give him help and assistance. Yet, he perceived that his father was hardly able to keep to his feet, and soon came the time of his death. Although Müller had come to believe that there were no more human feelings left inside him, he "mourned in pain and grief" and "the words of the traditional prayer gave me solace in this hour of sorrow" (48). Venezia also mentions men who prayed every day and appeared to gain solace from it, while he could not understand why they continued to call on God (2009, 100). These references to prayer in men's narratives are not replicated in female ones, suggesting that there was a gendered dimension to this aspect of life and death at Auschwitz.

Other aspects of normative male behavior include the use of alcohol and cigarettes, a recurrent theme in *Sonderkommando* accounts. Nyiszli describes instances of normative male conduct and details the use of both alcohol and cigarettes among his male colleagues in the *Sonderkommando*. Alcohol temporarily allowed them to clear their minds of the unpleasant thoughts that plagued them. He later describes brandy as "the blessing remedy of all *Sonderkommando* men"; alcohol was "a momentary but necessary respite" (Nyiszli 2012, 121, 132). This is a noteworthy point, because witness and perpetrator accounts document the presence and use of alcohol at killing sites for a variety of purposes. SS members and *Einsatzgruppen* routinely drank alcohol, and the male bonding camaraderie in its consumption was a way of dispelling the effects of their genocidal tasks. Indeed, Edward Westermann notes that "many *Einsatzgruppen* members used alcohol both as a means for preparing for mass murder and as a way of dealing with their role in it" (2016, 7). Likewise, it appears that the *Sonderkommando* used alcohol for similar purposes.

On another aspect of male normative behavior, Nyiszli even describes a football match between the *Sonderkommando* and the SS: "They put the ball into play. Sonorous laughter filled the courtyard. The spectators became excited and shouted encouragement at the players, as if this were the playing field of some peaceful town" (2012, 42).

Similar to other accounts, Venezia makes the point that those who came from less privileged backgrounds "had more of a chance of adapting to life in camp and surviving" (2009, 42). In order to survive, it was necessary to know "things that were useful" (42). In terms of the impact of conditions upon people's behavior, Nyiszli—similar to other survivors—explains how the stripping of all human dignity impacted the inmates at Auschwitz. "They pushed and shouted and bit and kicked each other in order to get a few more inches of space to sleep a little more comfortably" in the overcrowded barracks (2012, 6). Both male and female narratives make reference to this kind of conduct—although there is a sense that somehow it was less acceptable and more shocking for women to conduct themselves in this way as a result of expected gendered norms. For men to push and shove was not unexpected, as jostling for position and competition was more in line with male-gendered behavioral norms.

Venezia portrays an ambivalent experience in terms of the existence of solidarity between inmates at Auschwitz:

> There was solidarity only when you had enough for yourself; otherwise, you had to be selfish if you were going to survive. In the Crematorium, you could indulge in solidarity, since we each had enough to survive. I'm not talking about helping a friend in taking over from him to give him a chance to recuperate. I'm talking about having enough to eat. For those who didn't have enough to eat, solidarity was no longer an option. So even when you had to take something from someone in order to survive, many people did so. (Venezia 2009, 100–101)

His suggestion that solidarity occurred among men only when individual needs had been met was indeed an expected male-gendered behavioral norm.

There is an explicit statement about normative male behavior in Nyiszli's description of the *Sonderkommando* uprising at Auschwitz (October 1944). Although they wanted to live and get out of Auschwitz in order to tell the world about the events there, he notes that those who died in the action "despite overwhelming odds in both numbers and material . . . sowed death and destruction among their torturers before dying proudly like men," rather than being exterminated by the SS like all the other victims at Auschwitz (Nyiszli 2012, 92).

Like other male survivors, the *Sonderkommando* men explain the circumstances of the death marches from Auschwitz as well as the impact of their specific experiences on their future lives. For example, Nyiszli describes his death march from Auschwitz to Mauthausen concentration camp at the end of the war. Nobody, he writes, paid any attention to the prisoners lying on the ground, for each had all he could do to save himself. The description of the death march by Venezia suggests more solidarity among the prisoners: "There were some whom we tried to help when they were at the end of their strength. . . . Those of us who came from the *Sonderkommando* had a bit more strength than the others, and, as much as we could, we tried to help our friends" (2009, 129). In the end, Nyiszli states that his eight months "in the kommando of the living dead" had dulled his sense of good and evil (2012, 161). Once this experience became his past, he still had to cope with it in his thoughts and dreams. Venezia similarly describes what he calls "the survivors' disease":

> It's a disease that gnaws away at us from within and destroys any feeling of joy. I have been dragging it about with me ever since I spent that time suffering in the camp. This disease never leaves me a moment of joy or carefree happiness; it's a mood that forever erodes my strength. (Venezia 2009, 154)

Conclusion

Survivor accounts, as both narratives and testimonies, bear witness to the events of the Holocaust. They are undeniably important historical sources that allow us to reflect on this dark chapter of human history. A revisiting of men's testimonies previously regarded as "universal" through the lens of gender allows us to understand them as the testimonies of men specifically. Additionally, memoirs of the *Sonderkommando* allow us to begin to comprehend the ambivalent position of these male victims at Auschwitz, who served the machinery of death. A fresh reading of these accounts enables us to understand aspects that have not been previously analyzed in relation to the gendered experiences of male Holocaust victims. In the face of the situation at Auschwitz, it is important to note not only distinctions in how men and women have written their testimonies, but also that not all male behavior in the camp was homogeneous. The formation of close relationships was life sustaining when families were torn apart. While this is mentioned widely in female writings, it is also evident in some male writings. The forming of social bonds was an important survival strategy for both men and women, although women have tended to describe this more in their narratives. While sharing recipes and reminiscing were important survival strategies and coping mechanisms that many women utilized, men's narratives mention more the factors of work and prayer.

During their imprisonment at Auschwitz, male and female inmates had to opt for agency and make choices in a variety of ways. Frankl notes that the "choice of action" existed even in the face of the terrible privations they faced at Auschwitz (2004, 74–75).

In the end, all Jews were equally destined for death, but there were differences on the road to that destination for men and women. Women's and men's experiences of the Holocaust were not identical, but as Goldenberg has suggested, they were "different horrors" within the "same hell" (Goldenberg 1991, 150–166; also Goldenberg and Shapiro 2013).

This chapter has made visible the experiences and conduct of male Holocaust victims at Auschwitz specifically in relation to their gender. It has shown the significance men placed on work as a means of dealing with their situation, trying to gain control of it (in a similar way to which women used home-making skills) and surviving. As long as they could perform their work tasks, a chance of survival remained. Inability to work almost inevitably signaled selection and death. Men also chose to portray in their narratives the qualities of strength, courage, autonomy, and independence as expected gender norms. Once separated from their wives and children, an obvious aspect of their familiar pattern of behavior (responsibility for their family members) was taken away and this left them bereft and bewildered, along with the rest of the extreme circumstances in which they found themselves placed at Auschwitz. An analysis of gender-based distinctions in Holocaust experiences and the ways they have been narrated by men (and women) adds an important angle to our knowledge and understanding of life and death in Auschwitz.

References

Baer, Elizabeth, and Myrna Goldenberg, eds. 2003. *Experience and Expression: Women, the Nazis and the Holocaust*. Detroit: Wayne State University Press.
Bartrop, Paul. 2019. *The Holocaust: The Basics*. London: Routledge.
Berger, Maurice, Brian Wallis, and Simon Watson, eds. 1995. *Constructing Masculinity*. New York: Routledge.
Bettelheim, Bruno. 1986. *Surviving the Holocaust*. London: Fontana Paperbacks.
Boyarin, Daniel. 1997. *Unheroic Conduct: The Rise of Heterosexuality and the Invention of the Jewish Man*. Berkeley: University of California Press.
Cesarani, David. 2016. *Final Solution: The Fate of the Jews, 1933–1949*. London: Macmillan.

Dean, Carolyn. 2010. *Aversion and Erasure: The Fate of the Victim after the Holocaust*. Ithaca: Cornell University Press.
Des Pres, Terrence. 1976. *The Survivor: An Anatomy of Life in the Death Camps*. Oxford: Oxford University Press.
Fein, Helen. 1999. "Genocide and Gender: The Uses of Woman and Group Destiny." *Journal of Genocide Research* 1, no. 1: 42–63.
Felman, Shoshana, and Dori Laub. 1992. *Testimony: Crises of Witnessing in Literature, Psychoanalysis, and History*. New York: Routledge.
Frankl, Viktor. 2004. *Man's Search for Meaning*. London: Simon & Schuster.
Friedländer, Saul. 1997. *Nazi Germany and the Jews: The Years of Persecution*. London: Weidenfeld and Nicolson.
———. 2007. *Nazi Germany and the Jews: The Years of Extermination*. London: Harper Collins.
Friedler, Eric, Barbara Siebert, and Andreas Kilian. 2002. *Zeugen aus der Todeszone: Das jüdische Sonderkommando in Auschwitz*. Lüneburg: zu Klampen.
Goldenberg, Myrna. 1991. "Different Horrors, Same Hell: Women Remembering the Holocaust." In *Thinking the Unthinkable: Meanings of the Holocaust*, edited by Roger S. Gottlieb, 150–166. New York: Paulist Press.
———. 2003. "Food Talk: Gendered Responses to Hunger in the Concentration Camps." In *Experience and Expression: Women, the Nazis and the Holocaust*, edited by Elizabeth Baer and Myrna Goldenberg, 165–179. Detroit: Wayne State University Press.
Goldenberg, Myrna, and Amy Shapiro, eds. 2013. *Different Horrors, Same Hell: Gender and the Holocaust*. Seattle: University of Washington Press.
Greenspan, Henry. 2010. *On Listening to Holocaust Survivors: Beyond Testimony*. St. Paul: Paragon House.
Gurewitsch, Brana, ed. 1998. *Mothers, Sisters, Resisters: Oral Histories of Women Who Survived the Holocaust*. Tuscaloosa: University of Alabama Press.
Hardman, Anna. 2000. "Women and the Holocaust." *Holocaust Educational Trust Research Papers* 1, no. 3: 1–17.
Haynes, Stephen. 2015. "Ordinary Masculinity: Gender Analysis and Holocaust Scholarship." In *Genocide and Gender in the Twentieth Century: A Comparative Study*, edited by Amy Randall, 165–188. London: Bloomsbury.
Jones, Adam, ed. 2004. *Gendercide and Genocide*. Nashville: Vanderbilt University Press.
Kolinsky, Eva. 2004. *After the Holocaust: Jewish Survivors in Germany after 1945*. London: Pimlico.
Lagerwey, Mary. 1998. *Reading Auschwitz*. London: Sage.
Langer, Lawrence. 1982. *Versions of Survival: The Holocaust and the Human Spirit*. Albany: State University of New York Press.
———. 1991. *Holocaust Testimonies: The Ruins of Memory*. New Haven: Yale University Press.
Levi, Primo. 2000. *If This Is a Man*. London: Abacus Books.

Lothe, Jakob, Susan Suleiman, and James Phelan, eds. 2012. *After Testimony: The Ethics and Aesthetics of Holocaust Narrative for the Future*. Columbus: Ohio State University Press.
Matthäus, Jürgen, ed. 2009. *Approaching an Auschwitz Survivor: Holocaust Testimony and Its Transformation*. Oxford: Oxford University Press.
Müller, Filip. 1999. *Eyewitness Auschwitz: Three Years in the Gas Chambers*. Chicago: Ivan R. Dee.
Nyiszli, Miklos. 2012. *Auschwitz: A Doctor's Eyewitness Account*. London: Penguin.
Ofer, Dalia, and Lenore Weitzman, eds. 1998. *Women in the Holocaust*. New Haven: Yale University Press.
Petropoulos, Jonathan, and John Roth, eds. 2005. *Gray Zones: Ambiguity and Compromise in the Holocaust and Its Aftermath*. New York: Berghahn.
Pine, Lisa. 2015. "Gender and the Holocaust: Male and Female Experiences of Auschwitz." In *Genocide and Gender in the Twentieth Century: A Comparative Study*, edited by Amy Randall, 37–61. London: Bloomsbury.
Randall, Amy. 2015. *Genocide and Gender in the Twentieth Century: A Comparative Study*. London: Bloomsbury.
Rittner, Carol, and John Roth, eds. 1993. *Different Voices: Women and the Holocaust*. New York: Paragon House.
Rubin, Agi, and Henry Greenspan, eds. 2006. *Reflections: Auschwitz, Memory, and a Life Recreated*. St. Paul: Paragon House.
Schweitzer, Petra. 2016. *Gendered Testimonies of the Holocaust: Writing Life*. Lanham: Lexington Books.
Seidler, Victor. 2006. *Transforming Masculinities: Men, Cultures, Bodies, Power, Sex and Love*. New York: Routledge.
Smith, Roger. 1994. "Women and Genocide: Notes on an Unwritten History." *Holocaust and Genocide Studies* 8, no. 3: 315–334.
Turda, Marius. 2014. "The Ambiguous Victim: Miklos Nyiszli's Narrative of Medical Experimentation in Auschwitz-Birkenau." *Historein* 14, no. 1: 43–58.
Venezia, Shlomo. 2009. *Inside the Gas Chambers: Eight Months in the Sonderkommando of Auschwitz*. Cambridge: Polity Press.
Warren, Mary Anne. 1985. *Gendercide: The Implications of Sex Selection*. Totowa: Rowman & Allanheld.
Waxman, Zoë. 2006. *Writing the Holocaust: Identity, Testimony, Representation*. Oxford: Oxford University Press.
Wermuth, Henry. 1993. *Breathe Deeply My Son*. London: Vallentine Mitchell.
Westermann, Edward. 2016. "Stone-Cold Killers or Drunk with Murder? Alcohol and Atrocity during the Holocaust." *Holocaust and Genocide Studies* 30, no. 1 (Spring): 1–19.
Wiesel, Elie. 2006. *Night*. London: Penguin.
Wieviorka, Annette. 2006. *The Era of the Witness*. Ithaca: Cornell University Press.
Wijze, Louis de. 1997. *Only My Life: A Survivor's Story*. New York: St. Martin's Press.

Chapter 4

"Higher Reasons for Sending People to Death?"
Male Narrativity and Moral Dilemmas in
Memoirs and Diaries of Jewish Doctors

MONIKA RICE

The autobiographical writings of Jewish physicians about the Holocaust represent a challenging field of inquiry, given that these doctors were often responsible not only for life-saving treatment but also for life-and-death decisions regarding the persons in their charge. Within this data set, a separate challenge is to consider whether there is anything unique about the Holocaust-era autobiographical writings of *male* Jewish physicians. Did the male doctors construct their narratives in a significantly different mode than their female counterparts? This chapter analyzes the life writings of male Jewish doctors in Poland, investigating how gender affected their literary focus, the subject of their writing, its style, goal, and meaning. Research for this topic intersects three subfields of Holocaust scholarship: life writing, gender, and medical history. While early Holocaust scholarship produced, at least, singular works belonging to each of these subfields,[1] it was only in the 1980s that more concerted academic efforts were dedicated to the exploration of these subjects; since then there has been a blossoming of scholarship in all three areas.[2]

Among the writers of Holocaust-era autobiographies, physicians occupy a privileged position of knowledge. Medical doctors were able to become aware of the deadly aims of the German oppressors in occupied Poland, as well as prescient about the ultimate direction of their eventual actions, before anyone else did. What Marta Balińska and William

Schneider wrote about Dr. Ludwik Hirszfeld in this context could apply to all Jewish physicians: "Given his training and experience, he understood better than most around him what was happening, and his descriptions, especially of the typhus epidemics and starvation in the ghetto, contain a penetrating perspective without being cold or aloof" (Hirszfeld, Balińska, and Schneider 2010, xvi). While knowledgeable, the doctors were helpless; the impotence of their position as informed observers became manifest when they realized the perverse purposes of the actions in which they were obliged to take part. Nazi policies of delousing, for example, were designed to propagate lice infestation, and to increase the spread of typhus. Their medical vocation was hijacked as they were forced to participate in selections of their patients, or even of their colleagues. It was in that contemptible role that the Nazi machine ultimately sought to reverse the perception of their noble calling by twisting it around into something morally abhorrent.

In this chapter, I will first provide a general outline of gendered differences in life writing as they are distinguished by literary scholars; next, I will illustrate several types of masculine discourse present in Jewish physicians' autobiographies; finally, I will apply categories of gender to a short analysis of a moral discourse concerning the situation of those compelled to perform selections prior to deportations, as related in an archival source.

First, a methodological point. Among dozens of researched documents, in this chapter I focus on several sources that may aspire to represent a larger group. What is discussed here as autobiographical writing includes works that extend beyond the classic genre of autobiography. Following the well-known definition of the French literary scholar Philippe Lejeune, I am employing the term "autobiography" to indicate a "retrospective prose narrative written by a real person concerning his existence, where the focus is his individual life, in particular the story of his personality" (Lejeune and Eakin 1989, 4).

Lejeune later broadened this definition, characterizing autobiography simply as "a narrative that recapitulates a life" (128). Expanding on this broadening, based on the attention to kinds of *discourse* that governs literature (rather than formulaic genre distinctions), postcolonial and postmodern theorists have recently considered autobiographies, diaries, and memoirs as all forming part of a self-referential discourse that belongs to an expansive category of life writing, even while the genres are technically distinct (Smith and Watson 2010, 3). That same wider understanding of autobiographical writing will be applied to the texts discussed in this chapter. The inclusiveness is partly dictated by the fluidity and hybrid nature of the documents under consideration: some began as war diaries and were completed after the war as extended memoirs or "classic" autobiographies; one was rewritten after the war "from memory" to replace a lost diary; another is an oral life narrative transcribed by someone other than the protagonist; still another is a collection of autobiographical stories written in the third person. What connects these sources is their authorship by Jewish doctors describing their lives in occupied Poland during the Holocaust.

The category of "Jewishness" denotes both ethnic origins and, at least, a partial self-identification. Whether agnostic, atheistic, or baptized, none of the authors discussed here considered himself a religious Jew, although all of them retained a strong sense of solidarity and of commitment to their people.

General Differences of Male and Female Autobiographies

In 1956, the French critic Georges Gusdorf authored a seminal essay, "Conditions and Limits of Autobiography," which established the grounds for the notion of the autonomous, self-examining subject of autobiography that is culturally imbedded in Western tradition. That condition of authorship—similarly hinging on the European concept of individualism in Lejeune's work—became, later, the object of criticism, for the autobiographical authors were envisioned as privileged, white males, while the autobiographical writings of women or writers coming from "peripheral" backgrounds were not included in that definition (Eakin 1999, 47).

In particular, feminist critics objected to this exclusive autobiographical model. Mary Mason, who first challenged it, claimed that it was relationality rather than the overcoming of personal obstacles that characterized the experience of the female half of humanity and therefore should inform the process of defining this literary genre:

> Nowhere in women's autobiographies do we find the patterns established by the two prototypical male autobiographers, Augustine and Rousseau. . . . The dramatic structure of conversion that we find in Augustine's *Confessions*, where the self is presented as the stage for a battle of opposing forces and

where a climatic victory for one force—spirit defeating flesh—completes the drama of the self, simply does not accord with the deepest realities of women's experience and so is inappropriate as a model for women's life-writing. (Mason 1980, 210)

Mason distinguishes in women's autobiographies a formation of identity by relation to another autonomous being (friend, husband, child, et al.); a single, transcendent other (e.g., God); or a kind of multiple collectivity (e.g., nation) (1980, 231).

At the same time as the publication of Mason's challenges to Gusdorf's portrayal of "classic" autobiography, Estelle Jelinek (1980) created an anthology dedicated to women's autobiographies. In it, she distinguished some of the fundamental literary gender differences of life writing, which influenced the exclusion of female autobiographies from the "canon," and which are important for my analysis.

One profound difference between male and female autobiographies, for Jelinek, is "a restrictive male view of history": while men's autobiographies reveal their "connectedness to the society" and "concentrate on chronicling the progress of their authors' professional or intellectual lives," women's autobiographies "rarely mirror the established history of their times" (Jelinek 1980, 7). Instead of emphasizing the public aspect of their lives, the affairs of the world, even women famous for their professional successes concentrate, in their life narratives, on the details of their personal lives. Another critical gender difference that Jelinek identifies is related to how the universal tendency to abstain from revealing embarrassing, uncomfortable memories is displayed. In handling this predicament, men and women exhibit their detachment in different modes: "men tend to idealize their lives or to cast them into heroic molds," as well as to emphasize overcoming crises, while women project a different self-image, one that "[reveals] self-consciousness and a need to sift through their lives for explanations and understanding" (14–15). A third, crucial difference is a question of the linear nature and the cohesion of autobiographical narrative as a genre. Jelinek reports that, although male autobiographies generally create the impression of a coherent, logically developed whole, women's life narratives are characterized by a lack of orderliness and by irregularity. Women's self-portraits appear, not in chronological order, but fragmentary and disconnected, "organized into self-sustained units rather than connecting chapters" (17).

Paul John Eakin has recently raised an interesting challenge, however, to this binary model developed by feminist scholars. While acknowledging that the feminist critique of "the Gusdorf model" brought about a momentous development in the study of women's autobiography, Eakin contends that it also froze male life writing within the limitations of that model. Men were now to be relegated to what Nancy K. Miller has called "the model of imperial masculinity," while all the nuances of subjective, volatile, relational subjects were to be assigned to women's life writing (Eakin 1999, 49–50). Although Eakin proposes no definitive solution to this binary "straightjacket," he does call for the acknowledgment of universal relational and autonomous dimensions, common to both genders, without requiring that they be assigned necessarily either to female or male lives. One means to achieve such recognition might lie in a study of infant psychology that stresses the intersubjective dimensions of the acquisition of an autonomous identity (Eakin 1999, 51).

In the following pages, I will discuss whether, and to what extent, that traditional binary model may apply to the Holocaust autobiographies of Jewish male doctors, and what types of discourses their writings may create.

Scientists in Search of Healing the World: A Positivistic Outlook

A tendency to craft an autobiographical narrative in the style of a wise scholar who wishes to enlighten the audience and to heal a wounded civilization appears to be characteristic of the memoirs of a number of male physicians, among them Dr. Ludwik Hirszfeld, who has left us the most famous autobiography of a Jewish physician in Poland.

Hirszfeld (1884–1954) was born into an assimilated family from Łódź. He discovered the inheritance of ABO blood types and developed the science of population genetics. He earned a reputation as a leading immunologist during the first part of the twentieth century. During World War I, he volunteered his medical services in Serbia. Upon returning to the newly reconstituted Poland after World War I, he received baptism. Motivated by a strong sense of Polish patriotism, he anticipated, apparently, that his conversion would help him "fit" better in Polish society. Even before World War I, in fact, he had identified himself more as a Pole than as a Jew. It seems, then, that at least one likely reason for Hirszfeld's acceptance of Christianity may have been its utility as a step toward full cultural assimilation. He would later experience marginalization in the Warsaw Ghetto, however, for his religious allegiance and for his attending Catholic Mass with other Jewish converts.

In his memoir, nevertheless, Hirszfeld declares that the main purpose of his writing is the commemoration of the Jewish victims. The most heart-wrenching part of that commemoration was that the Hirszfelds lost their daughter, an only child, in the ghetto. Her death is attributed to natural causes, possibly anorexia (Hirszfeld, Balińska, and Schneider 2010, xxvi). Her death and the murder of other Jews were not to be relegated to silence; their eloquent stillness cried out to be memorialized in testimony:

> May this book be a monument to those who departed prematurely—among them my daughter. And to my associates for whom I wished to be a father.
>
> I had the impression that those who perished and those who are still suffering were standing behind me and bidding me to write the tale of their torture and the guilt of their contemporaries. (Hirszfeld, Balińska, and Schneider 2010, 296)

The testimony answered a *call* to be written; it was something that had to be done. Even apart from its necessity, however, the act of testifying on behalf of the tortured and the dying was also intended as a *diagnosis* to precede appropriate healing measures:

> Out of my pain, I decided to forge a weapon to move the public conscience. I would show the endless pain of parents whose children have died. No, not who died. But who were murdered before their parents' very eyes. . . . [I] will write about the death of the victim whose last impression is befouled with the sight of a murderer or a murdering robot, and is burdened with the loss of faith in man, with the complaint of senseless torture, and with the question cast in the last moment: "For what sins?" (Hirszfeld, Balińska, and Schneider 2010, 296)

Knowledge about what happened to the European Jews would have the power of engaging the conscience. Witnessing to personal tragedies as well as to the murder of a nation would become a useful tool ("a weapon") through which people could be "rendered better." It is the curative, "redemptive" function of the testimonial diagnosis that stems from a positivistic hope in moral improvement following civilizational progress.[3] The fundamental paradigm, in fact, within which the Polish scholars worked, and through which they attempted to understand and explain the world, was a positivistic outlook. This outlook appears as the philosophical perspective most frequently encountered in the background of the masculine Polish medical autobiographies of the time.

A similarly neo-Socratic conviction that knowledge will improve the world, fostered by the positivistic optimism of European technological progress, runs through the memoir of another Jewish physician, Dr. Julian Aleksandrowicz. In his preface he outlined how a scholarly observation of the effects of Hitler's regime on human nature led him to realize what might be the most effective cure for oppression and violence:

> We shall see how easy it is to make an evil man out of *Homo sapiens*. Hitler's scientific educational method achieved it. We shall see also that in order to make a good man out of a human being, it is not enough to feed him on some humanistic philosophy, or religion. Biological similarity, and not a declared idea, determines a man's attitude. I saw the most beautiful humanistic attitude in people of similar character, similar dynamic stereotype, therefore in people similar biologically, even though they differed in their opinions of the world. . . . Only based on the knowledge of this psycho-physical essence may we realize that mutual kindness among people is a condition of a successful evolution of the species *Homo sapiens*. Kindness is a most powerful factor that prevents not only many nervous diseases of individuals, which destroy their hearts and brains, but most of all the tragic social disease, which is the mutual destruction of human beings, caught up in the passion of hate, which, as a consequence, leads to a collective psychosis: war. (Aleksandrowicz 1955, n.p.)[4]

Beyond giving expression to a positivistic outlook, Hirszfeld's memoir also testifies to the deep need to alleviate the human suffering that he encountered and experienced in the ghetto. After surreptitiously obtaining from the Germans permission to lecture to other ghetto doctors (under the cover of instructing them on infectious diseases), Hirszfeld set out not only to save their medical knowledge but also "to keep up their morale" (Hirszfeld, Balińska, and Schneider 2010, 202). He confessed that his listeners appeared to him

> as little, frightened chicks. I would look at their young faces and think how few of them would survive. . . . Should I, one day before their death, talk about pathogens and require condemned men to take an exam in bacteriology? No, I would capture their imagination with lofty ideas and alleviate their pain by satisfying a desire that is very strong in Jews: their hunger for knowledge. . . . Thus, I gave them a vision of strong experiences, distant travel, and intense thoughts. I took those poor children by the hand and led them to the summits where the air was pure, where people prayed in ecstasy at sunrise, and no one despised them, and where, in the glory of mankind, they could build, think, and dream.
>
> From below, I could hear shots and cries of victims. But the students sat looking at me and were completely absorbed in what I was saying. . . .
>
> There, I found myself as a gardener of human souls. I always wanted my words to create meaning out of chaos and to shape human souls. Now, moreover, I was giving them oblivion. Did I reach the Jewish soul? I do not know; I only know that I reached very, very unhappy people. (Hirszfeld, Balińska, and Schneider 2010, 202)

From the distance of the knowledge that very few of his compatriots had managed to survive, Hirszfeld paints an image of himself as a healer of souls, reaching to the ancient ethos of a profound medical vocation that goes beyond "merely" curing bodily ailments. The project of saving the dignity of the human soul in the inhuman conditions of the ghetto, and of bringing spiritual healing to a horribly disfigured world, was an expression of resistance that many Jews, including those who were active in education and culture, maintained throughout their captivity in the ghetto. We find another example of a doctor embracing this healing mission in Dr. Janusz Korczak, who gathered the orphans under his care to prepare a play by

Rabindranath Tagore about a dying boy whose innocence radiated to others, a few weeks before these orphan children would be deported to Treblinka (Lifton 1997, 318).

Hirszfeld's life narrative, therefore, was made to be commemorative and salvific, in keeping with the positivistic tradition in which European scholars of his time were steeped. At the same time, his autobiography is typical of the genre, in that it is also an identity-building enterprise (Eakin 2008). One important motif of his memoir is his introspective "research" into the mind of a scholar who, witnessing the annihilation of his people, grapples with a difficult doubt about the very positivism that is the source of his other (curative) hope:

> Thus, I decided to write the story of my life. How my spirit was shaped in those remote times when the air was not imbued with hate. My dreams and my aspirations. How I believed that creators of science could sculpt human souls. And about their great guilt and betrayal of the Truth. (Hirszfeld, Balińska, and Schneider 2010, 296)

In its personal, introspective aspect, Hirszfeld's autobiography has elements of a classic *Bildungsroman*, with a typical structure of apprenticeship, education "in life," renunciation, and civic integration into society (Smith and Watson 2010, 119–120). Nearly half of his memoir is devoted to his youth and to the periods during and after World War I. Describing these times, he depicts happy years of international scientific collaboration, during which German scholars ruled the roost according to objective academic standards. In contrast to the scholarly explorations chronicled in the first part of his memoir, the second part tells the story of the destruction of his people by the methodical acts of relentless Nazi occupiers. It is also the record of a disappointed academic—one disappointed not so much in science as in its betrayal by German scientists and, generally, by the European scientific community.

Although Hirszfeld, significantly, avoids the discussion of his childhood years, he instead begins with the narration of his studies in Germany ("the apprenticeship"), the stages of "testing" that education, and of gaining experience "in life" during his years in the ghetto. When, after the war, he is invited to reestablish his scholarly activities, the positivistic premise once again motivates him to remain in communist Poland, thus helping him not only to regain his lost position as a productive member of society but also to return to the practice of a science that suffered betrayal during the war:

> Poland was threatened by the fact that she might not be able to create her intelligentsia, which was essential for the country's cultural life. . . . Who was to rebuild the lost or destroyed schools? How could one require of such a consciously destroyed nation, bled white, to reconstruct buildings on its own, to organize laboratories, to write and print burned manuscripts? And thus I decided to take upon myself the difficult task of organizing a Medical Faculty at the University of Wroclaw. I did not wish for Poland to be an eternal beggar especially where the most difficult values to create were concerned—the values of culture. (Hirszfeld, Balińska, and Schneider 2010, 353–354)

To conclude the discussion of Hirszfeld's autobiography, this work remains, in its most consistent form, a classic, heroic, male life writing of the "Gusdorf model." Even though Hirszfeld does not build his narrative around his medical achievements, it represents a solitary mental and moral evolution: the individual, internal struggle he waged against the betrayal of the values of the destroyed world, and "the destiny of one man against the background of history of his time" (16), through which he managed to emerge victorious.

The memoir of Dr. Mordechai Lensky is another example of an attempt to make an accurate, exhaustive "diagnosis" of the Nazi "pathology." Lensky had managed to escape the ghetto on the "Aryan" side in 1943 to hide with Poles. In *A Physician Inside the Warsaw Ghetto*, Lensky is primarily concerned with the medical infrastructure of the ghetto, and with the unfolding sufferings of its inhabitants. He strives to achieve objective, "neutral" descriptions, which, written in the third person, sound particularly detached. For example: "If the Jews' intuitive assessment of the general political situation was precise, crystal-clear even, their assessment of their own situation as Jews was faulty. Only a small part of the population felt jeopardized" (Lensky 2009, 33).

At the beginning of Lensky's memoir, the first-person pronoun appears almost exclusively only when he presents a strictly personal mental guess or a conviction. In this approach, his memoir even more approximates the style of a scientific report accompanied by critical annotation. For example:

> I have often asked myself this question: what could the Jews have done, had they properly assessed their situation, had they realized that the Nazis wished to annihilate them, to physically destroy them? . . . As I have already stated before, the vast majority of the Jews were not aware of the dangers ahead. (Lensky 2009, 36)

Such a detached perspective was part of the scholarly paradigm mentioned earlier; specifically, it was a reflection of the German academic tradition of an impersonal narrative of investigation, ostensibly free from subjective influence, which dominated the Polish academy of the time. Lensky's linguistic detachment is a means through which he asserts the veracity of what he describes, which might not, in ordinary circumstances, even be believable. Like other Holocaust autobiographies authored by male doctors, his document is a solid source of historical information, one that is able to enrich formal studies of the Warsaw Ghetto. It includes extensive reports on the mechanics of the daily functioning of the ghetto, its chief administrators, its major events, and also its social moods, its current customs, and its hopes, gossips, and jokes. Nevertheless, as a "cold" narrative might not sufficiently capture the depraved cruelty of the Nazi treatment of the Jews, Lensky breaks from the "objective" mode when writing about children—for example, when he described his medical treatment of little smugglers. He tenderly confesses:

> At times a brother or sister [of a wounded smuggler] would arrive, bringing them some food. They would kiss each other and weep silently. I always felt challenged witnessing their encounters. These wounded children embodied for me the moral courage of the entire Warsaw ghetto population. (Lensky 2009, 42)

Similarly, following an account of deportation witnessed from his hospital, Lensky is suddenly gripped by a vision:

> From the windows of the hospital I often saw the horrifying sight: a mass of bent-over Jews, their bags on their shoulders, led by the Nazis. Their faces haggard with fatigue and suffering, tripping along, humiliated and robbed of everything, carrying with them the remains of their earthly belongings:

> an old garment, a dry piece of bread, an onion slice, and a herring. . . . And I see myself together with all my colleagues from the hospital, marching single file, led by two or three Nazis in a long procession, further along Leszno St. All the Jews—men, women, and children—come out of the houses and join us. We all proceed in the wrong direction, out of the city. Others are entering Warsaw; we are coming out of the ghetto. Where are we headed? To the ghettos of Białystok, Równo, Słonim? But these are only transit stations. The final station will come later, the death stop that will be our end. When I opened my eyes, the procession had passed. A door opened noisily. Another wounded person was carried in on a stretcher. (Lensky 2009, 42–43)

This dreamlike reflection could be interpreted as contemplating realistic possibilities: Lensky knows that he might be the next in the "procession" heading to the "death stop." The only sensible thing to do is to take care of the next patient. His melancholy and the despair of his vacant emotions are palpable.

As Lensky's memoir progresses in time, he continues discussing the "historical" aspects of ghetto existence: the various public functionaries, the health department, the *Judenrat*, the Jewish historians, the soup kitchens, and so on. Sometime during 1941, he receives multiple testimonies from his patients concerning Jewish massacres in the East. These, again, affect the tone he has adopted as a "factual" chronicler, within which he begins to report on the terrible news:

> He [the patient] spoke Lithuanian Yiddish. There were many Lithuanian Jews in Warsaw, but their own brand of Yiddish had already been affected by the surrounding Polish-Yiddish sounds. It was no longer sharp and witty as before. . . . "Where are you from?" I asked the patient. "I arrived in Warsaw from Słonim last week. I managed to escape in time," he answered. "Escape from Słonim? What happened? Disaster?" I asked fearfully. "The Nazis carried out a horrible massacre in Słonim," he answered, his voice quivering. . . . My wife and son were murdered, and only I survived, hiding in the cellar. . . ." The patient told me this and his tears flowed. He turned his face,

probably not wanting me to see him break down like a woman, overcome with emotion. He was trying to save face. Innocent Jew! Your pure tears embody a martyred, tormented and humiliated people, upon which—in the words of the prophet Isaiah—"the Lord hath laid the iniquity" of all nations. (Lensky 2009, 75–76)

With a similar account heard from his friend, Lensky's narrative becomes more personal and revealing of his own state of mind, even as he avoids directly describing it. The first-person account allows him to signal a retreat into his own gloomy interior: "Dismal thoughts gripped me. Suddenly I couldn't stop yawning. Fatigue set in and I could neither sit nor stand. I barely made it to bed, took off my clothes and tucked myself in. I was asleep in an instant" (80).

More interior torment is revealed when Lensky visits a refugee home (organized by the *Judenrat* for Jews deported from other communities) and considers working there, attracted by the extremely harsh and filthy conditions amid which he would have an opportunity to bring the refugees some meager degree of medical relief. His wife is concerned that he might be risking his own life, a fear confirmed when he falls ill with typhoid fever. His sickness, though, follows an amazing heavenly dream, in which he visits a perfect fairytale land ("marvelous and enchanting"), enters a magnificent palace, and is affectionately welcomed by a man and a woman whose faces are familiar to him. He realizes that these were the patients in the refugee home he just saw and treated during the day. "A sob escaped," he wrote, "followed by uncontrollable weeping, tears streaming out of my eyes. I woke up, my eyes opened wide" (87). The incursion of deep, surreal tenderness, compassion, and the will to heal overflow through his ordinarily restrained narrative, which shies away from directly revealing his emotions. On the other hand, when, in the following pages, Lensky tried again to contain, to understand, and to explain what he has witnessed, he occasionally falls into unexpected sarcasm:

> Life in Warsaw took its course; Jews left this course for the next that was all bounty, at least for simple, honest folk. This happened for various reasons: hunger, typhoid fever, tuberculosis and colitis. Most of them left without much ado, nor the slightest protest. Mr. Pinkert's business—delivering the bodies

of the dead to the cemetery—flourished daily: 200–300 bodies a day, 6,000–9,000 bodies a month. No wonder Pinkert could afford to sit at a restaurant and order a fat duck and wine for lunch, then get up patting his paunch, and throw some alms to the beggars outside. (Lensky 2009, 93)

Bitter conclusions might be a natural, human response to a situation of unmitigated, pointless, massive death. Lensky, for example, faces his own impotence in the face of Jewish suffering: "There is not much work at the hospital. The doctors pass the time either telling jokes or looking out the window, to watch out for deportation—a general state of terrified boredom" (134).

Such interludes seem to push Lensky's objective, scholarly style in the direction of acerbic wit. Both are, functionally, a means of detaching oneself and of preserving a necessary distance, even while the very need to do so is a manifestation of the perception of his own powerlessness.

In the middle of the memoir, Lensky has placed a short literary story, "Three Sisters" (107–111). In evocative language that is distinct from that of the rest of the memoir, Lensky focuses on the character of the eldest of three sisters, Esther, who dies on the way to the *Parówka* (a compulsory steaming that supposedly had a delousing effect but was really just a Nazi method of humiliating the Jews). In an image eerily resembling Hans Christian Andersen's "The Little Match Girl," Esther is called by the dead to enter heaven:

In winter, the river Vistula (Wisła) freezes over, but under the top layer of ice, stormy waves pound away. And here she was seeing Jews wrapped in their prayer-shawls, praying with joyous devotion, to the sound of the cantor and the choir . . . From the top galleries of the synagogue women were gesturing to her with their fingers. . . . Suddenly her face shone—the women were signaling her to join them. She heard their voices calling out to her, "Esther, don't be afraid. Hurry up and join us up here, don't go to the bathhouse. The devil lives there, and he will contaminate you. This is the last *Parówka*, there won't be any more. All Jews will come to us from Warsaw, Brześć, Łódź, Siedlce, from every big city, from the smallest outlying hamlet: rabbis, shopkeepers, doctors and lawyers, beggars—they will all come together, leave hell with its filthy Nazis, and join us. Together we shall hold prayers to the God of Israel, sing His praises, divine chants to our God in heaven. (Lensky 2009, 111)

Esther leaves the line and intentionally falls down to the ground in a nearby ruin, "trying to push her way into the beyond, into a world of truth and holiness." An angry Jewish policeman who supervises the group follows her, intending to do her harm; when he leans over her, however, he sees that she is already dead. Perhaps, "Esther" is a composite character; or, she may have been modeled on one or another person whom Lensky knew in real life. Either way, this heart-wrenching story, which paints for the reader the actual conditions and internal dilemmas of the ghetto inhabitants, offers a symbolic vision of religious hope in a God who is—paradoxically and yet, without question—worthy of praise. In this instance, as with other realistic portraits of persons living and dying in the ghetto, Lensky appears to introduce his characters to illustrate certain, definite ideas, including heroism, courage, faith, and rebellion.

Before the Great Deportation in the summer of 1942, Lensky becomes intensely sick, suffers a heart attack, and declines into a state of feverish delirium. When he recovers, he describes, in short, ironic sentences, his miraculous escapes from being caught up in the daily deportations, even while he experiences this period as one in which he was only half aware of his surroundings: "I felt no fear, just hollow and indifferent. 'My fate is in Thy hands' describes my mood at the time" (131). Realizing the increasing futility of working at a hospital with fewer and fewer patients, while awaiting yet another deportation, the Lenskys move out of the ghetto to a hideout.

Until the Ghetto Uprising in April 1943, the memoir will be punctuated with mournful, spiritual passages that invoke God in the martyred nation. These are interwoven with the "factual" chronicle of an annihilated community. "Hearing" the howls emanating from the apartments being forcefully emptied by the ghetto police intent on providing the daily contingent of victims to the *Umschlagplatz* drives Lensky to run away madly, with his heart pounding, yet recalling the Psalms and the book of Zohar (146–148). Anger that the Jews "delude" themselves, and so deliver themselves without any resistance, chokes him. The only resistance, in fact, was displayed by the children, who were taken to the cattle wagons kicking and screaming. Bitter, mournful words are interlaced with a "cold" analysis of how the Jewish "classes" were "disintegrated" (162–168). The memoir ends, then, with a short description of the uprising, and of the Jewish moods leading up to it.

Lensky's memoir is a courageous attempt to produce a "scientific analysis" of the murder of the Warsaw Jews. In the process of writing it, his emotions and religious expressions break through his detached style, as he allows them to surface at key moments. His is thus a less self-consciously chiseled portrait of himself; he does not seem to have the objective of forging an identity for himself as he writes, which is patent in Hirszfeld's and Aleksandrowicz's narratives. His document resembles some kind of material body, tightly wrapped in a rope that tries to contain it, yet bursting its bonds, so that, here and there, the rope begins to break.

Husbands and Wives: On Interiority

Among the dozens of doctors' diaries and memoirs I researched, there are four documents that may provide a unique opportunity for analyzing masculine perspectives: these are the four life narratives of two married couples: Drs. Noemi Makower and Henryk Makower and Drs. Alina Margolis Edelman and Marek Edelman. This rare material provides near-laboratory conditions to compare gender perspective: in each case, both spouses worked in the same profession; witnessed and went through almost the same events; and shared intimate memories, confidences, impressions, opinions, and judgments on what was likely to be the darkest period of their lives. A comparative analysis of the perspectives of these husbands and wives may provide material for a more generalized discussion about masculine Holocaust life writing.

Dr. Noemi Makower's memoir *Love in the Shadow of Death* is an example of a personal, relation-based narrative. It is a document written in hiding after the Warsaw Ghetto Uprising and, therefore, in conditions of relative peace and safety, which allowed a certain amount of room for her to reflect on and assess her situation. Noemi's first husband had escaped to the East at the start of the war; after he left, stung by his abandonment of her, she became involved with Dr. Henryk Makower, whom she would later marry. Noemi's style is careful and slightly detached; she appears aware of the insufficiency of language, as when she writes, "The word *terrible* was very much abused before the war" (Makower 1996, 7). She confesses, for example, that she was unable to communicate "the terrible things" to her then-lover Henryk, as he was facing his own gruesome experiences. They have both had their "fill" of it all. She pours out her reflection, therefore, on paper. In the style of a historical narrative, she describes the liquidation of the Warsaw Ghetto with chilling accuracy, tightly focused on the panic of the people. Her narrative of Jewish attempts at hiding during a *kocioł* (cauldron; a method of entrapping Jews in a small area before a deportation) provides a unique glimpse into the emotions of fear and desperation, interspersed with spasms of hope, during the most brutal hunts of the Jews in hiding.

While her matter-of-fact narrative gives us an invaluable depiction of what was occurring, Noemi also describes individuals: children in distress, helplessly attempting to save their parents by engaging in smuggling and incurring deep bodily wounds; adults looking for a last-minute shelter; other people, dear to her, who meet their death. Here, Noemi mourns the demise of one of her friends:

> The image of Bronka still haunts me. A young, twenty-six-year-old psychology student, tall and shapely, with a sweet little face surrounded by dark-blond hair. . . . A prominently Nordic type. She had a lot of friends on "the other side," who urged, asked, insisted on the phone—"come to us, do not wait, you will die." Bronka did not want to leave her husband, her parents and parents-in-law. She belonged to those who waited till the last minute to cross to the Aryan side and lived to see the deportation on January 18, 1942. . . . My beloved Bronka was fainting, because the air was foul, she was fainting after four years of war starvation. Only a week ago she aborted her pregnancy. I imagine her surprised, wide-opened childish eyes at the moment in which a brutal rifle butt and a whip of the beaters pushed her to the wagon. For what? To death? Why? Has she ever hurt anyone in her life?
>
> But why write about Bronka, there were crowds of little children, children suckling breast . . . , etc. But I loved Bronka and I can do nothing about it that not Mr. Józef, noble, intelligent, that not his wife, whom I knew much longer than Bronka, that not Michał and the other ten thousand people—small and big, gray and famous ones, but just Bronka keeps standing in front of my eyes when I think of the January action. (Makower 1996, 100)

Such passages, full of sketches of personal idiosyncrasies, convey instantly the uniqueness of each individual victim of the Holocaust. It is not what Bronka might have stood for, not any symbolic "role" for which she could be cast in a "story about the Holocaust," but Bronka herself, with her childish eyes and her tragic abortion, which momentarily connect the reader with the "real" experiences of the Jews. Such narratives, heartfelt close-ups of beloved individuals, are not often found in male autobiographies and are one of the important marks of a gendered literary difference.

A major distinctive feature of Noemi's memoir is that other large parts of it are deeply concerned with the emotional life of the author. Her work is a painfully revealing, alarmingly honest confession of Henryk's indifference, his betrayal, his illicit liaisons, her abortions, the growth and maturing of Henryk's love, and, finally, marriage and survival under the most dire human circumstances.

Comparing her diary with the memoir written by her husband, it is clear that Noemi writes, primarily, about herself and the evolution of her love with Henryk; she approaches all other observations—concerning the ghetto population, family, patients, and so forth—from the perspective of the emotions and psychological effects that they produce. Henryk's document, *Memoir of the Warsaw Ghetto*, on the other hand, which he wrote while he and Noemi were in hiding after the annihilation of the Warsaw Ghetto, presents a broad panoramic view of the organization and day-to-day functioning of the ghetto, the diseases and epidemics of its population, and other such matter-of-fact details. His memoir informs the reader more broadly than does Noemi's, not only on "the anatomy of the ghetto" but also by providing a detailed narrative of what happened to his and Noemi's extended families. His account incriminates strongly the Jewish police for the process of brutal deportations. It highlights the perversity of the Nazi order, which divided the Jewish population between those who would be complicit in Nazi crimes and those who would be their victims. It provides sweeping images of a starved, lice-ridden, terror-stricken population on the brink of extermination. In this respect, Henryk's memoir closely follows the positivistic, scholarly, informative, and educational perspective present in the autobiographical writings of Hirszfeld, Aleksandrowicz, and Lensky.[5]

There is also a noticeable difference between Noemi's and Henryk's accounts when it comes to fleshing-out portraits of characters in the ghetto and the camps. When Henryk describes an individual, it is in rather quick, matter-of-fact strokes that exemplify a larger reality. These portraits seem always to illustrate something else, to signify one aspect of the dehumanization occurring under the Nazis or, conversely, to display aspects of a morally victorious resistance. A similar approach to human portraiture is found in Lensky's *Three Sisters*, and again and again in other male diaries and memoirs. On the other hand, when Noemi and the other female physicians whom I researched incorporate individual examples—little vignettes of ghetto behavior—into their narratives, it is the people themselves who take center stage; we see them for who and what they are, as themselves. We do not perceive a need to provide a moral to their stories; we do not feel rushed to know what they "symbolize" or even what happened to a population "at large"; each description focuses on the specific sufferings of particular individuals, presented in poignant, compassionate detail.

Turning to the documents published by the Drs. Edelman, Marek has enjoyed a certain fame as the only leader of the Warsaw Ghetto Uprising to remain in Poland after the war. A book based on his oral narrative, *Shielding the Flame* (Krall and Edelman 1986), is an account of a conversation with Hanna Krall. Marek's style is cynical and impatient; he does not mince words and he does not tolerate it when notions that function in the "traditional" world, the world before Auschwitz, are applied to the Holocaust. His mockery of a traditional understanding of heroism, for example, is acerbic. Describing the "public" rape by Ukrainian guards of a girl waiting in a crowd to be loaded on the trains on the *Umschlagplatz*, Marek explains to Krall why nobody made a move to save her: "Well, nobody got up. Nobody was any longer capable of getting up from that floor. Those people were capable of only one thing: waiting for the trains" (Krall and Edelman 1986, 44). Apparently realizing the objective difficulty for an outside observer to grasp such an ethical universe, he provokes his interviewer with the rhetorical question: "But, why are we talking about it?" (45). Such a line of questioning surfaces often in his narrative, in which he sometimes seems to be telling a good joke and realizes, too late, that nobody has the tools to understand it. Even Krall, herself a child survivor of the Holocaust, is treated with mocking derision when Marek attempts to explain to her what true heroism meant in the ghetto: "You see, Hanna, you don't understand anything. . . . this doctor had given *her own* cyanide to kids who were complete strangers! . . . She saved these children from the gas chamber. People thought she was a hero" (9). Interestingly, Marek doesn't state directly that he considered the female doctor a hero; he seems only to pose such an interpretation *ad populum*, as he calls into question traditional notions of morality.

There are a few events that seem to have been experienced together by Marek and his future wife, Alina Margolis Edelman. One of them concerns the occurrence of infanticide during the *Aktion*. In *Shielding the Flame*, Marek recounts:

> When the liquidation action started and they were gathering up people from the first floor of our hospital, one woman upstairs was in labor. A doctor and a nurse were with her. And when the baby was born, the doctor handed it to the nurse, and the nurse laid it on one pillow, and smothered it with another one. The baby whimpered for a while and then grew silent. This woman was nineteen years old. The doctor didn't say a thing to her. Not a word. And this woman knew herself what she was supposed to do. (Krall and Edelman 1986, 47)

Compare this rendering with Alina's description of what was likely the very same event:

> I ran up to the first floor. . . . In the depths of the room, among empty beds, a young woman was in labor. Without a word, without a cry. . . . Next to the bed stood a girl in the pink dress of a student of Nursing School [Alina was a student there herself], my friend from an older group. Next to her a doctor. I knew him, he lived in our house. He was young, funny, he whistled, and used to say when passing me by: "How are you, colleague?" I stopped, I secretly came closer. They didn't notice me. After a moment I heard a sharp crying. In the doctor's large hands a newborn covered in mucus was straightening up his head. He cried! I saw everything as if in a sharp light. I saw a questioning look of the doctor directed to the mother. I saw how, with barely visible gesture she nodded her head. I saw a second look, thrown to the pink dress of the nurse. And immediately after that, her move. She grabbed a pillow from the next bed and pressed it on the newborn. The cry was barely audible now. The action was over. From afar one could still hear some shots. (Margolis-Edelman 1994, 64)

Comparing the two passages suggests the possibility that Marek may have known of the event from Alina's narrative of her firsthand experience. In Marek's conversation, the story is short, and concise, and its point is that the nurse who smothered the child "knew herself what she was supposed to do." As in other instances, for Marek, the "moral" is that morality itself had changed during this time of horror, and that we should not judge the participants by any absolute standard. Alina's narrative, on the other hand, seems to be concerned more with the very act of an innocent life meeting its end amid the surrounding catastrophe. She perceives the silent communication between mother, nurse, and doctor, and allows us to approximate the despairing feelings of a mother, who, "with a barely visible" nod, permits a new life that has just left her womb to be suffocated. The closing of the narrative has a double meaning: the *Aktion* of the Nazis is over, and so is the tragic killing by the Jews of their own children. In some sense, Alina's text invites a more open-ended reflection on the nature of morality in times of unprecedented terror, for it poses questions without imposing definitive conclusions.

Other passages in Alina's memoir, which we do not have the space here to analyze, testify to a "feminine" tendency to focus on the concrete and personal. Several moving portraits of ghetto victims, friends, and particular characters among the nurses demonstrate the pointlessness of logical categories when considering the chances of survival in the ghetto. They also manifest numerous examples of truly heroic, sacrificial attitudes among some of the people trapped there. Marek, for his part, also focuses, occasionally, on a personal story. When he saves his patients, for example, he describes them as his closest people; he knows everything about them. Yet it is hard to avoid the impression that his focus is primarily on a "fight with death." Saving lives, for him, is more of a strategic principle; it does not represent an actual, sustained interest in any one particular person, as one can certainly verify in the female narratives (Krall and Edelman 1986, 87).

Answering the Moral Question: A Postmodern Outlook

Aside from being a medical doctor in the Łódź Ghetto, Dr. Arnold Mostowicz was also a literary, artistic man. His fascinating memoir, *With a Yellow Star and a Red Cross: A Doctor in the Lodz Ghetto*, takes the form of a collection of stories written in the third person. Focusing on various aspects of the ghetto experience, his is generally a detached narrative, interspersed with the sort of short distraction and rhetorical question often used by Marek Edelman, a device meant to question the very purpose of one's giving the testimony.

Mostowicz's stories generally provide unique glimpses into the Łódź Ghetto. He includes, for example, a description of a Gypsy camp, into which only very few Jews were allowed, a fact of which only sparse documentation otherwise remains. I intend to focus on one chapter, "The Second Last," that tackles a matter of uncommon moral weight. This chapter is the best example I have found in which the morality of cooperating in the selections for deportation—something in which Jewish doctors were normally forced to participate under the threat of death—is discussed "to its logical end." In the life narratives of other Jewish physicians, all manner of questionable moral practices are implicitly presented as, at least relatively, justifiable, insofar as they had the potential effect of saving Jewish lives. For the Drs. Edelman or for Dr. Irene Blady-Szwajgier, collaborating in the selections of some people for deportation was justifiable if it was accompanied by an intention to save others, for example, those who might have been more useful for the Underground. For Dr. Giselle Perl and Dr. Olga Lengyel (who performed abortions to save mothers' lives) or for Dr. Baruch Milch (who with astounding honesty described his nephew's death in hiding, *at the hands of his father*), even the deaths of children could likewise be *relatively* excusable, although they were always to be regarded as horrific. While the doctors clearly did not relish standing in judgment of who, ultimately, should be allowed to survive at least a little longer, they all seemed to subscribe to the idea that rescuing a few individuals for a proportionate reason (such as usefulness to the Underground) is understandable. The end—defeating the Nazis—justified the means of putting the survival of those more likely to contribute to that end ahead of the lives of those who might not have as constructive a role in the resistance. With similar moral reasoning, the means of taking the life of a fetus in the womb or a newborn freshly out of it is justified by the end of saving the life of an expectant mother who might otherwise have been killed in Auschwitz, or of saving Jews in hiding whose lives might otherwise have been endangered by the newborn's cry. These utilitarian choices are uniformly presented as morally acceptable, especially to the extent that they are seen as reluctant or even "choiceless" choices, which Lawrence Langer defines as "crucial decisions . . . between one form of abnormal response and another, both imposed by a situation that was in no way of the victims' own choosing" (1982, 72).

Mostowicz is unique in his efforts to supply a comprehensive consideration of the morality of acts like these. This he accomplishes by relating the story of a doctor (himself?) who is ordered to examine and select candidates for a proximate deportation. This doctor belongs to an underground organization, and so he knows the ultimate destination of the transport, which is why he had been chosen to perform what he calls "this disgusting work" (Mostowicz 2005, 99). The organization desired to "save from deportation some persons from among those whom the ghetto authorities had designated to be deported by qualifying them as capable of working inside the ghetto." Mostowicz justified his own presence at the post by claiming that, "regardless of whether he was there or not, in any event 800 people were destined for death in the trucks" (99). In his account, however, the doctor-narrator comes to be confronted by the eponymous "second last" potential deportee. The unfortunate man is a certain Albert Cohen, a middle-aged man from Prague, now working in the ghetto as a garbage man, but a philosophy professor in the past, who had published extensively on Schopenhauer. This man, then, first gently and hesitantly, asks the narrator if he knows where the transport is going. The narrator declines to give a straight answer; had he done otherwise, it would have been very dangerous for him. Nor, however, does he build any false façade, for he sees that Cohen already realizes what awaits the deportees. He decides to let him come to his own conclusions, at the same time that he offers him a certificate that would allow him to stay in the ghetto (and save his life, for the present time). Cohen, the philosopher, refuses to accept it, observing that some other person would have to be selected in his place. As the conversation develops, we learn that Cohen has no family in the ghetto; his mother committed suicide at the time of the deportation from Prague. The doctor continues to evade the heart of the matter. Suddenly, Cohen launches an ethical question at the doctor: whether his "sitting here and sending people to death makes sense?" (102). The directness of the question places the narrator on the defensive; from this point forward, the contest is joined. The doctor seeks to place the ultimate responsibility on the Germans, where it rightfully belongs, but Cohen is now firmly determined to clarify his moral position against that of the doctor. He offers two reasons for his moral refusal to consent to be saved. First, there is a question of dignity:

> Instead of dying in some hole, rotting from filth, spitting out my decaying lungs, I shall try as long as possible to have my Jewish eyes open that the transition into nothingness that the Germans have planned for Albert Cohen from Prague occurs in the most dignified manner. (Mostowicz 2005, 103)

The second reason appears equally "simple": "I do not want, I do not wish someone else to die for me."

> "You probably did not learn that from Schopenhauer," said [the doctor] sarcastically, and again immediately regretted it.
> "No, doctor, from the Greeks. . . . But at the time I studied them it did not occur to me in what circumstances I should have use of their teachings." (Mostowicz 2005, 193)

The doctor is ready to end the conversation, but the philosopher from Prague will not let it go:

> Do you know, sir, why I asked you if this transport is destined for death? I wanted from your answer, from the tone of your voice, or perhaps from your eyes, to see clearly whether you are doing what you are doing consciously. . . . You received a recommendation, and perhaps even an order. An order is an order. I wish you never in your life to be forced to execute similar orders. But even such a recommendation does not justify you. The fact that you, knowing what fate awaits the people deported, are letting some stay in the ghetto and sending others to death, that is unforgivable! . . . You are like God. To one person life, to the other death. . . . According to a list. (Mostowicz 2005, 104)

Outraged, now, the doctor attempts to defend himself by questioning Cohen about whether it did not also happen to him, that he, Cohen, "acted in the name of some higher reasons which dictated that different rules of morality be applied?" "Higher reasons for sending people to death?" Cohen cuts to the chase. No, of course; the doctor only thought of sparing "people of special value in the ghetto," as determined by the judgment of people from his underground organization (Mostowicz 2005, 105). As the time passes and the doctor is urged to finish with the examination, he faintly defends his reasons by saying that he is certain they are true but, perhaps, he lacks the eloquence and logic of the philosopher's arguments. Indeed, Cohen retorts that he knows with "absolute certainty that the correctness of [his] arguments is supported by thousands of years of culture and civilization." At last, the doctor seems to have found an easy moral loophole:

"Do you not think that everything that is happening around us is evidence that the thousands of years of culture and civilization were cheapened and dirtied? . . . That in the struggle to survive they are as useful as a spear in modern warfare?" (105–106). Again, to Cohen's asking what he could propose "instead of the culture that has not defended Europe from savagery," the doctor offers "another morality. . . . Different values. No, perhaps the same values but differently defended" (106).

There is nothing left to say, and Cohen gets dressed. At this point, however, the doctor's disturbed moral sense gropes for reassurance: "Do you not have any doubts as to the fate of the whole ghetto?" he asks, suggesting that a calculated ethics could make sense if a few are to be left alive. Cohen will not go for that lead:

> I understand. . . . You want me to tell you that I have no doubt about the end of this spectacle. . . . This would mean that I am certain that the same fate as mine and this transport of deportees waits for everyone here. Then my decision would be only a hastening of the inevitable. No, I will not relieve you from the burden of responsibility for what you are doing here, doctor. (Mostowicz 2005, 107)

The narrator counters by suggesting that, possibly, some fighters he might save today would be useful in the future, but Cohen rejects all such logic and annunciates his credo:

> You will be shocked by it, but I am completely indifferent to that. Perhaps this is the most important difference between us. You divide people according to some criteria . . . you are giving them grades. As far as I am concerned, nothing would free me from the burden of knowing that someone was sent to death instead of me. . . . The garbage man Albert Cohen from the ghetto and the capable philosopher Albert Cohen from Prague are equally undeserving that someone should die for them . . . (Mostowicz 2005, 107)

The story ends with the mundane comment from the ghetto policeman ending the selection: "Well, the last one today, doctor. . . . Thank God!" (107). This statement, reminiscent of Marek Edelman's style, seems intended to nullify the validity of the stark moral judgment on the doctors' participation in the process of Nazi selections, something quite uncommon in Holocaust life writing.

Conclusions

The life narratives of male Jewish doctors of the Holocaust era seem to confirm the general literary gender differences delineated in the field following the debate of the "Gusdorf model," according to which male autobiographies present a more autonomous individual who overcomes difficulties encountered on his way, while female autobiographies are more concerned with forming relationships and recording their experiences, not according to progressive chronologies that are more typical of male autobiographies, but attaching meaning to experiences according to the value of the relationships.

In Holocaust life writing, a sharper personal perspective and focus on emotional life is a prism through which female doctors more typically observe their surroundings in their memoirs and diaries. In the writings of the male doctors, one more often encounters an organizing principle that shapes the autobiography according to a positivistic hope in improving the world, even if the project breaks down under the burden of the realization of the unprecedented scope of the catastrophe (Lensky), or else is consciously subverted through a cynical approach to positivistic values (Marek Edelman, Mostowicz).

As far as the consideration of "relationality" as a distinctive feature of women's experience and women's writings, my research supports the notion that the characters in female doctors' autobiographies serve the purpose of displaying an empathic connection with the author. In the male life writings, the individuals described tend to stand up for some "meaning" or principle, usually fulfilling a symbolic role to convey some element of the larger story of a Jewish community, or even something universal about human behavior.

Although the Holocaust provides major moral challenges for both men and women, it is the male physicians who seem to be able to acknowledge and redefine these challenges more definitely. A case in point is Mostowicz's narrative, which starkly incriminates the narrator himself (and, by implication, any other Jews who cooperate in Nazi selections) on the basis of appropriating the Nazi ethical principles of proportionalism and utilitarianism. Such clearly stated moral reasoning is not verified in a similar manner, or to a similar extent, in the life writings of the female doctors.

Notes

1. Holocaust testimonies, diaries, and memoirs were the foundational sources for a nascent Holocaust historiography (Jockusch 2015). Gender perspectives were present in the relatively numerous initial publications of women's life writings (e.g., Rittner and Roth 1993). Finally, Holocaust medical history was also studied in the context of perverted Nazi medicine (e.g., Mitscherlich and Mielke 1949).

2. While there is no space here to do justice to the scope of that vast and fast-growing literature, several major recent works in these areas are included in a section listing further reading at the end of this chapter.

3. An additional practical purpose of publishing Hirszfeld's story was to influence the postwar negotiations with Germany, which he hoped to achieve when trying to arrange, unsuccessfully, for the American publication of his memoir in 1946 (Hirszfeld, Balińska, and Schneider 2010, xxxvi).

4. Julian Aleksandrowicz, "Kartki z dziennika doktora Twardego" (Pages from the diary of Doctor Tough), *Yad Vashem Archives*, O.33/190. Aleksandrowicz's memoir was published later in Poland in three different editions, each expanding the positivistic concept of morality derivative from knowledge. Since I have analyzed Aleksandrowicz's memoirs in two other works (Rice 2017, 2015), I will not treat them more extensively in this chapter.

5. Two other memoirs that belong to this category but could not be treated in this study for reasons of limited space include: Baruch Milch's *Can Heaven Be Void?* (2003) and Edward Reicher's *Country of Ash: A Jewish Doctor in Poland, 1939–1945* (2013).

References

Aleksandrowicz, Julian. 1955. "Kartki z dziennika doktora Twardego" (Pages from the diary of Doctor Tough), manuscript. *Yad Vashem Archives* O.33/190.
Baer, Elizabeth Roberts, and Myrna Goldenberg, eds. 2003. *Experience and Expression: Women, the Nazis, and the Holocaust*. Detroit: Wayne State University Press.
Blady-Szwajgier, Adina. 1990. *I Remember Nothing More: The Warsaw Children's Hospital and the Jewish Resistance*. New York: Pantheon Books.
Eakin, Paul John. 1999. *How Our Lives Become Stories: Making Selves*. Ithaca: Cornell University Press.

———. 2008. *Living Autobiographically: How We Create Identity in Narrative.* Ithaca: Cornell University Press.
Garbarini, Alexandra. 2006. *Numbered Days: Diaries and the Holocaust.* New Haven: Yale University Press.
Gusdorf, Georges. 1980. "Conditions and Limits of Autobiography." In *Autobiography: Essays Theoretical and Critical*, edited by James Olney, 28–48. Princeton: Princeton University Press.
Hirszfeld, Ludwik, Marta A. Balińska, and William H. Schneider. 2010. *Ludwik Hirszfeld: The Story of One Life.* Rochester: University of Rochester Press.
Jelinek, Estelle C. 1980. *Women's Autobiography: Essays in Criticism.* Bloomington: Indiana University Press.
Jockusch, Laura. 2015. *Collect and Record! Jewish Holocaust Documentation in Early Postwar Europe.* Oxford: Oxford University Press.
Krall, Hanna, and Marek Edelman. 1986. *Shielding the Flame: An Intimate Conversation with Dr. Marek Edelman, the Last Surviving Leader of the Warsaw Ghetto Uprising.* New York: Henry Holt and Co.
Langer, Lawrence L. 1982. *Versions of Survival: The Holocaust and the Human Spirit.* Albany: State University of New York Press.
Lejeune, Philippe, and Paul John Eakin. 1989. *On Autobiography.* Minneapolis: University of Minnesota Press.
Lensky, Mordechai. 2009. *A Physician Inside the Warsaw Ghetto.* New York: Yad Vashem.
Lifton, Betty Jean. 1997. *The King of Children: A Biography of Janusz Korczak.* New York: St. Martin's Griffin.
Makower, Henryk, and Noemi Makowerowa. 1987. *Pamiętnik z getta warszawskiego: pazdziernik 1940-styczen 1943.* Wrocław: Zakład Narodowy im. Ossolińskich.
Makower, Noemi. 1996. *Miłość w cieniu śmierci: wspomnienia z getta warszawskiego.* Wrocław: Erechtejon.
Margolis-Edelman, Alina. 1994. *Ala z elementarza.* Londyn: Aneks.
Mason, Mary G. 1980. "The Other Voice: Autobiographies of Women Writers." In *Autobiography: Essays Theoretical and Critical*, edited by James Olney, 207–235. Princeton: Princeton University Press.
Milch, Baruch, and Shosh Milch-Avigal. 2003. *Can Heaven Be Void?* Jerusalem: Yad Vashem.
Mitscherlich, Alexander, and Fred Mielke. 1949. *Doctors of Infamy.* New York: Schuman.
Mostowicz, Arnold. 2005. *With a Yellow Star and a Red Cross: A Doctor in the Lodz Ghetto.* London: Vallentine Mitchell.
Rice, Monika. 2019. "Doctor's War Testimony: The Four Incarnations of Dr. Twardy." In *Jewish Medicine and Healthcare in Central Eastern Europe: Shared Identities, Entangled Histories*, edited by Marcin Moskalewicz, Ute

Caumanns, and Fritz Dross, 199–217. Cham: Springer International Publishing AG, part of Springer Nature.
Rittner, Carol, and John K. Roth, eds. 1993. *Different Voices: Women and the Holocaust*. New York: Paragon House.
Smith, Sidonie, and Julia Watson. 2010. *Reading Autobiography: A Guide for Interpreting Life Narratives*. Minneapolis: University of Minnesota Press.

Further Reading

Baumel, Judith Tydor. 1998. *Double Jeopardy: Gender and the Holocaust*. London: Vallentine Mitchell.
Dean, Carolyn J. 2010. *Aversion and Erasure: The Fate of the Victim after the Holocaust*. Ithaca: Cornell University Press.
Finnegan, Marianne Gilbert. 1995. "Bibliographic Essay: The Inclusive Past: Forms of Modern Autobiography." *Soundings* 78, nos. 3–4: 611–645.
Fuchs, Esther. 1999. *Women and the Holocaust: Narrative and Representation*. Lanham: University Press of America.
Goldberg, Amos. 2008. *Holocaust Diaries as "Life Stories."* Göttingen: Wallstein.
Lengyel, Olga. 2005. *Five Chimneys: A Woman Survivor's True Story of Auschwitz*. Chicago: Chicago Review Press.
Lentin, Ronit. 2000. "Expected to Live: Women Shoah Survivors' Testimonial of Silence." *Women's Studies International Forum* 23, no. 6: 689–700.
Ofer, Dalia, and Lenore J. Weitzman, eds. 1998. *Women in the Holocaust*. New Haven: Yale University Press.
Perl, Gisella. 1948. *I Was a Doctor in Auschwitz*. New York: International Universities Press.
Reicher, Edward. 2013. *Country of Ash: A Jewish Doctor in Poland, 1939–1945*. New York: Bellevue Literary Press.
Rice, Monika. 2015. "Holocaust Diaries: On Postwar Death and Resurrection: A Tale of Two Doctors." *Yad Vashem Studies* 43, no. 2 (December): 109–141.
Roland, Charles G. 1992. *Courage under Siege: Starvation, Disease, and Death in the Warsaw Ghetto*. New York: Oxford University Press.
Stewart, Victoria. 2003. *Women's Autobiography: War and Trauma*. Houndmills: Palgrave Macmillan.
Waxman, Zoë. 2006. *Writing the Holocaust: Identity, Testimony, Representation*. Oxford: Oxford University Press.
Wieviorka, Annette. 2006. *The Era of the Witness*. Ithaca: Cornell University Press.

Chapter 5

Muselmänner in Nazi Concentration Camps
Thinking Masculinity at the Extremes

MICHAEL BECKER AND DENNIS BOCK

The so-called *Muselmann*, a starving concentration camp prisoner on the brink of death, was a phenomenon that nearly all prisoners in Nazi concentration camps encountered. A vast number of testimonies mention *Muselmänner*, and the term itself is widely understood even by non-Holocaust survivors. Both male and female concentration camp prisoners have been labeled *Muselmann*. However, it was a gendered experience, a dimension that finds its expression in various testimonies and in several gender-specific synonyms. As men and women prisoners usually lived in separate quarters in the concentration camps, homosocial settings are of crucial interest for an understanding of gendered social orders. Consequently, this chapter makes the social situation of *Muselmänner* its point of departure. Even though male and female concentration camp prisoners experienced the *Muselmann* condition, our focus is primarily on male inmates.

Since the literature on *Muselmänner* is almost as scarce as that on the relation between the Holocaust and masculinities, research on the subject of the *Muselmann* demands a rather exploratory approach. A crucial aspect of the representation of *Muselmänner* is the discrepancy of their omnipresence in Holocaust testimonies and their absence from historical research at the same time (see Becker and Bock 2015; Bock 2015, 2017, 161–215). Accordingly, Ryn and Kłodziński's lone systematic study of the *Muselmann* concludes that survivor accounts "unequivocally show that the

Muselmann is not an exceptional appearance but, on the contrary, was an everyday occurrence in the camps" (Ryn and Kłodziński 1987, 104).[1]

However, these findings have rarely been reflected in contemporary studies on camp life and prisoner societies. Thinking about masculinity in the case of the physically weakest concentration camp prisoners contributes to shaping a more complex and comprehensive view on *Muselmänner* and their social position in the camps.

This chapter is based on the findings of a larger research project on the *Muselmann*. We will consider three different angles, beginning with a brief examination of the existing *Muselmann* narratives and their impact on the representation of this particular group. Next, the word's history and origin, particularly the lexeme *-mann*, and its usage in concentration camps, is a central aspect of this chapter. The word's sexist and racist connotations are of particular interest with regard to the construction of weakness, powerlessness, and unmanliness. Finally, we argue that the ascription of these characteristics has notably influenced the shaping, arrangement, and maintenance of the social order and hegemony in prisoner societies. We will conclude this chapter by suggesting a new understanding of *Muselmann*. Instead of solely being an "impossible Holocaust metaphor," as Sharon Oster (2016) put it, we address *Muselmänner* as prisoners with agency who participated in the daily and economic life of concentration camps and had a major impact on the symbolic, material, and social order of camp inmates' societies.

Shaping Narratives: Presence and Absence of the *Muselmann*

Even though *Muselmänner* have been mentioned in most testimonies and literary accounts, they appear as passive victims of starvation, exhaustion, and violence, maltreated by guards and fellow prisoners. This is emblematically expressed in Primo Levi's claim that "all the musulmans . . . have the same story, or more exactly, have no story; they followed the slope down to the bottom, like streams that run down to the sea" (1959, 103).

Primo Levi's autobiographical account *If This Is a Man?* was particularly influential in shaping the concept and narrative of the *Muselmann*. We argue that this narrative requires revision. Levi's descriptions of the appearance, mental constitution, and social situation of the *Muselmann* are repeatedly addressed in the literature and, as one may argue, therefore became an archetype in Holocaust literature and current research. In his text, Levi first and implicitly mentions a *Muselmann* when he remembers his former fellow prisoner "Null Achtzehn" (Zero Eighteen).

> He is Null Achtzehn. He is not called anything except that, Zero Eighteen, the last three figures of his entry number; as if everyone was aware that only a man is worthy of a name, and that Null Achtzehn is no longer a man. I think that even he has forgotten his name, certainly he acts as if this was so. When he speaks, when he looks around, he gives the impression of being empty inside, nothing more than an involucre, like the slough of certain insects which one finds on the banks of swamps, held by a thread to the stones and shaken by the wind. (Levi 1959, 42)

In Levi's representation, "Zero Eighteen" is no longer a man, although he is still alive—this description constitutes a leitmotif within the *Muselmann* narrative. Descriptions of weakened and emaciated prisoners as nonhumans, living dead, or walking corpses can be found in almost all literary accounts of the Holocaust. Descriptions of the *Muselmann*'s deep-set eyes, sometimes sparkling, sometimes dull, and of their blank stares, like in Levi's account, repeatedly occur in many such texts. While the *Muselmann*'s appearance has often been the focus of scholars and readers of Levi's work, the double meaning of "man" (*uomo* in the Italian original) as *man* and *human* has not been examined.

Levi's chapter "The Lost and the Saved" includes arguably the most important reflections on the *Muselmann* in his literary memoirs. He writes:

> But with the musselmans, the men in decay, it is not even worth speaking, because one knows already that they will complain and will speak about what they used to eat at home. Even less worthwhile is it to make friends with them because they have no distinguished acquaintances in camp, they do not gain extra rations, they do not work in profitable Kommandos and they know no secret method of organizing. (Levi 1959, 101–102)

The passage makes clear that *Muselmänner* belonged to the lowest class of prisoner society. Without any privileges and in a pitiful physical and mental state, *Muselmänner*, in the eyes of other prisoners, had simply become a "handful of ashes" (Levi 1959, 102). Thus, a new norm was established: such men were to be avoided. In addition, the appearance of the *Muselmann* demonstrated to other prisoners what fate probably awaited them all. Therefore, Levi and numerous other authors describe a process of social distancing toward and isolation of the *Muselmann*. This process can be interpreted as an act of displacement, a strategy to obscure the seemingly inevitable, that is, to evade the ever-present reality of an agonizing death from malnutrition, exhaustion, and mental destruction. In *If This Is a Man?* Levi writes:

> Their life is short, but their number is endless; they, the Muselmänner, the drowned, form the backbone of the camp, an anonymous mass, continually renewed and always identical, of non-men who march and labour in silence, the divine spark dead within them, already too empty to really suffer. One hesitates to call them living: one hesitates to call their death death, in the face of which they have no fear, as they are too tired to understand. They crowd my memory with their faceless presences, and if I could enclose all the evil of our time in one image, I would choose this image which is familiar to me: an emaciated man, with head dropped and shoulders curved, on whose face and in whose eyes not a trace of a thought is to be seen. (Levi 1959, 103)

It is important that Levi calls the *Muselmann* the "backbone of the camp." In his reflections on the essence of Nazi persecution politics, the *Muselmann* is assigned not a subordinate but a central role within the camp. His metaphor indicates that the *Muselmann* is precisely that phenomenon from which Levi derives the semantics of the camps. The figure of the *Muselmann* distills the experiences in Nazi concentrations camps and is therefore an image and symbol of genuine agony and misery.

While Levi mentions the *Muselmann* quite prominently in his writings, the figure holds a rather marginal place in many other key texts of Holocaust literature. Quite often, descriptions of *Muselmänner* are consigned to footnotes. Nevertheless, the *Muselmann* is an integral part of survivor accounts. The recurring reproduction as well as the recurring reception of the *Muselmann* narrative and its associated motifs have led to an unquestioned understanding of the conditions of *Muselmänner* in Holocaust literature and scholarship. Historical and sociological studies have stayed relatively close to narrative judgments found in Holocaust testimonies, and they therefore have reproduced those motifs outlined earlier. For example, the *Encyclopedia of the Holocaust*, edited by Israel Gutman and published in 1990, contains the following entry:

> *Muselmann*, German term, meaning "Muslim," widely in use among prisoners in concentration camps to refer to inmates who were on the verge of death from starvation, exhaustion, and despair. . . . *Muselmänner* were identified by such marks as the lack of flesh on their bodies and the tight yellow skin over their bones, a dull and expressionless look in their eyes, and the inability to stand upright for any length of time. They were indifferent to their surroundings, apathetic, and listless. . . . Most of the prisoners avoided contact with *Muselmänner*, afraid that this condition could be in store for them. A person who had reached the *Muselmann* stage had no chance of survival, and did not remain alive for more than a few days or weeks. (Gutman 1990, 1009)

"Levi's designation of the *Muselmänner* as 'the drowned,'" Oster argues, has been "uncritically adopted." Scholars, therefore, "have overlooked many of 'the saved,' in oral accounts, interviews, and less widely circulated narratives in which survivors *refer to themselves* as one-time *Muselmänner*" (Oster 2016, 305–306). Ultimately, it seems evident that there is a general shared knowledge of the *Muselmann*'s appearance that is formed and informed by photographs, film documentaries, medical-historical studies, and literary forms of representation. At the same time, however, the question of the *Muselmann*'s position within the prisoner society seems to be much more complex; it demands a critical literary and historical reexamination of the *Muselmann* and his representations.

Historical Origin and Usage in the Camps

Early research has shed light on the origins of the term *Muselmann*, but we suggest that we gain further insights into its diverse pre-Holocaust usage by shedding light on its etymologies, cultural employments, semantic layers, and interpretations. Scholars, surprisingly, have ignored the sociohistorical layers of the term and how these may have affected its usage in the camps.

The German term *Muselmann* is significantly older than the existence of the National Socialist concentration camp system. The word's colloquial use can be traced to the eighteenth century; its original meaning was already out of fashion in the 1930s and 1940s. Around 1800, *Muselmann* was a common and derogatory term used for Muslims or Turks. With the beginning of the nineteenth century, *Muselmann* was replaced by, or at least a variant of, the phrase *Mohammedaner* (Eng., Mohammedan). Yet, it was the term *Muselmann* that became a common term in the camp language. The most conceivable explanation for this dissemination lies in the popularity of an "anti-coffee rhyme" from the nineteenth century, which became a folk tune and is being taught in German schools even today. The song contains seven lines that admonish the audience of the dangers of drinking Turkish coffee. According to Carl Gottlieb Hering (1766–1853), who wrote the tune, drinking coffee leads to illness, weakness, and nervous debility. Consequently, Hering ends his rhyme with an imperative in the second to last line: "Sei doch kein Muselmann" (Don't be a *Muselmann*).

The racist undertone can be better grasped when seen in the context of the political climate in nineteenth-century Germany and the eventual fall of the Ottoman Empire. Muslims had become stereotyped as the enemy of the Western world and Islam depicted as a despised religion compared to the Christian-European tradition. Against this backdrop, the topos of the "sick man of Europe" was born, which led to the tune's popularity. "With its folk-etymological derivation, the term *Muselmann* offers a range of quips that deal with political and physical potency, thus varying the topos of the 'ill Turk.' Considering this logic 'Musel-Mann' is an ill, weakened, unmanly man" (Wittler 2012, 1051). A *Muselmann* was associated with political impotence and damaged manliness, a perception that continued to exist well into the twentieth century (Wittler 2012, 1052).

These etymological remarks not only help to explain the term's origin and legacy but are also essential for understanding how the phrase was used in National Socialist concentration camps. Marie Simon, for example, claims that the SS introduced the word *Muselmann* into the camps. Emaciated prisoners and those allegedly evoking images of praying Muslims or Bedouins were labeled as such. Because of the mobility of the SS, Simon further asserts, the term spread throughout the camp system (Simon 1992, 204). However, this view neglects to take into consideration the forced mobility of the prisoners, many of whom were deported and shuffled around to many camps as a result of the continuous development of the camp system. "Seeing them from afar," Elie Wiesel, for example, writes, "one had the impression of looking at Arabs praying. This image was the origin of the term used at Auschwitz for people dying of malnutrition: Muslims" (1995, 58).

While Simon focuses on the term's usage by the SS and its pejorative character, Kathrin Wittler approaches *Muselmann* through the lens of weakness and unmanliness, claiming that only a reading of both meanings, "Muslim" and "weakened man," leads to a broader understanding of this term (2012, 1055). Danuta Wesołowska also focuses on weakness, noting that *Muselmann* entails an important semantic shift: within the concentration camp system, to be "weak and unfortunate" meant to be "despised" (1998, 119). In her study of camp language, Nicole Warmbold discusses the term *Muselmann* in a paragraph on "invectives, scorn and derision" (Warmbold 2008, 272). She argues that the traditional, ostracizing meaning of invectives coincides with camp-specific survival strategies. Invectives thus suggest to prisoners not to help marginalized or unexperienced inmates, but to avoid them. Taking these crucial aspects into account, we would like to add a sociohistorical perspective to the discussion that will help us to understand the relation between masculinity, weakness, and social order.

Muselmann as a Principle of Gendered Social Classification

Such a sociohistorical perspective aims to trace these semantic layers of the term *Muselmann* to the social processes within prisoner societies. In the following, we will argue that *Muselmänner* had a central role for shaping the social order in Nazi concentration camps. On the one hand, we will outline the processes of marginalization and exclusion that weakened prisoners faced when labeled as *Muselmänner*. On the other hand, we will focus on the *Muselmann*'s strategies of self-assertion and survival.

In a second step, we will try to specify these processes as gender specific in the homosocial environments of the concentration camp system. The processes of marginalization as well as the strategies of self-assertion can be analyzed as gender-specific processes, with actors on both sides referring to or drawing on aspects of masculinity (or, in the case of women prisoners, of femininity). We argue that the existence of *Muselmänner* not only shaped the social order of prisoner societies and established social relations between prisoners along a divide of hegemonic and subordinated actors; it also established relations between men along the divide of hegemonic and subordinated masculinities, with masculinity being a core principle of individual and collective identity that subordinated prisoners tried to uphold in their quest for self-preservation.

In Primo Levi's narrative, *Muselmänner* do not belong to prisoner society. According to Levi, they had lost their agency and they did not form lasting relationships with other prisoners. In short, they were no longer individuals with a personal history. Levi describes that process as a "single and broad . . . path to perdition" (Levi 1959, 103). Hence, *Muselmänner* had no importance for the social order of prisoner societies. Other testimonies, however, depict a more complex picture and direct our attention to the process of becoming a *Muselmann*. Camp language even comprised a specific term for this process: *muzułmaniec*, a verb modeled after the Polish expression for *Muselmann*, as well as the noun *muzułmanienie*. For lack of a better term, this might be translated as *Muselmanization*. These terms indicate its importance for prisoners' concentration camp experience. They indicate that *Muselmann* was not a static and irrevocable but rather a transitory condition of the prisoner's body and psyche; it was the result of individual interaction as well as social relations between prisoners. To be clear, the overwhelming majority of prisoners suffering from the *Muselmann* condition eventually died and the relationships between *Muselmänner* and non-*Muselmänner* were marked by violence and extreme hierarchies. Nevertheless, important insights into the workings of prisoner societies can be gained by analyzing *Muselmanization* as the social consequence of its extreme context.

Based on testimonies of former *Muselmänner*, it is almost impossible to define the psychological condition of these prisoners. Without doubt, many of them had given up the hope to survive and lost their sense of agency.

> If one never had been a *Muselmann*, one cannot imagine how profoundly the psychological changes affected a person in that situation. One became so indifferent to one's own fate that one resigned oneself to everything and awaited death calmly. One no longer had any energy and passion to fight for daily survival. . . . I became indifferent to everything, my surroundings, work, and the future. (Karol Talik, qtd. in Ryn and Kłodziński 1994, 122)

Other survivors, however, report the exact opposite:

> Back then, perhaps I was not aware of the gravity of the situation. I did not think about all the perils of the camp, and I vegetated from one day to the other. . . . But all this did not penetrate my awareness, I balked at the thought that I could die and I believed with the tenacity of a maniac that we would survive. (Ignacy Sikora, qtd. in Ryn and Kłodziński 1994, 122)

According to Jerzy Mostowski, many prisoners labeled as *Muselmänner* did not even see themselves as such:

> I too was a *Muselmann* in 1942 and in the beginning of 1943. I was not even aware of that. I believe that many *Muselmänner* did not count themselves among this group. During the assignment of prisoners, however, I was placed among the group of Muselmänner. In many cases the appearance of a prisoner determined his assignment to this group. (Jerzy Mostowski, qtd. in Ryn and Kłodziński 1994, 122)

While the experience of being a *Muselmann* differed radically, it seems plausible to speculate about the psychological effects of *Muselmanization* for other prisoners, as the appearance of *Muselmänner* demonstrated to their fellow prisoners the fate that potentially awaited them all. "Reaching the state of *Muselmann* was the prisoners' dread, because no one knew when they would meet this fate themselves—a safe candidate for the gas chamber or another kind of death" (quoted in Langbein 1995, 157).

Sociologist and former Auschwitz-Birkenau prisoner Anna Pawełczyńska describes the range of possible reactions to the presence of *Muselmänner*:

> For the living this landscape of deaths constituted a permanent element of camp life. It codetermined their attitudes and either led to a complete breakdown or liberated the mechanisms of self-defense. The living could identify with the dying through compassion or through the vision of their own fate. They could also strive to detach themselves from the dying—ranging themselves with the world of the living, the others with the

world of the dead. . . . By imagining their own fate prisoners lost the remains of their psychic strength, which they needed for self-defense. (Pawełczyńska 1979, 77)

Warmbold interprets this detachment as the result of a perfidious strategy by the SS. They managed to deflect the prisoners' fear and anger to the *Muselmänner* (Warmbold 2008, 283). Closely related to these psychological effects, the transitory *Muselmann* condition most notably had an impact on the prisoners' social situation. Prisoner society, Wolfgang Sofsky asserts, "tried to draw a new line of separation. By treating the semidead as irksome individuals, banning them from social intercourse, it anticipated their final end" (Sofsky 1997, 205). "Physical emaciation," he argues, was "closely linked . . . with the destruction of social relations. Immiseration implies a simultaneous destruction of the social sphere, the *vita activa* and *vita mentalis*" (200). This "line of separation" served to classify *Muselmänner* as a nonhegemonic group of emaciated and powerless prisoners. A *Muselmann*, therefore, belonged to a multifaceted social category. On the one hand, the separation was an attempt of other inmates to handle their insecurity at the prospect of death and to develop strategies of social self-affirmation by labeling someone a *Muselmann*. On the other hand, social exclusion of the *Muselmann* was not merely an act of avoidance but also opened opportunities for fellow prisoners by influencing the distribution of essential goods. Both the privileged prisoner functionaries and the nonprivileged rank-and-file prisoners could benefit from marginalizing *Muselmänner*. "Prisoners who relegated the dying to the world of the dead could look the other way and pass them by or take their shoes and ration of bread" (Pawełczyńska 1979, 77). Marginalization and social exclusion of *Muselmänner* therefore became an important mechanism of self-preservation for other prisoners.

However, as Sofsky reminds us, "the system was not static: power was not distributed irreversibly once the positions had been staffed. The gradation of power was a constant process of displacements, coalitions, and intrigues. Although it was a formal structure, self-administration was also a political process, a figurative movement" (1997, 136).

Consequently, prisoner functionaries faced great pressure to retain their dominant positions within prisoner societies. Symbolic and physical violence was a proven way to maintain social order in concentration camps. *Muselmänner*, however, were continuously disrupting social order with their behavior and weak work performance. Accordingly, "some prisoners, especially block elders, have exceedingly mistreated *Muselmänner*, because they were disrupting social rules" (Ryn and Kłodziński 1987, 127). Gawalewicz remembers: "In spring 1941, the camp leaders apparently came to the conclusion that my *Muselmann* work commando fulfilled its function insufficiently or, put differently, that it liberated the camp from useless eaters too slowly. Hence, they occasionally organized downright manhunts against *Muselmänner*" (1998, 66).

For fear of a loss of their privileges and, ultimately, their lives, prisoner functionaries had to maintain order by distinguishing hegemonic from nonhegemonic groups. Violence in the case of prisoner societies has not only a destructive but also a "productive" and regulatory dimension (see Meuser 2002, 54; Bock 2017, 287–291). While *Muselmänner* were perceived as a danger to fellow prisoners who were still stronger or enjoyed limited privileges, they also had a function for social classification into hegemonic and subjugated groups. *Muselmänner* were at the bottom of the social hierarchy (Kautsky 1946, 167ff.) and a prime example of social exclusion (Levi 1959, 99–103); they thus constituted a crucial element in the social order of the camps.

While these remarks illustrate the character of *Muselmanization* as a social process—"a figurative movement"—within prisoner societies, they also highlight the fact that *Muselmänner*, contrary to Levi's account, were an integral part of prisoner society. They participated in the social and economic life of concentration camps. The "line of separation" between *Muselmänner* and non-*Muselmänner* was frequently crossed with the help of other prisoners.[2]

Manliness and Male Honor

Prisoners used an array of strategies to marginalize *Muselmänner* (Becker and Bock 2015). We will focus here on the gender-specific aspects of social exclusion and marginalization. Concepts of hegemony and hegemonic masculinity, especially in the context of the *Muselmann*'s social situation, help to describe "how particular groups of men inhabit positions of power and wealth, and how they legitimate and reproduce the social relationships that generate their dominance" (Carrigan, Connell, and Lee 1985, 592). Aspects of weakness and unmanliness legitimized the marginalization of *Muselmänner*: to be weak in the concentration camps meant to be despised.

The prisoner's apparent awareness "that only a man is worthy of a name" and that a *Muselmann* "is no longer a man" (Levi 1959, 42) evokes a range of patriarchal attributes by which men asserted their gendered identity even in the camp hierarchy. In other words: The SS tried to take away their humanity *and* their manliness. A positive relation to masculinity was denied, a humiliating and violating act that deeply affected *all prisoners'* chances of survival.

As an act of self-preservation, however, male prisoners tried to uphold their manliness and male honor. With regard to Pierre Bourdieu's concept of *Masculine Domination* (2001) and on the basis of survivor accounts, sociologist Maja Suderland gives insight into the homosocial and male-dominated environment of the concentration camps. According to former Dachau and Buchenwald prisoner Paul Martin Neurath, male honor—which can be considered "one of the 'basic concepts' of society" (Suderland 2013, 206)—could be defended "using strategies specially adapted to the camp" (207). One very important strategy was to exclude the violent SS man from the human society, so that in "a reversal of perspective, the prisoner himself—who was at best a sub-human in the eyes of the SS—was able to remain a man and thus a human being" (207).

> The second important aspect of the prisoners' strategy to preserve their male honour entailed viewing the other prisoners as the sole social reference for their behaviour. . . . By orienting himself on the other prisoners and certifying his "membership of the group of 'real men,' " the humiliated prisoner could still feel like a man as long as he fulfilled the requirements that characterized a "real man" in the concentration camps: he was not allowed to wail or scream when he was hit. (Suderland 2013, 208)

Former Auschwitz prisoner Adolf Gawalewicz contrasts the behavior of the weakest inmates of the *Isolierstation* in Birkenau—he calls this sector "Warteraum zum Gas" (Waiting Room for the Gas)—with those "who still believed to manage the impossible" (Gawalewicz 1998, 93). While the situation in the *Isolierstation* is described as "scrambling, wailing, [and] disputes over trivialities" that did not "fall silent until the next morning," Gawalewicz asserts that, in order to survive, "one had to become an active *Muselmann*" (92–93). He thus distinguishes between *passive* and *active Muselmänner*. While the former are characterized by their unmanly behavior, the latter, according to Gawalewicz, are scrambling to remain part of the hegemonic group. Since "only the community of men could judge who was a man and who was not" (Suderland 2013, 211), appreciation from the group was one of the most important factors, as Gawalewicz affirms regarding his own survival: "Władysław Fejkiel, former clerk in the camp hospital, said to me: You pulled our legs very well. I was sure you wouldn't make it until the morning roll call and I already had your death certificate ready" (65). In light of Gawalewicz's recollections, "it is entirely understandable that in the gender-homogeneous society of male prisoners, male honour was of essential importance to personal identity" (Suderland 2013, 211).

These related strategies—the exclusion of the "non-human" other and the adaption of the social frame of reference—were not only effective instruments to uphold manliness and male honor against the attempts of the SS, but they also maintained hegemonic and subordinated masculinities according to the "line of separation" within prisoner society. Just as prisoners excluded the SS man from human society to preserve male honor, the *Muselmann* was excluded from the hegemonic group in order to perpetuate and rearrange group affiliation. While for some prisoners obtaining manliness was an act of self-preservation, we can also see that, in the case of the *Muselmann*, "the sense of honor, virility, 'manliness' . . . is the undisputed principle of all duties towards oneself," so that "the impossible ideal of virility" could have been "the source of an immense vulnerability" (Bourdieu 2001, 51; also Suderland 2013, 211). The symbolic and social deprivation of virility thus affected the process of becoming a *Muselmann*.

While men suffered from their loss of male identity by being deprived of respectability and power and by their ability to protect their families—especially since "masculinity is clearly viewed as a particular form of honor and power" (Suderland 2013, 211)—women suffered similar attacks on their identity as women through the assault on their bodies. The loss of their hair in particular was experienced as an assault on their sense of womanhood. Women survivors repeatedly testified that hair was an important symbol of their femininity (Hájková 2005, 210) and that the forced cutting of all hair was one of the most radical experiences for them (Amesberger, Auer, and Halbmayr 2007, 88ff.).

It is perhaps telling that in the camp language the most common female synonym for *Muselmann* is *Schmuckstück* (jewel). Emaciated female camp inmates were sarcastically labeled *Schmuckstück*, ridiculing and negating their sense of femininity, comparable to male prisoners being called *Muselmann*. *Muselmann* and *Schmuckstück* became counterimages of masculinity and femininity, and these terms haven been employed and perpetuated also in survivor accounts.

While Suderland reads these accounts as sources for a sociological study of prisoner societies, literary theorist Margret Graf focuses on their function for their authors. By referring to these men as *Muselmänner*, Graf argues, writers of Holocaust testimonies explicitly contrast their past camp life with the experiences of *Muselmänner*. In case of a damaged male identity, these labels put on fellow prisoners also re-gender their male identity in the process of writing: by distancing themselves from the weakened, unmanly other, their own masculinity was retrospectively restored in their narratives (Graf 2015, 109).

Outlook: Toward a New Understanding of the *Muselmann*

The literature on the topic of *Muselmänner* portrays these men as those who had fallen to a near-death condition and lost their human features, thus turning the *Muselmann* into the extreme embodiment and emblem of Nazi atrocities. Previous studies have addressed the *Muselmann* primarily from medical, etymological, or philosophical points of view. In this chapter we have suggested a sociohistorical reading of the condition and social position of the *Muselmann*. Furthermore, we focused on the process of becoming a *Muselmann* as a gendered experience. We understand *Muselmann* not as an *irrevocable* condition that inevitably ended in death, but as a *transitory* condition of the human body and psyche, determined also by group affiliation. We have argued that this condition is in part the result of social interactions in extreme situations, and hence it must be addressed as such (Becker and Bock 2015, 147–162).

Investigating the condition and position of the *Muselmann* offers insights into structures and processes within National Socialist concentration camps. It furthermore poses questions regarding social relations, ethics, and power. Since almost any prisoner could have become *Muselmänner*, their condition allows us to study camp inmates across categories of gender, age, nationality, and class as well as labels by which Nazi classified the persecuted. In this regard, three crucial approaches seem relevant to us.

(1) *Muselmänner as important witnesses*. "For many years," former Auschwitz prisoner Adolf Gawalewicz writes, "my fate was . . . closely

bound to those who balanced on that dangerous ridge on the border of life and death—the *Muselmänner*. Together with them, as one of them, I had survived until the dawn of freedom. So I will write about them because they are familiar; their fate was mine" (1998, 144). Indeed, on closer inspection, we have come across a striking number of testimonies by surviving *Muselmänner*, in addition to those mentioned in the important early study by Ryn and Kłodziński (1987). These include court testimonies, oral interviews, and fictional accounts (Becker and Bock 2015). They clearly refute Levi's claim that *Muselmänner* have "the same story, or more exactly, have no story" (1959, 103) and question Agamben's (1999) well-known assertion that *Muselmänner* cannot bear witness.

(2) *Muselmänner and prisoner societies*. As almost any prisoner could become a *Muselmann*, these testimonies are indispensable for a comprehensive understanding of social structures and processes within prisoner societies. Instead of grasping the *Muselmann* as a mere figure in literary accounts and philosophical explorations, prisoners classified as *Muselmänner* actively participated in daily and economic life. Their existence shaped the social order of prisoner societies. Indeed, for many concentration camps, at least since 1944, *Muselmänner* represented a majority of the prisoners.[3] Questions regarding agency, gender, and social interaction can help us understand better the social realities of *Muselmänner* inside the concentration camps. While many survivor accounts confirm that a "new line of separation" (Sofsky 1997, 205) between *Muselmänner* and fellow prisoners existed, it is also true that former prisoners have testified to a wide range of acts of empathy and assistance for *Muselmänner*—often depending on group affiliation, personal relationships, and availability of material resources (see Kłodziński and Ryn 1987; Becker and Bock 2015). These gestures of solidarity refute the simple assumption that *Muselmänner* were automatically victims of mechanisms of social death. Such acts of solidarity did in no way diminish the masculinity of those helpers or the masculinity of others. Had *Muselmänner* not received some assistance, we would not be able to draw on their testimonies of survival today.

(3) *Masculinity at the extremes*. The *Muselmann* condition was a gendered experience. Its analysis provides important insight into homosocial settings under extreme conditions. We have argued that social exclusion and marginalization in same-sex prisoner societies were gender-specific social processes that established relations between men along the divide of hegemonic-subordinated masculinities. The SS targeted the prisoners' male identity as part of their attempt to dehumanize them. Prisoners

reacted by redefining the frame of reference for manliness and male honor. On the one hand, the violent SS men were excluded from human society. On the other hand, prisoners also distanced themselves from the weakened, unmanly inmates labeled *Muselmänner* who, as a consequence, were excluded from the hegemonic group. These acts of exclusion enabled prisoners to uphold their manliness as an integral part of their humanity.

Acknowledgments

We would like to thank Björn Krondorfer and Ovidiu Creangă for inviting us to contribute to this volume and for their valuable comments and corrections.

Notes

1. All translations are by the authors.
2. Help and solidarity, without which we could not draw on the numerous testimonies of surviving *Muselmänner*, have curiously been excluded from scholarly reflections. The best-known example of such neglect is arguably Giorgio Agamben (1999), who extensively cites testimonies of former *Muselmänner* while conceptualizing them at the same time as those who could not bear witness. See Becker and Bock (2015).
3. See, for example, the consultation of Dr. Tadeusz Kowalski, Military Court for the trial of war criminals, held at the Curiohaus, Hamburg, March 22, 1946, The National Archives, WO 235/162 (transcript Neuengamme Concentration Camp Memorial). For estimations by former prisoners and surviving Muselmänner, see Ryn and Kłodziński (1987, 102ff.).

References

Agamben, Giorgio. 1999. *The Remnants of Auschwitz: The Witness and the Archive.* Translated by Daniel Heler-Roazen. New York: Zone Books.

Amesberger, Helga, Katrin Auer, and Brigitte Halbmayr, eds. 2007. *Sexualisierte Gewalt: Weibliche Erfahrungen in NS-Konzentrationslagern.* Vienna: Mandelbaum Verlag.

Becker, Michael, and Dennis Bock. 2015. "Muselmänner und Häftlingsgesellschaften: Ein Beitrag zur Sozialgeschichte der nationalsozialistischen Konzen-

trationslager." *Archiv für Sozialgeschichte* 55: 133–175.
Bock, Dennis. 2015. " 'Nie chodzi o to, czy nienawidzi czy nie. Muzułmanie mu przeszkadzali'—kategoria zakłócenia w narracjach o muzułmanie w literaturze Szoa." *Poznańskie Studia Polonistyczne: Seria Literacka* 25, no. 45: 137–163.
———. 2017. *Literarische Störungen in Texten über die Shoah: Imre Kertész, Liana Millu, Ruth Klüger*. Frankfurt a. M.: Peter Lang.
Bourdieu, Pierre. 2001. *Masculine Domination*. Cambridge: Polity.
Carrigan, Tim, Bob Connell, and John Lee. 1985. "Towards a New Sociology of Masculinity." *Theory and Society* 14, no. 5 (Fall): 551–604.
Gawalewicz, Adolf. 1998. *Überlegungen im Warteraum zum Gas: Aus den Erinnerungen eines Muselmanns*. Gütersloh: van Hoddis.
Graf, Margret. 2015. *Erinnerung erschreiben: Gender-Differenz in Texten von Auschwitz-Überlebenden*. Frankfurt a. M.: Campus Verlag.
Gutman, Israel. 1990. "Muselmann." In *Encyclopedia of the Holocaust*, volume 3, edited by Israel Gutman, 1009–1010. New York: Macmillan.
Hájková, Anna. 2005. "Strukturen weiblichen Verhaltens in Theresienstadt." In *Genozid und Geschlecht: Jüdische Frauen im nationalsozialistischen Lagersystem*, edited by Gisela Bock, 202–219. Frankfurt a. M.: Campus Verlag.
Kautsky, Benedict. 1946. *Teufel und Verdammte: Erfahrungen und Erkenntnisse aus 7 Jahren in deutschen Konzentrationslagern*. Zurich: Büchergilde Gutenberg.
Langbein, Herrmann. 1995. *Menschen in Auschwitz*. Vienna: Europaverlag.
Levi, Primo. 1959. *If This Is a Man*. New York: Orion Press.
Meuser, Michael. 2002. "Doing Masculinity: Zur Geschlechtslogik männlichen Gewalthandelns." In *Gewalt-Verhältnisse: Feministische Perspektiven auf Geschlecht und Gewalt*, edited by Regina-Maria Dackweiler and Reinhild Schäfer, 53–78. Frankfurt a. M.: Campus Verlag.
Oster, Sharon. 2016. "Impossible Holocaust Metaphors: The *Muselmann*." *Prooftexts* 34, no. 3 (Fall): 302–348.
Pawełczyńska, Anna. 1979. *Values and Violence in Auschwitz*. Berkeley: University of California Press.
Ryn, Zdzisław, and Stanisław Kłodziński. 1987. "An der Grenze zwischen Leben und Tod: Eine Studie über die Erscheinung des 'Muselmanns' im Konzentrationslager." *Die Auschwitz-Hefte. Texte d. poln. Zeitschr. 'Przegląd Lekarski' über histor., psych. und med. Aspekte d. Lebens u. Sterbens in Auschwitz* 1: 89–154.
Simon, Marie. 1992. "Das Wort 'Muselmann' in der Sprache der deutschen Konzentrationslager." In *Aus zweier Zeugen Mund: Festschrift für Pnina Navè Levinson und Nathan Peter Levinson*, edited by Julius H. Schoeps, 202–211. Gerlingen: Bleicher.
Sofsky, Wolfgang. 1997. *The Order of Terror: The Concentration Camp*. Princeton: Princeton University Press.
Suderland, Maja. 2013. *Inside Concentration Camps: Social Life at the Extremes*. Cambridge: Polity.

Warmbold, Nicole. 2008. *Lagersprache: Zur Sprache der Opfer in den Konzentrationslagern Sachsenhausen, Dachau, Buchenwald*. Bremen: Hempen.
Wesołowska, Danuta. 1998. *Wörter aus der Hölle: Die 'lagerszpracha' der Häftlinge von Auschwitz*. Krakow: Impuls.
Wiesel, Elie. 1995. " 'Stay together, always.' " *Newsweek*, January 16.
Wittler, Kathrin. 2012. " 'Muselmann': Anmerkungen zur Geschichte einer Bezeichnung," *Zeitschrift für Geschichtswissenschaft* 61: 1045–1056.

Chapter 6

Tests of Manhood
Alcohol, Sexual Violence, and Killing in the Holocaust

Edward B. Westermann

During the rise of National Socialism and over the course of the Third Reich, violence—ranging from beer hall brawls and street fights during the "time of struggle" to organized acts of mass murder in the killing fields and death camps of the Occupied Eastern Territories—emerged as a hallmark of the Nazi regime. The orgy of violence that characterized the regime expressed its genocidal aim, but it also served as an "expression of *male* politics" in which "toughness, readiness to stand one's ground and 'never quit the field' . . . were values associated with manliness" and defining characteristics of masculinity within the movement (Bessel 1986, 144; emphasis in the original). Indeed, violence constituted a central element of the worldview and identity of the Nazi Party's paramilitary arms in which one's "readiness for violence" served as a marker of masculinity and gained the "admiration" of one's peers (Reichardt 2002, 457). As Detlev Peukert argued, this exaltation of the "'soldierly' man, with an inner hardness" would find its ultimate "fulfillment in acts of terror and mass slaughter" (1987, 205). This concept of "hardness" and of being "unconditionally tough" or "tough and determined men" was one of the defining features of masculinity within the Nazi Party's paramilitary organizations and extended into the entire SS and police complex, a trait that became especially pronounced after the outbreak of the war in 1939 (Haynes 2015, 170).

In this arena of conflict and struggle, it was the dominant male or the "most brutal comrade [who gained] the greatest respect" (Kühne 2011, 239). From a broader perspective, the National Socialist regime employed violence "not only as a way of defeating its opponents but, more importantly, as a way of creating the new virile man" (Wieland 2015, 130). This chapter examines the interrelationships of three specific attributes that underlay National Socialist concepts of masculinity: alcohol use, sexual violence, and killing.[1]

Defining Masculinity in the Third Reich

With respect to the Third Reich, numerous historians have used the term "hypermasculinity" to refer to the Nazi male gender ideal, whether related to one's prowess in impregnating German women or linked to the longer standing tradition of Prussian militarism (Cocks 2012, 105).

For example, Jane Caplan identified a "troubling relationship between power and masculinity, between absolute power and hypermasculinity—cultivated by the SS" and present within the concentration camp system (2010, 86). In contrast to hypermasculinity, other scholars have focused on the concept of "hegemonic masculinity" to describe the interplay between the factors of gender, power, and community to create a dominant, if contested and malleable, paradigm of masculinity within a given social and cultural context.[2] While accepting the premise of hegemonic masculinity, this chapter adopts the term hypermasculinity in describing the Nazi masculine ideal by framing this term within the discourse of National Socialism that established a specific racial, biological, and gender ideal with respect to both masculinity and femininity. In this regard, race became a key symbol in the creation of a "hierarchy of masculinities" and was tied to a belief in superior virility (Moore 2010, 9).[3] Likewise, sexual violence and killing emerged as defining characteristics of the National Socialist ideal of hypermasculinity within the SS and the police complex and both of these activities frequently intersected with the use and abuse of alcohol by the perpetrators.[4]

Masculinity and Alcohol in Germany

The idea that "men affirm their manliness by drinking" constitutes a traditional aspect of Western culture extending back to Imperial Rome when male citizens expressed their superior masculinity through the amount of alcohol they could consume (Lemle and Mishkind 1989, 214). In the case of Germany, the belief linking masculinity with a man's ability to hold his liquor predated the Third Reich and was a "class-cutting phenomenon" that found reflection within German society during the *Kaiserreich* (1871–1918) (Spode 1993, 261). In Imperial Germany, taverns became sites of both heavy drinking and ritual, a trend exemplified in the drinking rituals and ceremony of the *Burschenschaften* (student fraternities) in which the consumption by members of a thousand liters of beer was not exceptional (Spode 1991, 262). In a similar way, drinking among members of the nineteenth-century working class was "an essential ingredient of masculine sociability" and served both physiological and psychological functions, with the tavern emerging as an important locus of social and political interaction (Roberts 1984, 47, 129). For the paramilitary arms of the Third Reich, ritualized community drinking bouts (*Trinkgelage*) served an "important integration mechanism" for establishing group camaraderie and identity and played a "central role" in violent confrontations with political adversaries (Reichardt 2002, 455).

During the Weimar Republic (1919–1933), taverns and the beer halls served as sites of political exhortation and mobilization for party activities from across the political spectrum (Freudenthal 1968, 334–337). For the *Sturmabteilung* (Stormtroopers or SA), political theater, alcohol, and violence were intrinsic elements of public meetings held in beer halls throughout Germany. In the case of the former, *Saalschutz* (meeting or hall protection) served a defensive and offensive purpose with both roles tied explicitly to the threat or actual use of force. Under Weimar, beer halls and taverns emerged as locations dominated by expressions of "male politics" and way points of acts of political violence (Walter 1999, 214; Schönstedt 1934, 11–32).[5] Similarly, contemporary research on gang use of alcohol and violence has revealed that alcohol plays "an integral and regular part" of group socialization in which "drinking works as a social lubricant, or social glue, to maintain not only the cohesion and social solidarity of the gang, but also to affirm masculinity and male togetherness" (Hunt and Laidler 2001, 66).[6] This observation aptly describes SA and SS units under National Socialism. Describing this dynamic Christopher Dillon remarked, "Vast consumption of alcohol could fuel an intense, fiercely emotional camaraderie within local *Stürme* [SA units], banter and masculine horseplay came to the fore." He continues, "Heavy drinking sessions might spill over into 'punitive expeditions' to working-class enclaves and thence public violence" (2015, 183). In this regard, the barroom became more than just a site for political rhetoric, but more importantly a realm of political mobilization and radicalization where words would be turned into concrete deeds of political violence. "Unleashing brutality in bar brawls, fighting together furiously in the streets and committing murder together," according to Thomas Kühne, not only promoted social bonding and male comradeship, but such "ruthless violence guaranteed public attention and established community" (2011, 239). Additionally, SA men returned to their taverns after battles against their communist adversaries in order to boast of their actions and to toast these "triumphs" with their comrades (Reichardt 2002, 457).

To be sure, "martial masculinity" was not an invention of the Nazis, but it was "glorified" under National Socialism and transformed into a "cult of masculinity" (Kühne 2006, 69). Under National Socialism the concepts of maleness and masculinity were inextricably tied to toughness and hardness from male prepubescence into adulthood. While Hitler exhorted the boys of the Hitler Youth to be "quick like greyhounds, tough like leather, and hard like Krupp steel," the education system under National Socialism stressed "the spirit of Prussian militarism, the spirit of manliness, armed strength, breeding, honor, [and] loyalty" (Koch 1975, 238; Blackburn 1985, 95). According to the historian Sven Reichardt, "Through their violent actions, the unit's members could confirm the meaning of comradeship." He continued, "To that extent the community forming violence was a premise for ideological integration: through his actions, the individual became successively more entangled in the SA, which operated as a closed community in which security and violence, hierarchy and solidarity were closely interwoven" (2013, 276). Moreover, SA units were expressly designed as "women free zones" in which masculine ideals were "cultivated" (Frevert 2004, 245).

In addition to serving social functions, the SA taverns and SA *Heime* (homes) served as designated meeting sites with the requirement that all members attend a weekly fellowship evening. During these gatherings, the ability to drink large amounts of alcohol and to "hold one's liquor," without demonstrating visible effects of intoxication, served as one marker of masculinity. In such cases, the object was not to drink oneself into a stupor or to lose control of one's faculties, but rather to demonstrate one's ability to continue to function despite a high level of alcohol consumption as a visible sign of superior manliness. Not coincidently, female "visitors" were expressly prohibited from engaging in these masculine demonstrations and were limited to soft drinks (*Limonade*) or water, a clear reflection of expected gender behavior (Longerich 1989, 127).[7]

The use of fellowship evenings extended beyond the SA and into the SS and the concentration camp system. For example, one survivor of Buchenwald remarked on the ritual associated with the introduction of these evenings at the camp in 1938, "They were eating and drinking sprees that almost invariably ended in wild orgies" (Kogon 1950, 118). The public nature of such rituals and their conduct within or near the camp complex offers insight into the way in which the perpetrators remade the camp spaces into sites of celebration. Such activities also underline the way in which perpetrators used alcohol to engage in orgiastic excess, whether related to alcohol, sexual activity, or physical violence. Additionally, the culinary and sexualized extravagance of such celebrations, especially within sight of the prisoners, served as a further symbol of the ritualistic dehumanization and emasculation of the inmates.

Fellowship evenings proved one mechanism for weaving together these communities of violence and were organized around specific political and martial themes. SA fellowship evenings included a martial ritual with the initial military formation of the members, roll call, uniform inspections, and the announcement of orders. Concluding rituals included the singing of SA and party songs and an emphasis on male bonding. In the words of Peter Longerich, "These training objectives make it apparent, that National Socialist depictions of the time of struggle testify to raw masculinity as the ideal of the SA, and robust carousers (*trinkfreudig*) with a combative nature dominated the scene" (1989, 141). Once again, masculinity, the ability to hold one's alcohol, and the willingness to fight emerged as the hallmarks of such men and the entire SA organization. In this sense, heavy drinking was an expression of one's masculinity and toughness rather than a manifestation of weakness or loss of self-control. Likewise, the refusal to take part in such rituals stigmatized one as an "outsider" and could result in threats of violence against those electing not to participate (Benz 2015, 219).

Domination, (Sexual) Power, and Violence

By refusing to participate in drinking rituals, the individual was not only seen as having rejected the group and its actions, but his actions were also viewed as manifestations of weakness or feminized behavior; traits associated in Germany with the Jew as the "feminised man" (Wieland 2015, 135). One contemporary study focusing on the relationship of male alcohol use and expressions of masculinity argues that alcohol use forms a method in which masculinity can be affirmed by the amount of alcohol consumed and one's tolerance to its effects. In a similar sense, those incapable of "holding their liquor" are correspondingly characterized as weak or feminine. The author of this study contends that "men use alcohol to express their presumed superiority over women and marginalized men," with heavy drinking providing manifestations of male power and strength (Peralta 2007, 743). In this regard, it is not surprising that one of the expressions of this "power" was reflected in the act of sexual violence. For example, one male participant explicitly linked alcohol consumption with sexual assault: "Men drink. They get violent, rape." Likewise, a female participant expressed her fear of becoming a victim of alcohol-related violence, both physical and sexual, by noting, "I think especially with guys . . . when they are drunk their drinking gives them this power" (Peralta 2007, 747, 749). In a similar sense, the concept of "masculine behavior" by "Aryan" men was a "red thread" linking crimes of physical and sexual violence against women within Nazi Germany. In a study of gender and power in the Third Reich, Vandana Joshi writes that "men become visible as oppressive sexual beings." Furthermore, she asserts that women were denied legal protections since the Gestapo "considered cases of violent outbursts by men in a drunken state, arguments between couples resulting in physical abuse and so on as 'private matters' not worthy of consideration" (2003, 189–190). In this view, "Aryan" masculinity found "legitimate" expression in acts of physical or sexual domination over women.

Based on the clear relationship between masculinity, alcohol, sexual aggression, and violence, it is not surprising that drinking played a role in acts of sexual violence, ranging from voyeurism, sexual humiliation, and rape in a regime that glorified a hypermasculine ideal. Research on sexual violence against women, especially Jewish women, has revealed the widespread sexual predation by German forces in the Occupied Eastern Territories (Hedgepeth and Saidel 2010; Mühlhäuser 2010). Acts of sexual violence by SS and police forces were commonplace despite the Nazi regime's own prohibition against race defilement (*Rassenschande*), an act punishable by death or imprisonment as witnessed in numerous cases in the "Old Reich" (Grunberger 1971, 123). In the Occupied Eastern Territories, far away from the centers of power in Berlin, these prohibitions were widely ignored and the abuse of alcohol often proved to be a key contributing factor (Beorn 2014, 172). Likewise, SS and police murder squads committed rapes in the killing fields, while drunken SS personnel in the concentration camps and the ghettos of the East sexually humiliated and brutalized Jewish women (Sinnreich 2010, 112–115).

The combination of alcohol, sexual predation, and murder can be seen in numerous cases involving a broad range of sexual violence. For example, the widespread act of making women undress before executions was not merely associated with the plundering of their clothes and a search for valuables; it also served the purpose of sexually humiliating the victims and sexually arousing the perpetrators as demonstrated by one mass execution of Jews in Odessa. A participant in this execution remarked that the SD men involved were "so drunk that they could barely conduct their duties." He continued by describing the operation: "Finally the victims at the orders of the SD [Security Service] had to undress. This was demanded above all of the women. . . . The victims then had to pass through a gauntlet of SD men whereby primarily the women were beaten with dog whips" (Mallmann, Rieß, and Pyta 2003, 153). In another case, intoxicated Security Policemen in German-occupied West Galicia forced two Jewish girls to pull down their pants in order to expose their buttocks before they shot them (Mallmann 2002, 119). In some cases, SS and policemen selected attractive young girls during the killing operations and forced them in sexual bondage in exchange for a temporary reprieve. These types of arrangements might last as little as a day or two or even for several weeks, completely at the discretion of the perpetrators (Mallmann, Rieß, and Pyta 2003, 155). One Ukrainian woman remembered how the Germans had spared a number of beautiful Jewish girls as concubines, but "when the girls got pregnant, they were killed" (Desbois 2008, 126).

The combination of alcohol and sexual coercion can be found in the actions of members of Einsatzgruppe D. The unit's members formed a "theater group" composed of attractive Russian women who were forced to put on a show. After the performance, the assembled SS men and the women "danced" and "drank" together before reaching an "arrangement" (Angrick 2003, 448). For these women, the arrangement most likely included the promise of better rations along with alcohol in exchange for sex. Such behavior was not limited to the SS, as one Wehrmacht soldier wrote in his journal: "We sang over claret and liqueurs, vodka and rum, plunged into intoxication liked doomed men, talked drunkenly about sex . . . made a Russian woman prisoner dance naked for us, greased her tits with boot polish, got her as drunk as we were . . .." (Reese 2005, 149). In two other examples, three Wehrmacht soldiers, occupying a house in a Russian village, raped a young girl while two drunken German officers murdered a family in their billet (Stahel 2015, 206; Shepherd 2016, 98).[8] Similarly, members of an SS killing unit forced attractive Jewish women to perform chores in the nude and to bathe naked in front of them. Not surprisingly, rumors circulated that these men were sexually assaulting their female prisoners after their nightly card games and heavy drinking (Angrick 2003, 187). As noted in this example, reports of "drinking binges" (*Sauftage*) were often associated with gambling and such games frequently involved the money and valuables plundered from the murdered victims (Mallmann 2002, 122).

As can be seen from the preceding examples, the dynamic between sexual aggression and power was prevalent in the Occupied East among soldiers, policemen, and members of the SS. The historian Annette Timm contends that under National Socialism "sexual gratification" was equated "with masculine power to a degree unprecedented in Germany." She also notes that "masculine vitality was thus viewed as highly dependent on sexual gratification. . . . Masculine sex drives . . . were to be channeled into the purpose of achieving the racial state" (2005, 227). While Timm focuses on prostitution and the soldiers' use of brothels, the power dynamic she describes related to sexual domination reflects a generalizable mentality among members of the SS and police complex in the Third Reich, especially in the Occupied Eastern Territories. SS men on duty in the East routinely employed sexual violence as a means for the "total exploitation of power and the demand for total subjugation [of the victims]" (Benz 2015, 213). An SS judicial investigation of cases of rape and gang rape by SS men estimated that "at least 50 percent of all members of the SS and the police violated the 'ban on undesirable intercourse with ethnically alien women'" (Mühlhäuser 2009, 203). When SS authorities chose to prosecute cases related to sexual assault in the East, judicial officers received instructions to consider the "lack of opportunity for sexual intercourse as well as excessive alcohol consumption" as extenuating factors in sentencing, a view that "propagated" the Nazi concept of masculinity and legitimized sexual violence, "especially if it was committed against women from an 'inferior race'" (Beck 2002, 266). In this sense, rape and acts of sexual violence were simply one aspect "of a continuum of violence that resulted from genocide" and a brutal expression of the perpetrator's "power and dominance through the humiliation and degradation of the other" (Halbmayr 2010, 30–31).

At the individual level, these acts of sexual violence by German forces in the East reflected male power and domination, but at a broader level they also "symbolize[d] both the military defeat and humiliation of the [subject] male population" (Mühlhäuser 2009, 201). Alcohol consumption often played a prominent role in acts of subjugation. In August 1941, Genia Demianova, a Russian schoolteacher, was interrogated by a German soldier who tortured, whipped, and brutally raped her. She remembered:

> There is a roar of cheering, the clinking of many glasses. The sergeant is standing in the open doorway: "The wild cat is tamed," he is saying. "Boys, she was a virgin. What do you say to that?" Another burst of cheering. . . . The others came in. Ten, a hundred, a thousand, one after another. The[y] flung themselves upon me, digging into my wounds while they defiled me. (Demianova 1941, 58–59)

After the attacks ended, she lay naked and battered on the floor and heard "the sound of a sentimental Schumann song. . . . the sounds came from the next room where my executioners were singing" (1941, 59). Genia Demianova's horrific ordeal raises two important points. First, the German perpetrators engaged in rape not only to demonstrate their masculinity and power over a woman and a "racial inferior," but these men also used gang rape as a mechanism for "fraternal" and "male bonding" in which they demonstrated their allegiance to the social group (Reeves Sanday 2007, 82). Second, the act of toasting the initial rape followed by the additional rapes points to the use of alcohol in a celebratory fashion, much in the way that mass killing actions would be celebrated with banquets or post-killing drunken revelry, a process that combined aspects of "alcohol, cruelty, rage, and possession" (Ingrao 2011, 117).

In some cases alcohol served a celebratory function among the murderers either in the wake of mass killings or as part of a surreal sexualized courting ritual. Some perpetrators combined the elements of a traditional picnic, including alcohol consumption, with the activity of a hunt in which the Jews became the intended prey. A Jewish survivor recalled being tasked to flush rabbits for a senior German official, his staff, and their wives and girlfriends:

> They were all drunk, lying around their seats in the carriage hugging and shouting, their peals of laughter echoing in the distance. . . . One of the drunken officers aimed his hunting rifle and started shooting at Jews to the raucous pleasure of his staff. The bullets struck some marchers who collapsed in pools of blood. (Qtd. in Lower 2013, 106)

In another example, Leo Kahn recalled a group of Nazi officials returning from an unsuccessful hunt who, after a "drunken lunch," decided to round up a group of forty Jews. These Jews were told to scatter throughout the countryside and perpetrators rode in trucks "as if they were on an African safari" and shot them all (1978, 57). Wilhelm Westerheide, a Nazi regional commissar in Ukraine, participated in a two-week-long massacre of an estimated fifteen thousand Jews. During the shootings Westerheide and his accomplices "caroused at a banquet table with a few German women . . . drinking, and eating amid the bloodshed" while music played in the background during a surrealistic killing party (Lower 2013, 128). From a social and historical perspective, the hunt in a European context was an almost exclusively male rite of passage and deeply embedded with a "masculine martial ideal" (Mangan and Mckenzie 2010, 7; Mckenzie 2005, 545–562). In this sense, the "hunting" of Jews served not only to dehumanize the victims but also to manifest the strength and potency of the hunter, especially when such acts were performed in front of a female audience.

Participation in mass killing as a means of seeking female approval or sexual gratification offers another insight into the method by which murder became an overt symbol of masculine prowess. One German policeman, after returning from a killing action, sought to impress a German secretary by showing her his blood-stained boots and uniform. Similarly, a Gestapo agent in the Polish city of Tarnów brought his seventeen-year-old son with him to work in order to "teach him how to shoot the Jewish captives" (Grabowski 2013, 94). These acts of performative masculinity also intersected with acts of sexual violence as exemplified by SS men who "often returned drunk from the *Aktion* and went to the [German] women's dormitory . . . they dragged women from their rooms and, as another secretary put it delicately, 'sought our company'" (Lower 2013, 110–111).

Another reflection of performative masculinity was a practice that mirrored trophy-taking rituals for hunting in which policemen kept running totals of the number of their victims. A former policeman with Police Battalion 9 testified, "I also know, that several [men] kept exact count of the number of people they had shot. They also bragged among themselves about the numbers" (Mallmann, Rieß, and Pyta 2003, 132) For the men of Police Battalion 61, the bar (*Kneipe*) became a site for celebrating mass executions in "drinking orgies" (*Sauforgien*) (Klemp 1998, 27, 48). Individual policemen also participated in "shooting contests" in which they competed against one another for the highest murder totals. The unit's glorification of the act of murder found its expression in the hundreds of notches carved in groups of five on the bar's door and in the drunken celebrations that occurred in the wake of these killings (Klemp 1998, 49). Another German official recalled witnessing an intoxicated Gestapo agent in 1942 leaving a bar with a beer coaster pinned to his blouse with the number 1,000 inscribed in red ink. The Gestapo man drunkenly exalted, "Man, today I'm celebrating my thousandth killing [*Genickschuß*]," as he and his colleagues caroused in a "drinking-bout" (*Zechgelage*) (Mallmann, Rieß, and Pyta 2003, 37). Another perpetrator boasted about having killed two thousand people, and, when told that this was a "reason to celebrate," he "beamed with joy" and responded, "That's what we did!" (Mallmann, Rieß, and Pyta 2003, 47). These celebrations in some cases led to acts of additional killing. A Jewish survivor of the Miedzyrec Ghetto recalled how drunken Gestapo men came into the ghetto on New Year's Eve 1942: "They [the Gestapo men] invaded the ghetto and embarked upon a so-called 'killing spree.' They went from house to house shooting people as they lay in their beds. These Gestapo men killed lots of people 'as a sport'" (qtd. in Mallmann, Rieß, and Pyta 2003, 110).

Celebratory banquets absent documented sexual violence also took place in the wake of killing actions, like the notorious massacre at Babi Yar near Kiev in 1941 and after the liquidation of the Mir Ghetto in 1942. In the case of the former, members of Police Battalion 303 not only received extra alcohol rations for their participation in the murder of almost thirty-four thousand Jews in a two-day killing operation on September 29 and 30, the battalion's men attended a banquet at the invitation of the Higher SS and Police Leader Friedrich Jeckeln, who gave a speech at the event in which he referred to the "necessity of the execution of the Jews" (Schneider 2011, 469–471). In the case of the Mir Ghetto, a joint killing operation conducted by German gendarmes and Belorussian auxiliary policemen was followed by a banquet that included "excellent food, vodka, and a variety of wines" that "led to a more relaxed mood and lively conversations" including that of a German policeman who "became very talkative, very gay" (Tec 1990, 123). In another grotesque example, a police official supervised the burning of some eight hundred Jewish corpses by tapping a keg of beer. This policeman, based on his leading role in the murders, was given the "honor" of setting fire to the bodies and when the fire department arrived to investigate the blaze, he sent them away by stating, "It's only the Jews burning" (qtd. in Mallmann, Rieβ, and Pyta 2003, 52). This grisly "cremation kegger" was not simply an isolated case; one Gestapo man recalled the smell of burning flesh as he and his colleagues sat around a bonfire made with Jewish bodies, singing and drinking after a killing operation in Przemyśl (Mallmann 2002, 119).

The Sexualized Semantics of Alcohol Use

The words used to describe the process of drinking by SS and policemen during occupation duties offer important insights into some of the ways alcohol consumption was framed and intended. Victor Klemperer's oft-cited *LTI-Lingua Tertii Imperii* examines the National Socialist perversion of the German language in a process by which "Nazism permeated the flesh and blood of the people through single words, idioms and sentence structures" (2000, 15). In fact, the use of words such as *Zechgelage, Trinkgelage, Sauftage,* and *Sauforgien* offers revealing insights into the conceptualization of drinking, the ritualistic use of alcohol, and the ultimate meaning and importance of the process of drinking itself. For example, the German verbs *saufen* and *zechen* both are linguistically tied to *excessive* drinking, with the former often being used to describe animal drinking behavior. These two terms also have sexualized connotations of carousing or orgy. Likewise, the use of the word *Gelage* connotes acts of carousal, revelry, and drinking bouts (*Cassell's* 1939). The sexualized nature of such activities is most apparent in the term *Sauforgien* (lit., drinking orgies), a word that explicitly combines the act of extreme alcohol consumption with the concept of unrestrained sexual activity. The perpetrators' use of these terms to refer to the act of drinking intersected with their views of masculinity at two levels. First, it highlighted their ability to consume large quantities of alcohol in an almost animalistic sense, and, second, the act of drinking was explicitly tied to an expression of virility and sexual prowess. Indeed, such linguistic constructions perfectly reflect drinking rituals to celebrate rape, gang rapes, and murder in the East (Mühlhäuser 2009, 199–202).

Sexual Violence

While words and their meanings can be used to justify actions, it is ultimately the actions themselves that serve as the clearest indicator of intent. The relationship of alcohol and physical or sexual violence perpetrated against women offers another perspective for evaluating the actions of individual SS men both within the camps and in the killing fields. Numerous academic studies have examined the linkage between alcohol consumption and aggression. In reviewing this literature, one study notes: "It is now well established, by both correlational and experimental studies, that alcohol consumption facilitates aggressive behavior" (Giancola et al. 2002, 64). While researchers and scholars debate whether there is a direct causal linkage between alcohol consumption and sexual assaults, numerous studies have identified the increased prevalence of violence and sexual assault when one or both of the parties involved have been drinking (Abbey 2002, 118–128). Similarly, acts of sexual aggression by men, against both women and other men, are tied to the concept of masculinity and hypermasculinity and have been described as "promoting forms of dominant hegemonic heterosexuality" (Gregory and Lees 1999, 131; Crawford 2014).

With respect to alcohol and sexual assault, one investigation found that "men anticipate feeling more powerful, sexual and aggressive after drinking alcohol" (Abbey 2002, 121). Feelings of power or dominance, whether physical or sexual in nature, characterized the male ideal in Nazi Germany. In fact, one postwar German observer bemoaned the fact that "the dominance of the man, which was so strongly emphasized in the Third Reich, has collapsed" (qtd. in Herzog 2005, 86). The National Socialist preoccupation with procreation was an area in which the concept of hypermasculinity found its most visible expression, and, therefore, the manifestation of hypersexual activity, both consensual and transgressive, should not be surprising, especially in the presence of alcohol consumption (Timm 2005, 225–227).

In the East, acts of sexual aggression not only demonstrated male dominance but also male bonding. "Abusing women in the occupied areas was the ultimate performative masculinity, that is, an assertion of the sovereignty of the male bond" (Kühne 2011, 245). Examples of sexual violence, including sexual assault and acts of sexual humiliation, are readily apparent in the actions taken by members of the SS, the police, and soldiers of the Wehrmacht in both the Occupied East as well as in the confines of the concentration and extermination camps. The combination of sexual humiliation and violence can be found in a number of examples involving SS guards and auxiliaries in the camps. Acts of sexual humiliation might embrace psychological or physical violence, but in either case they served as expressions of male physical and sexual domination over the victims. In the case of the former, Chil Rajchman, a survivor, recalled German SS men and SS foreign auxiliaries at Treblinka watching naked women and girls being led to the gas chamber. During the process, the men amused themselves by making "jokes" about the women and "laughing," incidents that continued "throughout the entire winter" (quoted in Benz 2015, 229).

Sanjay Palshikar argues that the use of humiliation in wartime is "predicated upon already existing notions of manhood and glory" (2005, 5430). In this sense, such acts are an overt expression of masculinity and male power and these traits are perhaps most clearly seen in acts of sexual humiliation involving physical violence against the victims, both males and females. In the summer of 1943, four SS men found a group of Jews hiding in a bunker in Warsaw. According to a witness statement, they ordered the men and women to undress: "SS men were lifting women's breasts, looking inside their mouths, they inspected their sexual organs. They were putting their fingers into their colons groping them like good housewives at the market searching for a fatty goose for lard." The witness statement continued: "Everybody, women, children and men were subjected to these unheard of inspections. . . . The SS-men jeered and enjoyed the sight of the inhuman suffering of their victims" (Gross 2012, 91–92). Similar scenes were repeated at Auschwitz during the first Slovakian deportation as SS men conducted "gynecological exams" under the pretext of searching for valuables before engaging in mass rapes (Levenkron 2010, 18). The ghettos, the camps, and the killing fields all provided a singularly suitable environment for acts of humiliation and sadism that preceded the murder of the victims.

At Auschwitz, several survivors testified on the actions of SS guard Otto Moll at the cremation pits. A Jewish prisoner, Mel Mermelstein, recalled a case in which Moll had selected twenty "beautiful" women from a newly arrived transport. "He had them undress and stand naked facing him in a single row. He then shot all of them, one by one, in full view of witnesses" (1979, 152). In fact, Moll routinely engaged in a ritual of the sexual humiliation of his victims before he killed them. *Sonderkommando* member Filip Müller also recalled:

> Moll had a morbid partiality for obscene and salacious tortures. Thus it was his wont to turn up in the crematorium when the victims were taking off their clothes. . . . Like a meat inspector he would stride about the changing room, selecting a couple of naked young women and hustling them to one of the pits. . . . In the end he shot them from behind so that they fell forward in the burning pit. (Müller 1979, 141)

For Moll, sexual titillation and murder were conjoined in an act where the sexual humiliation of the victim became a key part in the ritual of destruction.

Müller's description of Moll as "sexually excited" by the nakedness of his victims combined with their punishment can also be found in the accounts of sexual aggression against males. At Dachau, SS men used eighteen-inch-long dried ox penises as pizzles to flog prisoners, a device that at one and the same time symbolized the virility and hypermasculinity of the perpetrator and reinforced the submissiveness or femininity of the victims (Ryback 2014, 150). Heinz Heger, a concentration camp survivor, "witnessed innumerable ritual floggings" of male prisoners in several camps. "The victim was tied to the notorious 'whipping post' in such a way as to make his buttocks arch upward above the rest of his body." Heger then described the reaction of the camp commandant supervising the flogging: "His eyes lit up with every stroke; after the first few his whole face was already red with lascivious excitement" (qtd. in Theweleit 1989, 300–301). The ritualistic form of violence in this case was not only sexualized in nature but also embraced elements of male dominance. In fact, Heger identifies these floggings as "celebrations of torture" and he contends that he witnessed SS concentration commanders who masturbated on "more than thirty occasions" as male prisoners were being beaten on their bare buttocks (Theweleit 1989, 301).

The "celebration of [sexual] torture" was a frequent occurrence in areas under German occupation. In many cases, alcohol not only proved to be a catalyst for acts of sexual violence, but its use continued after these assaults in a festive ritual. In the case of SS auxiliaries, whether Ukrainian, Lithuanian, Latvian, or Russian, their use and abuse of alcohol and their resulting acts of brutality are noted repeatedly in the scholarship of the Holocaust (Black 2011; Browning 1992, 80; Salton 2002, 116; Tory 1990, 37–38, 40–42, 58). For Ukrainian auxiliaries, their acts of drunken violence led even their German SS masters to describe them as "a wild race without self-restraint, especially when they drank" and as "wild animals" who were "uncouth and unreliable, especially under the influence of alcohol" (qtd. in Black 2011, 35). At Sobibor, the Ukrainian auxiliaries "consumed large quantities of alcohol," which they usually attained either from trade with locals for plundered Jewish goods or as part of their weekly rations from the SS (Schelvis 2007, 35). Similarly, SS auxiliaries in Belarus traded plundered goods for homemade schnapps, which then initiated "a new wave of violence" that often included sexual assaults by the perpetrators. Indeed, historian Bernhard Chiari notes that "in general, schnapps played an important role in the abuse . . . [and] rapes were not uncommon" (1998, 192–193).

Conclusion

"Sexuality in the Third Reich was after all," Dagmar Herzog argues, "also about the invasion and control and destruction of human beings" (2005, 6). In a study of Wehrmacht operations in the East another historian concluded that, "at the local level, sexuality in the East seems to have operated under a moral code different from that observed in Western Europe. . . . German civil authorities (as well as military men) frequently abused alcohol to excess and participated in depraved sexual acts outside the pale of acceptability in the West" (Beorn 2014, 172). In the East, physical conquest of territory, racial and gender-based concepts of superiority, and perceptions of male dominance combined with excessive alcohol consumption to create a mind-set among the perpetrators in which acts of sexual aggression were either overlooked or even encouraged at the local level by military and SS officers as the right of the victor.

For the political soldiers of the Third Reich, the military campaigns in the East offered the ultimate arena for displaying "masculine virtues like will, determination, and action" as part of an "active and aggressive concept of masculinity" in which geography itself was represented in the gendered space of the "manly battlefront" and the "womanly home front" (*weibliche Heimat*) (Werner 2008, 12, 20). In this environment, physical and sexual violence against women and girls emerged as a fact of daily life in which male fellowship and self-conceptions of masculinity found expression in "gang rapes, torture, and drink" that often preceded the murder of the victims (Matthäus, Böhler, and Mallmann 2014, 77; Ingrao

2011, 85; Hedgepeth and Saidel 2010, 2). As Wehrmacht soldiers, policemen, and SS personnel marched East prepared to test their manhood, they imagined themselves as protecting German women from falling victim to the Russian "hordes" and the "Asiatic enemy" (Werner 2008, 16). By 1945, however, the actions of German forces in the East had resulted in a self-fulfilling prophecy as Soviet forces stormed westward toward Berlin intent on reaping their own revenge. In a diary entry of May 13, 1945, a German woman in Berlin reflected on the role of alcohol in the sexual assaults by Soviet soldiers: "I'm convinced that if the Russians hadn't found so much alcohol all over, half as many rapes would have taken place." She continued:

> Next time there's a war fought in the presence of women and children (for whose protection men supposedly used to do the fighting out on the battlefield, away from home), every last drop of drink should be poured into the gutter, wine stores destroyed, beer cellars blown up. . . . Just make sure there's no alcohol left as long as there are women within grabbing distance of the enemy. (Anonymous 2005, 173)

For this woman, German soldiers had failed in their duties as soldiers and men, and she and many other women would suffer the consequences. However, in focusing on the result of a lost war, she had lost sight of the cause of her condition. For it was the National Socialist ideal of hypermasculinity that had created the conditions for a war in which alcohol, sexual violence, and killing were given free rein. Countless women in the East had previously payed the physical and psychological price for German SS and policemen "testing their manhood" in a racial war of annihilation.

Notes

1. These specific factors along with drug use have been identified as "key elements of masculinity" in contemporary culture as well. See De Visser and Smith (2007).

2. For an excellent review of this research, see Connell and Messerschmidt (2005).

3. While Moore's claim in this case pertains to the issue of race on the nineteenth-century Texas frontier, it is equally applicable to the Nazi case.

4. For an extended discussion of the relationship between alcohol and atrocity in the Third Reich, see Westermann (2016).

5. For a contemporary popular culture depiction of this process, see Schönstedt (1934). This popular novel, although written by a German communist exile in Paris with an anti-Nazi moral, still captures the atmosphere of the *Sturmlokal* as a site of male camaraderie, ritual, and political violence.

6. The formation of SA and SS units, especially in the period prior to the Nazi seizure of power, reveals a number of similarities with respect to the culture, rituals, and activities of contemporary organized gangs.

7. Beer was the primary drink for such occasions and SA men who demonstrated an inability to drink and maintain control were served low-alcohol-content beer (*Malzbier*) instead.

8. Shepherd (2016) notes that drunken violence was also prevalent in occupied France, with one French police commissioner blaming such cases on "the mingling of males and females and above all because of the abuse of alcohol."

References

Abbey, Antonia. 2002. "Alcohol-Related Sexual Assault: A Common Problem among College Students." *Journal of Studies on Alcohol Supplement* 63, no. 2 (March): 118–128.

Angrick, Andrej. 2003. *Besatzungspolitik und Massenmord: Die Einsatzgruppe D in der südlichen Sowjetunion, 1941–1943*. Hamburg: Hamburger Edition.

Anonymous. 2005. *A Woman in Berlin: Eight Weeks in a Conquered City*. Translated by Philip Boehm. New York: Metropolitan Books.

Beck, Birgit. 2002. "The Military Trials of Sexual Crimes Committed by Soldiers in the Wehrmacht, 1939–1944." In *Home/Front: The Military, War and Gender in Twentieth Century Germany*, edited by Karen Hagemann and Stefanie Schüler-Springorum, 255–273. Oxford: Berg.

Beorn, Waitman. 2014. *Marching into Darkness: The Wehrmacht and the Holocaust in Belarus*. Cambridge: Harvard University Press.

Benz, Angelika. 2015. *Handlanger der SS: Die Rolle der Trawniki-Männer im Holocaust*. Berlin: Metropol.

Bessel, Richard. 1986. "Violence as Propaganda: The Role of the Storm Troopers in the Rise of National Socialism." In *The Formation of the Nazi Constituency, 1919–1933*, edited by Thomas Childers, 131–146. Totowa: Barnes and Noble Books.

Black, Peter. 2011. "Foot Soldiers of the Final Solution: The Trawniki Training Camp and Operation Reinhard." *Holocaust and Genocide Studies* 25, no. 1 (Spring): 1–99.

Blackburn, Gilmer W. 1985. *Education in the Third Reich: A Study of Race and History in Nazi Textbooks.* Albany: State University of New York Press.
Browning, Christopher. 1992. *Ordinary Men: Reserve Police Battalion 101 and the Final Solution.* New York: Harper Collins.
Caplan, Jane. 2010. "Gender and the Concentration Camps." In *Concentration Camps in Nazi Germany: The New Histories,* edited by Jane Caplan and Nikolaus Wachsmann, 82–107. New York: Routledge.
Cassell's New German Dictionary. 1939. New York: Funk and Wagnalls.
Chiari, Bernhard. 1998. *Alltag hinter der Front: Besatzung, Kollaboration und Widerstand in Weißrußland, 1941–1944.* Düsseldorf: Droste Verlag.
Cocks, Geoffrey. 2012. *The State of Health: Illness in Nazi Germany.* Oxford: Oxford University Press.
Connell, R. W., and James W. Messerschmidt. 2005. "Hegemonic Masculinity: Rethinking the Concept." *Gender and Society* 19, no. 6 (December): 829–859.
Crawford, Michael T. 2014. "A Culture of Hypermasculinity is Driving Sexual Assault in the Military." *Huffington Post* http://www.huffingtonpost.com/michael-t-crawford/a-culture-of-hypermasculi_b_5147191.html (accessed 23 October 2016).
Demianova, Genia. 1941. *Comrade Genia: The Story of a Victim of German Bestiality in Russia Told by Herself.* London: Nicholson and Watson.
Desbois, Patrick. 2008. *The Holocaust by Bullets: A Priest's Journey to Uncover the Truth Behind the Murder of 1.5 Million Jews.* New York: Palgrave Macmillan.
De Visser, Richard O., and Jonathan Smith. 2007. "Alcohol Consumption and Masculine Identity among Young Men." *Psychology and Health* 22, no. 5 (July): 595–614.
Dillon, Christopher. 2015. *Dachau and the SS: A Schooling in Violence.* Oxford: Oxford University Press.
Freudenthal, Herbert. 1968. *Vereine in Hamburg: Ein Beitrag zur Geschichte und Volkskunde der Geselligkeit.* Hamburg: Museum für Hamburgische Geschichte.
Frevert, Ute. 2004. *A Nation in Barracks: Modern Germany, Military Conscription and Civil Society.* Translated by Andrew Boreham and Daniel Brückenhaus. Oxford: Berg.
Giancola, Peter R., Emily L. Helton, Abigail B. Osborne, Michael K. Terry, Angie M. Fuss, and Johnna A. Westerfield. 2002. "The Effects of Alcohol and Provocation on Aggressive Behavior in Men and Women." *The Journal of Studies on Alcohol* 63, no. 1 (January): 64–73.
Grabowski, Jan. 2013. *Hunt for the Jews: Betrayal and Murder in German-Occupied Poland.* Bloomington: Indiana University Press.
Gregory, Jeanne, and Sue Lees. 1999. *Policing Sexual Assault.* London: Routledge.
Gross, Jan Tomasz, with Irena Grudzińska Gross. 2012. *Golden Harvest: Events at the Periphery of the Holocaust.* Oxford: Oxford University Press.

Grunberger, Richard. 1971. *The 12-Year Reich: A Social History of Nazi Germany, 1933–1945*. New York: Holt, Rinehart and Winston.

Halbmayr, Brigitte. 2010. "Sexualized Violence against Women during Nazi 'Racial' Persecution." In *Sexual Violence against Women during the Holocaust*, edited by Sonja Hedgepeth and Rochelle Saidel, 29–44. Waltham: Brandeis University Press.

Haynes, Stephen R. 2015. "Ordinary Masculinity: Gender Analysis and Holocaust Scholarship." In *Genocide and Gender in the Twentieth Century: A Comparative Survey*, edited by Amy E. Randall, 165–188. London: Bloomsbury.

Hedgepeth, Sonja M., and Rochelle G. Saidel, eds. 2010. *Sexual Violence against Jewish Women during the Holocaust*. Hanover: University Press of New England.

Herzog, Dagmar. 2005. "Hubris and Hypocrisy, Incitement and Disavowal: Sexuality and German Fascism." In *Sexuality and German Fascism*, edited by Dagmar Herzog, 3–21. New York: Berghahn.

———. 2005. *Sex after Fascism: Memory and Morality in Twentieth-Century Germany*. Princeton: Princeton University Press.

Hunt, Geoffrey P., and Karen Joe Laidler. 2001. "Alcohol and Violence in the Lives of Gang Members." *Alcohol Research and Health* 25, no. 1: 66–71.

Ingrao, Christian. 2011. *The SS Dirlewanger Brigade: The History of the Black Hunters*. Translated by Phoebe Green. New York: Skyhorse.

Joshi, Vandana. 2003. *Gender and Power in the Third Reich: Female Denouncers and the Gestapo, 1933–1945*. New York: Palgrave Macmillan.

Kahn, Leo. 1978. *No Time to Mourn: A True Story of a Jewish Partisan Fighter*. Vancouver: Laurelton Press.

Klemp, Stefan. 1998. *Freispruch für das "Mord-Bataillon."* Münster: LIT Verlag.

Klemperer, Victor. 2000. *The Language of the Third Reich: LTI-Lingua Tertii Imperii, a Philologist's Notebook*. Translated by Martin Brady. London: Athlone Press.

Koch, H. W. 1975. *The Hitler Youth: Origins and Development, 1922–1945*. New York: Dorset.

Kogon, Eugen. 1950. *The Theory and Practice of Hell: The German Concentration Camps and the System Behind Them*. Translated by Heinz Norden. New York: Farrar, Straus and Giroux.

Kühne, Thomas. 2006. *Kameradschaft: Die Soldaten des nationalsozialistischen Krieges und das 20. Jahrhundert*. Göttingen: Vandenhoeck and Ruprecht.

———. 2011. "The Pleasure of Terror." In *Pleasure and Power in Nazi Germany*, edited by Pamela Swett, Corey Ross, and Fabrice d'Almeida, 234–255. New York: Palgrave Macmillan.

Lemle, Russell, and Marc E. Mishkind. 1989. "Alcohol and Masculinity." *Journal of Substance Abuse Treatment* 6, no. 4: 213–222.

Levenkron, Nomi. 2010. "'Prostitution,' Rape, and Sexual Slavery during World War II." In *Sexual Violence against Jewish Women during the Holocaust*, edited by Sonja M. Hedgepeth and Rochelle G. Saidel, 13–28. Hanover: University Press of New England.

Longerich, Peter. 1989. *Die braunen Bataillone: Geschichte der SA*. Munich: C. H. Beck.
Lower, Wendy. 2013. *Hitler's Furies: German Women in the Nazi Killing Fields*. New York: Houghton Mifflin Harcourt.
Mallmann, Klaus-Michael. 2002. "'Mensch, ich feire heut' den tausendsten Genickschuβ': Die Sicherheitspolizei und die Shoah in Westgalizien." In *Die Täter der Shoah: Fanatische Nationalsozialisten oder ganz normale Deutsche?*, edited by Gerhard Paul, 109–136. Göttingen: Wallstein Verlag.
Mallmann, Klaus-Michael, Volker Rieβ, and Wolfram Pyta, eds. 2003. *Deutscher Osten 1939–1945: Der Weltanschauungskrieg in Photos and Texten*. Darmstadt: Wissenschaftliche Buchgesellschaft.
Mangan, J. A., and Callum Mckenzie. 2010. *Militarism, Hunting, Imperialism: "Blooding" the Martial Male*. New York: Routledge.
Matthäus, Jürgen, Jochen Böhler, and Klaus-Michael Mallmann. 2014. *War, Pacification, and Mass Murder, 1939: The Einsatzgruppen in Poland*. Lanham: Rowman & Littlefield.
Mckenzie, Callum. 2005. "'Sadly Neglected'—Hunting and Gendered Identities: A Study in Gender Construction." *The International Journal of the History of Sport* 22, no. 4 (July): 545–562.
Mermelstein, Mel. 1979. *By Bread Alone: The Story of A-4685*. Huntington Beach: Auschwitz Study Foundation.
Moore, Jacqueline M. 2010. *Cow Boys and Cattle Men: Class and Masculinities on the Texas Frontier, 1865–1900*. New York: New York University Press.
Mühlhäuser, Regina. 2009. "Between 'Racial Awareness' and Fantasies of Potency: Nazi Sexual Politics in the Occupied Territories of the Soviet Union, 1942–1945." In *Brutality and Desire: War and Sexuality in Europe's Twentieth Century*, edited by Dagmar Herzog, 197–219. New York: Palgrave Macmillan.
———. 2010. *Eroberungen: Sexuelle Gewalttaten und intime Beziehungen deutscher Soldaten in der Sowjetunion, 1941–1945*. Hamburg: Hamburger Edition.
Müller, Filip. 1979. *Eyewitness Auschwitz: Three Years in the Gas Chambers*. Edited and translated by Susanne Flatauer. Chicago: Ivan R. Dee.
Palshikar, Sanjay. 2005. "Understanding Humiliation." *Economic and Political Weekly* 40, no. 51 (December 17–23): 5428–5432.
Peralta, Robert L. 2007. "College Alcohol Use and the Embodiment of Hegemonic Masculinity among European American Men." *Sex Roles* 56 (June): 741–756.
Peukert, Detlev. 1987. *Inside Nazi Germany: Conformity, Opposition, and Racism in Everyday Life*. Translated by Richard Deveson. New Haven: Yale University Press.
Reese, Willy Peter. 2005. *A Stranger to Myself: The Inhumanity of War: Russia, 1941–1944*. Translated by Michael Hofmann. New York: Farrar, Straus and Giroux.
Reeves Sanday, Peggy. 2007. *Fraternity Gang Rape: Sex, Brotherhood, and Privilege on Campus*, 2d ed. New York: New York University Press.

Reichardt, Sven. 2002. *Faschistische Kampfbünde: Gewalt und Gemeinschaft im italienischen Squadrismus und in der deutschen SA.* Cologne: Böhlau Verlag.

———. 2013. "Violence and Community: A Micro-Study on Nazi Storm Troopers." *Central European History* 46, no. 2 (June): 275–297.

Roberts, James. 1984. *Drink, Temperance and the Working Class in Nineteenth-Century Germany.* Boston: George Allen and Unwin.

Ryback, Timothy W. 2014. *Hitler's First Victims: The Quest for Justice.* New York: Alfred A. Knopf.

Salton, George L. 2002. *The 23d Psalm: A Holocaust Memoir.* Madison: University of Wisconsin Press.

Schelvis, Jules. 2007. *Sobibor: A History of a Nazi Death Camp.* Oxford: Berg.

Schneider, Karl. 2011. *"Auswärts eingesetzt": Bremer Polizeibataillone und der Holocaust.* Essen: Klartext Verlag.

Schönstedt, Walter. 1934. *Auf der Flucht erschossen: Ein SA Roman 1933.* Paris: Éditions du Carrefour.

Shepherd, Ben H. 2016. *Hitler's Soldiers: The German Army in the Third Reich.* New Haven: Yale University Press.

Sinnreich, Helene. 2010. "The Rape of Jewish Women during the Holocaust." In *Sexual Violence against Jewish Women during the Holocaust*, edited by Sonja M. Hedgepeth and Rochelle G. Saidel, 108–123. Hanover: University Press of New England.

Spode, Hasso. 1993. *Die Macht der Trunkenheit: Kultur- und Sozialgeschichte des Alkohols in Deutschland.* Opladen: Leske and Budrich.

Stahel, David. 2015. *The Battle for Moscow.* Cambridge: Cambridge University Press.

Tec, Nechama. 1990. *In the Lion's Den: The Life of Oswald Rufeisen.* Oxford: Oxford University Press.

Theweleit, Klaus. 1989. *Male Fantasies: Psychoanalyzing the White Terror*, vol. 2. Translated by Erica Carter and Chris Turner. Minneapolis: University of Minnesota Press.

Timm, Annette F. 2005. "Sex with a Purpose: Prostitution, Venereal Disease, and Militarized Masculinity in the Third Reich." In *Sexuality and German Fascism*, edited by Dagmar Herzog, 223–255. Austin: University of Texas Press.

Tory, Avraham. 1990. *Surviving the Holocaust: The Kovno Ghetto Diary.* Translated by Jerzy Michalowicz. Cambridge: Harvard University Press.

Walter, Dirk. 1999. *Antisemitische Kriminalität und Gewalt: Judenfeindschaft in der Weimarer Republik.* Bonn: J. H. W. Dietz Nachfolger.

Werner, Frank. 2008. "'Hart müssen wir hier draußen sein': Soldatische Männlichkeit im Vernichtungskrieg 1941–1944." *Geschichte und Gesellschaft* 34, no. 1 (March): 5–40.

Westermann, Edward B. 2016. "Stone-Cold Killers or Drunk with Murder? Alcohol and Atrocity during the Holocaust." *Holocaust and Genocide Studies* 30, no. 1 (Spring): 1–19.

Wieland, Christina. 2015. *The Fascist State of Mind and the Manufacturing of Masculinity: A Psychoanalytic Approach.* New York: Routledge.

Chapter 7

Catholic Seminarians and *Vernichtungskrieg*
How Nationalism, Religion, and Masculinity Mattered

LAUREN FAULKNER ROSSI

In late August 1941, the young seminarian WS found himself in Russia, part of the German military behemoth that had violated an international treaty and invaded Soviet territory two months earlier. To his seminary director, Johann Westermayr, he wrote, "One must experience Russia for oneself and march 1,400 kilometers on foot through this so-called paradise to appreciate seriously how superior German civilization is . . . [here there are] no men to be seen, with bodies and souls, but rather individuals resembling animals."[1] A classmate, MH, reflected a month later on the reasons they had been sent into Russia. If he noticed anything about the inferior culture he encountered, or its peoples, he did not mention it and instead chose to concentrate on the urgency of their mission: "I have followed many comrades and confreres into the East, to fulfill my duty here in the battle against Bolshevism. Indeed, it is a fine thing to know that we stand here against the enemy of all God-given order and religion."[2] Both of these Catholic seminarians were conscripts in the Wehrmacht and served on multiple fronts. Neither mentioned Hitler or Nazism in their letters, but concentrated on their task that was simultaneously spiritual, cultural, and political: the defeat of Bolshevism.

There were a total of 452 Catholic German seminarians conscripted out of their classrooms in the archdiocese of Munich and Freising, in Bavaria. Analyzing their experiences as Wehrmacht soldiers, this chapter asserts that these men were complex individuals living in a stressful, volatile environment, whose daily lives were neither constant nor predictable. Dichotomies such as resistance and collaboration, opposition and accommodation, dissent and assent fail to capture the moral ambiguity in their writings, nor do they adequately describe the nature and depth of the compromise they made and their understanding of the war they were fighting. Primo Levi spoke of a nebulous gray zone that "shuns half-tints and complexities" and complicates the black-and-white, Manichean categories of good and evil, or friend and enemy (Levi 1989, 22). While Levi conceptualized his paradigm to describe individuals within the extermination camps, this gray zone, which at its core seeks to complicate, problematize, and redefine conventional categories of behavior, might be applied to the Catholic German men who are the subject of this essay. Within this gray zone, many of these seminarians were able to carve out a space for themselves in the Wehrmacht that Nazi ideology neither defined nor sustained. While it is problematic to use this space as evidence of either resistance or complicity, it demonstrates very real limits to the persuasive power of Nazi ideology. This does not make the war they fought any less criminal, but it does suggest that the army was not entirely "Hitler's army" (see Bartov 1992; also Förster 1998, 266–283).

I also seek to challenge the argument that members of the Catholic Church enjoyed a unique imperviousness to Nazism that others in Germany at the time did not. Historian Martin Broszat pointed to the apparent immunity of Catholic Germans to certain aspects of Nazi rule, specifically the regime's attempts to infringe on the autonomy of the Church in administrative or religious matters. He called this immunity *Resistenz*. Controversial when it was introduced in the early 1980s, this supposedly neutral concept was responsible for nuancing and elaborating our understanding of possible reactions to the regime. However, immunity to Nazism is difficult to apply to the sphere of the military, particularly when considering these Catholic seminarians. Nazism was neither necessary persuasion to motivate them nor effective dissuasion that kept them from going. Just like the vast majority of bishops and priests on the home front, seminarians drafted into the Wehrmacht understood the war as a fight against an enemy of the Catholic Church, and they saw themselves as essential participants in that battle. The decisions that they made about wartime behavior were guided by three salient points of self-identity: their German nationalism, their Catholic faith, and their masculinity. They had no need of Nazi propaganda to encourage them to enlist in order to defend their families, their homes, and their faith, even their whole way of life, from Bolshevism.

In focusing on their military service, these seminarians contribute something original to the study of conflict and consensus between Catholic clergy-in-training and Nazi ideology. It proves that one did not have to be a Nazi to fight willingly in the Wehrmacht and for Hitler's objectives. It highlights the overlap as well as the tension between the military world and the seminary, between training to be a soldier and training to be a priest: both were highly masculine spheres, dominated exclusively by men (women did not serve on the frontlines in the Wehrmacht), though the manhood of supposedly celibate Catholic seminarians may not have been understood as the same kind of manhood that defined other soldiers. It also proves the longevity of traditional Christian mores and beliefs in the military, beliefs that clearly survived Nazism's concerted efforts to extinguish them by substituting its own racial-biological worldview. Arguably, members of the Catholic Church were most successfully coordinated with the regime's modus operandi and end goals while serving in the military; ironically, this was also the atmosphere in which the Christian faith of those members proved particularly resilient, providing a bulwark against criminality and terror, deprivation and certain death, while simultaneously enabling them, as soldiers, to keep fighting.

Vocational Conviction and Military Conscription

The seminarians hardly present an undifferentiated group. The primary unifying elements of this group were their Catholic faith, their gender, and their enrollment in the Freising seminary in Bavaria. Lying just north of Munich, Freising was a major artery in medieval Germany and a center of learning. Prior to German unification in 1871, the kingdom of Bavaria was one of the most densely Catholic areas of Central Europe (Schwaiger 1989, 16–37). After unification, Germany's Catholics, constituting about 30 percent of the population of the new German Reich, self-identified as a marginalized minority.[3] By the early twentieth century, Freising's religious significance had waned but its role in the education of future priests remained intact. In addition to the seminary, it was also the site of a junior seminary (*Knabenseminar*) and a theological college (*philosophische-theologische Hochschule*). Founded in 1826, Freising's clerical seminary was a locus for young Bavarian Catholic men drawn to the priesthood. Their seminary education was an essential and rigorous part of the ordination process and would have normally taken about eight years.[4]

During the course of the Second World War, 452 seminarians from the Freising clerical seminary were called up to fight.[5] They were encouraged to correspond with seminary director Johann Westermayr, who used the correspondence to monitor the spiritual and physical health of his charges. A few seminarians wrote only once or twice during their entire service; others wrote prolifically, every two weeks or fortnight. For those who were conscripted as early as the war's outbreak in September 1939, this amounts to dozens of letters and a significant dedication of time and mental energy. The themes that surface in the letters are as varied as the letter writers, though perhaps a dozen occur with regularity. These include nostalgia for the seminary and Freising; concerns for families and friends back home, especially after the Allied bombing campaign began in earnest in 1943; encounters with other priests and clergy in the army; the need to guard against the apathy and fatalism of other soldiers; their experiences as tourists in foreign lands; and their interactions with foreign civilian populations.

I will focus primarily on the three most frequently recurring themes: descriptions of religion and their vocation as a source of strength and conviction in their current mission; conditions on the Eastern Front and their reactions to the Russians they encountered; and their understanding of Bolshevism as the primal enemy against which they were waging a crusadelike, and very necessary, war of extermination (*Vernichtungskrieg*). These areas demonstrate that, while most seminarians seem to display a *Resistenz*-like inoculation from Nazi propaganda in terms of what motivated them to go to war, the effects of their behavior furthered the regime's war goals. Once in the ranks of the military, most seminarians tried to be good soldiers within the parameters of their personal belief system and convictions, which entailed a familiarity with a highly masculine environment that, on this basis, may have been reminiscent of the seminary. Religious fervor was one of several reasons that men fought in the ranks of the Wehrmacht. Nazi ideology was hardly the totalizing impetus it strove to be, even in Hitler's own armed forces.

Catholic seminarians from the Munich and Freising archdiocese understood the war into which they had been conscripted as an interruption of indeterminate length in their studies for the priesthood. Not surprisingly, there is no evidence of enthusiasm for war in their early letters. Seminarians performed military service for the most part because they had to, not because they felt a keen desire to.

A loss of faith, doubts about the priesthood, or a loss of vocational conviction were not uncommon. Statistics indicate that at least fifty-eight seminarians withdrew from their seminary studies during the course of the war.[6] But it was more often the case that seminarians used their war experiences to rededicate themselves to the priestly life. For some, such as AB, the war brought clarity, insight, and the patience to endure the present in order to prepare for the future as a priest: "I have seen how the world today needs priests, and I am calm, knowing that for now I must be a soldier and can wait until I have achieved the goal of my desire . . . fully prepared for this great charge."[7] Another seminarian echoed this, declaring, "My wish to continue studying in order to prepare myself for the greater vocation and become a priest is stronger than before and grows each day, even here in the army."[8] Serving in the army, and all the attendant trials and hardships that this entailed, was for some the best preparation for becoming a priest.

Some seminarians, such as AN, indicated that the army was perhaps an even more appropriate training environment than the seminary was: "Today this battle is more an inner battle, one that builds character and strengthens courage. In this way, time in the military is the best school for future officers of Christ . . ."[9] Finding spiritual significance for the indeterminate interruption in their priestly training was important because this allowed the seminarians to come to terms with their new way of life, one that they did not choose. TW asked himself, "Is this time in the military a lost time specifically for us theology students? Others will frequently answer yes, but we must deny this. We undertook a life in and with Christ through our vocation, so the first goal is perfection in order to serve others . . ."[10] Although no letters that I read explicitly mentioned this, the new, militarized environment was, like their seminary classrooms, almost exclusively populated by men. The only women they would have encountered were either nurses in the rear area hospitals or among foreign civilian populations, making a female presence peripheral. This highly militarized, masculine atmosphere likely would have felt familiar to many seminarians, whose chosen vocation would have taken them into an exclusively male-dominated sphere, the Catholic Church. As a matter of fact, the concept of "militarized masculinity" might be of some help here. It refers to the idea that men are not naturally soldiers but are trained to become soldiers through the acquisition of certain traits typically considered "male," such as strength, discipline, endurance, and courage. But the embrace, enactment, and embodiment of these idealized male traits through military service and combat is uneven among men. The ideal construct of militarized masculinity is not the same for all soldiers, and seminarians in uniform may have held different conceptions of masculinity during their military service and combat during the Second World War. Militarized masculinity is constructed against others, first and foremost against women and femininity—and seminarians were already familiar with and socialized into a homosocial environment through their seminary training—even when the concept is malleable enough to be manifested in multiple and diverse ways.[11]

There is also considerable evidence that, in the minds of these young men, their religion was inseparable from their national identities. In this remarkable but (especially given their youth) not unexpected synthesis of spiritual affiliation and national belonging, seminarians found further justification for their presence on the front lines: "Our history," declared AF, "is so intrinsically connected with Christianity, like no other land and no other culture. . . . And so there is a self-understanding and a duty to be examined in this 'yes' that we say to our German Fatherland, a holy duty besides, because this 'yes' is a genuine mission in the realm of culture as much as in the realm of that which is 'beyond nature.'"[12] There was no distinction between the territorial *Heimat*—Germany—that needed to be saved and the corresponding spiritual homeland—the Church and Christianity—whose existence was at stake. On this basis, talk of hardship, necessity, and sacrifice was not uncommon. JR lamented that comrades had to sacrifice themselves in the battle "against the world enemy of Christianity and also of our German culture."[13] JHR expressed this even more explicitly, declaring, "As a German and a Christian I have to fight, and gladly, against Bolshevism and godlessness."[14] Christian and German national identity, fused together, propelled these men more effectively than Nazi propaganda. (This kind of motivation hardly contradicted Nazi ideology, which advocated its own, eliminationist brand of German uniqueness.) This had a direct effect on seminarians' comprehensions of civilians and the way of life they encountered in the East, especially in the Soviet Union.

There is some evidence that their relatively tranquil acceptance of duty was more effortlessly maintained when they were stationed on the Western Front. Here, seminarians were no different in their reactions than other German soldiers, who criticized the decadence and immorality of the French and upheld German civilization as the mainstay of Christianity.[15] The Eastern Front, though, was another world entirely and the seminarians struggled to square what they saw and experienced with what they had been told to expect by their superiors, both spiritual and secular, back home in Germany. The Catholic German view of Russia, often expressed distinctly from Bolshevism, predated Nazism and was bound up in religious complexities (e.g., the division between the dominant Russian Orthodox Church and the suppressed Uniate Church, the latter which had historically close ties to Rome) and ethnic considerations about Slavs. From 1918, when the Bolsheviks emerged as the winners of the Russian Revolution, to 1945, Catholics in Germany generally perceived a riven Russia: the true, persecuted Russia, which was deeply (if not in an approved "Catholic" way) religious, and the concrete power and politics of the atheistic Bolsheviks. A Russian was not automatically a Bolshevik; the two terms were not interchangeable. Bolshevism was above all a threat to culture, especially religion, its lethality embodied by its commitment to the total destruction of institutionalized religion. Cultural bolshevism, the target of numerous German social and religious groups throughout the Weimar era, including the Protestant churches and women's organizations, became associated with anything under the rubric of *Schmutz und Schund*, or filth and trash (Smolinsky 1994, 326, 336).

This distinction holds in the letters of many seminarians who interacted with Russians. More than a few expressed wonder at encountering the persistence of faith among Russians, particularly the elder generation. "Here in Russia," wrote JL, "where Bolshevism wanted to exterminate all religion, one can clearly observe how little this godless movement has actually achieved: in the houses of this wretched, believing people, many religious images testify still to their strong religious convictions."[16] HÖ mentioned, "I've already found, often, holy images and images of Christ in houses, and seen religious postcards among POWs that were undoubtedly Russian representations. So religiosity among the population has not been completely eradicated."[17] Another seminarian confessed in dismay that he had not "been able to make out much about what these people think about religion and Christ. The older generation cannot be dechristianized—everywhere icons are appearing again. But the younger generation! The prisoners of war! For the first time I encountered here people truly without God. And how terrible it was!"[18]

Others were less convinced about the manifestations of belief they witnessed and they expressed bewilderment over the evident paradoxes presented by foreign civilians. Referencing cultural stereotypes about Russians that included primitiveness, savagery, and naïveté, WM stated, "The faith of this land is as enigmatic as its geography and its people.... New, childlike beliefs coexist with fanatical, passionate faith, and honest will and severe ethical principles coexist with bestial sadism."[19] Other seminarians evaluated and understood their experiences in Soviet Russia only through the lens of ethnic or racial superiority in a cultural (not evidently eugenic) sense, which the teachings of Church leaders had reinforced for years. In this way, seminarians, like German soldiers generally, were often well prepared to have their expectations confirmed upon setting foot in the East.[20] This buttressed their overall perceptions of German preeminence and the entire war effort. "I've always known," wrote WS, and quoted at the beginning of this essay, "even in the thickest shellfire, why we're fighting here, above all to protect our beloved *Heimat* from the terror that we've lived through. One must experience Russia for oneself, and must have marched 1,400 kilometers on foot through this so-called paradise to appreciate seriously how superior German civilization is and how deeply sunk this unfortunate country is, in which God has been trampled underfoot for twenty years."[21] This is no strident Nazi racism being expressed—there is no mention of subhumans but rather pity and a more broadly Western "civilizing mission," or "white man's burden" kind of ethnic antipathy.

Fighting a Just War against Bolshevism

The Soviet Union proved to be a complex entity that confirmed some stereotypes and contradicted others, but one element remained clear: Bolshevism was a force that needed to be destroyed before it could destroy faith in God, and the German army had come to do precisely that. In the minds of these seminarians, and no doubt many Christian Germans as well, other considerations were secondary. Thus, they might have reasoned, the invasion of the Soviet Union was a defensive war, and entirely just.[22]

Throughout the early twentieth century, the Catholic Church across Europe had watched the development of Bolshevism in Russia with fear and aggressive vigilance. This definitive anti-Bolshevism held common ground with the Nazis, whose ideology had made explicit the eradication of Bolshevism since the 1920s. Before the party came to power, early Nazi ideologues and Catholic proponents of the movement had pushed conceptions of Bolshevism in ways designed to garner support and solidarity in the name of German and Christian civilization (Hastings 2010, esp. 107–142). Being faithful to the German nation, to *Volk* and Fatherland, meant being prepared to fight the red menace in the East. Seminarians were not immune to such nationalistic motivations. This sociopolitical interpretation of Bolshevism offers another way to understand seminarians' motivations, with one distinction worth noting.

With a few exceptions, the seminarians' letters suggest that the rigid racial aspect of Nazism failed to penetrate the beliefs of Catholic seminarians. Equivalences of Bolshevism and Judaism are also largely absent: the seminarians generally did not fuse the two in their letters. The language they use to describe Bolshevism reveals a deep hatred, fear, and mistrust of it, but based almost entirely on its perceived dangers to religion and Christendom. Explicitly racial references are usually absent. "I have followed many comrades and confreres to the East, in order to fulfill my duty here in the battle against Bolshevism," confessed MH in 1941, as quoted earlier. "Until now Saint Michael, my patron saint, was at most an ideal for me during my inner struggles, but now he will be my role model in this external battle against the Satanism of the twentieth century."[23] FV echoed this: "I can do nothing but bristle [when I see] the cultural nadir [that is] Russia. Only in this [atmosphere] can Bolshevism thrive. The soldiers are really beasts . . . we're fighting not just against Bolshevism but also against the archenemy of Christendom. . . . With these thoughts one can endure the hardships much more easily."[24] Not unlike WS's observations, FV and MH exhibit a cultural, even ethnic, aversion to their enemies, likening them to animals and to Satan, but explicitly neither to subhumans nor to Jews. When faced with such an enemy, their national and religious identities became inseparable. JR revealed that "[here] one must battle the tendency to follow the herd; one must be ever ready to say yes to the moment. . . . This is never easy, but our Christian faith obliges us . . ."[25]

There are very few overt mentions of Jews, and only one explicit mention of "Judeo-Bolshevism," further suggesting that the racial antisemitism spewed continuously by the Nazi propaganda machine made few inroads into the mentalities of seminarians. In a rare identification of Bolshevism with Jews, LS portrayed the war as a conflict being "slugged out between two worldviews, between the civilization of the Christian world and that of the Judeo-Bolshevik will to destruction."[26] But this was not nearly as prominent in their letters as observations about cultural degeneration or poverty. There are almost no unambiguous mentions of Jews; HR is anomalous rather than representative when he described what he had witnessed regarding Jews: "The sniper war behind the front continues, in its most recent manifestation as a civil war between the Ukrainians and the Jews[!]. Close to our current quarters, Ukrainians slew some two hundred Jews, since the Jews committed egregious atrocities against the Ukrainians, who apparently refused to join the red fighting units [Bolsheviks]. The Jews had to exhume the mutilated bodies of the Ukrainians, and one witnessed a horror for which sanity cannot account. The revenge was fearsome, it became a virtual manhunt."[27] Even if Ukrainians were responsible for the atrocity alluded to in HR's mention of revenge, the seminarian could hardly have been ignorant of a significant instigating factor: the presence of the German Wehrmacht and the SS-*Einsatzgruppen* death squads, who in early July 1941 had barely begun their murderous work. But HR stands out from the group. If the seminarians' letters alone are used to depict the war experience, their battlefront world was essentially bereft of Jews and Jewish influence.[28]

Does the absence of racism indicate a certain immunity to Nazism? Does the fusion of nationalism and religious faith prove that Nazism was not a motivating factor? The answer to both of these questions must be no, because the dearth of evidence proves only that there is no evidence. However, the preceding statements do demonstrate the enduring importance of religious and spiritual influences, acting at least as a supplement to, and at most as a substitute for, Nazi antisemitism and racism.

There is also a clear sense that the war in which Germany and the Soviet Union were engaged was an *Endkampf* in the literal meaning of the term: a final, decisive battle in which the very existence of German—and Christian—civilization was at stake. It was for this reason that Nazism, if these men understood Nazism as an opponent of any kind, was a lesser evil. This would not have been mentioned in the letters anyway; criticism of the regime in a soldier's letter was dealt with swiftly and brutally.[29] Bolshevism took on the qualities of an impersonal, supernatural, monstrous evil that the seminarians did not always equate with the armies they were fighting, at least not on paper. It was instead a nebulous, intangible presence, not unlike the objects of worship in their own faith, including God and grace. Such an enemy could only be defeated with similar weapons—transcendent, unyielding belief in God and Christ. That the war was an all-or-nothing endeavor is encapsulated by JF's simple proclamation: "Bolshevism must be annihilated. Otherwise, all that we hold dear and holy is done for."[30]

One particularly striking letter using this language to describe an almost apocalyptic setting was concerned with the dire moral consequences of a war of extermination. The seminarian who wrote it was stationed in Łódź in 1943. This was the site of the second-largest Jewish ghetto in Nazi-occupied Europe, and though he did not mention Jews explicitly, one might read between the lines and surmise that, at the very least, he had witnessed something deeply unsettling. It is worth quoting at length:

> Indeed, we have a true war of extermination now, with the words "hate—revenge—blood—extermination." This is the end of human wisdom; it's a fiasco that cries to heaven. The end of this war cannot be foreseen; in any case its consequences are catastrophic in every way for victor and vanquished alike, above all morally. Only on the basis of religion can this sunken humanity be repositioned gradually as an ethical civilization. . . . The spirit of the era and years of propaganda have subverted and undermined Christianity. Such an operation's success is greater than one might think, particularly among the younger generation. . . . There is much pastoral care to be done, actually I would say missionary work, but the workers are few, and will be even fewer because of the war, the death of heroes at the front and the lack of recruits to follow them. . . . We are living in a colossal dispute that is religious and ideological, that will get duked out along with the political, military, and economy battle. May God give us the enthusiastic, worthy champion-priests who will recognize and understand the suffering of the world and so heal it.[31]

JR's sentences are ambivalent enough that it is difficult to comprehend with any certainty who he held responsible for the moral dissolution he witnessed. But he was addressing more than the Poles and Russians he must have encountered, and he was by no means defending the Germans with whom he was fighting. No one was unblemished in his perspective. He was also writing toward the end of 1943, more than two years after the beginning of the war in the Soviet Union and well after the Wehrmacht had suffered significant military losses, especially at Stalingrad and Kursk. Disillusionment had set in.

It was in the context of Bolshevism that seminarians frequently identified the war in the East between Germany and the Soviet Union as a crusade, sometimes explicitly. They were encouraged to by their spiritual superior in the military, Reich Catholic Field Bishop Franz Justus Rarkowski, whose pastoral letters referred to the war against Soviet Russia as "a European crusade."[32] The words the seminarians chose to describe it reveals the extent to which anti-Bolshevik propaganda had permeated them: "Hopefully this bloody battle will soon find a good end, and with it, Bolshevism will be extirpated once and for all. Otherwise, the many victims of this crusade against the world enemy would have died in vain."[33] To them as well as to the soldiers with whom they marched, the material conditions they encountered as they made their way into Russian territory proved that Bolshevism was the most destructive force in existence, because "the impoverishment, the depletion, the decrepitude is terrible . . . every village has a church [in Polish territory], but here [in Russia], such cannot be found anywhere, for even in our own quarters, it exists only as a ruin."[34]

It is on the basis of this shared perception of Bolshevism as a deadly enemy, articulated ad nauseam for years if not decades prior to the war by both Church and secular leaders, that Catholic seminarians were most deeply complicit with the Nazi regime's war aims. Certainly they were familiar with the racial antisemitism of Nazism via the Hitler Youth, of which all boys in Germany were required to be members after 1936. This is why any apparent immunity to Nazi ideology failed to be significant: there was another ideology at play, and plenty of personal motivation to fight a defensive war on behalf of one's culture, one's family, one's way of life.

Complicity, Compliance, or Resistance?

More than six years prior to the war's outbreak, in July 1933, Nazi Germany and the Vatican finalized a treaty intended to normalize relations between them, and to extend a measure of protection to Germany's Catholics. Few individuals were aware of the "secret appendix" to the Reich concordat, an appendix that concerned itself with the possibility of a general mobilization and, in four concise bullets, detailed the guidelines by which priests and other clergy would be affected should war break out.[35] Consequently, approximately seventeen thousand Catholic priests and seminarians at various levels of ordination served in the German military between 1939 and 1945.[36] Could the men have said no to the conscription order? Given that the core of Nazi ideology consisted of the belief in the racial superiority of Germans, and the necessity of propagating the German race through the acquisition of territory, one of the regime's priorities from its inception was the build-up and maintenance of a strong military, which in turn demanded the availability and militarization of all battle-able men. Men (and boys) of the cloth, *as men*, were no exception. Conscientious objection was an unequivocal threat to this, and was treated with no leniency, as those who opposed the conscription order found out. Of the approximately half-dozen conscientious objectors who were Catholic clergy, all but one were executed for their refusal to serve, documenting the lethal coercion that was doubtless a factor in determining a priest's or seminarian's response to the conscription order.[37]

However, their lack of refusal does not automatically equate with enthusiastic support; many indicate the contrary, that they felt little or no loyalty to the Nazi regime. Nor should we read this silence vis-à-vis the party and its leaders as resistance, because there were no explicit rejections of Nazism. Nor can the coercive element of the regime and its insistence on military service satisfactorily explain it, or the timidity of the seminarians in the face of martyrdom, though doubtless for some these were factors. Fear of execution does not account for why seminarians would respond positively to the call to serve an openly anti-Christian regime. Coercion fails to address the fact that most of these men found confirmation of their spiritual values and their vocation itself during their time in Wehrmacht uniform. Most seminarians greeted their service, if not with enthusiasm, then with a voluntary willingness and submission, an attitude reinforced by their faith.

This acceptance of their duty to render military service may have been determined by conceptions of national obligation, but also by their gender. Though I found no examinations of gender and its role in any seminarian's letters, given the broader social and political context, they likely understood military training as a man's work, and not incompatible for a priest-in-training. To shirk this duty would have indicated their own lack of manliness not only in the eyes of German society but also in their own self-understanding: they ran the risk of others seeing them as weak, feminine, even servile and immoral (Mosse 1996, 6). Their membership in the militant Hitler Youth had prepared them for such service; the seminary's rigidity and regulations would have supplied further grounding for military life. Their aspiration to the priesthood, a vocation exclusive to men who were called to be defenders of Christ and the Church, may well have made it easier for them to accept a (temporary) position as a soldier, which they could have interpreted as merely a different kind of warrior.

Did their decision to serve in the Wehrmacht on their own terms constitute a form of indirect resistance to Nazism, an attempt to remake the Nazi-directed war effort into a more religiously inspired "crusade" to defeat an existential enemy? Did their own reasons for serving indicate a special immunity to Nazi ideology? In considering these questions, we must acknowledge that the seminarians belonged to two spheres whose resistance activities have been catalogued elsewhere and at length: the military and the Catholic Church. Because the contours of these spheres, and the possibilities and limitations of resistance within each, informed their choices and behavior, they are worth outlining here very briefly.

Within the military, the resistance of officers who participated in the July 1944 plot to kill Hitler has long been the core of resistance literature.[38] Conscientious objectors have also received attention as resisters, thanks to the 1938 Special Wartime Penal Code (*Kriegssonderstrafrechtsverordnung*) that criminalized any form of dissent or opposition to military leadership. This included conscientious objection under the broader, deliberately ambiguous term *Zersetzung der Wehrkraft*, or the undermining of military force (Paul 1994; Ausländer, Haase, and Paul, 1995). Resistance to Nazism in the military, however, remains a complicated topic. As Peter Hoffmann points out, the hold of a soldier's oath of loyalty is not immaterial; on the contrary, solidarity with one's comrades in the face of an enemy made it difficult for individuals to decide on their own what the limits of their loyalty were, or to refuse obedience to criminal orders. Subverting military leadership not only put them in breach of military conduct, which was punishable by death, but also would have isolated them from their comrades (Hoffmann 1988, 74). For this reason, tracing out soldiers' resistance activities is complicated, not only because they were in an active war environment that posed serious obstacles for resistance, but also because the evidence is scarcer.

The history of the resistance of the churches, both Catholic and Protestant, has proliferated since the 1960s and is equally voluminous and controversial. Resistance figures such as the Protestant pastor Dietrich Bonhoeffer and the Catholic Jesuit Alfred Delp stand out as a stark minority, as the German spiritual and lay leaders of both denominations ultimately, and for various reasons, chose not to protest the regime publicly (Lewy 1965; Conway 1968; Denzler 1984; Scholder 1988). But historians disagree about the definition and nature of resistance and point to discrepancies between how actions were interpreted at the time and how they are understood today. As Donald Dietrich has argued, "What is perceived by [some scholars] as capitulation or, at the very least, lack of resistance was viewed by Nazi leaders as posing a very serious threat" (Dietrich 1988, 182). This absence of open resistance lies at the heart of the controversies about the concept of Catholic resistance as a form of "institutional protectionism," directed toward the survival of the Catholic Church as institution.[39]

Those who resisted the regime because they could not bring themselves to agree with its policies often met with death. They have been praised in postwar historiography as heroes and martyrs. But they were a small fellowship. Resistance in both the military and the churches was a minority affair; the majority of Germans declined to protest or resist, and instead either actively supported the regime or found ways to compromise. Of the seminarians conscripted out of the Munich and Freising archdiocese, none refused to serve, and there is no evidence that any had ties to resistance circles in either the military or the Church at home.

Martin Broszat developed his controversial term *Resistenz* in the late 1970s to describe how individuals and institutions evaded the regime's claims on total power.[40] He defined it as "all forms of refusal, of individual or collective protest, of dissidence or non-conformity that were directed against certain coercive ideological, disciplinary, or organizational measures and impositions of the NS regime" (Broszat 1983, 300, also 1987). The emphasis is placed squarely on deeds, not what the actors intended by them. It is the story of behavior, not of ideology, mentality, or motivation. He makes a further qualification to distinguish his term from the more ubiquitous "resistance":

> This *Resistenz* differentiates itself from political resistance carried on by those who fundamentally opposed the regime in that proponents of *Resistenz* were not essentially against Nazism, or in any case did not evince such fundamental enmity. They comprised only partial opposition, were in no way always politically motivated, and acted prevalently to ensure individual and social interests and the maintenance of autonomy in religious, spiritual, cultural, economic, or other occupational [*berufliche*] or private areas of life. (Broszat 1983, 300)

The Catholic Church is one of his preferred examples. Its leaders in Germany never challenged the authority of the Nazi Party or Hitler's government. The Church "was able to retain a relative immunity and self-determination" to Nazism that insulated it from becoming completely dominated by and subservient to the regime (Broszat 1983, 300).

The term *Resistenz* had its critics and is not often used today except in historiographical reviews of literature on resistance and complicity. There are many reasons for this. One of the primary reasons why it did not acquire wider usage is its untranslatability: there is no English equivalent beyond "immunity." There is also a problem with the elasticity of the term, which embraces everything from silent acceptance to apathy. Closely connected to this is the difficulty in divorcing the moral implications of an action from its effect. There is no easy separation of an action from the intention behind it, because it matters whether an individual was acting purely spontaneously or in a burst of emotion, or whether the action was premeditated and deliberate. To use Broszat's own example against him, when Church leaders objected in written letters to the wartime deportation of "Aryan Christians"—that is, Catholics who had converted from Judaism—they did so because in the eyes of the Church, they were Catholic, not Jewish. They did not raise similar protests over the deportation of "Aryan non-Christians," that is, Jews.

Still, the term is valuable. The Bavaria Project, an intellectual collaboration of German scholars that Broszat pioneered in the late 1970s that produced a six-volume series highlighting the concept of *Resistenz*, established that viewing resistance behavior and its close corollaries—dissent, opposition, refusal—as a gray spectrum rather than a black-and-white binary is useful. Those who stood openly against Nazism, such as Georg Elser and the Scholl siblings, Dietrich Bonhoeffer, Bernhard Lichtenberg, and Claus von Stauffenberg, were simply not characteristic of German society; they were incongruous. Far more likely behavior is exemplified by those who attended Nazi parades in March 1933 and yet shopped in Jewish stores on April 1 of that year, ignoring the boycott, or those who wholeheartedly supported the "defensive war" against Soviet Russia in 1941–1942 but snuck home to listen to forbidden BBC radio broadcasts. These actions do not constitute resistance, nor do they toe the Nazi line. They may not be solid examples of ideological immunity, or *Resistenz*, but they demonstrate that Nazi ideology had its limits. This is an essential component in the reality of the Third Reich: this was a one-party dictatorship that attempted to establish total control over German society and that came up against very real limits. The ability of individuals to remain aloof from Nazism's totalizing program renders the idea of the truly totalitarian state a myth.

On the other hand, as Ian Kershaw points out, Broszat's *Resistenz* exposed the social context in which opposition to the regime formed new angles and avenues of inquisition. In highlighting the possibility of resistance, one is also confronted with both its absence as well as its opposite, "the wide areas of underlying social consensus in major aspects of Nazi rule" (Kershaw 2000, 203). If a key element of *Resistenz* is immunity to certain Nazi goals, this nevertheless is not tantamount to a total rejection of Nazism or outright opposition. The fact remains that these individuals also complied, maybe even most of the time, with the regime. In other words, why did people choose not to conform to certain regulations and prohibitions that Nazi Party leaders set forth and cooperate with others?

Despite a growing accumulation of studies about the complicity of German society with the Nazi regime, there remain several unanswered questions, especially if resistance and complicity are considered together (Kershaw 1983; Peukert 1987; Barnett 1999; Gellately 2001; Ericksen 2012). Often these two kinds of behavior occurred in the same individual or social groups, suggesting that change over time and in context is significant for understanding an altered stance vis-à-vis the regime. It also becomes more challenging to divorce motivation from the equation. How else to explain the ways in which one slides from supporter of Nazism to indifference to outright resistance? Moreover, how can we explain the side-by-side appearance of complicity and resistance looking no further than the example of the Catholic Church, whose leaders refused to accept Nazism's sterilization policies or its racist language but looked on passively as discrimination against Jews became persecution and deportation? In some cases, conventional explanations such as material or political self-interest, moral cowardice, or latent (and not so latent) antisemitism suffice. In other cases, they are less persuasive.

Comradeship and Brotherhood

There is no easy answer for all the men in the German military. From the outset, the fundamental distinction between home front and battlefront must be acknowledged: German soldiers did not have access to the same spectrum of behavioral choices that civilians did, nor did they have the same freedoms. Their daily routine was no longer their own. Thomas Kühne provides one of the most unflinching descriptions of life in the Wehrmacht, relating that the daily life of a soldier was "governed by formal and informal hierarchies, material and psychic deprivation, loneliness, isolation, egoism, indignity, intrigue and brutality, by direct, structural, and cultural violence" (1999, 540–541). Undoubtedly, these conditions had an effect on seminarians in the ranks. Moreover, this was the Wehrmacht, one of the pillars of the regime. Even if soldiers refused to embrace Nazi propaganda about the reasons for the war or the subhuman races they were fighting, that worldview had permeated the ranks from the officer corps down, and they had been subjected to it for years before the war's outbreak. Nor was Nazi racial ideology the only impetus driving soldiers to view the war as necessary, even defensive: prewar German conceptions of the East, of Russians and Bolsheviks (not to mention Jews), even of cleanliness and filth worked just as well (see, e.g., Latzel 1999, 573–588; Volkmann 1994; Thum 2006; Koenen 2005).

Kühne's recent work on Wehrmacht cohesion and togetherness and what he calls "the myth of comradeship" addresses most directly the relationship between soldiers' diverse motivations for going to war and issues of complicity and resistance. He speaks of "a huge brotherhood of crime and bad conscience" of which soldiers became part during the war, a brotherhood defined by the military system of rule, the material and physical deprivation of the front, and the widespread emotional depravity soldiers suffered there (Kühne 1999, 538–540, also 2010, 97). Brotherhood is no incidental term, either, although Kühne does not explore the gendered aspect of it—inclusion in this group was predicated on one's manliness, and one's ability to prove it to one's comrades (in this context, through participation in war and atrocity). The seminarians would not have been exceptions to this.[41] The myth of comradeship is one of the most helpful conceptual tools in understanding German soldiers, including Catholic seminarians, and the environment in which they operated. Additionally, many ultimately found the experience career- and vocation-affirming, and even explicitly observed the similarities between the two: "Service and comradeship, these are now the two north stars, the new concepts of my life . . . [the priestly life and the military life share the same goal,] to be a comrade, to live for and help others. . . . In this way the present is the best preparation for my vocation, if God wills it. This is how I see this life."[42]

To some extent, these seminarians were like many other able-bodied German soldiers after 1939: they had not volunteered for service, they had had no intentions of a military career, but they were conscripted into the military. They were young and had been inundated with Nazi propaganda throughout their childhood; they had spent time in the Hitler Youth. Some manifested a genuine German nationalism in the traditional, pre-Nazi sense: an attachment to the Fatherland and a desire to defend their family, faith, and nation from a perceived mortal enemy, Bolshevism. Over the course of the war, they found ways to justify their service and the lethal activities in which they were engaged, whether through a conviction such as AB's, that the world needed priests, or, as with AF and JHR, through the fusion of Germany and Christianity. It is also possible that some seminarians found the hierarchical organization and routinization of military life reminiscent of the seminary. Though the latter world was marked by quiet meditation and prayer, rather than the drills and physical exertions of the former, both were characterized by discipline, regimentation, competition, and a conscious striving for development and survival in the face of self-denial and hardship. Both were also, literally, a man's world. While the comparison on this point can only be taken so far—one's physical survival was at stake incessantly on the frontlines, whereas one had the option of withdrawing from the seminary if mental or spiritual well-being was in question—it is worth noting.

There was one fundamental distinction that made them different than other German soldiers: their plan to become priests, at once a career and a vocation. These were young men who enrolled in a seminary in pursuit of a life of faith and service to others. The war was an indefinite interruption of that training. While all conscripted Germans could claim the war was an interruption, the seminarians had an external motivation for remembering their prewar vocations, a particular way of justifying the war, and a support system that reinforced that justification: their correspondence with their seminary director, Johann Westermayr.

Catholic German seminarians may have worn a soldier's uniform and fought alongside other German soldiers, experiencing the same deprivations and challenges as their comrades. They faced trials that even their spiritual brothers, particularly those more advanced in the process of ordination, normally did not face.[43] And as other soldiers turned to the tenets of Nazi ideology in the midst of a brutal and brutalizing war, so did many of these seminarians cling to their Catholic faith. This served to set them apart. They had recourse to different strategies for dealing with and making sense of their experiences. While they reacted to circumstances in ways similar to their secular counterparts, they had also been molded by the seminary classroom and clerical teachers, and they made sense of the battles they fought, and the larger war environment, through the lens of their faith. Theirs was an explicitly religious mission. After attending a mass that was also attended by Russian civilians in early August 1941, AA wrote, "We contribute in a small way to bringing back the faith to this godless country, and in a certain sense we are trailblazers for the Lord, so that He can return . . ."[44] Less than a month later, his fellow seminarian SE prayed fervently, "So may I be a warrior in the first line in this war against Bolshevism, and may our deeds be capped off with the proclamation of the Christian Gospel to these poor people."[45]

The Church enjoyed a relative autonomy in Nazi Germany that few other institutions were permitted. But does the fact that many seminarians found affirmation of their vocation in time of war, or used their faith as a bulwark of support, lend credence to the theory that the Catholic faith inoculated them against Nazi ideology? How can we explain the willingness of these young seminarians to serve a regime for which they professed to have no liking? There has been no systematic study of Catholic seminarians in the Wehrmacht, how many might have served over the course of the war, how many abandoned their vocation during or after the war, or how many went on to be ordained.[46] A rigorous investigation of this would provide a much-needed "history from below" to complement what we know of the Catholic Church's leadership echelons, both ecclesiastical and lay.

Outlook

It is difficult to gauge with any accuracy how representative these seminarians were. An estimated seventeen million men served in the Wehrmacht between 1939 and 1945; the several hundred that anchor this study are admittedly a mere drop in a much larger ocean.[47] But it is not their representativeness that makes them worth studying; it is their very presence in the military that intrigues. The seminarians' justifications for serving tend to center on a Christian-based aversion to Bolshevism, which hardly constitutes a form of resistance (*Widerstand*) or even immunity (*Resistenz*) to Nazism. In fact, this crucial intersection of Nazi and Christian interests invited many Germans, not just Catholic seminarians in the military, to conform to the regime's goals. There are other ways to explain why the language in seminarians' wartime letters, subject as it was to rigorous censorship, contains no hint of animosity toward the regime and its racist, antisemitic goals. Men were wearing military uniforms and fighting in an arena that left no room for dissent. Other scholars have outlined the positively murderous policies employed by the German military during the war to enforce discipline (Bartov 1992; Messerschmidt and Wette 1996). They were no longer in their seminary classrooms. They had entered a world governed by different rules entirely. For soldiers, Catholic or no, it was impossible to engage in resistance of the kind displayed by Münster bishop Clemens von Galen in his 1941 sermons, or by Bishop Konrad von Preysing in his regular missives to Pope Pius XII bemoaning Nazi anti-Jewish policies.[48]

There were reasons to go to war. All able-bodied German men were conscripted; seminarians were able men and likely conscious of this even if their letters do not mention it. As well, in their own words, the war as they lived it affirmed for the majority their decision to become priests. More significantly, it reinforced for many their conviction that Bolshevism was a deadly enemy, threatening the existence of Germany as well as Christendom. Their service was not merely negatively motivated by a fear of the consequences of saying no to conscription, but positively provoked by the certainty that their participation in a battle to defend their home and their faith was necessary. In this sense they participated in the war by redefining "militarized masculinity" in such a way that it reconciled, at least to a large extent, their vocational conviction with military conscription. In forming their anti-Bolshevik opinion, they were just as much (if not more so) influenced by their Catholic spiritual advisers, their seminary teachers and directors, than by the regime's anti-Bolshevik propaganda. It is difficult to argue which influence was more discernable, as no seminarian was explicit in his letters, but both ideologies, the Catholic and the Nazi, must be considered.

The war, particularly on the Eastern Front, had a tremendous impact on how seminarians viewed their vocation, their conceptions of masculinity and brotherhood, their responsibilities as soldiers and as spiritual guides, and the role of religion in their lives. Most found ways to salvage something positive from it: noble self-sacrifice, a strengthening of vocational conviction, the satisfaction of having been called to an arduous task that they saw through to the bitter, often fatal end. Countless other men, both believing and nonbelieving, surely followed the same path, categorizing military service between 1939 and 1945 as a defense not necessarily of Nazism but of *Heimat*. This left little space for comprehending, or even acknowledging, the darker, more troubling aspects of Germany's war in the East. The genocidal impulses of the Wehrmacht and its collaboration with the *Einsatzgruppen*, the treatment of Jews, civilians, and POWs, are literally absent from this written record. This silence is deeply troubling but not surprising, for the letters of these seminarians suggest a Manichaean understanding of the world in which they lived. The war was a crusade in which Christians were called to defend their way of life; in this life-and-death face-off, exterminating Bolshevism, and thereby saving Germany and Catholicism, was the only priority. If they witnessed firsthand or participated in atrocities—I found no evidence of this in their letters—this may have been how the seminarians justified them.

Whether or not they endorsed Nazism, these men were complicit. Kühne's observation about another soldier who did not fully embrace Nazi ideology is apposite: "By wearing a German uniform and following orders, he [and the seminarians] supported not only the institutional and social basis of this war, but also confirmed its moral framework" (Kühne 2010, 127). Some of them used Nazi language to articulate rationalisms about the war, though not often to express overtly racist or antisemitic sentiments. Yet there is a striking resonance between Nazi and Catholic articulations, particularly about the meaning of suffering and redemption. The entire enterprise of collaboration between the Nazi regime and the Catholic Church in Germany, from the latter's perspective, was premised on the implacable opposition that both parties bore for Bolshevism. As shown earlier in this chapter, there is occasional, considerable overlap.

But to come close to the seminarians and their reasons for going to war, this complicity must be articulated in terms of how they understood their role: it by no means indicates an active, all-consuming conviction in favor of Nazism. A German did not have to be a Nazi to fight in the Wehrmacht or to desire the destruction of Soviet Russia. In fact, one could even dislike Hitler's regime, its leaders, and certain elements of its ideology, and still justify one's service at the front. These were men whose beliefs vacillated, whose ideas changed over time, who may have voluntarily cooperated in furthering certain goals of the regime while being totally against other central tenets of its ideology. This demonstrates a limit within the Wehrmacht to Nazi ideology, at least in terms of why Germans chose to fight.

This is not an apology for what they did. It does not elide the consequences of their wartime participation or absolve them of their responsibility: their presence, along with the millions of other German soldiers, made possible the perpetration of genocide. Rather, I have tried to understand why these seminarians behaved as they did, and why they chose to become complicit. Their examples, grappling with their service in Hitler's army, show that they were mostly immune to the insidious racial aspects of Nazi ideology, but that same immunity enabled them, even invited them, to interpret the goals of the war as a defense of Catholicism. The consequences of this religious and nationalist motivation are the same as those who were convicted Nazis: they participated in an undertaking that seemed justifiable at the time and, only after military defeat, was understood in its full criminal, genocidal reality. They were there on their terms, trying to take some benefit from a situation that was not of their choosing. They retained enough freedom to articulate for themselves what their purpose in the war was, a purpose resonant with and bolstered by their Catholic faith and vocation, even in the rigidly controlled world of Hitler's army.

Acknowledgments

I wish to thank Sebastian Rosato, John Deak, and Denise Della Rossa for encouragement on an early version of this chapter, and Björn Krondorfer, who played a seminal role in supporting it to its finish.

Notes

1. Erzbischöflichesarchiv München und Freising, Bestand Priesterseminar Freising (henceforth EAM Priesterseminar), seminarian WS, August 23, 1941.

2. EAM Priesterseminar, seminarian MH, September 30, 1941.

3. For more about the turmoil and challenges facing Catholic Germans in the nineteenth century, which included the menaces of secularization, modernization, and the Bismarck-directed *Kulturkampf*, see Anderson (1988, 350–378), Gross (2004), Walser-Smith (1994), and Ross (1998).

4. This included the completion of theological studies and practical liturgical studies. On the process of becoming a priest in Germany at this time, see Seibel (1994, esp. 13–37).

5. This number includes both seminary students and theology students, the latter who were not yet formally part of the seminary. Using my primary source material as a model, I will refer to both groups together as seminarians unless otherwise noted.

6. EAM Priesterseminar, "Kartei," including lists of the fallen (*Gefallene*) and withdrawals (*Austritt*).

7. EAM Priesterseminar, seminarian AB, November 16, 1944.
8. EAM Priesterseminar, seminarian JH, September 17, 1942.
9. EAM Priesterseminar, seminarian AN, October 26, 1941.
10. EAM Priesterseminar, seminarian TW, July 12, 1942.
11. Militarized masculinity tends to reinforce gender inequality but also manifests in multiple and diverse ways; it should more accurately be referred to in the plural as "militarized masculinities"; see Eichler (2014).
12. EAM Priesterseminar, seminarian AF, August 21, 1943.
13. EAM Priesterseminar, seminarian JR, March 31, 1942.
14. EAM Priesterseminar, seminarian JHR, August 27, 1944.
15. See, for example, seminarian HR's comments on France: "I know that nowhere in the world are cathedrals and brothels standing so close together, that nowhere else are the gaps between classes so dire, that the most Christian country of all, France, has no grounds upon which to designate itself as the preserver of Christian culture. If somebody has to defend Christian culture, well, we're already doing that. German soldiers speak less about Christianity, but display more of it. We found smutty literature in the knapsacks of French soldiers, which really puts them in a bad light. Marshal Pétain himself appears to understand the roots of the French downfall: *Peu d'enfants* [Few children]!" EAM Priesterseminar, September 8, 1940.
16. EAM Priesterseminar, seminarian JL, August 9, 1941.
17. EAM Priesterseminar, seminarian HÖ, August 11, 1941.
18. EAM Priesterseminar, seminarian GW, September 23, 1941. Of course, the Wehrmacht kept Russian POWs in conditions designed to kill them—that they did not manifest religious inclinations for their captors while they were starving to death is perhaps not surprising.
19. EAM Priesterseminar, seminarian WM, July 2, 1944.
20. This is the argument made by Bartov (1992, esp. chap. 4).
21. EAM Priesterseminar, seminarian WS, August 23, 1941.
22. Förster underscores this: "The majority of commanders [on the Eastern Front] either believed or allowed themselves to be convinced that the war of destruction against the Soviet Union required such harshness [i.e., atrocities such as the shooting of civilians, including all Jews]. Even opponents of National Socialism, such as Erich Hoepner and Carl-Heinrich von Stüplnagel, were able to combine this attitude with a militant anticommunism" (see 1998, 279).
23. EAM Priesterseminar, seminarian MH, September 30, 1941.
24. EAM Priesterseminar, seminarian FV, December 27, 1941.
25. EAM Priesterseminar, seminarian JR, March 31, 1942.
26. EAM Priesterseminar, seminarian LS, February 7, 1942.
27. EAM Priesterseminar, seminarian HR, July 5, 1941. This is rare evidence of the success of typical Nazi antisemitic propaganda, of the kind pedaled by *Der Stürmer*, which emphasized global Jewish conspiracies and the innate Jewish

tendency to plunge nations into civil war and chaos. This is the only reference I found among all the letters I read.

28. Another unpublished study of these letters offers the same observation; see Kislinger (2006-2007). This contrasts with studies of other letters from the front, in which racism and antisemitism are cited relatively frequently; see Buchbender and Sterz (1983, esp. 68-106). One might argue that the term "Bolshevism" would have been understood by any German soldier using it as an inherently racist term interchangeable with Judaism by 1941, but this is not clear to me with the seminarians, whose letters generally do not include racist language or connotations.

29. Seminarian Franz Wipplinger was hung on August 31, 1944, because of remarks made in his diary that were critical of Hitler and the regime; see Kislinger (2006-2007, 31).

30. EAM Priesterseminar, seminarian JF, April 15, 1944.

31. EAM Priesterseminar, seminarian JR, November 4, 1943.

32. See Rarkowski, "Pastoral Letter to the Catholic Soldiers in the Wehrmacht Regarding the Great Decisive Battle in the East," July 29, 1941, as reprinted in Missalla (1997, 56-59). The pertinent sentence reads, "Many European states that have existed until now under the threatening shadows of the Bolshevik danger, and that have had many of the most bitter experiences with the destructive effects of Bolshevik teaching within their state structures, know that the war against Russia is a European crusade."

33. EAM Priesterseminar, seminarian GG, July 28, 1941.

34. EAM Priesterseminar, seminarian JM, July 23, 1941. These findings are echoed in Heribert Smolinsky's research. Of the letters written by Catholic soldiers, mostly theology students, to Konrad Gröber, archbishop of Freiburg, Smolinsky found no mention of "Judenherrschaft," but rather a focus on Russia as a land of official godlessness, along with a fear of dechristianization taking place on the home front [*zuhause*] (Smolinsky 1994, 354-355).

35. The full text of the *Reichskonkordat*, including the secret appendix, is available in Volk (1972, 234-244).

36. For more information about the appendix's impact on the priests and seminarians who were conscripted, see Faulkner Rossi (2015).

37. Gordon C. Zahn conducted a study more than forty years ago that found only seven Catholics in the Greater German Reich who could be considered conscientious objectors—these were Franz Reinisch; Josef Fleischer; Franz Jägerstätter, an Austrian peasant beatified by Pope Benedict XVI in June 2007; Josef Mayr-Nusser, the Catholic Action leader of Austria; and three men associated with the religious community Christkönigsgesellschaft: Max Josef Metzger, Brother Maurus, and Brother Michael; see Zahn (1962, 55). Heinrich Missalla contradicts some of these names, pointing to unresolved discrepancies in more recent German-language historiography. Other names that he cites from Albrecht and Heidi Hartmann, Thomas Breuer, and Jakob Knab concerning Catholic

conscientious objectors include Michael Lerpscher, Josef Ruf, Ernst Volkmann, and Richard Reitsamer. On one thing they all seem to agree: Josef Fleischer, from Freiburg, was the only survivor (Missalla 1999, 228n41).

38. The work of Peter Hoffmann (1996) remains the cornerstone in this field as well as his compilation of documents (2011). See also Ian Kershaw's overview of the historiography of resistance (2000) and Geyer and Boyer (1994).

39. Scholars who make this argument include Spicer (2004) and Breuer (1992).

40. Broszat, along with Hans Mommsen, Ian Kershaw, and other historians, was not convinced of the accuracy of the totalitarian model in describing Nazi Germany. One of the consequences of their work—and *Resistenz* is an integral part of this—was a move in the field away from the use of the term "totalitarian" in relation to Hitler and Nazi rule, a move that became more popular in the 1980s in connection with trends in other social-scientific fields as well as contemporary events, not the least of which was the ascendancy of Gorbachev and the fall of the Berlin Wall.

41. Ramon Hinojosa's concept of masculinities within the military is relevant here, as he subdivides the category of "masculinity" into several kinds, including hegemonic (dominant), subordinated (oppressed), marginalized (neither dominant nor oppressed, but somewhere in between), and others. Given the lack of explicit statements about gender and masculinity and how they perceived others' views of them, the seminarians are difficult to conceptualize beyond the arena of speculation, but their vocation, which entailed a lifelong commitment to celibacy, may have made it difficult for other soldiers to accept them as true, manly equals (Hinojosa 2010, 180–181).

42. EAM Priesterseminar, seminarian AH, November 16, 1939.

43. Armed Forces High Command (*Oberkommando der Wehrmacht*) decree, October 14, 1939, as cited in Brandt and Katholisches Militärbischofsamt (1994, 18–19). This stands in contrast to various regulations put in place, in accordance with stipulations laid down in the secret appendix of the concordat, to ensure that fully ordained priests, deacons, and subdeacons were not placed in weapons-bearing positions.

44. EAM Priesterseminar, seminarian AA, August 8, 1941.

45. EAM Priesterseminar, seminarian SE, September 1, 1941.

46. The most thorough diocese-centered study is Schwaiger (1984). A comparable study, focused more narrowly on one of Würzburg's clerical seminaries, is also useful (Hillenbrand and Weigand, 1989). See also Kershaw (1983) and Hummel and Kißener (2009).

47. Müller-Hildebrand, *Das Heer 1933–1945* (1969) as cited in Kühne (2010, 97).

48. The two bishops, because of their connections, survived the war, though the Nazi leadership was particularly irked by Galen's sermons and considered him

persona non grata from 1941 on. Documentation indicates that he would have been arrested and executed had the war ended in victory for Germany. A third example, Bernhard Lichtenberg, provost of Berlin's Catholic cathedral, dared to pray publicly for the Jews after *Kristallnacht* in 1938 and was not so lucky. He was arrested in 1941 for misuse of the pulpit and slandering the party (under the *Heimtückegesetz*); he died in Dachau in 1943. Pope John Paul II beatified him in 1996.

References

Anderson, Margaret L. 1988. "Interdenominationalism, Clericalism, Pluralism: The Zentrumsstreit and the Dilemma of Catholicism in Wilhemine Germany." *Central European History* 21, no. 4: 350–378.

Ausländer, Fietje, Norbert Haase, and Gerhard Paul. 1995. *Die anderen Soldaten: Wehrkraftzersetzung, Gehorsamsverweigerung und Fahnenflucht im Zweiten Weltkrieg*. Frankfurt a. M.: Fischer.

Barnett, Victoria J. 1999. *Bystanders: Conscience and Complicity during the Holocaust*. Westport: Praeger.

Bartov, Omer. 1992. *Hitler's Army: Soldiers, Nazis, and War in the Third Reich*. New York: Oxford University Press.

Brandt, Hans Jürgen, and Katholisches Militärbischofsamt, eds. 1994. *Priester in Uniform: Seelsorger, Ordensleute und Theologen als Soldaten im Zweiten Weltkrieg*. Augsburg: Pattloch Verlag.

Breuer, Thomas. 1992. *Verordneter Wandel? Der Widerstreit zwischen nationalsozialistischem Herrschaftsanspruch und traditionaler Lebenswelt im Erzbistum Bamberg*. Mainz: Matthias-Grünewald.

Broszat, Martin. 1983. "Zur Sozialgeschichte des deutschen Widerstands." *Vierteljahreshefte für Zeitgeschichte* 31, no. 1 (January): 293–309.

———. 1987. "Resistenz und Widerstand: Eine Zwischenbalanz des Forschungsprojekts 'Widerstand und Verfolgung in Bayern 1933–1945.'" In *Nach Hitler: Der schwierige Umgang mit unserer Geschichte*, Martin Broszat, 68–91. Munich: R. Oldenbourg Verlag.

Buchbender, Ortwin, and Reinhold Sterz, eds. 1983. *Das andere Gesicht des Krieges: Deutsche Feldpostbriefe 1939–1945*. Munich: C. H. Beck.

Conway, John. 1968. *The Nazi Persecution of the Churches, 1933–45*. New York: Basic Books.

Denzler, Georg. 1984. *Widerstand oder Anpassung? Katholische Kirche und Drittes Reich*. Munich: Piper.

Dietrich, Donald J. 1988. "Catholic Resistance in the Third Reich." *Holocaust and Genocide Studies* 3, no. 2: 171–186.

Eichler, Maya. 2014. "Militarized Masculinities in International Relations." *The Brown Journal of World Affairs* 21, no. 1 (Fall/Winter): 81–93.

Ericksen, Robert P. 2012. *Complicity in the Holocaust: Churches and Universities in Nazi Germany*. Cambridge: Cambridge University Press.

Faulkner Rossi, Lauren. 2015. *Wehrmacht Priests: Catholicism and the Nazi War of Annihilation*. New York: Oxford University Press.

Förster, Jürgen. 1998. "Complicity or Entanglement? Wehrmacht, War, and Holocaust." In *The Holocaust and History: The Known, the Unknown, the Disputed, and the Reexamined*, edited by Michael Berenbaum and Abraham J. Peck, 266–283. Bloomington: Indiana University Press.

Gellately, Robert. 2001. *Backing Hitler: Consent and Coercion in Nazi Germany*. Oxford: Oxford University Press.

Geyer, Michael, and John W. Boyer. 1994. *Resistance against the Third Reich, 1933–1990*. Chicago: University of Chicago Press.

Gross, Michael B. 2004. *The War against Catholicism: Liberalism and the Anti-Catholic Imagination in Nineteenth-Century Germany*. Ann Arbor: University of Michigan Press.

Hastings, Derek. 2010. *Catholicism and the Roots of Nazism: Religious Identity and National Socialism*. Oxford: Oxford University Press.

Hillenbrand, Karl, and Rudolf Weigand, eds. 1989. *Mit der Kirche auf dem Weg: 400 Jahre Priesterseminar Würzburg 1589–1989*. Würzburg: Echter.

Hinojosa, Ramon. 2010. "Doing Hegemony: Military, Men, and Constructing a Hegemonic Masculinity." *The Journal of Men's Studies* 18, no. 2 (Spring): 179–194.

Hoffmann, Peter. 1988. *The German Resistance to Hitler*. Cambridge: Harvard University Press.

———. 1996. *The History of the German Resistance*. Montreal: McGill-Queen's University Press.

———. 2011. *Behind Valkyrie: German Resistance to Hitler*. Montreal: McGill-Queen's University Press.

Hummel, Karl-Joseph, and Michael Kißener, eds. 2009. *Die Katholiken und das Dritte Reich: Kontroversen und Debatten*. Paderborn: Schöningh.

Kershaw, Ian. 1983. *Popular Opinion and Political Dissent in the Third Reich*. New York: Oxford University Press.

———. 2000. *The Nazi Dictatorship: Problems and Perspectives of Interpretation*, 4th ed. New York: Bloomsbury.

Kislinger, Florian. 2006–2007. "Zwischen Front und Heimat: Kontakte zwischen Soldaten bzw. Feldgeistlichen und der Erzdiözese München und Freising 1939–1945." Unpublished MA thesis (*Hausarbeit*), Ludwig-Maximilians-Universität München.

Koenen, Gerd. 2005. *Der Russland-Komplex: Die Deutschen und Der Osten 1900–1945*. Munich: C. H. Beck.

Kühne, Thomas. 1999. "Gruppenkohäsion und Kameradschaftsmythos in der Wehrmacht." In *Die Wehrmacht: Mythos und Realität*, edited by Rolf-Dieter Müller and Hans Erich Volkmann, 534–549. Munich: R. Oldenbourg Verlag.

———. 2010. *Belonging and Genocide: Hitler's Community, 1918–1945*. New Haven: Yale University Press.

Latzel, Klaus. 1999. "Wehrmachtsoldaten zwischen 'Normalität' und NS-Ideologie, oder: Was sucht die Forschung in der Feldpost?" In *Die Wehrmacht: Mythos und Realität*, edited by Rolf-Dieter Müller and Hans Erich Volkmann, 573–588. Munich: R. Oldenbourg Verlag.

Levi, Primo. 1989. *The Drowned and the Saved*. London: Abacus.

Lewy, Guenter. 1965. *The Catholic Church and Nazi Germany*. New York: McGraw-Hill.

Messerschmidt, Manfred, and Wolfram Wette. 1996. *Was damals Recht war: NS Militär- und Strafjustiz im Vernichtungskrieg*. Essen: Klartext.

Missalla, Heinrich. 1997. *Wie der Krieg zur Schule Gottes wurde: Hitlers Feldbischof Rarkowski*. Oberursel: Publik-Forum.

———. 1999. *Für Gott, Führer, und Vaterland: Die Verstrickung der katholischen Seelsorge in Hitlers Krieg*. Munich: Kösel.

Mosse, George. 1996. *The Image of Man: The Creation of Modern Masculinity*. New York: Oxford University Press.

Müller-Hildebrand, Burkhart. 1969. *Das Heer 1933–1945: Entwicklung des organisatorischen Aufbaus*, vol. 3. Darmstadt: Verlag von E.S. Mittler & Sohn GmbH.

Paul, Gerhard. 1994. *Ungehorsame Soldaten: Dissens, Verweigerung und Widerstand deutscher Soldaten 1939–1945*. St. Ingbert: Röhrig Universitätsverlag.

Peukert, Detlev. 1987. *Inside Nazi Germany: Conformity, Opposition, and Racism in Everyday Life*. New Haven: Yale University Press.

Ross, Ronald J. 1998. *The Failure of Bismarck's Kulturkampf: Catholicism and State Power in Imperial Germany, 1871–1887*. Washington, DC: Catholic University Press of America.

Scholder, Klaus. 1988. *The Churches and the Third Reich*, 2 vols. Philadelphia: Fortress Press.

Schwaiger, Georg, ed. 1984. *Das Erzbistum München und Freising in der Zeit der nationalsozialistischen Herrschaft*, 2 vols. Munich: Schnell und Steiner.

———. 1989. "Das Erbe des 19. Jahrhunderts in der katholischen Kirche Bayerns." In *Das Erzbistum München und Freising im 19. und 20. Jahrhundert*, vol. 1, edited by Georg Schwaiger, 16–37. Munich: E. Wewel.

Seibel, Paul. 1994. *Priester: Ausbildung und Verfolgung*. Frankfurt: Haag and Herchen.

Smolinsky, Heribert. 1994. "Das katholische Russlandbild in Deutschland nach dem Ersten Weltkrieg und im Dritten Reich." In *Das Russlandbild im Dritten Reich*, edited by Hans-Erich Volkmann, 323–355. Cologne: Böhlau.

Spicer, Kevin P. 2004. *Resisting the Third Reich: The Catholic Clergy in Hitler's Berlin*. DeKalb: Northern Illinois University Press.
Thum, Gregor, ed. 2006. *Traumland Ost: Deutsche Bilder vom östlichen Europa im 20. Jahrhundert*. Göttingen: Vandenhoeck and Ruprecht.
Volk, Ludwig. 1972. *Das Reichskonkordat vom 20. Juli 1933*. Mainz: Matthias-Grünewald-Verlag.
Volkmann, Hans-Erich, ed. 1994. *Das Russlandbild im Dritten Reich*. Cologne: Böhlau.
Walser-Smith, Helmut. 1994. *German Nationalism and Religious Conflict: Culture, Ideology, Politics, 1870–1914*. Princeton: Princeton University Press.
Zahn, Gordon C. 1962. *German Catholics and Hitler's Wars: A Study in Social Control*. New York: Sheed and Ward.

PART II
AFTERMATH

Chapter 8

Contested Manhood
Autobiographical Reflections of German Protestant Theologians after World War II

BENEDIKT BRUNNER

Church historians and scholars of religious history have neglected autobiographies as a source of understanding the past for quite a long time (Krondorfer 2014, 2006; Staats 1994; Nowak 1994). This is somehow surprising, as the remembrance of the Third Reich played an important role in the many autobiographies that were published after World War II. Many theologians participated in this activity to explain their views of the past. Too little is known about the gender relations that these sources reveal. This chapter will contribute a gender analysis of these texts (see also Brunner 2015).

What influence did the experience of the Third Reich and World War II have on the ways in which German theologians wrote about masculinity? This case study provides some answers to this question. A few essential points need to be stated at the outset. First, for a thorough understanding of postwar German memory, the autobiographies of important and influential public figures need to be taken into account. In the 1950s and 1960s, the years in which all these books were published, "Germany engaged in reconstructive and restorative work on many levels, not only economically and politically, but also literarily, biographically, and through public representations of the self" (Krondorfer 2014, 105). Furthermore, the written self-representations of that time were "textual witnesses to these processes of self-exculpation" (105). As Krondorfer and others have shown, the case of the German Protestant theologians is more ambiguous in terms of self-representation and self-exculpation, and my chapter will also demonstrate this.

Second, it is important to take into account that the authors of these autobiographies were all men; yet, surprisingly the gender category is scarcely used in research about contemporary church history. In my case study, I will follow Krondorfer's suggestion and "apply a male-gendered analysis so that we can learn something about men's identities, self-perceptions, self-representations" by "investigating their practices and textual witnesses as gendered expressions in a given cultural moment of history" (Krondorfer 2014, 102).

Third, men wanted "to talk about themselves to assert their male subjectivity and moral agency, and yet not reveal too much about themselves in order to elude levels of complicity and culpability" (Krondorfer 2014, 105–106). It is important to take into account that these voices of theologians were influential among German Protestant circles and beyond. The question of their contribution to the "normalization" of gender relations in the postwar years needs further scrutiny (Schissler 2001).

Otto Dibelius (1880–1967), a famous participant in the "Church Struggle" (*Kirchenkampf*) during the Nazi years, described his experiences as a "fierce fight" (1961, 173).[1] This martial image was a characteristic element of the Protestant remembrance of the Nazi years. It was, furthermore, closely connected to a discourse about masculinity. The references to the Church Struggle were of vital importance for the constitution of Protestant identity after 1945 (Fischer-Hupe 2002). The leading question of my chapter is: To what extent did the experiences in the Third Reich influence the postwar discourses about Protestant identity and masculinity?

I will first clarify my methodological premises and explain why autobiographies are important sources for historians. I will then sketch the historical context of the "long sixties," the years approximately between 1958 and 1977, in which most of the autobiographies examined in this chapter were published. In a third step, I will analyze the ways manhood is reflected in these autobiographies and show which facets of masculinity are most important.

Methodological Reflections

For a long time, autobiographies were seen as a chronically unreliable and problematic source for historians (Machtan 2013; Rödder 1997). What, however, is an autobiographical work? The philosopher Wilhelm Dilthey believed that the "self-biography . . . is the highest and most instructive form, in which the understanding of life comes to us" (Dilthey 1927, 198). The person who understands the course of life becomes identical with the person who creates it through writing. Between the different parts of the course of life, Dilthey sees connections that can be hermeneutically understood. "Insofar as in memory we look back, we grasp the connections of the bygone parts of the course of life under the category of their meaning" (Dilthey 1927, 201).

It is not necessary to delve into the depths of Dilthey's hermeneutics (Lessing 2008). Suffice it to say that for him autobiographies are the most important sources for a recapitulation of a life. At the same time, long before Bourdieu's warnings of an *illusion biographique* (Bourdieu 1986; see also Hildenbrand 2012), Dilthey clarifies that autobiographies are not a pure image of one's life, but a process in which one (re)constructs oneself.

Presently, there is little consensus about how to define autobiography. The French literary scholar Philippe Lejeune proposes the following: "Retrospective prose narrative written by a real person concerning his own existence, where the focus is his individual life, in particular the story of his personality" (1989, 4). Holdenried states that the moments of retrospection and the description of the genesis of one's personal history are central aspects of an autobiography (2000, 20; see also Wagner-Egelhaaf 2005). For Georg Misch, an autobiography "can hardly be more closely defined than by the explanation of the term itself: the description (*graphia*) of the life (*bios*) of an individual person by himself/herself (*auto*)" (1989, 38). It is quite obvious that based on such general definitions many questions remain open (Finck 1999). Is an autobiography a factual or fictional work? What role does the author play in this genre? Trying to answer these questions will help to clarify the value of autobiographies as sources for historians.

Renate Dürr, a historian of Early Modern Germany, makes clear that the "question regarding the relationship between reality and fiction can barely be answered satisfactorily" 2007, 20) through a genre-theoretical (*gattungstheoretischen*) approach. She argues, instead, for an understanding of autobiographical memory as a communicative act:

> The reflection of one's own life path, one's own self, or certain experiences in the course of life can only be understood as dialogical, and this in two respects: in light of the remembered

past on the one hand . . . [and] on the other hand, as external communication geared toward a potential circle of readers. (Dürr 2007, 21; see also Lehmann 1988)

This means that autobiographies not only construct the identity of the individual in the act of writing, they also constitute a space of social reality by keeping in mind their potential readers. The Americanist Volker Depkat rightfully states that "autobiographical writing is an act of social communication through which the writer relates himself to his environment. His narration is, at the same time, influenced by this specific environment" (2003, 442, also 2007; Heinze 2010). Depkat understands the autobiography as an expression of a certain group membership and as "the result of a social practice that determines how the members are supposed to describe their lives at a certain time" (2003, 442–443; also Landwehr 2008; Kleinberg 2007; Alheit and Dausien 2000).

Depkat's approach focuses on the group dynamics that influence the process of the organization of particular memories to give them a socially acceptable form. How do the memories of the theologians I am examining in this chapter reflect and reproduce discourses that were socially accepted in certain milieus? My reading of select autobiographies will reveal how the language employed by several theologians has strong gender implications, especially when those theologians relied on militaristic tropes. In this sense, my work is somewhat related to what George Mosse presented in his pathbreaking works *The Image of Men* (1996) and *Nationalism and Sexuality* (1985).

Ulrike Auga (2013) states that gender and religion are interdependent categories of knowledge. Hence, when analyzing the autobiographies of theologians, we need to ask the following questions: How is the relationship between religion and gender conceived in these texts (Fulda 2005)? What is the nature of dominant or hegemonic discourses in these texts (Mouffe and Laclau 1986; Martschukat and Stieglitz 2008, 64–73)? Are there silences in those text, and if so, when?[2]

Historical Contextualization

This chapter is based on a sample of thirteen autobiographies, which all were published between 1959 and 1977. This roughly covers the time span that the historian Arthur Marwick called "the long 1960s" (1998). Recent research has made clear that those were years of a fundamental and irreversible change, especially for the churches (Kanis, Billie, and Pasture 2010; McLeod 2007; see also Großbölting 2013). Regarding West Germany, the immediate postwar years, even into the 1950s, were described as a time of "restoration," which was not always meant in a negative way, as a widely known article by the left-leaning Catholic intellectual Walter Dirks implies (Dirks 1950). Nevertheless, the euphoric hopes for a rechristianization of German society were eventually dashed, although the church as an institution experienced an extremely successful period of reconstruction.

In the 1950s, the churches in Germany had gained a high reputation in both political and societal respects. They were a sought-after interlocutor with respect to ethical questions, such as on issues of rearmament or marriage and sexuality (see Rahden 2008; Chappel 2017). All of this changed in the following decade. The 1960s were a time of crisis for the Western churches. A massive pluralization and politicization in the religious field put the churches into a defensive position (Großbölting 2013, 120–148). Growing skepticism and a general crisis of authority affected the churches in multiple ways.

One last point is decisive for analyzing these autobiographies, namely the impact of the historicization or nonhistoricization of the *Kirchenkampf* (Church Struggle). All of the theologians who wrote their autobiographies experienced the Nazi period firsthand, and all of them wanted to express their views on how the Protestant church "struggled" with the Nazi regime. After World War II, a certain master narrative of this conflict developed.[3] The goal of this narrative was to remember the Confessing Church as resisting National Socialism, which in reality it did partially at best. It still needs to be deconstructed properly. Thomas Seidel has pointed out that the aspect of masculinity remains a desideratum for research on the Church Struggle (Seidel 1999, 333). He believes that Protestant theologians and church leaders adhered to a *Gesinnungsmilitarismus*, a way of thinking that embraced militarism as part of their national identity. We can assume that such *Gesinnungsmilitarismus* affected their postwar autobiographies.

"Manhood" during the Third Reich and in Postwar Autobiographies

What is the significance of the militaristic attitude in Protestantism? What role does war rhetoric play in the descriptions of the Church Struggle? To what extent is autobiographical language influenced by gender?

Seidel (1999) claims that theologians belonging to the Religious Socialist movement[4] were the least affected by militaristic attitudes and language. The analysis of the autobiographies of Emil Fuchs (1874–1971) and Günther Dehn (1882–1970)—two leading protagonists among Religious Socialists—proves him right. Commenting on a search of his home by the Gestapo in 1933, Fuchs states that he and his sons took the following for granted: "That we only fight with spiritual weapons and that we don't have material weapons in our homes" (Fuchs 1959, 221). Similarly, Dehn writes that it took a while for him to recognize "that the church would have to fight against the ruling state . . . , but only with the single weapon that only the church possesses: the Word of God" (Dehn 1962, 295).

Dehn and Fuchs, however, were the exception: a strong and manly war rhetoric was far more common among German Protestant theologians. This is especially true for those who participated in World War II as soldiers. Wilhelm Niemöller (1898–1983), for instance, fought as a Wehrmacht officer at the Eastern Front between 1942 and 1944. Since 1923, he also had been a member of the National Socialist Party. His accounts of the unifying and bonding experience of comradeship are numerous.[5] Still, it might be surprising to hear from Niemöller—the leading postwar German voice that constructed an unblemished view of the "Confessing Church" (Protestant clergy that opposed Nazism in the 1930s)—how he described his superiors in the German military. In his words, they were "only upright, capable, sincere and pious men" (Niemöller 1961, 265).

Heinz-Dietrich Wendland (1900–1992), the founding father of social ethics in postwar Germany,[6] with a personality more down to earth than the lofty Niemöller, also emphasizes courage and comradeship in his recollection of his war experiences. "An incredible amount of courage, strength and confidence was necessary to not lose the heart," he wrote in his 1977 memoirs (Wendland 1977, 159). Comradeship among soldiers was, in his opinion, crucial to get through the war. During his time as a Russian prisoner of war, he remembers, almost all of his experiences were good (171).

We find another variation on this theme of comradely, national unity in Wolfgang Trillhaas's (1903–1995) autobiography. Trillhaas, a rather conservative professor of systematic and practical theology at the University of Erlangen, writes: "Now here in the air-raid shelters the much acclaimed people's community [*Volksgemeinschaft*] constituted itself from one alarm to the other" (1976, 87). More critically, Trillhaas also writes about his experiences in a "paramilitary sport camp for [university] lecturers," which took place in March 1934. Through the "cheerfully rude behavior" of the SA leader, the "community of the gathered lecturers was changed into a bunch of recruits" (162). The Third Reich "now got to them physically" (163). Sports were an important aspect of those paramilitary camps, with the purpose to prepare the recruits to fight. No "happy and manly eruption of comradeship was harmless under these circumstances. You learned to behave in a natural way without losing your self-control for a single moment" (163; see also Diem 1974, 30).

A militaristic rhetoric is often used to describe the events of the Church Struggle as such. For instance, Hanns Lilje (1899–1977), a Lutheran theologian and bishop with conservative convictions, writes about the congregational struggle between the "German Christians" (*Deutsche Christen*) who constituted those parts and members of the Protestant Church that supported the Nazi Party, and the so-called "intact churches," those Protestant congregations that neither joined the Nazified German Christians nor the oppositional Confessing Church. The "German Christians" tried to realize the racist agenda of the Nazis within the realm of the church and to establish a *Reichskirche* (church of the Reich), a hierarchical national church body led by a *Reichsbishop*.

According to Lilje, congregations led by German Christians witnessed "fights [that] were fiercer than those in the 'intact' ones" (1973, 127). But Lilje also regrets that "the leading figures of the Confessing Church lacked war experiences at all" (137). Hermann Diem, who was a member of the radical wing of the Confessing Church formed around Bonhoeffer, and hence on a different side than Lilje with respect to the political spectrum within the Protestant Church during the Nazi regime, speaks of a "war on two fronts, with the leadership of the church on the one hand, and the Nazi Party on the other hand" (Diem 1974, 124). Finally, Otto Dibelius, a more conservative-leaning member of the Confessing Church, remembers to have felt the necessity to tell the congregations "that the fight is grave and everything is at stake" (Dibelius 1961, 185).

These authors rarely speak about women. The exceptions, though, are quite telling regarding the relationships they reveal. Hermann Diem (1900–1975) is such an exception. He was a systematic theologian and Lutheran disciple of Karl Barth and also a member of the Confessing Church. Diem reports that during his time in the military service his wife Annelise fulfilled his duties as a pastor. After his return, a member of the presbytery told him he "should let his wife preach again, she was better at it." Diem comments dryly: "My return, therefore, was not triumphant, but rather adequate regarding the circumstances" (Diem 1974, 144).

An unusual example of an autobiography that relies on militaristic language was actually written by a woman, Guida Diehl (1868–1962). She was a Protestant pedagogue and founder of the "Neulandbund," a right-wing conservative organization of the women's movement in Germany. In 1959, she published her memoir, *Christ sein heisst Kämpfer sein* (Being a Christian means to be a fighter). Her rhetoric exceeds the militaristic tone of any other writer in my sample, with the exception perhaps of Wilhelm Niemöller. Despite her strong views, she was marginalized even among the "German Christians," as historian Doris Bergen has pointed out (1996, 136). Despite her marginalization, Diehl felt close to this pro-Nazi group, an affection that endured until the end of the war. Many former "German Christians" after the end of World War II did not agree with the militant tone of her book. "Presumably, the men concerned found Diehl's image of herself as a fighter too strident for a woman in the manly church" (Bergen 1996, 136). Diehl was obviously perceived as a threat to those who believed that manliness in the church had to be represented by men only.

Diehl, however, did not seem to care. In her memoir, she focused on her courage to tell the truth and that she wanted to mediate between different parties of the Church Struggle (Diehl 1959, 244). In her own words, she fought "an open fight against the anti-Christian spirit" (256) of the National Socialist German Workers Party (NSDAP). With special intensity, she writes, she combatted the instruction of SS leader Heinrich Himmler who had called SS men to engage in reproductive acts. The order had stated that "the girl who says no is as bad as an objector of war" (258). Diehl was infuriated then and she used her 1959 autobiography to express again her disapproval of this order. Her memoir is intended to convey her important role during the Nazi years, with the aim to affirm her usefulness as a role model in the late 1950s.

Her own calling had been inspired by Johann Hinrich Wichern, the founder of the "Innere Mission."[7] Diehl believed that Wichern had taught German Protestants that a Christian had to become a fighter in public life. "This is a difficult but also a great task, and for women the service of motherly love in particular and in small things has to be added" (Diehl 1959, 274). In other words, Diehl sees herself as a fighter, which she blends with her role as a mother. At the end of her book, she states that writing about her life was necessary because of the "great task that was put on . . . Germans" in her lifetime (275).

Diehl is a telling example of how "manly" concepts can be adopted by a woman in her self-portrayal.[8] We can compare her writing, which reveals her complicity with Nazism as a church member, with the autobiography of theologian Walter Birnbaum, another member of the pro-Nazi "German Christians." According to Krondorfer, "more than other theological autobiographies, Birnbaum's language is saturated with martial images of camaraderie, soldiership, protection of soil, defense of order, manly postures, and distaste for 'intellectualized' talk" (2014, 115). In his 1973 memoir, forty years after the *Kirchenkampf*, Birnbaum still complained that "the victory of the Confessing Church was the defeat of the true Church" (1973, 287). Birnbaum's postwar autobiography, like Diehl's book, illustrates a typical way of "German Christians" remembering the Third Reich after 1945. Perhaps surprisingly, Nazified rhetoric is still being used decades after the end of the war.

The Case of Heinrich Grüber: Experiences in Concentration Camps

On the other end of the spectrum we have Heinrich Grüber, a reformed theologian, pacifist, and opponent to Nazism. His case is particularly important for an understanding of the relationship between the Holocaust and masculinity. Among Protestant theologians writing their autobiographies after the war, Grüber is the only one who experienced the Holocaust in its worst form, as a prisoner in a concentration camp (Wachsmann 2016; Benz and Diestel 2015; Kundrus 2017). In 1938, Grüber founded the so-called "Bureau Grüber," or "Relief Center for Protestant Non-Aryans," the purpose of which was to enable non-Aryans to leave Germany safely. In 1941, Grüber was arrested by the Gestapo and imprisoned, first in the Sachsenhausen concentration camp and later (in September 1941) in Dachau until his release in June 1943.

Violence is a significant and almost omnipresent aspect in his recollections of his time in the concentration camps. Upon his arrival at Sachsenhausen, he was beaten up by SS members who assaulted some detainees of every transport. Usually, they chose Jews, but this time, they decided to target Grüber. Grüber also did not experience a sense of comradeship among his fellow sufferers (Grüber 1968, 148). He was eventually detained in the *Pfaffenblock*, an area where only priests and pastors were imprisoned. Among the "SS-*Leute*," Grüber writes, brutality and sentimentality could be present at the same time. Despite their viciousness, they still wanted to sing Christmas songs with him and the other detainees of the *Pfaffenblock*. Occasionally, they even listened to him preach: "'How do we want to live here together?' I asked, 'Do we want to be like mud or like steel? If steel is squeezed, it becomes stronger and more persistent. When mud is squeezed it spills in all directions.' The SS soldiers listened and remained silent" (150).

Grüber was a kapo in Sachsenhausen, one of the so-called privileged prisoners whom the SS put in charge to supervise forced labor. Grüber finds it necessary to defend himself in his memoir for his role as kapo. He concedes that sometimes it was necessary to punish someone who endangered "order and cleanliness" (152), for otherwise the SS would punish the whole group, and not just the individual transgressor.

Compared to the experiences of Wolfgang Trillhaas and Heinz-Dietrich Wendland, who had been compelled as university lecturers to participate in the National Socialism sport camps, Grüber describes his imprisonment in harsh and nonromanticizing ways. "The first weeks in the camp were ineffably difficult. Like many others I had to experience that suffering together doesn't bring people together, but creates hostility against one another" (153). Some of the detainees imitated the cruelty of their tormentors to survive. Violence was always present, such as the hangings they had to witness. He tells the story of two Jehovah's Witnesses, father and son. When the father was hanged and shot, the son stood next to him, with no expression in his face. After the hanging, the son left "like a winner, with a superior calmness which only his solid faith made possible" (159).

The language in Grüber's memoir shares similarities with the autobiographies of the Religious Socialists Emil Fuchs and Günther Dehn. Like them, the significance of spiritual weapons is emphasized. Time and again, Grüber describes how he reacted to the SS brutality and injustice in a Christlike manner. He endured it and accepted his suffering (160). He also writes much about the spiritual care he administered to the camp inmates and about the ways he tried to help them. In this respect, the time in the camp was, in his perception, a continuation of what he did before in the "Bureau Grüber": to be present for those who were alone, with no one to help them (155). His autobiography tells various stories about how faith comforted detainees, independent of confessional or religious boundaries. In addition to being the suffering Christlike figure, Grüber can also be seen as the Good Samaritan (Barwich 2014).

The Good Samaritan figure is exemplified in the case of the death of Pastor Werner Sylten. Due to illness, he had been selected to the "commission of invalids," as the Nazis called it. They chose several hundred detainees with the intention to kill them, and it was forbidden to meet them. Grüber describes the different ways in which the SS guards punished and tormented detainees. But despite of the threat of punishment, he tried to see Sylten anyway (176). When he succeeded in talking to Sylten, he tried to rescue him from certain death, but he was unable to do so. This story is important for two reasons. First, it shows the compassionate male figure of the "Good Samaritan" that Grüber represents, trying to save a friend while putting his own life in danger. Second, it demonstrates that even in the circumstances of a Nazi concentration camp, there was space for "agency" (McNay 2000, 1–30) among some of the detainees.

Grüber writes that an inner morale (*Haltung*) was necessary to survive the camps and that some inmates died because they lacked such morale. He told newly arriving detainees, "nur Haltung garantiert Erhaltung" (only morale/attitude guarantees survival) (163–164). Strong smokers, he writes, were less able to resist and were the first to die in difficult times. Here we have an instance of moral and theological convictions intersecting with particular images of masculinity. A morally strong man would have had higher chances of survival, according to Grüber's autobiographical recollections.

Grüber describes himself as someone who tried to get things done in the name of Christian *diakonia*. "I often found possibilities to help someone spiritually or physically. I learned that one's own need for help never goes so far that one wouldn't be able to do something for someone else" (182). Grüber helped others until he was completely exhausted; he suffered a heart attack. His diaconical service, we could say, reveals an ascetic component. But Grüber hesitated to call it martyrdom. "The concentration camp is no visible martyrium. Martyrium means testimony, but our sufferings didn't become public. A true martyrium can strengthen other people. But when you died wretchedly here, that was no testimony which was effective beyond this place" (185).

In Grüber's memories, women play a rather important role compared to the other autobiographical writings by male theologians. His book, for one, is dedicated "to my courageous wife"; furthermore, we learn a lot about the many things his wife tried to do to ease the burden of her husband and to free him from the concentration camp (197–198). Instructive also is his report on the installation of a brothel in Dachau, though in the end it was not created because of the unanimous resistance of most of the inmates (188ff.). Grüber also complains about unpleasant (sexual) relationships between older men and boys, and that he often admonished those who participated in such actions (191).

While largely rejecting a masculinity based on militaristic rhetoric, as we have seen in other autobiographies of German theologians of this time period, Grüber embraces the manly roles of a Good Samaritan and Suffering Christ; yet, his stern moral judgments concerning certain behaviors among male inmates also betray his belief in traditional gender roles. What is intriguing is that he so openly writes about them.

Outlook

Gender knowledge and gender relations, as regulated, enacted, and policed during the Third Reich, play important roles in the postwar autobiographies of these theologians. A close reading of select examples renders gender and male agency visible in these texts. Traditional gender roles remain largely unquestioned. The idea that men are the leading figures in history remains mostly intact, with women occupying supportive roles as wives. Certainly, the influence of the "German Christian" cult of masculinity, as we have seen it evidenced in Guida Diehl's and Walter Birnbaum's memoirs, can benefit from further examination (Bergen 1996, 61–81; Blaschke 2013). Comparing those memoirs with autobiographical texts written by members of the Confessing Church might yield further insight into the use of gendered language within divergent cultural and theology contexts.

Seidel's thesis about a "militaristic attitude" (*Gesinnungsmilitarismus*) seems convincing based on most texts analyzed in this chapter. A combative rhetoric and the topoi of comradeship, courage, and bravery are almost omnipresent. For these male theologians, it seems that the "sexual revolution" and other changes of the 1960s have left only a minimal impact on their ideas of masculinity. It might be rewarding to compare these results to autobiographies written by later generations of German theologians, and to embed their writings into the general history of gender and gender relations. A multipronged approach might shed more light on the specifics of a gender concept influenced by religion and theology (Dietrich and Heise 2013).

Notes

1. From 1949 to 1961, Dibelius—one of the most important church leaders of his time and part of the *Kirchenkampf*—was the bishop of the Evangelical

Church in Berlin and Brandenburg as well as chairman of the Evangelical Church in Germany. The standard work on the *Kirchenkampf* is Meier (1976–1984). For a concise overview, see Strohm (2011). All translations from the German are my own.

2. Regarding the importance of asking the "right" questions for which autobiographical writings can provide answers, see Depkat (2004, 2010) and Günther (2001).

3. Wilhelm Niemöller, the brother of Martin Niemöller, was a leading figure in this process of creating a normative narrative of the *Kirchenkampf*; see Ericksen (2005).

4. Religious Socialists are members of a religion (in this case Christianity) who are convinced that socialism is the only appropriate societal order. Most of them believe that capitalism has to be overcome and they see rightly practiced Christianity as a way to do so. The German Paul Tillich and the American Reinhold Niebuhr were two leading theological thinkers in this movement in the 1930s.

5. About comradeship, see the important work by Kühne (2006); from a sociological perspective, see Kühl (2014, 147–174).

6. Wendland started his career as a professor at the university in Kiel in 1950 before he moved to Münster in 1955, where he taught until 1970.

7. The "Innere Mission" was directed toward one's own society with the intention to bring people back into the church, to educate, and to help the poor. There is a certain similarity to the Social Gospel Movement in the United States; see Wu (2009).

8. One should not forget that the people's community made social advancement possible for non-Jewish women. The women's organizations of the NSDAP were as antisemitic and racist as other NS Party organizations. "Die nationalsozialistische Frauenpolitik zeigt noch einmal die ganze Widersprüchlichkeit der nationalsozialistischen Gesellschaftspolitik: den Widerspruch zwischen der Propaganda von der Volksgemeinschaft und dem Fortbestand sozialer Barrieren und Ungleichheit; den Widerspruch zwischen bürgerlich-traditionellen Leitbildern und rassistischen Ideologemen; schließlich den Widerspruch zwischen den frauenpolitischen Vorurteilen bzw. Vorgaben und der sich verändernden Wirklichkeit" (Thamer 2002, 264–265).

References

Alheit, Peter, and Bettina Dausien. 2000. "Die biographische Konstruktion der Wirklichkeit: Überlegungen zur Biographizität des Sozialen." In *Biographische Sozialisation*, edited by Erika M. Hoerning, 257–283. Stuttgart: Lucius & Lucius.

Auga, Ulrike. 2013. "Geschlecht und Religion als interdependente Kategorien des Wissens: Intersektionalitätsdebatte, Dekonstruktion, Diskursanalyse und die Kritik antiker Texte." In *Doing Gender—Doing Religion: Fallstudien zur Intersektionalität im frühen Judentum, Christentum und Islam*, edited by Ute E. Eisen, Christine Gerber, and Angela Standhartinger, 37–74. Tübingen: Mohr Siebeck.

Barwich, Beate, ed. 2014. *Veni Creator Spiritus: Heinrich Grüber—Gerechter unter den Völkern*. Leipzig: Evangelische Verlagsanstalt.

Benz, Wolfgang, and Barbara Diestel, eds. 2015. *Der Ort des Terrors: Geschichte der nationalsozialistischen Konzentrationslager, Bd. 2: Frühe Lager. Dachau, Emslandlager*. Munich: C. H. Beck.

Bergen, Doris L. 1996. *Twisted Cross: The German Christian Movement in the Third Reich*. Chapel Hill: University of North Carolina Press.

Birnbaum, Walter. 1973. *Zeuge meiner Zeit: Aussagen zu 1912 bis 1972*. Frankfurt: Musterschmidt.

Blaschke, Olaf. 2013. "'Wenn irgendeine Geschichtszeit, so ist die unsere eine Männerzeit': Konfessionsgeschichtliche Zuschreibungen im Nationalsozialismus." In *Zerstrittene "Volksgemeinschaft": Glaube, Konfession und Religion im Nationalsozialismus*, edited by Manfred Gailus and Armin Nolzen, 34–65. Göttingen: Vandenhoeck & Ruprecht.

Bourdieu, Pierre. 1986. "L'illusion biographiques." *Actes de a Recherche en Sciences Sociales* 62: 69–72.

Brunner, Benedikt. 2015. "Geschlechterordnung im Kirchenkampf: Konstruktionen von Gender in der autobiografischen Aufarbeitung des Nationalsozialismus." In *Sichtbar Unsichtbar: Geschlechterwissen in (auto-)biografischen Texten*, edited by Maria Heidegger et al., 103–117. Bielefeld: Transcript.

Chappel, James. 2017. "Nuclear Families in a Nuclear Age: Theorising the Family in 1950s West Germany." *Contemporary European History* 26: 85–109.

Dehn, Günther. 1962. *Die alte Zeit—die vorigen Jahre: Lebenserinnerungen*. Munich: Kaiser.

Depkat, Volker. 2003. "Autobiographie und die soziale Konstruktion von Wirklichkeit." *Geschichte und Gesellschaft* 29: 441–476.

———. 2004. "Nicht die Materialien sind das Problem, sondern die Fragen, die man stellt: Zum Quellenwert von Autobiographien für die historische Forschung." In *"Quelle": Zwischen Ursprung und Konstrukt: Ein Leitbegriff in der Diskussion*, edited by Thomas Rathmann and Nikolaus Wegmann, 102–117. Berlin: Erich Schmidt Verlag.

———. 2007. *Lebenswenden und Zeitenwenden: Deutsche Politiker und die Erfahrung des 20. Jahrhunderts*. Munich: Oldenbourg.

———. 2010. "Zum Stand und zu den Perspektiven der Autobiographieforschung in der Geschichtswissenschaft." *BIOS* 23: 170–187.

Dibelius, Otto. 1961. *Ein Christ ist immer im Dienst: Erlebnisse und Erfahrungen einer Zeitenwende*. Stuttgart: Kreuz-Verlag.

Diehl, Guida. 1959. *Christ sein heisst Kämpfer sein: Die Führung meines Lebens*. Giessen: Brunnen.

Diem, Hermann. 1974. *Ja oder Nein: 50 Jahre Theologe in Kirche und Staat*. Stuttgart: Kreuz-Verlag.

Dietrich, Annette, and Ljiljana Heise, eds. 2013. *Männlichkeitskonstruktionen im Nationalsozialismus: Formen, Funktionen und Wirkungsmacht von Geschlechterkonstruktionen im Nationalsozialismus und ihre Reflexion in der pädagogischen Praxis*. Frankfurt a. M.: Peter Lang.

Dilthey, Wilhelm. 1927. "Entwürfe zur Kritik der historischen Vernunft: Erster Teil: Erleben, Ausdruck und Verstehen." In *Gesammelte Schriften, Volume VII: Der Aufbau der geschichtlichen Welt in den Geisteswissenschaften*, edited by Wilhelm Dilthey, 191–245. Leipzig: Teubner.

Dirks, Walter. 1950. "Der restaurative Charakter der Epoche." *Frankfurter Hefte* 5: 942–954.

Dürr, Renate. 2007. "Funktionen des Schreibens: Autobiographien und Selbstzeugnisse als Zeugnisse der Kommunikation und Selbstvergewisserung." In *Kommunikation und Transfer im Christentum der Frühen Neuzeit*, edited by Irene Dingel and Wolf-Friedrich Schäufele, 17–31. Mainz: Verlag Philip von Zabern.

Ericksen, Robert. 2005. "Wilhelm Niemöller and the Historiography of the Kirchenkampf." In *Nationalprotestantische Mentalitäten in Deutschland (1870–1970): Konturen, Entwicklungslinien und Umbrüche eines Weltbildes*, edited by Manfred Gailus, 433–452. Göttingen: Vandenhoeck & Ruprecht.

Finck, Almut. 1999. *Autobiographisches Schreiben nach dem Ende der Autobiographie*. Stuttgart: Erich Schmidt Verlag.

Fischer-Hupe, Kristine. 2002. "Der Kirchenkampfdiskurs nach 1945: Wie katholische und evangelische Theologen in der frühen Nachkriegszeit über den Kirchenkampf der Jahre 1933–1945 sprachen." *Contemporary Church History* 15: 461–489.

Fuchs, Emil. 1959. *Mein Leben: Zweiter Teil: Ein Christ im Kampfe gegen den Faschismus, für Frieden und Sozialismus*. Leipzig: Koehler & Amelang.

Fulda, Daniel. 2005. "Hat Geschichte ein Geschlecht? Gegenderte Autorenschaft im historischen Diskurs." In *Historisierte Subjekte—Subjektivierte Historie: Zur Verfügbarkeit und Unverfügbarkeit von Geschichte*, edited by Stefan Deines, Stephan Jaeger, and Ansgar Nünning, 185–201. Berlin: De Gruyter.

Großbölting, Thomas. 2013. *Der verlorene Himmel: Glaube in Deutschland seit 1945*. Göttingen: Vandenhoeck & Ruprecht.

Grüber, Heinrich. 1968. *Erinnerungen aus sieben Jahrzehnten*. Cologne: Kiepenheuer & Witsch.

Günther, Dagmar. 2001. "'And now for something completely different': Prolegomena zur Autobiographie als Quelle der Geschichtswissenschaft." *Historische Zeitschrift* 272: 25–61.

Heinze, Carsten. 2010. "Autobiographie und zeitgeschichtliche Erfahrung: Über autobiographisches Schreiben und Erinnern in sozialkommunikativen Kontexten." *Geschichte und Gesellschaft* 36: 93–128.

Hildenbrand, Bruno. 2012. "Objektive Daten im Gespräch: Die biographische Illusion: Der Gang der Argumentation bei Pierre Bourdieu." *Sozialer Sinn* 13: 57–100.

Holdenried, Michaela. 2000. *Autobiographie*. Stuttgart: Reclam.

Kanis, Leo, Jaak Billie, and Patrick Pasture, eds. 2010. *The Transformation of the Christian Churches in Western Europe 1945-1990*. Leuven: Leuven University Press.

Kleinberg, Ethan. 2007. "Haunting History: Deconstruction and the Spirit of Revision." *History and Theory* 47: 113–143.

Krondorfer, Björn. 2006. "Nationalsozialismus und Holocaust in Autobiographien protestantischer Theologen." In *Mit Blick auf die Täter: Fragen an die deutsche Theologie nach 1945*, edited by Björn Krondorfer, Katharina von Kellenbach, and Norbert Reck, 23–170. Gütersloh: Gütersloher Verlagshaus.

———. 2014. "Gender and Post-Conflict Self-Representation: Autobiographical Writings of German Theologians after 1945." *Contemporary Church History/Kirchliche Zeitgeschichte* 27: 102–119.

Kühl, Stefan. 2014. *Ganz normale Organisationen: Zur Soziologie des Holocaust*. Frankfurt a. M.: Suhrkamp.

Kühne, Thomas. 2006. *Kameradschaft: Die Soldaten des nationalsozialistischen Krieges und das 20. Jahrhundert*. Göttingen: Vandenhoeck & Ruprecht.

Kundrus, Birthe. 2017. *"Dieser Krieg ist der große Rassekrieg": Krieg und Holocaust in Europa*. Munich: C. H. Beck.

Künneth, Walter. 1979. *Lebensführungen: Der Wahrheit verpflichtet*. Wuppertal: Brockhaus.

Landwehr, Achim. 2008. *Historische Diskursanalyse*. Frankfurt: Campus.

Lehmann, Jürgen. 1988. *Bekennen—Erzählen—Berichten: Studien zu Theorie und Geschichte der Autobiographie*. Tübingen: Niemeyer.

Lejeune, Philippe. 1989. *On Autobiography*. Minneapolis: University of Minnesota Press.

Lessing, Hans-Ulrich. 2008. "Der Zusammenhang von Leben, Ausdruck und Verstehen: Diltheys späte hermeneutische Grundlegung der Geisteswissenschaften." In *Dilthey und die hermeneutische Wende in der Philosophie: Wirkungsgeschichtliche Aspekte seines Werkes*, edited by Gudrun Kühne-Bertram, 57–76. Göttingen: Vandenhoeck & Ruprecht.

Lilje, Hanns. 1973. *Memorabilia: Schwerpunkte eines Lebens*. Nuremberg: Laetare.

Loewenich, Walther von. 1979. *Erlebte Theologie: Begegnungen, Erfahrungen, Erwägungen*. Munich: Claudius-Verlag.

Machtan, Lother. 2013. "Autobiographie als geschichtspolitische Waffe: Die Memoiren des letzten kaiserlichen Kanzlers Max von Baden." *Vierteljahrshefte für Zeitgeschichte* 61: 481–512.

Martschukat, Jürgen, and Olaf Stieglitz. 2008. *Geschichte der Männlichkeiten*. Frankfurt: Campus.

Marwick, Arthur. 1998. *The Sixties: Cultural Revolution in Britain, France, Italy, and the United States, c. 1958–c. 1974*. Oxford: Oxford University Press.
McLeod, Hugh. 2007. *The Religious Crisis of the 1960s*. Oxford: Oxford University Press.
McNay, Lois. 2000. *Gender and Agency: Reconfiguring the Subject in Feminist and Social Theory*. London: Polity.
Meier, Kurt. 1976–1984. *Der evangelische Kirchenkampf*, 3 vols. Göttingen: Vandenhoeck & Ruprecht.
Misch, Georg. 1989. "Begriff und Ursprung der Autobiographie (1907/1948)." In *Die Autobiographie: Zu Form und Geschichte einer literarischen Gattung*, edited by Günter Niggl, 35–55. Darmstadt: Wissenschaftliche Buchgesellschaft.
Mosse, George. 1985. *Nationalism and Sexuality: Respectability and Abnormal Sexuality in Modern Europe*. New York: Howard Fertig.
———. 1996. *The Image of Man: The Creation of Modern Masculinity*. New York: Oxford University Press.
Mouffe, Chantal, and Ernesto Laclau. 1986. *Hegemony and Socialist Strategy: Towards a Radical Democratic Politics*. London: Verso.
Niemöller, Wilhelm. 1961. *Aus dem Leben eines Bekenntnispfarrers*. Bielefeld: Bechauf.
Nowak, Kurt. 1994. "Biographie und Lebenslauf in der Neueren und Neuesten Kirchengeschichte." *Verkündigung und Forschung* 39: 44–62.
Rahden, Till van. 2008. "Paternity, Rechristianization, and the Quest for Democracy in Postwar West Germany." In *Forschungsberichte aus dem Duitsland Instituut Amsterdam*, vol. 4, edited by Duitsland Instituut bij de Universiteit van Amsterdam, 53–71. Amsterdam: Duitsland Instituut bij de Universiteit van Amsterdam.
Rödder, Andreas. 1997. "Dichtung und Wahrheit: Der Quellenwert von Heinrich Brünings Memoiren und seine Kanzlerschaft." *Historische Zeitschrift* 265: 77–116.
Schissler, Hanna. 2001. " 'Normalization' as Project: Some Thoughts on Gender Relations in West Germany during the 1950s." In *The Miracle Years: A Cultural History of West Germany, 1949–1968*, edited by Hanna Schissler, 359–375. Princeton: Princeton University Press.
Seidel, Thomas A. 1999. "Im Wechsel der Systeme: Anmerkungen zur evangelischen Landeskirche Thüringens 1919 bis 1989." In *Von der babylonischen Gefangenschaft der Kirche im Nationalen: Regionalstudien zu Protestantismus, Nationalsozialismus und Nachkriegsgeschichte, 1930 bis 2000*, edited by Manfred Gailus and Wolfgang Krogel, 331–359. Berlin: Wichern.
Staats, Reinhart. 1994. "Die zeitgenössische Theologenautobiographie als theologisches Problem." *Verkündigung und Forschung* 39: 62–81.
Strohm, Christoph. 2011. *Die Kirchen im Dritten Reich*. Munich: C. H. Beck.
Thamer, Hans-Ulrich. 2002. *Der Nationalsozialismus*. Stuttgart: Reclam.

Trillhaas, Wolfgang. 1976. *Aufgehobene Vergangenheit: Aus meinem Leben*. Göttingen: Vandenhoeck & Ruprecht.
Wachsmann, Nikolaus. 2016. *KL: A History of the Nazi Concentration Camps*. London: Little, Brown.
Wagner-Egelhaaf, Michaela. 2005. *Autobiographie*. Stuttgart: J. B. Metzler.
Wendland, Heinz-Dietrich. 1977. *Wege und Umwege: 50 Jahre erlebte Theologie, 1919–1970*. Gütersloh: Gütersloher Verlagshaus.
Wu, Albert. 2009. "'Unafraid of the Gospel': Johann Hinrich Wichern and the Battle for the Soul of Prussian Prisons." *Church History* 78: 283–308.

Chapter 9

Post-Holocaust Conceptualizations of Masculinity in Austria

CARSON PHILLIPS

> The current tendency to pluralize masculinities and deconstruct gender is heavily influenced by postmodern philosophical currents that arose after WWII. . . . Postmodernism was born, however, not just out of a particular time but out of a particular place as well. That place was Auschwitz. It was there that modernity, humanism, figuratively and literally, went up in smoke.
>
> —Harry Brod, "Some Thoughts on Some Histories of Some Masculinities"

At the end of World War II, Austria required a massive effort to rebuild both its physical and societal structures. Vienna, the former imperial capital characterized by its splendorous Baroque and *Jugendstil* architecture and compact, chocolate-box inspired Innere Stadt, was in ruins. It was devastated by a bombing campaign that left a substantial segment of housing either fully or partially destroyed, with many apartments deemed uninhabitable. Compounding the situation were the several thousand bomb craters that permeated the city, making daily life in the "City of Dreams" anything but idyllic. The extensive physical damage extended to the infrastructure of sewers, gas, and water pipes and created a chaotic and disordered living condition. However, it was not only the city's material foundation that was shattered: the constructions of fascist masculinity that developed and flourished under nearly eight years of National Socialist regime were also in ruins.

As the city and country rebuilt, new models of masculinity emerged to define a new generation of men, paralleling at times the forging of a new Austrian national identity. This new post–World War II identity stressed Austrian*ness* as separate from German*ness*, and so Austrian masculinity defined itself as separate and different from German masculinity. Forging a new national identity and constructs of masculinity also meant confronting the realization that "600,000 registered Nazis made up one-third of the population" (Bukey 2000, 228); in addition, "1.2 million Austrian soldiers served in the German army and while many may not have been enthusiastic, most accepted the *Wehrmacht* as legitimate" (Fritsche 2012, 39). Compounded by the 1943 Moscow Declaration, which declared Austria the first victim of Nazi Germany aggression, the seeds were seemingly, yet unwittingly, set for new models of masculinity to emerge that resisted grappling with the nation's initial complex embrace of German National Socialism and its Austrian-born leader, Adolf Hitler. The Moscow Declaration states:

> The governments of the United Kingdom, the Soviet Union and the United States of America are agreed that Austria, the first free country to fall a victim to Hitlerite aggression, shall be liberated from German domination. They regard the annexation imposed on Austria by Germany on March 15, 1938, as null and void. They consider themselves as in no way bound by any charges effected in Austria since that date. They declare that they wish to see re-established a free and independent Austria and thereby to open the way for the Austrian people themselves, as well as those neighboring States which will be faced with similar problems, to find that political and economic security which is the only basis for lasting peace. Austria is reminded, however that she has a responsibility, which she cannot evade, for participation in the war at the side of Hitlerite Germany, and that in the final settlement account will inevitably be taken of her own contribution to her liberation.[1]

The last sentence to this declaration was forgotten by a country in the throes of reimagining itself, and consequently it remained dormant for several decades after the end of World War II. Denazification proceedings began systematically and in earnest. "Between 1945 and 1948 Austrian tribunals tried and convicted 10,694 persons for war crimes (usually committed on Austrian soil) and sentenced 43 to death" (Bukey 2000, 228). However, as the challenge of investigating Austria's vast party membership dragged on, the denazification process stoked resentment among a weary populace. The increasingly unpopular process was shelved as the "First-Victim myth" took on new relevance. In order to move forward and rebuild Austria, the foundational leaders of the Second Republic "were forced to conclude that economic reconstruction and social integration required the support of harmless followers and soldiers who believed that they were doing their duty" (228). Masculinity continued to be linked to national identity, just as it was during the National Socialist era.

During this period of flux, conceptualizations of masculinity encountered an important societal paradox. As Maria Fritsche has cogently argued, Austrian men who had deserted the *Wehrmacht* "frequently faced discrimination in their professional and social lives after the war, and they continued to be defamed as 'cowards' or 'traitors' for many decades" (2012, 38). Although deserters may have demonstrated a rejection of the fascist masculine ideal, they were not considered victims of National Socialism but rather a source of embarrassment. Deserters, it seems, broke the cardinal and time-honored tradition that intrinsically links masculinity to national identity. A man therefore must not renege on his military obligation to fight on behalf his homeland, regardless of whether the rationale provided by the regime for doing so calls into question the very nature of his masculinity. "In the eyes of the public, deserters had committed an unmanly action, which cast a suspicious light on their masculinity" (Fritsche 2012, 49).

It is in this cultural and historical milieu that the first of the new conceptualizations of Austrian masculinity emerged, once again synergistically linked to Austrian national identity. As historian Oliver Rathkolb has demonstrated, the overarching tenet characterizing this era was the emphasis on the cultural differences between Austrians and Germans and the cultural superiority of being Austrian. "The claim to higher cultural refinement was supposed to ensure for Austria the role of 'better Germany' and preferential treatment in the pan-German Reich" (Rathkolb 2010, 190). In the aftermath of World War II, the concept of Austrian cultural superiority was not only a founding characteristic for the national identity of the Second Republic, but it also influenced emerging constructs of masculinity.

As I will demonstrate in this chapter, Austrian maleness and gender performativity manifested themselves through a number of constructs that were linked to a new, burgeoning Austrian national identity. Complicity in the crimes of National Socialism was effectively silenced for several decades and did not, as I will elucidate later, influence Austrian maleness until the 1980s. The coalescence of these factors required men to carefully negotiate individual, community, and public manifestations of masculinity. Drawing on cultural representations in Austrian society, cinema, and literature, I examine four paradigmatic constructs of masculinity that emerged in postwar Austria: the Cultured Gentleman, the *Burschenschafter* (members of fraternities), the Soccer Player, and the Remembrance Activist. By following their trajectory from their origins in the immediate post–World War II period to representations in contemporary spheres of culture, politics, and society, I demonstrate that each of these four constructs has been and continues to be shaped by Austrian involvement with National Socialism. Although this is not an exhaustive investigation into each manifestation of maleness in Austria, it does provide a concise analysis of the foundational constructs. The representations I focus on have had a significant and enduring impact upon conceptualizations of Austrian masculinity.

The Cultured Gentleman

If there is one hegemonic model of masculinity that defines maleness in Austria since the end of World War II, it is the model of the "Cultured Gentleman." Derived from the foundational premise that equates Austrianness with being the better German, the cultured gentleman is manifested at all levels of society, such as business, politics, academia, and the arts and culture, thereby becoming the dominant model of hegemonic masculinity in Austria. This conceptualization is so enduring that it remains one of the defining characteristics of Austrian self-identification.

Rathkolb states that "the self-image of Austrians as a closed cultural nation was reflected in 1980 in a survey on 'Austria as the bearer of great cultural heritage,' a claim to which 47 per cent assented" (2010, 18). Remarkably, the percentage remained relatively stable over time. In 1987, 45 percent indicated agreement with this idea, while 74 percent of those surveyed additionally stressed Austria's cultural heritage in general. In the aftermath of World War II, this emphasis on the role of culture assisted in the rebuilding of the Austrian nation as well as new constructs of masculinity. Whether it was high culture, as in orchestral concerts and operatic performances, or the popular culture of the movie theaters, Austrian men were depicted as cultured, refined, and charming.

An early example of the emphasis placed on culture is the resumption of concerts by the Vienna Philharmonic on April 27, 1945. Austrian author Viktor Suchy describes the first announcement of concerts: "This city is bleeding from a thousand wounds; from millions of eyes flow tears of suffering and bitterness about the brown plague [National Socialism] that has ravaged this city of ours until recently. . . . Yet they have been unable, in spite of seven years of tyranny, to rob us of Austria, which has taken shape in our beloved music" (qtd. in Rathkolb 2010, 205). The resumption of concerts may have been an attempt of returning to normalcy, but it neglects the fact that "almost 50% of the musicians were card-carrying members of the NSDAP, compared with barely 20% in the Berlin Philharmonic."[2] Masculinity may have maintained an affinity to culture but the extent to which it embraced National Socialism was highly problematic. Far from coming to terms with the Philharmonic's close ties to National Socialism or acknowledging that the now-famous New Year Concert had been a Nazi creation, high culture was used to reinforce the First Victim myth; Austrian maleness was thus presented as the standard-bearer of a new Austria, separate and distinct from Germany.

The popular *Heimatfilm* genre that captivated German-speaking audiences after the war presented new models of masculinity that were in keeping with the cultured gentleman. "The most successful genre of the early postwar period has gone on to become one of the most critically disdained types of German films: namely, the *Heimatfilm*, which seemed to relegate the viewer to the cultural provinces" (Fehrenbach 1995, 8). As a genre, the *Heimatfilm* focused specifically on dramatic country landscapes and societal structuring, illustrating the connections between the countryside as represented cinematically and national identity and gender performativity. Film historian Johannes von Moltke comments, "Today the *Heimatfilm* has become virtually synonymous with the parochialism of German cinema during the Adenauer era, which more than one scholar prefers to remember as 'the Dark Ages,' nothing but *Heimatfilm* and reaction" (2005, 22). However, the genre is considerably more complex: It provided a site where 1950s film culture could negotiate central concerns with home, space, and belonging in the ongoing process of national construction, both in Germany and Austria. Culturally, the *Heimatfilm* represents an important domestic contribution to the construction of postwar Austrian masculinity. Although not immune to the influences of Americanism and the Western Allies, the *Heimatfilm* demonstrated an important and organic development of models of masculinity linked to the German-speaking lands and values that predated National Socialism.

As a cultural influencer, the *Heimatfilm* must neither be dismissed nor marginalized. From the regeneration of the *Heimatfilm* genre in the 1950s and 1960s, "approximately three hundred films were produced" (Zimmerman 2008, 175). Among the films that enjoyed commercial and critical success in Germany and Austria were: *Schwarzwaldmädel* (Black Forest girl, Berolina, dir. Hans Deppe, 1950), *Grün ist die Heide* (Green is the heath, Berolina, dir. Hans Deppe, 1951), *Die Fischerin vom Bodensee* (The fisher girl of Lake Constance, Neubach Film, dir. Harald Reinl, 1956), and *Hoch oben auf dem Berg* (High up on the mountain, Berolina, dir. Géza von Bolváry, 1957). Defining *Heimat* has been perhaps more difficult than describing what *Heimat* has come to represent or understanding what intrinsic meanings are associated with it. The Austrian-born, German Jewish author Jean Améry reflected on what *Heimat* meant from the perspective of someone who was forced into exile. He defines *Heimat* as a "land of childhood and youth," in which we have learned to control the "dialectic of knowing and perceiving, of trust and confidence" (qtd. in Vansant 2001, 36). Taking Améry's definition of *Heimat*, one can determine that Austrianness can be gleaned, at least for the many Austrian men of the postwar period, from an earlier period. Indeed, images of *Heimat* permeate the Romantic and *Bergfilm* genres that predate National Socialism. For the men who experienced their formative years during the German Reich, these earlier conceptualizations of *Heimat* were integrated into a new understanding of Germanness. The conceptualizations of *Heimat* were imagined, reconfigured, and represented for a new era of cinema.

As a domestic product, the genre of the *Heimatfilm* was important for relaying to the Austrian public a domestically occurring construct of masculinity. Undoubtedly, American films influenced the development of this genre, but the *Heimatfilm* also demonstrated the continuation of a domestic film industry rooted in German and Austrian traditions of land, culture, and community. However, it must be remembered that Austrians also took part in revitalizing and reestablishing the genre of the *Heimatfilm*. The masculinity exemplified in the *Heimatfilm* reinforced the concept of controlled masculinity that valued restraint over aggression and emphasized that the strength of a man's character could be demonstrated by responsible behavior rather than violent confrontation. This construct of nonaggressive masculinity shares similarities with the Soccer Player and the later construct of the Remembrance Activist; yet, and importantly, it was linked to the Austrian soil and tradition. I posit that the genre also influenced strongly the conceptualization and representation of a new Austrian masculinity. Often characterized by themes of blissful heterosexual domesticity and an idyllic rural lifestyle, the *Heimatfilm* offered the German-speaking public a sense of comfort and succor during the tremendous social upheaval of the postwar period. Rather than providing viewers with a sense of escapism, the *Heimatfilm* offered new constructs of masculine behavior where men overcame challenges and obstacles without resorting to armed or physical violence. These new conceptualizations helped to reestablish a separate Austrian national identity and masculinity.

Period pieces such as *Sissi* (Erma-Film, dir. Ernst Marischka, 1955), which recreated the specificity of Habsburg Vienna, also fall into the genre of *Heimatfilm*. It delivered surprisingly similar elements of egalitarianism, control, and independent thinking that came to characterize the new Austrian model of masculinity. Early in the film, when Sissi's family life in Bavaria is introduced, her father, the Baron, is portrayed as a purveyor of egalitarianism. The Baron prefers socializing in the unrestricted and open atmosphere of his local tavern, where class consciousness is barely recognized, rather than attending formal society functions. Even in the imperial Habsburg court, Franz Josef and his father are portrayed as responsible, sensitive men. A historical drama, it nevertheless intersects with the *Heimatfilm* in presenting its masculine characters very much in keeping with this construct of the new postwar Austrian male. Until recently, *Sissi* was one of the few Austrian films known outside of German-speaking countries. It was just one of the many historical costume films that were hugely profitable at the time. It offered hope during a time of rebuilding the Austrian nation and it provided comforting, responsible, and trustworthy depictions of masculinity that were embraced by the populace and came to permeate all levels and representations of Austrian society. In short, *Sissi* brought to life the new Austrian male, and this man was a figure the country was ready and eager to accept.

The *Burschenschafter*

The pan-Germanist ideals that characterized the National Socialist era lived on in the construct of Austria's academic *Burschenschaften*, right-wing male student fraternities that envisioned one culturally German state reunited with Austria and the autonomous region of Südtirol in northern Italy. *Burschenschaften* that embraced German *völkisch* nationalism were substantially different in nature and function from Catholic fraternities. Historian Bernhard Weidinger describes them as "acting as standard-bearers of German nationalism in Austria after 1945 and being strongly represented in the ranks of the Freedomite Party of Austria (*Freiheitliche Partei Österrreichs* / FPÖ), they have been able to maintain a degree of political relevance up until the present day—their intimate ideological, personal, and institutional entanglement with the National Socialist regime notwithstanding" (2014, 213).[3] To understand the longevity and the allure of these *Burschenschaften*, one must understand the conceptualization of masculinity they represent and their appeal to young Austrian males.

Foremost in an analysis of *Burschenschafter* masculinity is the homosocial dynamic within these groups, a reinforced masculinity, and the perception of belonging to a stable community in the midst of an unstable and ever-changing world. In a 2015 opinion piece, Jörg R. Mayer proudly self-identifies as a member of right-wing *Burschenschaft Teutonia*, which he describes in endearing terms: "Wegen der großartigen Menschen, die ich dort kennenlernen durfte. Wegen der Erfahrungen, die ich machen durfte. Wegen der Erlebnisse, an die ich mich mein Leben lang erinnern werde" (Because of the great people I could get to know there. Because of the experiences I could make there. Because of the experiences I will remember all my life).[4] Mayer's description is vague enough to encourage one to imagine that this is just another social club for likeminded Austrian university males. In reality, there is a darker and more problematic side to *Burschenschafter* masculinity.

First, the exclusionary nature of the *Burschenschaft* means that it cultivates a model of masculinity that harkens back to the National Socialist ideal of a *Volksgemeinschaft* (people's community). Quoting a publication of the Alemannia *Burschenschaft* in Vienna, Bernhard Weidinger states, "In order to keep German soil German, the people living on that soil—perceived more as vessels of German-*ness* than as individuals—are called upon to cultivate their German identity and wherever possible to isolate themselves from any alien [*volksfremd*] influence" (2014, 215). The *Burschenschaften* are also known for promoting far-right political opinions and historical interpretations. For example, in 2005 the Viennese fraternity Olympia invited convicted Holocaust denier David Irving to address their membership. More recently, Teutonia invited as speaker the rabble rousing, Turkish German author Akif Pirinçci, who has perplexingly embraced the far-right movement in Germany. Rather than a progressive model of masculinity and citizenship, the *Burschenschaft* is reinvigorating a pan-Germanic model of narrowly defined maleness intertwined with an exclusionary version of nationhood. In this way the *Burschenschaften* distinguish themselves from the "Corps," fraternal organizations that focus on developing the upper echelons of society regardless of ethnicity, and from German Catholic fraternities (or *Cartellverband*), which are not ethnically exclusionary and do not permit fencing.

Indeed, the ritual fencing duel, known as the *Mensur*, seems to be a defining characteristic of *Burschenschaft* masculinity. In what appears reminiscent of the nineteenth century, men fight as a point of honor and see any resulting scars in a similar manner. In the 2015 Vice Alps documentary *Ehre, Freiheit, Vaterland* (Honor, freedom, fatherland) *Burschenschaft* members described the ritual duel as something that bonds two men together.[5] It is a homosocial activity that defines masculinity through a potentially dangerous and bloody sport; it is a shared experience between two men fighting with swords for dominance and superiority over the other. In the Viennese fencing tradition of the *Burschenschaften*, duelers fight sixty rounds with four hits each, but commonly a person is eliminated before the duel gets to this point. Should either of the duelers be wounded on the face or head, they will likely be scarred for life. Scarification on the cheek, head, or chest—the so-called *Schmiss*—is a classic initiation rite in some fraternities.[6] Any resulting scarring becomes a symbolic badge of honor, and these young men end up wearing their *Burschenschaft* affiliation publicly for all to see. It is a mark most of the duelers are proud to wear, for it shows they have taken the *Mensur* challenge and not retreated from danger. Like the heroes of epic sagas, they have lived to tell others about their encounter and how they fought bravely to survive. In twenty-first-century Vienna, the *Burschenschaft* provides an opportunity for young men to participate in a nineteenth-century ritual within a pan-Germanic milieu.

At their social events and meetings, *Burschenschaft* members wear uniforms with gloves and hats that distinguish their fraternity from others. The uniforms invoke a nineteenth-century military tradition and are easily recognizable, strengthening a sense of belonging to an elite or exclusive club. In Vienna, this construct of masculinity is put on display at the Akademiker Ball, which occurs annually in late January or early February. The gala is a part of Vienna's annual ball season and attempts to normalize the far-right *Burschenschaften*. Holding the gala at the Hofburg palace, the seat of imperial power during the Habsburg monarchy, lends legitimacy to the event, to the *Burschenschaften*, and to the far-right construct of masculinity it promotes.

In 2012, UNESCO officially removed Vienna's ball season from its list of Austrian cultural heritage events, in part due to the public protest over the Akademiker Ball and its perceived links to far-right political parties and politicians. Ewa Nowotny, president of Austria's UNESCO commission, clarified that cultural events must represent the list's foundational principle, "which gives a special priority to tolerance and respect for other cultures, and to esteem for cultural diversity."[7] The decision indicates that there are at least some clear boundaries between the "cultured gentleman" of Austrian masculinity and the resuscitated, pan-Germanic, exclusionary model represented by the *Burschenschafter*.

Still, despite their high-profile gala and connections to the FPÖ political establishment, the men of the *Burschenschaften* frequently see themselves, at least superficially, in the tradition of being victimized for their ideas and activities. Claiming that the *Burschenschaften* are misunderstood in Austria, Jörg R. Mayer pleads: "Sometimes I just want to ask: What do you think is wrong with us? How did we harm you? And what can we do to help you just put up with us? Or are you only satisfied when we are all gone? If you have made us disappear? Why do not you just let me live my life according to how we want?"[8] Such shallow commentary indicates either an inability to recognize and admit the problematic connection to fascist masculinity that the *Burschenschafter* construct represents or a willingness to play the victim in hopes of currying favor with the general public. Or it might be an amalgam of both.

Similarly, when guests of the 2012 Akademiker Ball were subjected to anti-extremist protesters before entering the Hofburg, FPÖ leader HC Strache, who in 2017 became vice chancellor of Austria, compared the evening to the Nazi *Reichskristallnacht* of November 1938, when waves of anti-Jewish pogroms had been unleashed across the German Reich. Strache declared that the guests, consisting of far-right *Burschenschaft* members and far-right politicians, "are the new Jews."[9] In an astonishing appropriation of victimhood, it seems that this construction of masculinity invokes elements of fascist masculinity in the private sphere while claiming victim status in public. The appropriation is even more audacious when one considers that the 2012 gala was held on January 27, the United Nations designated International Holocaust Remembrance Day. Unfortunately, this problematic model of masculinity does not seem to be losing its traction in Austria despite its obvious far-right tendencies.

The Soccer Player

The construct of soccer player masculinity in Austria represents a more complex manifestation than might be imagined. It transcends generations, integrates ethno-cultural expressions of masculinity, and at times marginalizes nonconforming constructs of sexuality. It is characterized by the functions it attributes to men: producer, protector, and provider. It is one of the dominant and most influential models of Austrian masculinity today as exemplified by the immense popularity of the soccer-playing male in Austria (as in the other regions of German-speaking Europe). In postwar Austria the soccer player became, for some segments of society, an idealized male. Physically attractive and increasingly culturally diverse, the Austrian soccer player has become synonymous with masculinity on and off the sporting field.

The lithe athletic male as represented by the soccer player is distinctly different from the Aryan male that National Socialism sought to fashion. Addressing the Hitler Youth movement, Hitler described the Aryan masculinity he wished to infuse into German youth in the following infamous words: "der deutsche Junge der Zukunft muß schlank und rank sein, flink wie Windhunde, zäh wie Leder und hart wie Kruppstahl" (the German boy of the future must be slim and trim, swift as the greyhound, tough as leather and hard as Krupp steel; qtd. in Dearn 2006, 16). The lean, hard body encouraged by the Hitler Youth was in preparation for the role of the male warrior. "Physical exercise played a crucial part in forming the fascist male; fascism accepted the by then traditional notion that a fit body was the sign of a manly spirit. . . . The extreme of fascist manliness mattered, of course, for it brought into sharp relief the warrior elements of masculinity, even while it attempted to direct and channel manly aggression and energy" (Mosse 1998, 162). The postwar Austrian soccer player was indeed lean and swift, but he displayed flexibility, control, individuality, and frequently sensitivity—characteristics at odds with those of the fascist male. The athletic male in National Socialism was part of something greater than himself and his team: he was inextricably linked to the concept of nationhood and *Volksgemeinschaft*. The male body had been elevated as a symbol of nationalism.

Patricia Vettel-Becker argues that athletic competitions are akin to war. As such it is not surprising that athletic masculinity was readily accepted in postwar Austria. Indeed, the successful athlete required many of the same characteristics upon which warrior masculinity was constructed: courage, stamina, discipline, and physical strength (see Vettel-Becker 2005, 121). Unlike the warrior-soldier, however, the postwar Austrian soccer player does not require body-altering protective equipment. Indeed, the lean, muscled physique of the soccer player bears no resemblance to his counterpart the heavily padded North American football player or to the padded and helmeted player found in competitive hockey leagues. Rather, the soccer player relies upon his minimal clothing modifications—shin guards—and presents masculinity as competitive yet controlled, sculpted in physique but not overly muscular. He moves with agility rather than force. This new construct of Austrian masculinity as defined by the soccer player is a realistic body image that can be attained by the average male.

Indeed, the body culture of the soccer player is dissimilar to fascist aesthetics. This is not the image of the male body infused with strength and idealized beauty codified in Leni Riefenstahl's 1938 propaganda films, *Olympia 1: Teil—Fest der Völker* (Olympia part 1: Festival of nations) and *Olympia 2: Teil—Fest der Schönheit* (Olympia part 2: Festival of beauty). Riefenstahl's carefully shot and edited productions presented the athletic male as bodily perfection and heir to a legacy of greatness that was first established by the athletes of ancient Greece. Such a perfected human form was interpreted as the symbol for Aryan beauty and masculinity. George Mosse notes: "The male body had to be prepared carefully before it could be offered for public scrutiny. The skin must be hairless, smooth and bronzed. The body would thus be almost transparent; with as few individual features as possible, it would lose any sex appeal" (1998, 173). The condition of such a male body was elevated to symbolic and nationalistic proportions.

The soccer player, on the other hand, does not offer any hint of an innate racial purity to be juxtaposed against a supposedly racially impure male counterpart. One need to look only at the makeup of the Austrian National Soccer Team (*Österreichische Fußballnationalmannschaft*) to observe a new Austrian masculinity that embraces cultural and ethnic diversity within the rubric of Austrian maleness. Star defender David Alaba was born in Vienna to a Filipina mother and Nigerian father; goalkeeper Ramazan Özcan is of Turkish Austrian ethnicity; striker Rubin Okotie was born in Pakistan to an Austrian mother and Nigerian father; midfielder Valentino Lazaro was born in Graz to an Angolan father and

Greek mother; and defender Aleksandar Dragović was born in Vienna to parents who immigrated from Serbia. All were educated in Austria and self-identify as Austrians. Soccer has afforded opportunities for the opening up of the concept of Austrian maleness based on shared linguistic, educational, cultural, and social commonalities.

Nor is the Austrian soccer player synergistically linked to any ideology of sexual purity. Unlike the athletes in Riefenstahl's films, the soccer player is not indicative of fascist aesthetics. Susan Sontag argues:

> A utopian aesthetics (physical perfection; identity as a biological given) implies an ideal eroticism: sexually converted into the magnetism of leaders and the joy of followers. The fascist ideal is to transform sexual energy into a "spiritual" force, for the benefit of the community. . . . Fascist aesthetics is based on the containment of vital forces; movements are confined, held tight, held in. (Sontag 1975, 93)

In contrast, the soccer player represents a responsible and controlled construct of masculinity predicated on values of teamwork and accountability. Unlike the fascist warrior, the soccer player is competitive rather than destructive. He emerges as a positive form of masculine identification in the wake of the discrediting of National Socialism. In the postwar period, the sports movement was free from influences of National Socialism that had integrated athleticism into expressions of the dominance of the Third Reich and the new Aryan male.

From the 1920s onward, soccer in Vienna found its most fruitful terrain in the proletarian suburbs. "This was where it became a mass spectacle, where it had its most faithful and devoted fans, and where its transformation into a modern spectacle began" (Horak 2006, 27). Undoubtedly, the fact that soccer did not require expensive equipment or special training facilities made it accessible to young men and boys from underprivileged backgrounds. It became a sport that could neutralize the background of its players, providing an opportunity for players to succeed based upon individual merit. The lean athletic physique of the soccer player depended upon his skill on the field, not on the strength of his armaments or superiority of his tanks and weapons. Nor did it require an expensive education: anyone could play this sport. While soccer may provide a competitive opportunity analogous to war, it does not carry with it the consequence of life, death, and destruction.

The rise of soccer in the public consciousness mirrored a significant attitudinal shift among postwar Austrians: expressing national pride and masculinity became acceptable through soccer. For many men, rites of passage related to manhood are increasingly associated with sports rather than with military service. A sport without any type of object that could be conceived of as being a weapon (no hockey stick, no baseball or cricket bat), soccer relied upon controlled masculinity and teamwork in order to ensure success. Although the Austrian National Soccer Team enjoyed only limited success in recent years in its quest for a European soccer championship, it has aroused a sense and feeling of national pride that is rarely openly exhibited by Austrians.

Soccer continues to provide Austrian men with a concept of masculinity that is part of a shared group experience and reaches all segments of society. Through broadcasting of sporting events on television and internet, the prevalent depictions of Austrian masculinity are disseminated beyond Austria's geographic borders. It also provides men with the ability to perform their masculinity. As a sport that enjoys tremendous mass appeal, it offers men another model of controlled yet powerful masculinity, either as spectators participating in the massively popular public viewing of championship games, or participants in one of the many soccer clubs. Incontrovertibly, soccer fills an important void in the realm of masculine identity construction. Soccer provides men with the opportunity to work cohesively as members of a competitive team, experience same-sex camaraderie, and demonstrate the pride of a nation without the dangers or aggression of war.

Vettel-Becker succinctly posits that it is the physicality of the bodies of boxers that is integral to constructing a model of athletic masculinity. She writes that "the construction of hard, large muscles reinforces the phallus as the supreme emblem of power without necessitating focus on the penis, which not only fails to remain hard but carries too great a homoerotic charge" (2005, 122). Similarly, I argue that the physical appearance and the actions of the male soccer player's bodies are fundamental to defining and codifying new constructs of masculinity. For Austrian men, the sinewy yet supple, lithe yet powerful body of the soccer player came to represent the idealized form of the new Austrian male. Whether clothed or partially unclothed—as soccer players are notorious for removing their jerseys after scoring a goal—the aesthetic of the Austrian soccer player body is coded heterosexual. This aesthetic subsequently reinforced heteronormativity as the ideal and socially acceptable expressions of masculinity in generations of young Austrian men. At the same time, soccer provided an important homosocial context for men to gather together. It fulfilled not only the desire to compete in an athletic setting but it also allowed men to gaze upon the physicality of other men's bodies in an acceptable and admissible manner without the fear or threat of being labeled homosexual. Indeed, homosexuality, which remained a criminal offense in Austria until 1971. Given the societal constraints against homosexuality, the ability of sport to provide a legitimate venue to gaze upon the male body cannot be underestimated. The construct of soccer player masculinity, like military models of masculinity, developed as assumedly heterosexual, but it permitted a homosexual gazing within defined parameters.

The physical performativity of masculinity exhibited by star players such as Austrian National Soccer Team forward Marko Arnautovic influences younger generations of fans and players. Born in Vienna to an Austrian mother and Serbian father, Arnautovic has a penchant for changing his hairstyle and hair color and for decorating his body with tattoos symbolizing important life-cycle events and milestones. His extrovert personality as well as his athleticism on the field have made him a household name and a cultural signifier to young Austrian males. Whether it is his short, bleached-blonde haircut or the shaved sides with topknot that he sported at the EUFA Euro 2016, Arnautovic's athletic prowess allows him to experiment with male performativity in a sphere that is watched and emulated by generations of young Austrian males. He is able to take chances with his appearance, don an avant-garde hairstyle at the risk of ridicule, or show tenderness to another player without damaging his heterosexual identity. In the end, Arnautovic is protected by his athletic prowess and his heterosexuality. There is perhaps no stronger representation of a mass construct of masculinity in Austria than the soccer player.

The Remembrance Activist

The fourth paradigm evidenced in Austrian civil society is one that I call the "Remembrance Activist," who emerged in the late 1980s and early 1990s. Not surprisingly, this coincides with what is now known as the "Waldheim affair." A turning point in how the Second Republic imagined itself and how Austrian maleness dealt with its complicity in the crimes of National Socialism, the Waldheim affair was responsible for a new construct of masculinity. This "new man" rejected military service and attempted to come to terms with the past. In doing so, he brought awareness of Austrian complicity in National Socialism and the Holocaust to the forefront.

In 1985, Kurt Waldheim, former secretary general of the United Nations (1972–1981), launched a campaign for the office of president of the Federal Republic. When it was revealed that Waldheim had falsified his autobiographical account of wartime service by omitting crucial events, he became embroiled in an international controversy. Whereas he had declared that he had been discharged from active service in 1942 and had spent the remainder of the war in Vienna, documents proved that he returned to active service in 1943 with Army Group E of the *Wehrmacht* in the Balkans. Waldheim's unit had taken part in the violent deportations of the Jewish population to Auschwitz-Birkenau. The result of this discovery was an international episode that demanded a clear historical record documenting Waldheim's action and role in the *Wehrmacht*. "This successful playing of the Nazi card against a federal president—a move then unheard of in the history of the Second Republic—made it clear that the taboo of addressing NSDAP membership in a political context was broken" (Rathkolb 2010, 254).

Although Waldheim eventually won the presidential election and served from 1986 to 1992, he ended up paying a heavy price. Isolated by being placed on a watch list of people to be refused entry to the United States, Waldheim became persona non grata and was unable to fulfill many functions associated with the Austrian presidency. He did not seek reelection in 1992. An international committee of historians was appointed by the Austrian government to examine Waldheim's role in World War II and to provide conclusive answers. Although their report did not find any evidence of Waldheim being personally involved in any war crimes, the committee cited evidence that Waldheim must have known about war crimes that took place. The result was damning, and his political career was over. As historian Robert Herzstein argues, "The fact that Waldheim played a significant role in military units that unquestionably committed war crimes makes him at the very least morally complicit in those crimes" (1988, 260). Waldheim retreated into relative obscurity in private life, and a new chapter in Austrian maleness opened up, one in which Austria's complicity in World War II and the Holocaust was examined.

Part of this reawakening and discovery of Austrian involvement in World War II were young men who rejected the expected duty of mandatory military service. Although it was possible to be excused from mandatory military service upon completing high school, there was no official alternative, and each case was assessed and decided upon individually. In 1992, Andreas Hörtnagl and Andreas Maislinger successfully lobbied the Austrian government to accept the establishment of an alternative to mandatory military service. Their aim was to increase awareness about the Holocaust among Austrian youth, promote education, and demonstrate a tangible form of Austrian reconciliation with the past. With the creation of the Austrian Holocaust Memorial Service, young Austrian males, known as *Gedenkdieners* (Holocaust Memorial Servants), had the possibility to complete an equivalent form of civil service at Holocaust memorials and educational centers outside of Austria. Although the participant numbers remain relatively small—between forty and fifty young men are afforded this opportunity annually—the program is extremely popular with educational centers. The demand for *Gedenkdieners* far exceeds the number of accepted applicants.

Young Austrian males choosing to go abroad and perform Holocaust memorial service around the globe represent a newly emergent form of masculinity that could not have been imagined at the end of World War II. In doing so, these young men become de facto goodwill ambassadors for their country: non-Austrians are introduced to Austrian men embodying a soft masculinity created in direct opposition to militarized masculinity. It is a masculinity that is both resilient and stable. In some ways, it might resemble aspects of the "cultured gentleman," with the distinction that these young men are actively engaging with Austria's legacy of shared responsibility in National Socialism and are motivated by a strong desire to initiate change at home and abroad. This new form of maleness developed at least twenty years after soft masculinity had already spread in Germany. This delay can be explained in part as the lingering effect of the "First Victim" myth in Austria. Describing the origins of soft masculinity in Germany in the 1970s, literary theorist Barbara Kosta notes that it developed "in response to demands of the women's movement and a raised consciousness of power relations" when "masculinity/patriarchy came under rigorous scrutiny" (2001, 224). As this new, supposedly liberal-minded ideal of masculinity emerged, the tension between the spheres of sexuality, nationalism, and masculinity grew, culminating in the now iconic moment of German Chancellor Willy Brandt's *Warschauer Kniefall* in 1970. An act of humility to some, controversial to many more, there can be no doubt that this simple but dramatic gesture of kneeling at the foot of the Ghetto Fighters' Memorial in Warsaw, Poland, could only have been made by someone who had experienced the tension of masculinity so prevalent after the war. As a gesture of reconciliation and repentance, with its Christian overtones, Brandt was determined to prevent the Nazi version of militarized masculinity from becoming again a dominant expression of masculinity.

In Austria, an equivalent acknowledgment of responsibility for past actions took place on July 8, 1991, when Franz Vranitzky, chancellor of Austria, acknowledged unequivocally in a speech before the Austrian parliament his country's "shared responsibility for the suffering that was brought over other human beings and peoples, if not by Austria as a state, by citizens of this country."[10] It was an official statement that moved away from depicting Austria as "Hitler's first victim" to one of "shared responsibility" for World War II and the Holocaust. On June 9, 1993, on a state visit to Israel, Vranitzky was even more concise:

> We acknowledge all the facts of our history and the deeds of all parts of our population, the good as well as the bad. Just as we claim credit for our good deeds, we must beg forgiveness for the evil ones. Jews, gypsies, the physically and mentally handicapped, homosexuals, members of minorities, those who were persecuted for political and religious reasons.[11]

After several decades of declaring oneself to be the first victim of Nazi aggression, Austrian self-perceptions, along with new constructs of masculinity, began to change.

Although the number of young men carrying out Holocaust Memorial Service is relatively small, they represent an important and vital image. Many are multipliers who share their experiences with students, family members, and friends; many go on to study and work in areas of human rights and education and are committed to building a fair and equitable civil society. Perhaps most importantly, through their placement outside of Austria, they meet and work with Holocaust survivors and Holocaust educators who otherwise might not have an opportunity to engage with young Austrian men embodying a refreshingly alternative form of masculinity.

The Intersection of Sexuality and Gender

Before concluding, I want to add a few thoughts on the intersectionality of sexuality with masculinity—an important issue that can deepen and enrich the constructs I have presented in this chapter. In postwar Austria, it is evident that homosexuality remained outside the margins of hegemonic masculinity. Gay rights in Austria have followed a relatively slow pace due in part to the alpine nation's predominately Roman Catholic, conservative society and to the slow shift of perception from being the first victim of Nazi aggression to a shared responsibility regarding the crimes of National Socialism. Even the cultured gentleman, the dominant model of masculinity, remained until recently avowedly heterosexual. It was not until 2003 that cohabitating same-sex couples in Austria were given the same rights as cohabitating opposite-sex couples. This was followed by registered partnerships for same-sex couples in 2010; joint adoption rights for couples came into effect in 2016. Upon a ruling by Austria's Constitutional Court, same-sex marriage became legal on January 1, 2019.

This rather slow progression toward the acceptance of homosexuality within legal, sociopolitical, and business frameworks has kept homosexual men for a long time on the margins of society. Relationships between homosexual men were coded as being outside of the law; they were burdened by the weight of being perceived as immoral. Australian sociologist Raewyn Connell argues that "from the point of view of hegemonic masculinity the potential for homoerotic pleasure was expelled from the masculine and located in a deviant group, symbolically assimilated to women or to beasts" (2005, 196). In their expulsion from hegemonic masculinity, homosexual relationships were also silenced. This seems to have been the case of Jörg Haider, the controversial former leader of the FPÖ, affiliated first with the *Burschenschaft Albia* and later with *Silvania*. Although publicly outed in 2000 by the *Berliner Tageszeitung*, Haider deftly avoided any questions concerning his sexuality, even though it remained a subject of interest to Austrian media.[12] Undoubtedly, this reluctance to integrate homosexuals into hegemonic masculinity was partially due to the embedded privilege of heterosexuality in societal, cultural, and religious institutions.

A significant crack in the social authority of Austria's hegemonic masculinity appeared when then Chancellor Christian Kern addressed an at-capacity audience from the main stage at the festival that followed Vienna's gay pride parade in June 2016. When asked why he spoke at the festival in the Sigmund Freud Park, Kern replied, "Ja ich bin der Bundeskanzler und ich bin auf der Regenbogenparade, aber na und? Mein Gott, es ist 2016 und die Zeit dafür war überreif" (Yes, I am the chancellor and I am at the Rainbow Parade, so what? My God, it is 2016 and the time for this was overdue).[13] For many in the audience, Kern's words symbolically echoed those of Canadian prime minister Justin Trudeau, whose pithy comment a year earlier, when questioned on why he insisted on gender balance in the formation of his cabinet, was simply, "Because it is 2015."[14] Kern, the embodiment of the cultured gentleman construct of masculinity, demonstrated an openness and willingness to see hegemonic masculinity become more inclusive.

Conclusion

Arguably, perhaps more than other European nations (with the exception of Germany), Austrian conceptualizations of masculinity reflect an inherent connection to the National Socialist regime that ruled the small alpine nation for approximately eight years. This consanguinity may be because the small nation of 8.5 million people covers an area of approximately 84,000 square kilometers, all that remains of the former vast Austro-Hungarian Empire.[15] As a multinational and multiethnic state, the former empire spanned over 620,000 square kilometers, more than seven times its current size. As the bearers of a vast and rich history that harkens back to the glory days of the Habsburg Empire, Austria had to periodically readjust its concepts of nationhood, nationality, gender, and masculinity.

I have argued that Austria's slower-paced accounting for its complicity with the National Socialist past contributed to how masculinities were perceived. In the years following 1945, as Austria settled comfortably into its role as the first victim of Hitlerite aggression, new constructs of masculinity emerged in response to changing societal, political, and economic conditions. A major turning point resulted from the Waldheim affair in 1986 and irrevocably changed the Second Republic's sense of nationhood and masculinity. What I am suggesting is that the process by which Austria officially changed its position from "First Victim" to one of "Shared Responsibility" in the crimes of National Socialism shaped Austrian constructs of masculinities. The inquiry into representations of masculinities has the potential to transform our understanding of historical events; in turn, we can observe that masculinities are formed in response to the continual ebb and flow of historical and social crises.

Acknowledgments

I would like to thank Dr. Susan Ingram and Dr. Markus Reisenleitner for helpful advice with this chapter, and the Vienna Wiesenthal Institute for the fellowship that permitted the research to be conducted.

Notes

1. For the complete text of the Moscow Declaration, see http://avalon.law.yale.edu/wwii/moscow.asp.

2. "The Vienna Philharmonic's Nazi Past: Lifting the Veil of Deliberate Ignorance," March 16, 2013, by Fritz Trümpi, retrieved August 2016, https://www.theguardian.com/commentisfree/2013/mar/16/vienna-philharmonic-nazi-past.

3. Weidinger prefers this "translation as an alternative to the more common usage 'Austrian Freedom Party'. Apart from mirroring the German name more accurately, the term 'freedomite' accentuates the blend of liberal and nationalist traditions of thought that is characteristic of the FPÖ. . . . Other than liberalism, freedomite ideology emphasizes the collective dimension of freedom (the freedom of a people in an ethnic sense) at the expense of individual rights and freedoms" (2014, 213).

4. Jörg R. Mayer, "Warum ich Burschenschafter geworden bin," June 2016, http://www.vice.com/alps/read/warum-ich-burschenschafter-bin-715.

5. Burschenschaften in Österreich, July 2016, http://www.vice.com/alps/video/vice-alps-burschenschaften-oesterreich-teil-1-001.

6. Laurence Doering, Vera Mair, and Werner Reisinger, "Austria's Nazi Frat Boys?" *The Vienna Review*, March 5, 2012, retrieved July 2016, http://www.viennareview.net/news/front-page/austrias-nazi-frat-boys.

7. "Vienna Ball Dropped from UNESCO Austrian Heritage List," BBC.com, January 19, 2012, retrieved August 2016, http://www.bbc.com/news/world-europe-16636732.

8. See note 1. The original German reads: "Ich möchte manchmal einfach fragen: Was stört euch an uns? Was verdammt tun wir euch denn? Und was können wir tun, damit ihr ertragen könnt, dass wir auch da sind? Oder seid ihr erst zufrieden, wenn wir alle nicht mehr da sind? Wenn ihr uns weggemacht habt? Warum lasst ihr mich nicht einfach mein Leben nach meinen Wünschen leben?"

9. "Strache auf WKR-Ball: 'Wir sind die neuen Juden,'" *Der Standard*, January 29, 2012, retrieved August 2016, http://derstandard.at/1326504047903/STANDARD-Bericht-Strache-auf-WKR-Ball-Wir-sind-die-neuen-Juden.

10. Fund for Reconciliation, Peace and Cooperation, retrieved August 2016, http://www.reconciliationfund.at/db/admin/de/index_main9304.html?cbereich=3&ctchema=341&carticle=602&fromlist=1.

11. Fund for Reconciliation, Peace and Cooperation.

12. "HOSI Wien zum Outing Haiders als Homosexueller," March 20, 2000, retrieved May 2018, http://www.hosiwien.at/haiderouting/hosi-reaktion/.

13. "Kanzler Kern auf der Regenbogenparade: 'Na und? Es ist 2016,'" *Die Presse*, June 18, 2016.

14. "Trudeau's 'Because it's 2015' Retort Draws International Attention," *The Globe and Mail*, November 5, 2015, retrieved July 2016, http://www.theglobeandmail.com/news/politics/trudeaus-because-its-2015-retort-draws-international-cheers/article27119856/.

15. Today, the alpine republic is also characterized by a strong sense of regionalism. Austria's nine *Bundesländer* (provinces) allow for differences in how maleness is performed in combination with regionalism. The adherence to distinctive regional dialects and region-specific *Trachten* (traditional clothing) further reinforces a connection to regional identity, exposing gender performativity to more scrutiny and observations.

References

Bukey, Evan Burr. 2000. *Hitler's Austria: Popular Sentiment in the Nazi Era*. Chapel Hill: University of North Carolina Press.

Connell, R. W. 2005. *Masculinities*, 2nd ed. Berkeley: University of California Press.

Dearn, Alan. 2006. *The Hitler Youth 1933–1945*. Oxford: Osprey.

Fehrenbach, Heide. 1995. *Cinema in Democratizing Germany: Reconstructing National Identity after Hitler*. Chapel Hill: University of North Carolina Press.

Fritsche, Maria. 2012. "Proving One's Manliness: Masculine Self-Perceptions of Austrian Deserters in the Second World War." *Gender & History* 24, no. (April): 35–55.

Herzstein, Robert Edwin. 1988. *Waldheim: The Missing Years*. New York: Arbor House–William Morrow Press.

Horak, Roman. 2006. "Germany versus Austria: Soccer, Urbanism and National Identity." In *German Soccer: History, Culture, Society*, edited by Alan Tomlinson and Christopher Young, 23–35. New York: Routledge.

Kosta, Barbara. 2001. "*Väterliteratur*, Masculinity, and History." In *Conceptions of Postwar German Masculinity*, edited by Roy Jerome, 219–241. Albany: State University of New York Press.

Moltke, Johannes von. 2005. *No Place Like Home: Locations of Heimat in German Cinema*. Berkeley: University of California Press.

Mosse, George L. 1998. *The Image of Man: The Creation of Modern Masculinity*. Reprint. New York: Oxford University Press.

Rathkolb, Oliver. 2010. *The Paradoxical Republic*. New York: Berghahn Books.

Sontag, Susan. 1975. "Fascinating Fascism." *The New York Review of Books*, February 6, 1975. http://www.nybooks.com/articles/1975/02/06/fascinating-fascism/. Accessed July 16, 2016.

Vansant, Jacqueline. 2001. *Reclaiming Heimat: Trauma and Mourning in Memoirs by Jewish Austrian Reémigrés*. Detroit: Wayne State University Press.

Vettel-Becker, Patricia. 2005. *Shooting from the Hip: Photography, Masculinity, and Postwar America*. Minneapolis: University of Minnesota Press.

Weidinger, Bernhard. 2014. "'. . . in order to Keep German Soil German': Austrian *Burschenschaften*, National Ethnopolitics and the South Tirol Conflict after 1945." *Austrian History Yearbook* 45: 213–230.

Zimmerman, Stefan. 2008. "Landscapes of Heimat in Postwar German Cinema." In *The Geography of Cinema*, edited by Chris Lukinbeal and Stefan Zimmerman, 171–186. Stuttgart: Franz Steiner Verlag.

Chapter 10

Multiple Masculinities among German Jewish Refugees
A Transnational Comparison between Canada and Palestine/Israel

PATRICK FARGES

The Nazi seizure of power in 1933 resulted in several waves of forced emigration, first from Germany, later from the Saarland, Austria, and Czechoslovakia. Emigration proved a life-saving option for German-speaking Jews seeking to leave Europe. The migration process deeply affected men's life expectations, gendered roles, and gendered performances of Jewish masculinity. Given the recent interest in German Jewish masculinities (Baader, Gillerman, and Lerner 2012), it is time to focus on the multiple masculinities in the shadow of the Holocaust. This chapter, which is based on life narratives and oral history interviews, looks at the multiple masculinities of German-speaking Jews as they migrated to and settled in different countries. A transnational comparison between two very different destinations in the 1930s, Canada and Mandate Palestine/Israel, shows that these new countries determined available masculinity options during and after migration. Whereas Canada did not welcome Jewish refugees—considering them "non-preferred immigrants" and "enemy aliens" to be interned—an emigration to *Eretz Israel* meant that men had to conform to the Zionist injunctions of the "New Jew." How these masculinities played out in different contexts is the question pursued in this chapter.

German-speaking Jewish refugees were scattered to a number of countries after 1933, where they grew new roots. They became known as *Yekkes*, a term that connotes specific cultural and social ways of being (such as formal stiffness) and allegedly plays on their inadequate clothing and habitus as traces of their assimilated bourgeois past. The dissemination of German Jewry through forced emigration led to a form of "*Yekkish* diaspora" (Segev 2005, 30) by which "the accoutrements of German-Jewish life [were carried] to all corners of the globe" (Grossmann 2003, 97). By no means a homogeneous group, German-speaking Jews were, however, socially extremely diverse and they identified with being Jewish in different ways, thus constantly negotiating sociocultural dynamics of "assimilation" and "dissimilation" (Volkov 1990). Similar dynamics of distinction continued in the post-Holocaust world within the German Jewish diaspora: first-generation German and Austrian Jews did not mingle, nor did convinced Zionists and non-Zionists; assimilated Jews looked down on Jews with an *ostjüdisch* past; Orthodox German Jewish families did not socialize with nonreligious German Jews; and those who migrated in the 1930s were distinct from postwar Holocaust survivors. And yet *Yekke* families had *something* in common: they formed transnational networks, visited each other, wrote letters, sent packages, and knew about what was going on in their relatives' lives abroad. As Atina Grossmann writes, "The history of German Jews continued outside of Germany, in the exile communities, Washington Heights, Upper West Side, Golden Green and Hampstead Heath, Tel Aviv, Moshav Germanid and Rehavia, certain neighborhoods in Buenos Aires, Melbourne and elsewhere. In some ways they were all the same, the same china, the same doilies, the same accents" (Grossmann 2003, 121). Other places on the map of post-1945 German Jewry included Toronto and Montreal, as this chapter will show.

In this chapter, I pursue a transnational comparison between two very different destinations: Canada and Mandate Palestine/Israel. This work is based on self-narratives, memoirs, autobiographies, and correspondences of a generation born between 1900 and 1925. I also use oral history interviews conducted in the 1990s and 2000s with men of this generation who experienced an important postmigratory resocialization process. These sources convey *something* of the past events to us through individual and collective mediation. They contain statements about social, cultural, and historical realities. They also enable us to inquire into the sociocultural interpretations of historical experience and into the complex, multifaceted (and at times contradictory) nature of historical reality—which includes gender.

It seems particularly challenging to add gender and masculinity into a story that is already doubly marginalized with regard to the Holocaust. First, gender and masculinity are still perceived by some as marginal approaches in the field of Holocaust studies, despite years of scholarly research exploring the Holocaust's gendered aspects (Waxman 2017). Second, the German Jewish refugees were able to leave Europe *before* it was too late. Their forced migration located them at the margins of the Holocaust, and in their recollections they largely voiced this feeling. As a global phenomenon, however, the Holocaust affected multiple lives in multiple ways. While gender and masculinity as such are rarely explicitly mentioned in the sources, this chapter argues that the focus on multiple masculinities enables us to explore social, generational, as well as racial issues of the Holocaust. We will see how gendered power dynamics functioned between the sexes, and also among men, using Raewyn Connell's idea of a prism of difference that explores masculinities as an ongoing dynamic process producing hierarchies (Connell 1995).

Masculinity is simultaneously a place in gender relations, the practices through which both men and women engage that place in gender, and the effects of these practices in bodily experience and identity formation. Rather than defining masculinity as an object, we need to focus on the processes and relationships through which individuals conduct their gendered lives. This chapter thus presents an investigation of the lives, experiences, and gendered identities of young male emigrants from Nazi Europe who had partly been socialized in Europe, had interrupted their education, and were forced to realign their existential projections. It also centers on the question of what new theoretical insights the field of Holocaust studies might gain from integrating (largely invisible) masculinities as analytical categories (Hájková et al. 2018). Far from being invisible and disembodied, German Jewish masculinities at the margins of the Holocaust were marked through practices, constraints, and routines that affected the men's bodily and gendered selves.

Canada

Julius Pfeiffer was born in 1902 to an Orthodox family. He grew up in Düsseldorf, where his parents owned a clothes shop. After studying law in Cologne and Munich, he obtained the First State Examination in Law in 1929, completed his PhD in 1931, and passed the Second Examination magna cum laude in 1932. He was soon appointed judge. On March 15,

1933, however, Julius Pfeiffer forced a lawyer to remove his Nazi insignia before entering his court. This act had immediate consequences: Pfeiffer had to flee over the border to the Netherlands where his sister lived. A few weeks later, he was selling kitchen utensils door-to-door. His social and gendered identity as a skilled professional, a well-paid family provider, and a dominant man had dramatically and abruptly changed within just a few weeks:

> The merchandise was under my bed, next to my bed, on top of my bed, next to the door. I had to get used to it. . . . I had been a judge; people bowed to me and called me "Sir." Now, it was humiliating, but it was a good preparation for what was coming in the future. (Pfeiffer 1989, 210–211)

Julius's wife, Flora, soon joined him in Amsterdam. Two sons were born in the Netherlands. After Nazi Germany invaded the country in May 1940, each family member lived a different experience of the Holocaust. Gender was a central aspect of that experience. As a man, Julius thought at the time he was the one facing the greater danger. This is why he fled to England on a boat. Shortly after, he was interned as an "enemy alien" and sent to an internment camp. A few weeks later, the British authorities transferred him to an internment camp in Canada for two years. His wife Flora opened a Jewish home for the elderly in Amsterdam, but in 1943, as the situation became critical, she decided that her older son (who "passed" as non-Jewish because of the color of his hair) should be *ondergedoken* (hidden) in a Catholic family. She and her younger son were deported to Westerbork and Bergen-Belsen that same year. They survived with the help of Flora's social connections in the camp and thanks to her position in the camp's laundry facility, which ensured them heat and clean clothes. In March 1945, both mother and son were liberated on a train bound for Theresienstadt. Three months later, they were reunited with the older son who had survived in hiding. In 1946, Flora and her sons joined Julius in Canada. In 1947, a third, post-Holocaust, son was born. Julius Pfeiffer, the former judge in Germany, eventually became an accountant in Montreal. All his life, he—a true *Yekke*—continued reading the newspaper *Aufbau* as well as the *Rundbrief des Berliner Juristenverbandes*. He also chaired Montreal's German Jewish Heritage Association, which ceased to exist after his death (Meune 2003, 167). The *Aufbau* obituary, published in 1991, mentions the following anecdote: asked about how he should be addressed, "Dr. Julius Pfeiffer" of Montreal, who had been bereft of his PhD title by the Nazis, used to answer: "Call me Mr. Pfeiffer, call me Dr. Pfeiffer, I don't care. But don't be late!" (Vogt-Moykopf 1991).

Until recently, Canada was one of the lesser-known destinations of Jewish migration from Nazi Europe. Unlike its southern neighbor, Canada had offered limited opportunities for Jewish immigration. Irving Abella and Harold Troper's groundbreaking study of Canadian immigration policy in the years of National Socialism, *None Is Too Many: Canada and the Jews of Europe 1933-1948* (first published in 1983), convincingly shattered the illusion of Canada being a haven of refuge and an open society (Abella and Troper 1983; Klein 2012). In the last two decades, several international publications finally put Canada on the map of Jewish forced migration (Puckhaber 2002; Farges 2008 and 2015; Banauch 2009; Strutz 2012; Whitehouse 2016). Between 4,900 and 6,000 German-speaking refugees were allowed into Canada in the 1930s. Most of them were Jewish. Some entered because they had relatives who could sponsor them, others were able to demonstrate proficiency in a profession favored by immigration officials (and settled as farmers, for instance). In 1940, Canada took in over two thousand German and Austrian civilian internees—mostly refugees—from Great Britain. When the fear of a "Fifth Column" spread over the United Kingdom, reaching a peak in the spring of 1940, Winston Churchill decided to register and categorize all "enemy aliens," including the refugees, and to intern some of them (Kushner and Cesarani 1993). About two thousand male internees—the "Camp Boys"—were sent overseas to Canadian internment camps while others were sent to Australia. In imperialistic tradition, Great Britain had called on its former Dominions to take care of its unwanted.[1] The detainees were interned for several months, in some cases alongside German prisoners of war, some of whom were declared Nazis. In Canada, the detainees were located in eight internment camps: one in New Brunswick, five in Quebec, and two in Ontario (Draper 1983; Whitehouse 2016). While in July 1941 their formal status was finally changed from "Prisoner of War second class" to "refugees from Nazi oppression," little changed in their everyday internment routine.

The camp microcosm offers a pertinent space to study how interactions between men redefined multiple Jewish masculinities (Farges 2008, 104-141; 2012; 2015, 115-153). In this particular case, gender constituted a dimension present both in the rationale for interning solely "dangerous" men and in the everyday practices within the camps. In the camps, the internees' masculinity was under constant scrutiny. It was marked through a loss of privacy as well as various collective practices that ranged from wearing uniforms to repetitive constraints and routines affecting the men's bodies. "Being a (real) man" and performing manhood in such an environment were complex processes. Stigmatization, deportation, and internment covered a dense and intense period in these men's lives. The social, religious, and sexualized relations the Camp Boys were confronted with became part of their German Jewish masculine identity. They spent months (sometimes years) in a confined, all-male, but sociologically diverse environment. Their ages ranging from sixteen to sixty-five, the internees experienced an acute sense of disempowerment and a near complete loss of control over the workings of their life that unsettled assumptions linking masculinity with dominance, freedom, and also providing for family. This explains in part why they referred to themselves as "boys"—not as men.

At the mercy of authorities, they had to invent new recalcitrant forms of agency. Camp life was a small, men-only version of the outside world. It made unusual sociocultural face-to-face interactions possible, thus dissolving social and religious hierarchies. Carl Weiselberger (born 1900 in Vienna) recalls:

> The internees were a human mix of "liberal" German and Austrian Jews, of Orthodox *yeshiva bokher* [pupils in religious schools], rabbis, of German sailors, a few Italians (including the young *tenante* Levi from Venice who pretended he was a refugee), of enemy aliens who were twice victims—first, of Hitler, and then of an over-eager and panicky British Home Office, etc.[2]

Camp was the site of intense "biopolitics," as power hierarchies from men against men, which involved the guards, were used as micro-social regulators. In this context, the demonstration of (sometimes violent) power was a means of installing complex masculinity dynamics, performed for, and judged by, other men (Kimmel 2008). The various camps formed micro-social systems with little communication with the outside world, in which every individual performed social and gendered roles.

Reframing camp life in terms of masculinity dynamics sheds new light on the numerous debates, quarrels, fights, and (sexual) domination that took place in this microcosm, which in the camp vocabulary was called "the men's kitchen." Various chores and outdoor activities, aimed at channeling "dangerous" manly energies, created everyday opportunities for manly competition and identity work. On the other hand, intellectual activities provided by camp schools or theatrical events gave occasions to perform and reclaim alternative, "softer" forms of being a Jewish man (Boyarin 1997). Through these occupations, the Jewish internees established *multiple* masculine identities: they could be productive providers and even professionals again. Entertainment and cultural activities gave the internees opportunities to explore their musical, theatrical, or academic inclinations, thus regaining self-respect and dignity as a German Jewish *Bildungsbürger* (member of the educated, intellectual middle class). At a group level, social activities were an important safety valve that brought change in the internment routine. And for the camp authorities, they served as a micro-social instrument of domination over the internees.

Given the fluidity of the camps' social organization, the Camp Boys walked a fine line between gaining and losing manliness. Homosexual practices, fantasies, or mere rumors in an environment that was highly sexualized were easily instrumentalized. In Gregory Baum's recollection, the kitchens in particular served as strategic sites of power games:

> We had the black kitchen. Those were the rabbis, and so this was the black kitchen. Then we had the red kitchen. Those were the communists. And then we had the warm kitchen and those were the homosexuals who had also fled Germany. And in German, "warm" means "homosexual"—*ein Warmer, ein warmer Bruder* [a warm brother]. And so that was the "warm kitchen." So we had three kinds of crews.[3]

Any problem related to the kitchens—or to food—led to particularly irrational and violent reactions. One day, a camp leader had to deal with a serious problem: one of his cooks had been discovered having sexual intercourse with an internee in the kitchen area. This soon led to the wildest rumors about food.

> I was surprised by the vehemence of the response, because somehow people began to associate homosexual practices in the kitchen with food. It became an explosive issue, and the demand was made for the cook to be removed from the kitchen. This was one of those situations where it was difficult

> to restore reason through objectively orientated discussion. (Koch 1980, 158)

On a similar occasion, communist internees held a spectacular phony trial that ended in the condemnation of two boys. As punishment, they were ordered to fight each other "until there was a bloody mess" in order to prove their manliness. The public performance was aimed at reinstalling hegemonic, heteronormative masculinity, which was constantly challenged by the everyday environment of the camp. Such (hard-to-find) testimonies attest to the fact that there existed forms of domination of men over other men, as well as an economy of—at times sexualized—power within the camps. Domination was sometimes played out as sexual domination in the attempt to impose one pattern of hegemonic masculinity. But the Boys also had access to *alternative* forms of social and gendered interactions, such as nurturing roles, which also became part of their identity toolkit. Most self-narratives and memorializations silence, however, these crucial episodes of camp life. In retrospect, most ex-internees tended to recreate in their self-narratives "normal" masculine identities through erasure and cautious remembering of "deviant" masculinity.

The internment experience was a dense and intense period of (re) socialization. Through their common experience, the German Jewish internees were cemented into a masculine peer group that shared a collective memory. Internment had begun in the late spring of 1940 in England and was prolonged in Canada. Liberations started in 1941 and continued until 1943. About half of the liberated internees eventually chose to remain in Canada, thus becoming Canada's "accidental immigrants" (Draper 1983), while others asked to be transferred to the United States or back to the United Kingdom. After months of symbolic impotence, most Camp Boys were eager to regain "normal" masculine identities. This is what Ernst Friedrich Bergmann (born 1916 in Fürth), a former refugee who after being liberated joined the Canadian armed forces, wrote while he was stationed in Wilhelmshaven, Germany:

> July 10th, 1945 was the day when the Canadian Army Occupational Forces took up their positions inside Germany. . . . For me, and for some of my friends, this was quite a day. We re-entered the country, where we once had been born, and which we had left to escape the Nazis. This time we were on the upper side. . . . The Germans here do not look any too much

like the "Supermen" they claimed to be. . . . Since fraternizing has been permitted I have been out several times, mainly to get my laundry done. It is a good feeling to have some pure blooded Aryan doing a Jew's laundry.[4]

Most German Jewish refugees, however, felt somewhat marginalized in the postwar Jewish communities. In Canada, the low numbers of German-speaking Jews made it almost impossible to recreate "Little Jewish Germanies." Cultural transmission of a German Jewish heritage was relegated to private practices. Furthermore, it was for a long time practically impossible to "tell the story," as internment was in no way comparable with the horrors others had been through under Nazism. As Canada let in over twenty thousand Holocaust survivors in the late 1940s and 1950s, there was no doubt about the distinction that existed between a refugee and a Holocaust survivor. Some ex-internees, who had experienced Dachau or Sachsenhausen *prior to* leaving Germany, or those whose family members had been deported and killed, knew this all too well. The Boys, one can argue, were Holocaust survivors of a different kind. In a post-Holocaust world, the memories of wartime internment were obliterated. This also became an aspect of the former internees' masculine identity. Far from being manly and heroic, their story was merely "accidental."

Erwin Schild (born 1920 in Cologne), who became the rabbi of the Toronto Adath Israel Congregation in September 1947, is certainly one of the ex–Camp Boys who most deeply reflected on this issue. In his autobiography published in 2001, he—who had left Nazi Germany after the *Reichskristallnacht* and spent five weeks in Dachau—clearly distanced himself from claiming the status of a "Holocaust survivor": "What I have written was never intended as a Holocaust memoir; I do not claim the title of Holocaust survivor" (Schild 2001, 300). Schild also wrote that internment "was but a footnote because it was dwarfed by the Holocaust, and yet related to it as a footnote to a text. It could only have happened at that time, and only in a world that allowed the Holocaust to happen" (235). It is interesting to follow the evolution of his discourse in the span of the years in which he produced several self-narratives. When I interviewed Erwin Schild in 2004, he came back to the notion of a "footnote," calling it this time a "significant footnote":

[Our story] is not part of the Holocaust and yet it couldn't have happened without the war and without the Holocaust, so I figured that it's a significant footnote, an interesting footnote, but no more than that, except for the people who went through it. It shaped their lives, so it's no longer a footnote.[5]

On an individual basis, the German Jewish refugees were able, so it seems, to construct nonhegemonic masculinities by endorsing the paradoxical identity of male victims *and* "accidental immigrants." But private forms of memory reclaiming also existed among former Boys, who in the 1990s used to organize gatherings with "veteran" and "male-bonding" undertones. Helmut Kallmann (1922–2012) published ten issues of an *Ex-Internees' Newsletter*. In light of the destruction of European Jewry, the retrospective narratives tended to emphasize the success stories of "valuable" Jewish immigrants to Canada. Some published their autobiographies in Canada, the United Kingdom, or Germany, the most famous memoir being the *Kochbuch*, that is, Eric Koch's *Deemed Suspect: A Wartime Blunder*, published in 1980. The book's prevalent tone is that of the "good old days" in which the—now old—men were young, thus reversing the boy-to-man polarization process.

Mandatory Palestine/Israel

Approximately ninety thousand German-speaking Jews found refuge in Palestine in the 1930s and 1940s, thus constituting nearly 15 percent of the Jewish settlement (*Yishuv*). While in Zionist historiography this migration was often labeled "Fifth (or German) *Aliyah*," a majority of the German-speaking Jews had in fact not planned on "ascending" to the Promised Land. Most of them would have stayed in Europe had the Nazis not come to power. While the social and cultural aspects of the German Jewish emigration to Palestine have widely been researched (Greif, McPherson, and Weinbaum 2000; Zimmermann and Hotam 2005; Siegemund 2016), the multiple gendered masculinity dynamics at play still need to be explored.

In the *Yishuv* and the early Israeli society, Zionism combined a socialist discourse, collectivist values, and a secular national ethos. Since the end of the nineteenth century, Zionism had developed as an ideological means to address and fight antisemitism. In particular, Zionism sought to mold new Jewish masculinities in order to reverse antisemitic stigmas. The figure of the disciplined, agile, and strong "muscle Hebrew" was both a response to antisemitic stigmatization, which depicted Jewish men as weak, and the practical adaptation of a nationalist discourse (Presner 2007). Zionism in Mandatory Palestine advocated for a pioneering spirit, the use of Hebrew, physical labor, agricultural settlement, and military defense. The "New Hebrew," a man, a pioneer, and a citizen in arms, became the hegemonic model of masculinity. Zionist injunctions aimed at making productive, useful, and good New Hebrew men by reshaping masculinity through bodily and military training, thus paralleling European (and especially German) nationalistic masculinities (Mosse 1996). This translated into specific body cultures within those organizations that helped young Jews to emigrate, for example, the Youth *Aliyah*, the *Hachshara* (preparation), or the *kibbutzim*. Outdoor work and bodily training reinforced the hegemonic model of masculinity, which emphasized physical aptitudes over intellectual ones. This, however, rubbed against the tradition of the *Bildungsbürger* held dear by most of the German-speaking Jews arriving in Mandate Palestine; it would become an important aspect of their subsequent perceived and proclaimed collective identity as *Yekkes*.

When Ernst Loewy (1920–2002) was forced out of school in 1935, his parents immediately sent him to a farm belonging to the Zionist Youth *Aliyah* in order to prepare for emigration to Palestine. A year later, Ernst arrived at Kiryat Anavim, near Jerusalem. Between 1936 and 1938, he wrote long and frequent letters to his parents, describing his new surroundings and the hardships of *kibbutz* life. Despite the escalation of antisemitic persecution in Germany, he repeatedly discouraged his parents from joining him, warning them about the difficulties they, as urban *Bildungsbürger*, would undoubtedly face in Palestine. In 1938, however, as the situation in Germany became critical, he finally sponsored them on a tourist visa. They reached Palestine shortly after *Kristallnacht*. The correspondence between Ernst and his parents also reads as a report of the moral and physical transformations of a young man who is becoming a Zionist pioneer, a *Haluts*. In one of his last letters to his parents in October 1938, Ernst wrote:

> This might be my last letter to you in Germany. . . . I very much look forward to welcoming and hugging you. But please don't be surprised if you don't find your little "Ernstchen," the one you said farewell to over two years ago. Instead, you'll find a fully grown and changed man. One grows fast here. (Loewy 1997, 172)

In this passage, Ernst underscored his visible Zionist transformation to a new form of manhood. Leaving behind his bourgeois background, he no longer felt the young, unsexed, and unmanly "Ernstchen." On the contrary: his transformation, he claimed, showed physically, to the point that his parents might not recognize the earnest and serious (*ernst*) New Hebrew he had become. Interestingly, as Ernst was writing these lines, he had already begun to distance himself from the collective pioneer life and the hardships of rural labor. He later would write that he never really adapted to the norms of Hebrew masculinity. In fact, he eventually left Kiryat Anavim to be trained as a librarian in Tel Aviv, which he saw as a form of resistance toward Zionist masculinist injunctions. He thus reclaimed an alternative gendered identity, that of the learned *Bildungsbürger* working with books. In 1956, he even remigrated to East and later West Germany, a scandalous move in a post-Holocaust world. He pursued an academic career as the head of the Judaica section at the Goethe University Library in Frankfurt.

Inspired by contemporary European youth cultures (see Hotam 2009; Nur 2014), Zionist organizations intensely used peer socialization and group activities in which national, Jewish, generational, as well as gendered identities intensely intersected. As a Jewish nation was in process of being created, the youth, and especially the male youth, played a strategic role. Though the groups were generally mixed, in accordance with Zionist discourse, the actual pioneer was definitely seen as male. Consequently, even the female pioneer, the *Halutsa*, was highly masculinized in her clothing and attitude (Pilarczyk 2009).[6] Moreover, the creation of a highly gender-specific hegemonic Zionist masculinity excluded other, alternative forms of masculinity. Daniel Boyarin described this alternative ethos as *Edelkayt*, a gentler, "unmanned but not desexualized" form of Jewish masculinity resisting Western European nationalistic gendered injunctions (Boyarin 1997, 2). According to Boyarin, this counterhegemonic masculinity was that of the Eastern European rabbis and pupils of Jewish religious schools.

For German Jews, however, who looked down on *ostjüdisch* behaviors, the masculine identity of the *Bildungsbürger* served as a countermodel. Not all young German Jewish men conformed to the hegemonic ideal of the New Hebrew after they had reached Mandate Palestine. The process was particularly painful to those who did not fit the hegemonic standards. Gabriel Walter (born 1921) remembers that his older brother's condition did not enable him to adopt the manly rules of the *kibbutz*. Consequently, the younger Gabriel regularly stepped in and took over the chores of his older brother, who was regularly mocked and stigmatized.[7] Deviant behaviors were singled out and reported. In some cases, forms of gendered violence even served to train reluctant boys into becoming New Hebrews. Demonstrating one's adherence to Zionist ideals was a highly gendered act.

In the Zionist master narrative, the masculine pioneer, reenacting his mythical Jewish ancestors' gestures, was a builder in hostile lands. Arab as well as Sephardic and Arab-Jewish (*Mizrahi*) masculinities were instrumental in installing the New Hebrew *Ashkenazi* masculinities as hegemonic (Ben-Rafael and Sharot 2008). The *Yishuv* (and later Israeli society) was indeed characterized by racial differentiation. In the Israeli nation-building process, the *Ashkenazim* abandoned the stigma of otherness that was previously attached to Jews in Europe and came to represent a form of non-ethnically marked whiteness (Shohat 1999). Despite their difficulties of adaptation, the *Yekkes* were part of the dominant group and looked down on "Levantine" others.

In general, the *Yekkes* have been criticized for the positive quality of their initial everyday interactions with Arab populations. One can speculate whether this conciliatory attitude was partly due to the experience of violent racist discrimination in Germany and Austria. Using an Orientalist framework, they nonetheless projected cultural (and gendered) stereotypes onto the Arab populations of Palestine. In this context, man-to-man encounters with Arabs were particularly important narrative tropes, as they were altogether of ideological, biographical, and historical significance. Consequently, they were vividly recalled in the self-narratives. Until 1947–1948, the "Arab"—whether a Muslim, a Christian, or a Druze—was seen as a neighbor, a coworker, sometimes a friend. He certainly embodied a different, oriental, and exoticized masculinity, but beyond cultural differences, it was possible to get along. At the end of 1947, however, as the "war of independence" approached, man-to-man encounters turned violent. As Gad Landau (born 1909) remembers: "In Hebrew, there is a saying, 'honor him [the Arab] and mistrust him.' That's the general idea about our relationship."[8] According to Jakob Tachauer (born 1928):

> Before 1948 everything was normal and peaceful. We bought from Arabs, the Arabs bought from us, man-to-man. . . . But now the friendship is not as great anymore. I used to drive to Nablus and Jenin alone, I speak Arabic. . . . The Arab can be described as follows: for years, he gives you the keys to his

house, invites you to his daughter's wedding, but one day he takes revenge and stabs you. (Qtd. in Zinke 2003, 125)

Here the pre-1948 period appears idealized. The assumption inferred is that the Arab man, moved by his violent instincts, will eventually reveal his wild, untrustworthy side. The war of 1948 (and the following wars of 1967 and 1973) durably marked masculinities on both Arab and Jewish sides.[9]

The Israeli case is particularly relevant when studying the military. Due to the central place of wars and conflicts in Mandate Palestine/Israel, the "military ethos" permeated all relationships between army, state, and society (Maman, Ben-Ari, and Rosenhek 2001). War and the military became a key matrix of the new gendered Zionist repertoire, reshaping male body practices and comradeship among men in order to regulate physical proximity between men (Lomsky-Feder and Ben-Ari 2000; Kaplan 2006). The 1930s and 1940s were an early stage in the imposition of this military ethos. A majority of the young German Jews who arrived in those years participated in Jewish self-defense operations. Some joined the British army. For this generation, military experience strongly marked the social, professional, gendered integration and identity formation. Gabriel Walter distinctly remembers what it meant for a Jew who had just been forced out of Germany to carry a gun and regain some sense of male pride. For him, as for other German Jews of his generation, "fighting back" was a way of regaining manliness. "It was the first time in our lives that we carried a weapon and that we could defend ourselves. Until then, when someone in Germany attacked us, we couldn't fight back!"[10]

In 1941, the British supported the creation of an elite strike force in Mandate Palestine, the *Pelugoth Mahatz* (or *Palmach*), which recruited young cohorts. Among them were a significant proportion of young men from the Youth *Aliyah* who had emigrated from Germany and Austria. A German squad was even created, the *machlaka ha-germanit*, in charge of sabotaging behind enemy lines. Shimon Avidan (born Siegbert Koch, 1911–1994), a former member of the International Brigades who had migrated to Palestine in 1934, headed the squad. At the end of the war, the *Palmach* resumed the Zionist struggle against British authorities. In 1948, it comprised over six thousand combatants. After the foundation of Israel in May 1948, the *Palmach* and several other military formations—Haganah, Irgun, Jewish Brigade, and "Stern group"—merged to form the Israel Defense Forces (*Tsva Haganah le-Israel*, or *Tsahal*). The prestige of the *Palmach* as an elite group that actively contributed to the creation of Israel was widely celebrated. As much as it affirmed the equality and organic unity of all male Jewish combatants, it excluded women. The collective memory constructed a male "*Palmach* generation" of heroes, thus heroizing the "war of independence" (Shapira 1996). Yet, the collective memory was also subject to controversy. Anita Shapira has shown to what extent the *Palmach* generation was instrumental in Israel's transition from a "defensive" toward an "offensive ethos" (Shapira 1992, 358–359).

General Aharon Doron (born 1922), a *Yekke*, had a prestigious military career. He arrived in Palestine in 1939 with the Youth *Aliyah*. Like the majority of his peers, Doron first joined the *Yishuv*'s paramilitary organization, the *Haganah*, founded in 1920 to defend the Jews against Arab attacks. Within this organization, combatants as well as officers were volunteers; many came from local self-defense brigades. Young German Jewish immigrants who had arrived in Palestine in the 1930s and 1940s participated in those Jewish self-defense operations. The choice was to join either the British army, the Jewish Settlement Police controlled by the British, or the *Haganah*. Aharon Doron soon became a recruiter and started his military career. During the war of 1948, he was heading a training camp for high school recruits. According to him:

> The *Palmach* was a unit of the *Haganah*. [It] was an elite unit. . . . They recruited athletic boys, young men who somehow had been active and who knew what a rifle was. . . . It was a successful attempt to get the cream of the cream of Jewish male youth. They approached youth movements, because of the ideological proximity. The *Palmach* found excellent human material, including many high school graduates. . . . To this day, there is something left of that feeling of "we are just better."[11]

Usi Biran (born 1920) confirms this esprit de corps among elite men. First a member of the *Haganah*, he was later recruited to join the *Palmach*, where he mingled with native sons and became one of them:

> The *Palmach* was the group that really made me a Hebrew. For the most part, it was a group of Israeli-born Jerusalemites. The group was fairly close-knit. The boys had known each other for years, mostly from high school in Jerusalem. These Jerusalemites were nationalistic and spoke very good Hebrew. . . . The long marches of up to twenty, twenty-five

> kilometers were exhausting. So were the physical and military exercises. I wasn't physically strong back then, so I tried very hard. At the same time, this gave me strength and some sense of inner security. The group organized get-togethers, we drank and sang, and led an intense social life. . . . They accepted me as one of them, so I was no more the little *Yekke*.[12]

Adapting to Israel's masculinized and militarized "offensive *ethos*" involved adopting new forms of sociability and new bodily repertoires that had to be learned. It meant changing one's European habitus and posture as well as one's bourgeois gestures, like extending the hand as a form of salute, or automatically tipping one's hat as an expression of greeting. For German Jewish men who were newcomers to *Eretz Israel*, it was particularly crucial to be recognized as members of the *Palmach* generation, a generation that successively fought the Nazis, the British Mandatory Authorities, and the Arabs. This pride helps explain the discrepancy between the way this military experience is sometimes overstressed in retrospective narratives and the more general skeptic tone toward militaristic and masculinist values. Generally, the German-speaking Jews, as immigrants who needed social integration, strategically negotiated Zionist demands. But some voiced their reluctance toward endorsing militaristic and nationalistic defense values because they had witnessed firsthand the dangers of exacerbated militarism in Europe. Despite their "Ashkenaziness"—and hence their identification with some form of hegemony—*Yekke* masculinity in Israel remained a subordinate masculinity. The major reason for this seems to be the *Yekkes*' European-like bourgeois habitus, which was not in accordance with the New Hebrew masculinity. In some ways, they provided "an almost ideal projection surface for what the Israeli, the Hebrew Jew, should not be" (Diner 2000, vii).

Conclusion

After 1933, German-speaking Jewish men scattered around the world negotiated and navigated multiple masculinities, as refugees, spouses, sons, comrades, fighters, pioneers, professionals, and intellectuals. This chapter has analyzed the gendered aspects of sociocultural integration in two postmigration societies, with a focus on multiple masculinities.

Whereas Canada did not welcome (German-speaking) Jewish refugees, considering them "non-preferred immigrants" and "enemy aliens" to be interned, an emigration to *Eretz Israel* meant that one had to conform to Zionist injunctions. Both situations had gendered implications with respect to negotiating masculinity in and after migration. In Canada and Israel, the *Yekkes* remained somewhat marginal. A major reason seems to be the importance of *bildungsbürgerliche* values that contoured softer forms of masculinity. This may be why success stories abound—of *Yekke* men in academia, the arts, in libraries and museums. The *Yekkes* certainly represented a strange voice and often transmitted a specific and distinctive memory onto their children and grandchildren. Nowadays, more than seventy years after the Holocaust almost destroyed German Jewry, some people still identify with their (grand)parents' *Yekkishkeit* (Kranz 2016).

A close look at the sources shows that competing and overlapping masculinities were strategically used according to situational experiences. Masculinities were produced through complex processes involving negotiation in multiple social relationships, cultural settings, and specific historical circumstances. Different forms of masculinity existed in relation with each other, often in relations of hierarchy and exclusion, thus relying on power structures and forms of domination.

For a long time, German Jewish refugees' masculinities remained difficult to locate within the frame of Holocaust studies. This chapter has shown that German Jewish men's lives, behaviors, attitudes, and self-projections in the postmigration period were deeply affected by the Holocaust. Consequently, it also affected the way they constructed their gendered selves. It is important to continue writing integrated histories of the Holocaust that help us link the core of Holocaust studies to its margins (Waxman 2010). The history of the German-speaking Jews' forced migration and their subsequent lives did not occur within a vacuum, even though their history was for a long time minimized in the context of Holocaust historiography. They survived the Holocaust because they left Europe while it was still possible, but their story occurred in a world that allowed the Holocaust to happen. Their invisible story at the margins of the Holocaust is now gradually being traced. It is time to shed light on their experiences of masculinities in a way that renders them subject to study. The presence/absence of men will expand our understanding of the Holocaust by situating German Jewish masculinities in a broader, global, framework.

Acknowledgments

Parts of this chapter were presented at the 2018 American Historical Association Conference in Washington, DC. I would like to thank Jennifer Evans, Deborah Hertz, Thomas Kühne, and Paul Steege for their feedback and questions. I would also like to thank Ovidiu Creangă and Björn Krondorfer for their suggestions on the written version. Unless otherwise indicated, all translations are mine.

Notes

1. See the international conference on Emigration from Nazi-Occupied Europe to British Overseas Territories after 1933 that took place at the University of London (Institute of Modern Languages) from September 13 to 15, 2017, https://www.sas.ac.uk/events/event/6784 (accessed February 11, 2018).

2. Archive of the University of Victoria, 93-004, Carl Weiselberger, vol. 2, file 6, "Unclassified fragments," undated.

3. Gregory Baum (1923–2017), Personal Interview, Montreal, March 25, 2003. Christine Whitehouse has pointed out that the canteen was another strategic site within the internment camp (Whitehouse 2016, 78–80).

4. Alex Dworkin Canadian Jewish Archives (formerly known as the Canadian Jewish Congress Charities Committee National Archives), United Jewish Relief Agencies, Series Bc Internees, File Ernst Friedrich Bergmann, "Report on Entering Germany with the Canadian Occupational Forces," 1945.

5. Erwin Schild (born 1920), Personal Interview, Toronto, May 10, 2004.

6. In her brilliant visual history of German Zionist youth movements, Ulrike Pilarczyk (2009) has shown that the postures, gazes, poses, and the clothing of photographed young women read as gendered performances of masculinization. At the same time, the young men seem to exaggerate heroic and manly poses in front of the camera. These visual codes, Pilarczyk argues, enabled the young men and women to performatively project themselves as New Hebrews.

7. Israel Corpus 1st generation (IC1), Interview Anne Betten with Gabriel (Herbert) Walter (born 1921 in Kolberg, Pomerania), Sde Warburg, April 28, 1991. The corpus of interviews was put together between 1989 and 1998 by Anne Betten, Myriam Du-nour, and their collaborators. The interviews are archived at the Institut für Deutsche Sprache in Mannheim, and at the Oral History Division of the Hebrew University, Jerusalem.

8. IC1, Interview Kristine Hecker with Gad (Gustav) Landau (born 1909 in Lübeck), Haifa, November 7, 1990.

9. Samira Aghacy (2009) has addressed the issue of Arab masculinity in the Middle East, showing the disastrous effects of continuous conflict on representations of masculinity. In particular, she unveils the vulnerability and anxieties of Arab masculinity.

10. IC1, Interview Anne Betten with Gabriel (Herbert) Walter (born 1921 in Kolberg, Pomerania), Sde Warburg, April 28, 1991.

11. IC1, Interview Miryam Du-nour with Aharon Doron (Erwin Weilheimer, born 1922 in Ludwigshafen), Tel Aviv, November 4, 1994.

12. IC1, Interview Miryam Du-nour with Usi Biran (Edgar Birnfeld, born 1920 in Ludwigshafen), Jerusalem, May 11, 1991.

References

Abella, Irving, and Harold Troper. 1983. *None Is Too Many: Canada and the Jews of Europe 1933–1948*. Toronto: Lester & Orpen Dennys.

Aghacy, Samira. 2009. *Masculine Identity in the Fiction of the Arab East since 1967*. Syracuse: Syracuse University Press.

Baader, Benjamin Maria, Sharon Gillerman, and Paul Lerner, eds. 2012. *Jewish Masculinities: German Jews, Gender, and History*. Bloomington: University of Indiana Press.

Banauch, Eugen. 2009. *Fluid Exile: Jewish Exile Writers in Canada 1940–2006*. Heidelberg: Winter-Verlag.

Ben Rafael, Eliezer, and Stephen Sharot. 2008. *Ethnicity, Religion and Class in Israeli Society*. Cambridge: Cambridge University Press.

Boyarin, Daniel. 1997. *Unheroic Conduct: The Rise of Heterosexuality and the Invention of the Jewish Man*. Berkeley: University of California Press.

Connell, Raewyn. 1995. *Masculinities*. Berkeley: University of California Press.

Diner, Dan. 2000. "Geleitwort." In *Die Jeckes: Deutsche Juden aus Israel erzählen*, ed. Gideon Greif, Colin McPherson, and Laurence Weinbaum, i–xi. Cologne: Böhlau.

Draper, Paula Jean. 1983. "The Accidental Immigrants: Canada and the Interned Refugees." PhD dissertation. University of Toronto.

Farges, Patrick. 2008. *Le Trait d'union ou l'intégration sans l'oubli: Itinéraires d'exilés germanophones au Canada après 1933*. Paris: Éditions de la Maison des Sciences de l'Homme.

———. 2012. "Masculinity and Confinement: German-Speaking Refugees in Canadian Internment Camps (1940–1943)." *Culture, Society & Masculinities* 4, no. 1: 33–47.

———. 2015. *Bindestrich-Identitäten? Sudetendeutsche Sozialdemokraten und deutsche Juden als Exilanten in Kanada: Studie zu Akkulturationsprozessen nach 1933*. Bremen: Edition Lumière.

Greif, Gideon, Colin McPherson, and Laurence Weinbaum, eds. 2000. *Die Jeckes: Deutsche Juden aus Israel erzählen*. Cologne: Böhlau.

Grossmann, Atina. 2003. "Versions of Home: German Jewish Refugee Papers Out of the Closet and into the Archives." *New German Critique* 90 (Fall): 95–122.

Hájková, Anna, Elissa Mailänder, Doris Bergen, Patrick Farges, and Atina Grossmann. 2018. "Forum: Holocaust and the History of Gender and Sexuality." *German History* 36, no. 1: 78–100.

Hotam, Yotam, ed. 2009. *Deutsch-Jüdische Jugendliche im "Zeitalter der Jugend."* Göttingen: V & R Unipress.

Kaplan, Danny. 2006. *The Men We Loved: Male Friendship and Nationalism in Israeli Culture*. New York: Berghahn Books.

Kimmel, Michael. 2008. *Guyland: The Perilous World Where Boys Become Men*. New York: Harper.

Klein, L. Ruth, ed. 2012. *Nazi Germany, Canadian Responses: Confronting Antisemitism in the Shadow of War*. Montreal-Kingston: McGill-Queen's University Press.

Koch, Eric. 1980. *Deemed Suspect: A Wartime Blunder*. Toronto: Methuen.

Kranz, Dani. 2016. "Changing Definitions of Germanness across Three Generations of Yekkes in Palestine/Israel." *German Studies Review* 39, no. 1: 99–120.

Kushner, Tony, and David Cesarani, eds. 1993. *The Internment of Aliens in Twentieth-Century Britain*. London: Frank Cass.

Loewy, Ernst. 1997. *Jugend in Palästina: Briefe an die Eltern 1935–1938*. Edited by B. Eckert. Berlin: Metropol.

Lomsky-Feder, Edna, and Eyal Ben-Ari, eds. 2000. *The Military and Militarism in Israeli Society*. Albany: State University of New York Press.

Maman, Daniel, Eyal Ben-Ari, and Zeev Rosenhek, eds. 2001. *Military, State, and Society in Israel: Theoretical and Comparative Perspectives*. Piscataway: Transaction.

Meune, Manuel. 2003. *Les Allemands du Québec: Parcours et discours d'une communauté méconnue*. Montreal: Méridien.

Mosse, George L. 1996. *The Image of Man: The Creation of Modern Masculinity*. Oxford: Oxford University Press.

Nur, Ofer Nordheimer. 2014. *Eros and Tragedy: Jewish Male Fantasies and the Masculine Revolution of Zionism*. Brighton, MA: Academic Studies Press.

Pfeiffer, Julius. 1989. "Enemy Alien." In *New Immigrant Voices*, edited by Milly Charon, 206–226. Dunvegan: Cormorant Books.

Pilarczyk, Ulrike. 2009. *Gemeinschaft in Bildern: Jüdische Jugendbewegung und zionistische Erziehungspraxis in Deutschland und Palästina/Israel*. Göttingen: Wallstein.

Presner, Todd Samuel. 2007. *Muscular Judaism: The Jewish Body and the Politics of Regeneration*. New York: Routledge.

Puckhaber, Annette. 2002. *Ein Privileg für wenige: Die deutschsprachige Migration nach Kanada im Schatten des Nationalsozialismus*. Münster: Lit Verlag.

Schild, Erwin. 2001. *The Very Narrow Bridge: A Memoir of an Uncertain Passage*. Toronto: Malcolm Lester.

Segev, Tom. 2005. "Ach, gäbe es doch noch einmal Karpfen wie an der Rehwiese!" In *Die Jeckes: Jüdischer Almanach des Leo Baeck Instituts*, edited by Gisela Dachs, 28–40. Frankfurt a. M.: Jüdischer Verlag im Suhrkamp Verlag.

Shapira, Anita. 1992. *Land and Power: The Zionist Resort to Force, 1881–1948*. Stanford: Stanford University Press.

———. 1996. "Native Sons." In *Essential Papers on Zionism*, edited by Jehuda Reinharz and Anita Shapira, 791–821. New York: New York University Press.

Shohat, Ella. 1999. "The Invention of the Mizrahim." *Journal of Palestine Studies* 29, no. 1 (Fall): 5–20.

Siegemund, Anja, ed. 2016. *Deutsche und zentraleuropäische Juden in Palästina und Israel: Kulturtransfers, Lebenswelten, Identitäten—Beispiele aus Haifa*. Berlin: Neofelis.

Strutz, Andrea. 2012. "Sie kamen als 'enemy aliens': Kanadas verschlossene Grenzen für jüdische Flüchtlinge." In *Zonen der Begrenzung: Aspekte kultureller und räumlicher Grenzen in der Moderne*, edited by Gerald Lamprecht, Ursula Mindler, and Heidrun Zettelbauer, 47–60. Bielefeld: Transcript.

Vogt-Moykopf, Chaim. 1991. "Die letzten Jeckes: deutsche Juden in Kanada." *Aufbau: Deutsch-jüdische Zeitung*, April 30.

Volkov, Shulamit. 1990. "Die Dynamik der Dissimilation." In *Jüdisches Leben und Antisemitismus im 19. und 20. Jahrhundert*, edited by Shulamit Volkov, 166–180. Munich: C. H. Beck.

Waxman, Zoë. 2010. "Towards an Integrated History of the Holocaust: Masculinity, Femininity, and Genocide." In *Years of Persecution, Years of Extermination: Saul Friedlander and the Future of Holocaust Studies*, edited by Christian Wiese and Paul Betts, 311–322. London: Continuum.

———. 2017. *Women in the Holocaust: A Feminist History*. Oxford: Oxford University Press.

Whitehouse, Christine. 2016. "'You'll Get Used to It!' The Internment of Jewish Refugees in Canada, 1940–43." PhD dissertation. Carleton University Ottawa.

Zimmermann, Moshe, and Yotam Hotam, eds. 2005. *Zweimal Heimat Die Jeckes zwischen Mitteleuropa und Nahost*. Frankfurt a. M.: Beerenverlag.

Zinke, Peter, ed. 2003. *Flucht nach Palästina: Lebenswege Nürnberger Juden*. Nuremberg: Antogo.

Chapter 11

Redemptive Masculinity
American Images of Jewish Men from
the Holocaust to the Six-Day War

SARAH IMHOFF

On May 7, 1945, *Life* magazine published a now-iconic photograph of Buchenwald survivors. Just liberated, the emaciated, half-dressed men huddled together and looked at the camera. "In the barracks at Buchenwald, near Weimar, emaciated prisoners stare from their hard bunks at the Americans who liberated them." The photo beside it showed one man in the foreground and only shadowy figures behind him in the bunks. The caption reads: "Deformed by malnutrition, a Buchenwald prisoner leans against his bunk after trying to walk. Like other imprisoned laborers, he worked in a Nazi factory until too feeble."[1] The other photographs showed only the bodies of prisoners, both Jewish and non-Jewish, who had died at the hands of the Nazis. Some were burned, others were shot, a few had scraps of pajamalike clothing, most were naked, and all were gaunt.

Twenty-two years later, different Jews graced the pages of *Life* magazine. These Jews were Israeli soldiers, tanned and fit. The cover image showed a smiling uniformed man cooling off in the Suez Canal while holding his gun. The soldiers in other photographs did not stare out at rescuers; they stared out from tanks and half-tracks, confidently surveying and protecting their land.

How did American culture make sense of both the image of the emaciated and weak survivor and the strong, self-defending state-builder? This chapter suggests that the two sets of images have a significant cultural relationship: while the Holocaust images depicted Jewish men who did not match the dominate norms of American masculinity, the Israeli images offered a redeemed (and redemptive) Jewish masculinity. Though neither of these sets of images—the weak, passive male victim or the muscle-bound fighter-farmer—became the hegemonic American Jewish masculinity, they each served as a recognizable image of Jewish men abroad. That is, neither American Jews nor American non-Jews tended to see Jewish men as a group through the prism of these images. But they did become a widespread and implicitly redemptive narrative of Jewish life abroad, wherein Jews went from being seen as weak and powerless victims of a state to strong and powerful builders of their own state.

This chapter will explore how popular media and middlebrow literature shaped and reflected American post-Holocaust images of Jewish masculinity. These magazine images, along with middlebrow novels published and film adaptations released between the Holocaust and the Six-Day War, presented a Jewish masculinity that was not passive and desexualized but far more in line with hegemonic American norms of masculinity. Here I attend to these sources to elucidate the changing American portrayals of the Jewish male body, and then analyze the change as reflecting the creation of a narrative of redemption after the near-annihilation of the Jewish body.

Silence or Remembrance: A Gendered View

This work on masculinity also helps us better understand a scholarly debate: Was the American cultural conversation quiet about the Holocaust before it rose into popular consciousness until the 1960s, or did Americans discuss and commemorate the lost lives and atrocities committed in the late 1940s and 1950s? (Cesarani and Sundquist 2012; Diner 2009). One way to answer this is: yes and yes. The shared language of "Holocaust" to designate the Nazi murder of the Jews did not become widespread across American communities until the late 1960s and 1970s, and comparatively few memoirs, literature, or films about the atrocities were produced. Few museums existed, and they had only small numbers of visitors. But the trope of an "early silence" about the Holocaust is a myth.[2] Even before this shared vocabulary, many Jewish communities commemorated the losses of family members, Jewish communities, and their sense of the Jewish people. So while there was discussion and commemoration in the early years after the murder of Jews, it is also true that the vocabulary of the Holocaust and its dissemination in popular culture made the American conversation about it much more audible and widespread in the late 1960s and 1970s. That is, what historian Hasia Diner calls the "vast unorganized spontaneous project" of early commemoration in the United States became even more vast and pervasive, as well as more organized (2009, 12). We can see a narrative about Jewish masculinity—in which a tragic Jewish masculinity led to a redemptive Jewish masculinity—as part of the reason for this development.

As I will suggest here, part of what facilitated the growing conversation among Jewish and non-Jewish Americans about the Holocaust was the way that the story of its tragedy and tragic masculinity could be redeemed by the new masculinity associated with Israeli Jews. Put reductively (surely too reductively, but nevertheless suggestively): perhaps it was easier for Jews to represent and discuss male Holocaust victims when they could also point to the redemption of male Jewish bodies in Israel. And for non-Jews, too, a tale of atrocity with aspects of redemption made a more familiar narrative, and one that was more comfortable to assimilate with other narratives of the United States and their American identity.

There are already many narratives about the Holocaust and America, and so this chapter in no way seeks to be comprehensive. Rather, it seeks to show how images of the Holocaust, in conjunction with later representations of the new state of Israel, represented different Jewish masculinities to both Jewish and non-Jewish American audiences. It simultaneously suggests that masculinity is continually recoded both in the present and in its historical forms. Historical masculinities are subject to the narrative frame of the present. As the years after the Holocaust went on, even the weak, passive, desexualized male bodies of the Holocaust could be recoded as they took their place in a story of redemption.

Popular Culture and Jewish Masculinities

Late 1940s and early 1950s American popular culture looks like it gives relatively little airtime to Holocaust themes and images, especially compared to our own cultural context today in which the Holocaust is far more visible. This might initially strike us as odd, given that most historical events tend to recede from the popular imagination as time passes. And yet, at the time, there was no widely shared vocabulary for thinking about the murder of Jews as a distinct part of the atrocities of the Second World War, and before the Eichmann trial in 1961, many Americans had not read about or absorbed the extent and horror of the historical facts.

The images that were present suggested what I will call a *tragic Jewish masculinity*. The men pictured in the 1945 *Life* photograph epitomized this dominant sense of Jewish male victims of the Holocaust: They were weak. They were skinny. Some were disabled. They were unable to work. And all of the murdered bodies, mostly naked, represented exactly the opposite of what male bodies were ideally: they were emaciated, exposed, defenseless, twisted, disabled, and undifferentiable from one another. In publications that would never publish images of naked white Europeans, these bodies appeared, demonstrating that they were thought of as desexed and utterly desexualized. In all of these ways, the images of Jewish male Holocaust victims embodied a masculinity that contrasted American norms of masculinity in almost every facet. In the worst interpretation, these male victims were an embarrassment. They had gone "like sheep to the slaughter," in a particularly uncharitable but rather widespread simile.

To take another familiar artifact from the first decade after the Holocaust, the popularity of Anne Frank's diary (published in 1952, adapted into a play in 1955) also has a distinctly gendered element that provides a useful contrast to the images of tragic masculinity. Scholars have seen the book, and its adaptations, as a major player in the "Americanization of the Holocaust," and almost all agree that it brought the atrocities to the attention of far more Americans than other publications (Novick 2000). Because she was female and an adolescent, she already occupied a social position that was considered vulnerable. Her youth and feminine vulnerability could draw on readers' and viewers' empathy in an unambiguous way. Unlike adult men, Anne Frank was far less likely to be criticized or second-guessed for not adequately fighting because dominance and warfare tend not to be norms of femininity. Many scholars have noted how the American adaptations of Anne Frank's diary downplayed her Jewishness, but few note that her father's redaction of it before publication removed references to sexuality, female genitalia, and even menstruation, a presentation that comports with norms of feminine purity and American ideals of young womanhood. So much has been written about Anne Frank and her diary that it is not my goal to analyze it extensively here. But it is notable that, as the first major popularizer of Holocaust stories, it aligned with American norms of gender, in that it had a sexually pure young woman victim.

Jewish publications from this early period also suggest a nervousness about endorsing images of tragic Jewish masculinity. In 1952, *Jewish Currents* published an excerpt from a new novel, in which Chaver Paver (Gershon Einbinder) narrated "the heroic and important" and mostly real events. It valorized the Warsaw Ghetto uprising, but it also firmly reinscribed the value of strong, assertive, and military masculinity. When one character cried, the narrator described the crying as "not at all as befitted a guerrilla who had already killed a nazi [sic] and had also thrown a grenade." Another had been a "strong, fearless fighter" but had been rendered paranoid and needy by the loss of his five children and wife.[3] The partisans were a motley crew, but it was clear that the best mode of being was manly, aggressive, and willing to use violence.

The 1961 Eichmann trial and its written and televised coverage brought the extent of the Nazi atrocities to many Americans who had previously paid little attention to it. In retrospect, published coverage and analysis created narrative links between the past atrocities of Jewish suffering under the Nazi regime and the present Jewish state of Israel. Historian Anita Shapira writes, "The Shoah became the issue of the survivors in particular and that of the people of Israel as a whole" (qtd. in Ouzan 2007, 25).

The creation and strengthening of ties between the Holocaust and Israel in the minds of Americans also connected Holocaust victims and the new state of Israel with gendered images. Philosopher Hannah Arendt's now-iconic *Eichmann in Jerusalem*, first a five-part article in the *New Yorker*, supported narratives of Jewish passivity and lack of courage—both characteristics of tragic Jewish masculinity—and counterposed them to Israeli courage in her narration of the trial:

> The contrast between Israeli heroism and the submissive meekness with which Jews went to their death—arriving on time at the transportation points, walking under their own power to the places of execution, digging their own graves, undressing and making neat piles of their clothing, and lying down side by side to be shot—seemed a telling point, and the prosecutor, asking witness after witness, "Why did you not protest?," "Why did you board the train?," "Fifteen thousand people were standing there and hundreds of guards facing you—why didn't you revolt and charge and attack these guards?" (Arendt 1963, 42)

Arendt castigated what she saw as the complicity of the *Judenräte* and praised "the glory of the uprising in the Warsaw ghetto and the heroism of the few others who fought back." Although Arendt tempered the defense's indictments and characterization of passivity with her acknowledgment that "no non-Jewish group or non-Jewish people had behaved differently," these images still stood. For our purposes, the point was that she counterposed the Israeli masculinity embraced in the courtroom to the tragic masculinity of the Holocaust. Thus even before the Six-Day War, there was a narrative tie between the tragic Jewish masculinity of the European past and a redemptive Jewish masculinity of Israel.

Israeli society rejected tragic Jewish masculinity, not just in the impressions of Americans or observers of the Eichmann trial. One historian explained her findings: the image of survivors was "hardly complimentary because Israeli society emphasized 'heroism and resistance,' and suppressed narratives of vulnerability and victimization" (Cohen 2005, 230). In short, they did not fit Israeli norms of masculinity. Of course, American norms of masculinity were not identical with Israeli norms, but the idea of the state of Israel would nevertheless play a role in American Jews and non-Jews imagining a counterimage to the unmanly Holocaust victim.

Although far more would be published after the Six-Day War, even before 1967, several middlebrow American novels about the Holocaust and the early state of Israel appeared from major American publishers. Six novels featured Jewish men far more prominently than Anne Frank's diary and its many incarnations. In these novels, these Jewish men were far more than victims. Some were Holocaust survivors themselves, others were not, but none embodied a tragic Jewish masculinity. In Lester Gorn's 1958 novel *The Anglo Saxons*, the American World War II veteran Joe volunteers to fight for Israeli independence. His fellow soldier Mike crassly introduces himself: "'Phugging well right I'm a Jew.' Mike flexed a wiry arm. 'See that muscle? My Jew credentials, them muscles'" (Gorn 1959, 113). Mike's sentiment could have appeared in any one of the half dozen American Jewish novels written between the end of Second World War and the Six-Day War.

Along with *The Anglo Saxons*, five other American novels about Jewish characters were set in Israel/Palestine: Meyer Levin's 1947 *My Father's House*, Zelda Popkin's 1951 *Quiet Street*, Michael Blankfort's 1953 *The Juggler*, Leon Uris's 1958 *Exodus*, and James Michener's 1965 *The Source*. All six combined narration of historical events with portrayals of Jewish characters fighting to create a homeland. Many of these novels sold well, and they are best characterized as "middle-class novels": literature that strove to sell books and entertain a broad reading public with its accessible storytelling (Hutner 2009). Like *The Anglo Saxons* and its muscular brave Jewish men, these novels produced and valorized the image of a physically strong and assertive Zionism, an ideology that clearly resonates through their approving depictions of Israeli fighting supermen and valiant, hunky kibbutzniks.

Together they suggested the land of Israel could (and did) transform the passive, weak male Holocaust survivors into strong farmers and fighters. To their American audience, these largely depicted the nascent state of Israel as the savior of a Jewish male body emasculated by war. In the Israeli case, the Jewish male body could be (re)masculinized, often styling it as strong, fighting, and connected to the land. This image, often referred to as the "New Jew," gained popularity in American culture, less as an ideal for American Jews themselves, and more as a referent, as if to say, "Our Jewish brethren aren't passive and weak—they are strong nation-builders."

The image of the "New Jew" was not wholly new, however. It had its antecedents in nineteenth- and twentieth-century European Zionism, which promoted *Muskeljudentum*, or "muscle Jewry" (Nordau 1909; Presner 2007; Baader, Gillerman, and Lerner 2012). This gendered component of Zionism, in which the diaspora Jew was effeminate and the Jew in Palestine was manly, never became a central motif of American Zionism (Imhoff 2017). Yet, although American Zionism did not espouse a nationalist-gendered ideology identical to its European counterparts, these gendered themes influenced Zionists in Palestine (Nur 2014), who in turn became objects of the American Jewish imagination.

Each of these novels written by American authors between the time of Israel's independence and the Six-Day War also relied explicitly on historical narrative. Leon Uris's *Exodus* had a prefatory note: "Most of the events in *Exodus* are a matter of history and public record. . . . There may be persons alive who took part in events similar to those described in the book. It is possible, therefore, that some of them may be mistaken for characters in the book" (1986, front matter). In 1951, Zelda Popkin published *Quiet Street*, a novel about a Jerusalem neighborhood on the eve of the war of independence. The "author's note" prefacing the novel read:

> Although this book derives from certain historic events which took place between the first of February and the end of July, 1948, in the country now known as Israel, its characters are all

fictitious. Actual happenings and personalities offer a novelist only cues and any resemblance herein to people, living or dead, stems from the fact that persons as disciplined, as brave and as bewildered as those in the book were among the human components which made Israel. (Popkin 2002, front matter)

Like *Quiet Street* and its "disciplined" and "brave" men, all six of these novels used narration of historical events, especially the Holocaust, to frame the portrayals of Jewish characters fighting to create a homeland.[4] A Jewish past of persecuted bodies had led to a Jewish present of fit, tanned, farmer-fighters.

Despite their setting in the Palestinian landscape, these six novels illuminate little about Israeli gender roles and far more about American popular visions of male Jewishness. The literary representations here are American—they were written by Americans, for American readers—and they similarly trade in the production of myth and desire.[5] Literary critic Dan Wakefield wryly asked in his 1959 review of *Exodus*: "Is it any wonder that the novel of Israeli life Americans have been waiting for had to be written by an American?" (1959, 318–319). Analysis of first the Israeli Jewish male characters suggests that these midcentury American novels reflect a wholehearted endorsement of a martial Jewish masculinity as one available Jewish masculinity—and often one framed in contrast to a passive, weak image of Jewish male Holocaust victims.

In telling the stories about the founding of the modern state of Israel, these authors pushed readers to admire these Jewish male characters. In the words of Leon Uris, these new Israeli characters would be nothing like the familiar "clichéd" Jewish characters who

> cluttered up our American fiction—the clever businessman, the brilliant doctor, the sneaky lawyer, the sulking artist—all those good folk who spend their chapters hating themselves, the world, and all their aunts and uncles—all those steeped in self-pity—all those golden riders of the psychoanalysis couch—all these have been left where they rightfully belong, on the cutting room floor. (Qtd. in Silver 2010, 119).

Uris never hid his distaste for Philip Roth and others he saw as monopolizing the American imagery of Jewishness. True to the Zionist imagination, Uris's men were "fighting people": courageous, strong, capable, physically attractive, both ideological and pragmatic, and willing to take up arms for their cause. Gorn, Michener, Levin, Popkin, and Blankfort, all mirrored the hardy approval of these male Zionists as kibbutzniks, fighters, and farmers.

The majority of the main male characters across all six novels embody courage and strength, and often have remarkably parallel descriptions of male characters—"tall," "strong," "tanned," "muscular," and "quiet courage" describe almost every adult male Israeli character. The tall, strapping, capable Ari Ben Canaan, the hero of *Exodus*, is the most famous character of the Israeli fighter-farmer genre. The "strapping, handsome man" renders the beautiful American Christian nurse Kitty speechless (Uris 1986, 48). "What a man of action Ari Ben Canaan was!" one character exclaims upon meeting him (22). Ari himself articulates the militant philosophy, which elicits awe from his female companion: " 'The old men in there,' Ari explained, 'don't quite understand that the only messiah that will deliver them is the bayonet on the end of a rifle.' Kitty looked at Ari. There was something deadly about this man" (56). Even minor male characters frequently embody this vision of manhood. Joe, the American protagonist of *The Anglo Saxons*, recalled his father's stories about one kibbutz: "Ramat Boker. To hear his dad tell it, every pioneer went about the place clutching a rifle in one hand and a plow in the other. Joe smiled faintly. No doubt Dad's version of this paradise was exaggerated. Still, there was bound to be something special about people who voluntarily became pioneers" (Gorn 1959, 28).

While the dashing male fighter-farmer is nearly ubiquitous in American Zionist novels, the most striking example of the portrayal of this Jewish masculinity comes when Uris and Levin, in particular, and the other writers to lesser degrees, dramatically reverse the usual stereotypes about Holocaust victims. In these American novels, survivors were neither passive nor complicit in their own torture; many of the characters left the camps ready to be fighters. *Exodus* explained: "the concentration camps bred a mean lot" (Uris 1986, 110). The young Holocaust survivor Dov Landau goes from being a meek refugee to a fighter in the Irgun— and a lover of the young and beautiful Karen. In *My Father's House*, the kibbutznik Zev observes of the refugees furtively disembarking the boat in the dark of night, "They had fought to come this far, and they would fight" (Levin 1947, 28). When a fellow kibbutznik expresses concern about integrating newly arrived refugees into kibbutz life, the sabra patriarch Avram objects. "Why do you have to think of them as the sickly dregs of

Europe? They're just what we need.' Avram declared. 'Young and tough. Did you look at them?'" (49).

James Michener's characters likewise see the strength and courage as underlying potentials to be realized through working the land. Michener's *The Source*, his eighth novel but the only one set in the land of Israel, tells the story of the physical space of Palestine through flashbacks triggered by objects discovered at a contemporary archaeological dig. The saga sold over a quarter million copies in its first year, making it the bestselling book in 1965 (Hackett and Burke 1977, 15).[6] Like *Exodus*, which had sold almost five million copies by this time, *The Source* sought to use historical fiction to draw readers—both Jews and non-Jews—into the history and glory of the land of Israel and its inhabitants. Although Michener is the only non-Jew among the authors, *The Source* approaches Judaism in the same generalizing and diluted manner and portrays its main characters, kibbutzniks, and fighters in nearly identical terms to the other novels.

As the novel progresses through history from ten centuries BCE to the time of the dig, *The Source* narrates the stories of the archaeologists themselves, their lives on the kibbutz, and their lives before and during the war. When the main characters are poised to meet new Jewish immigrants to Israel, the Israeli archaeologist Ilan Eilav says to his American colleague John Cullinane: "I've got to warn you again that these aren't the handsome young immigrants that you accept in America, Cullinane. These are the dregs of the world, but in two years we'll make first-class citizens of them" (Michener 2002, 70). Despite their current state of downtrodden appearance, life on the kibbutz would transform them into strong, suntanned, and courageous citizens. War of Independence hero turned Israeli cabinet minister Teddy Reich routinely visits the kibbutz in order to "demonstrate to young members . . . that work, productive work, is the salvation of man, and especially of the Jew" (63). The American archaeologist Cullinane observes "the bronzed young men and women engaged in the work of the kibbutz. They were unusually attractive, and Cullinane thought: It took only a few years to change the hunched-up Jew of the ghetto into a lively farmer. Looking at the muscular young people, especially the free-moving women, he could not detect that they were Jews" (16). Michener described these tanned and muscular bodies as undetectably Jewish to Cullinane's eye. While the "hunched-up ghetto Jew" was presumably a visually identifiable type, the "lively farmers" were no longer physically marked as distinctively Jewish. The erasure of physical difference may have appealed to Jewish readers invested in improving images of weak or effeminate Jews and simultaneously reassured non-Jewish readers of the familiarity and assimilability of Jews. In the novels of Michener, Uris, and Levin, the land of Israel transformed the passive, weak refugees and victims of the Jewish past into strong farmers and fighters.

Michael Blankfort's *The Juggler* espouses a similar pattern of transformative masculinity. When it was released in 1952, the novel was not nearly as popular as *Exodus* or *The Source*, but it was widely reviewed in Jewish and non-Jewish publications and was later adapted for the screen. This is no surprise since Blankfort himself was primarily a screenwriter. The narrative is the story of Hans Muller, a Holocaust survivor who redeems himself from passivity, fear, and escapism through his travels through Israel and communal connections forged at a kibbutz. *The Juggler* engaged psychological issues of the aftermath of the Holocaust well before it became popular to do so. A *Variety* review even claimed that "the story-telling has one serious flaw: it fails to establish early the nature and cause of [Hans's] illness," as though surviving the Holocaust would not have been an obvious cause of the "neurosis."[7] Hans violently attacks a policeman in a haze of confusion—or, as one doctor diagnoses, "Nazi pneumonia," which "attacks the will to live" (Blankfort 1952, 29)—shortly after his arrival in Israel and spends the bulk of the novel running from both his imagination and the law. One night he finds himself hoping for an Arab raid on the kibbutz where he has been staying: "In a vague way, he was seeking an opportunity to fight, or more accurately, to fight back. . . . He had gone for so long without fighting back, the prospect was satisfying" (175). When thinking of Hans, the pursuing police officer thinks of the transformative quality of the land of Israel: "*We have all the chance to become men again*, the detective sang to himself; *we will be men at last!*" (163).

Twelve-year-old Yehoshua, the orphan boy who helps Hans discover strength in *The Juggler*, similarly echoes the new Israeli culture of masculinity. "He was native born, a sabra, and in style with the times, pretended to be excessively self-sufficient, rough, and unsentimental" (Blankfort 1953 53). Yehoshua later articulates these assumptions about Israeli men to himself, almost as a mantra: "A sabra doesn't cry; a soldier-pioneer, a hero, tough and hard. . . . A sabra had to be a master of himself" (90–91). Such a degree of self-sufficiency and strength borders on silliness in reference to a twelve-year-old orphan. In calling attention to the cultural contingency of this masculinity as a "style," *The Juggler* thereby opens a space for a critique of that masculinity. The novel nevertheless ultimately assents to those same values. This assent is clear in the transformation of Hans from a fleeing loner to a strong man willing to take responsibility for himself and others.

Assertive sexuality also emerges as an important aspect of this redeemed masculinity. Although he "felt himself unmanned" by his imprisonment during the Holocaust, his encounter with kibbutznik Yael reawakens his sexual desire (Blankfort 1953, 138). Once Hans joins the kibbutz community, his lover Yael sees "a real strength" in him. Six pages later, he heroically enters a burning barn to save first the cows and then an older kibbutznik named Mordecai from the flames (197). When, near the end of the novel, the policeman hunting Hans considers the opinion of a psychologist, he thinks to himself: "If Dr. Traube was right, Muller's sin was not of greed nor of violence for its own sake, but of fear and hopelessness" (72). In the new Israeli culture, seen through the eyes of American literature, male hopelessness and fear (tragic Jewish masculinity) was a much greater sin than violence.

When these novels narrate the history of the Holocaust, the land of Israel facilitates the rebirth of survivors. In *My Father's House*, rebirth is almost literal, when the eight-year-old main character Daavid undergoes a reversion to mental infancy and cleaves to sabra kibbutznik Avram as a surrogate father and fellow Holocaust survivor Miriam as a surrogate mother on a path to restart a life in Israel. This theme was not lost on readers. The glowing review in *Commentary* magazine summarized the novel's message: "In effect, he tells the most bitter and the most broken that all is not lost, that regeneration is open to all" (Becker 1947, 292).

This transformation takes Holocaust survivors from victims to agents and allows them to become the manly pioneers, farmers, and fighters they had the capability but not the circumstances to become. Daavid's friend and protector Stepan—a kind of friendly Goliath—takes to the fields of the kibbutz like a fish to water: "Stepan stood there staring at the people swinging their mattocks and hoes, and all the others stared too, as though this were something wonderful. Suddenly Stepan walked into the field and reached his hand out for a hoe. 'Give me one of those!' he said." Abba, the patriarch of the kibbutz, "tossed his mattock to Stepan, and it was like a twig in his giant hands. He bent and began to chop the earth, and they laughed and made jokes at his fervor." But almost instantly, other refugees joined in the labor. "But Lazar too had to start to work at once, and Dvora took a hoe from the pile on the ground, and soon they were mixed in among the others, and Daavid saw that in the clothes they had been given this morning it was not easy to tell his companions from the people of the place" (Levin 1947, 48). The physical labor of working the land on the kibbutz had created a physical transformation in these survivors, and they had turned from being persecuted and downtrodden to being strong and productive state-builders.

To symbolize their transformations, the survivors who reach Palestine on the same boat as Daavid and Miriam all change their names.[8] After Stepan reveals that he had escaped the ghetto but returned to help the others fight, the kibbutzniks decide that Stepan and the other survivors have "a whole new life" and so "you need a new name." Stepan asked, "'Isn't there a name, like after a fighter? A Jewish fighter?' Surely, Avram thought, they should have come to that themselves. 'Why not let him be called Maccabee?' he said. 'Maccabee?' Stepan repeated. 'Who was that?'" (Levin 1947, 54–55). This choice of name allowed Levin to narrate the story of the Maccabees and thereby give historical resonance to the figure of the fighting Jew.

The American Embrace of Redemptive Jewish Masculinity

These novels (and the film adaptations) appealed to broad American audiences, both Jewish and non-Jewish, which suggests that the idea of the Jewish male body as redemptive appealed beyond Jewish communities. After all, Michener was not Jewish, and Uris's *Exodus* became a bestseller. The film adaptation of *Exodus* became a blockbuster that quickly surpassed its $3.5-million-dollar production cost. In short, these stories and characters proved very popular among non-Jewish and Jewish audiences. One possibility is that American popular culture—novels, films, and magazines—picked up on a process of redemption as Jewish national self-fashioning in the Israeli project, and the narrative functioned as a story of gendered progress of an outside group. That is, American audiences could have seen Jewish redemptive masculinity as an appealing story about others. But also important is how Americans could see their own role in the story. While the United States more generally moved to place the Holocaust at the center of Second World War narratives, and as it loomed larger as a justification of the morality of war, Americans could see their own national story as helping to redeem Jewish masculinity. American forces intervened in the genocide of Jews, American GIs participated in liberating the camps, and in doing so Americans could see themselves and their own nation as part of the progress from tragic Jewish masculinity to redemptive Jewish masculinity.

When, in 1967, Americans saw images from the Six-Day War, it was less a pivot point and more a culmination of a cultural recoding of masculinity that had been under way for many years. When *Life* printed the photographs of Israeli soldiers on a half-track, many Americans already had a narrative in which the heroic masculinity of the Jewish farmer-fighter had come to oppose and redeem the tragic Jewish masculinity of the Holocaust. Perhaps they had encountered it in fictional form, such as reading one of these novels, or seen the film adaptation of *Exodus* or *The Juggler*. Or perhaps they had gleaned it from journalistic coverage or more philosophical analysis, such as Hannah Arendt's writings. For those Americans who did not have this narrative, the *Life* photographs and essay helped to create it. "On the slopes of Mount Zion, by David's tomb, is a memorial to the nameless millions of Jews murdered in Europe by Hitler," the interior article read. "In the underground grotto, by the light of flickering candles, one can read, smeared in black ash on the wall, in the Bible's Hebrew, 'The voice of your brother's blood screams to me from the ground.' Israelis are Jews who have declared they will not ever again be victims—and their army is an expression of this will."[9]

A tough-looking Moshe Dayan was on the cover of *Time* two weeks earlier; *Life* published its own ninety-six-page special entitled "Israel's Swift Victory" filled with photos of Israeli soldiers marching, fighting, wielding guns, inspecting tanks, and cooling off shirtless under running water. Even the humor valorized the redemptive masculinity of Israeli Jews. The *Time* issue contained jokes:

> At one point in the campaign, an Arab division spotted a lone Israeli sniper on a sand dune. The commander dispatched three men to get him. When they did not return, he sent a dozen. None of them came back. So he finally sent an entire company. Two hours later, one blood-splattered Egyptian soldier crawled back. "It was an ambush," he explained. "There were two of them."[10]

These were not men who went "like sheep to the slaughter"—they were tough, independent, and willing to do the slaughtering themselves.

This redemptive Jewish masculinity did not end the story of the American imagination of Jewish masculinities. In his work on later

American fiction, Paul Breines suggests the potential dark side of this redemptive Jewish masculinity (Breines 1990). As the 1970s and 1980s progressed, the character of the tough, often violent Jewish man became a central figure in a subgenre he calls "the tough Jewish novel." These characters enact vengeance, sometimes in retribution for the Holocaust, and more frequently against Arabs—a "brutalization" that Breines shows to be politically and morally problematic.

These post-Holocaust images did more than simply contrast with the earlier images of male victimized bodies: they also subtly changed the variety of ways those earlier bodies were gendered. Once situated in a narrative of redemption, these emaciated, passive bodies could also be seen as bodies that had an extraordinary ability to survive under wretched conditions and display remarkable perseverance.

Notes

1. The title of the *Life* article (May 7, 1945) reads: "Atrocities: Capture of the German Concentration Camps Piles Up Evidence of Barbarism That Reaches the Low Point of Human Degradation." The quotation appears on page 33.

2. Diner (2009) identifies the work of Leon Jick, Edward Linenthal, Edward Shapiro, Gerald Sorin, Alan Mintz, and Jonathan Sarna as key examples of scholarship that has helped perpetuate the myth of early silence, but she pinpoints Norman Finkelstein and Peter Novick as the two main architects of the myth.

3. "Jewish Partisans in the Woods," *Jewish Currents*, December 1952, 18–20.

4. Michener (2002) began his novel with a similar note about the historicity of his novel: "This is a novel. Its characters and scenes are imaginary except as noted. The hero, Rabbi Akiba, was a real man who died as described in 137 C.E. All quotations ascribed to him can be verified. King David and Abishag, Herod the Great and his family, General Petronius, Emperor Vespasian, General Josephus and Dr. Maimonides were also real persons and quotations ascribed to the last are also verifiable."

5. *Exodus*, *The Anglo Saxons*, and the other novels considered here are neither timeless classics nor have they received sustained critical acclaim. Literary critic Joshua Lambert, for instance, writes about the critical unanimity in the evaluation of "Uris's prose, which at its infrequent best is taut and simple and at its worst is riddled with grammatical errors and the flattest of clichés" (2009, 75). This is not a project to trumpet the aesthetic value of these novels, nor is it intended to recover forgotten authors. Scholars argue that even Israeli literature and culture is better characterized as the production of the myth rather than some historically transparent account of gender roles (Almog 2000).

6. *Exodus* spent nineteen weeks atop the *New York Times* bestseller list.
7. "The Juggler," *Variety*, May 6, 1953, 6.
8. In *Exodus*, brothers Yakov and Jossi Rabinsky likewise change their names to Akiva and Barak Ben Canaan upon reaching Palestine. In *The Source*, the German-born Itzhaak Gottesmann changes his name to Ilan Eliav during the War of Independence shortly after his arrival.
9. The *Life* article, which bears no title, was written by Theodore H. White (June 23, 1967). The quote appears on page 25.
10. "Blintzkrieg," *Time*, June 9, 1967, 39.

References

Almog, Oz. 2000. *The Sabra: The Creation of the New Jew*. Translated by Haim Watzman. Berkeley: University of California Press.

Arendt, Hannah. 1963. "Eichmann in Jerusalem." *New Yorker*, February 16, 40–113.

Baader, Benjamin Maria, Sharon Gillerman, and Paul Lerner, eds. 2012. *Jewish Masculinities: German Jews, Gender, and History*. Bloomington: Indiana University Press.

Becker, George. 1947. "My Father's House by Meyer Levin." *Commentary*, September 1.

Blankfort, Michael. 1953. *The Juggler*. New York: Dell.

Breines, Paul. 1990. *Tough Jews: Political Fantasies and the Moral Dilemma of American Jewry*. New York: Basic Books.

Cesarani, David, and Eric J. Sundquist, eds. 2012. *After the Holocaust: Challenging the Myth of Silence*. London: Routledge.

Cohen, Sharon Kangisser. 2005. *Child Survivors of the Holocaust in Israel: Finding Their Voice: Social Dynamics and Post-War Experiences*. Brighton: Sussex Academic Press.

Diner, Hasia R. 2009. *We Remember with Reverence and Love: American Jews and the Myth of Silence after the Holocaust, 1945–1962*. New York: New York University Press.

Gorn, Lester. (1958) 1959. *The Greater Glory* [*The Anglo Saxons*]. New York: Popular Library.

Hackett, Alice Payne, and James Henry Burke. 1977. *80 Years of Best Sellers, 1895–1975*. New York: R.R. Bowker Co.

Hutner, Gordon. 2009. *What Americans Read: Taste, Class, and the Novel, 1920–1960*. Chapel Hill: University of North Carolina Press.

Imhoff, Sarah. 2017. *Masculinity and the Making of American Judaism*. Bloomington: Indiana University Press.

Lambert, Joshua. 2009. *American Jewish Fiction: A JPS Guide*. Philadelphia: Jewish Publication Society.

Levin, Meyer. 1947. *My Father's House*. New York: Viking Press.
Michener, James. (1965) 2002. *The Source*. New York: Dial.
Nordau, Max. 1909. "Muskeljudentum." In *Zionistische Schriften*. Cologne: Juedischer Verlag.
Novick, Peter. 2000. *The Holocaust and American Life*. Boston: Mariner Books.
Nur, Ofer Nordheimer. 2014. *Eros and Tragedy: Jewish Male Fantasies and the Masculine Revolution of Zionism*. Brighton, MA: Academic Studies Press.
Ouzan, Françoise. 2007. "The Eichmann Trial and American Jewry: A Reassessment." *Jewish Political Studies Review* 19, nos. 1–2 (Spring): 25–38.
Popkin, Zelda. (1951) 2002. *Quiet Street*. Lincoln: Bison Books.
Presner, Todd. 2007. *Muscular Judaism: The Jewish Body and the Politics of Regeneration*. New York: Routledge.
Shapira, Anita. "Hannah Arendt et Haim Gouri: Deux perceptions du procès Eichmann." *Revue d'Histoire de la Shoah* 182 (2005): 301–23.
Silver, M. M. 2010. *Our Exodus: Leon Uris and the Americanization of Israel's Founding Story*. Detroit: Wayne State University Press.
Uris, Leon. (1958) 1986. *Exodus*. New York: Bantam Press.
Wakefield, Dan. 1959. "Israel's Need for Fiction." *The Nation*, April 11.
White, Theodore H. 1967. [No title]. *Life*, June 23.

Epilogue
The Holocaust and Masculinities

Thomas Kühne

The Holocaust is one of the best if not *the* best explored events in human history, with some fifteen to twenty thousand books catalogued in the Library of Congress, written by historians and scholars of all disciplines in the humanities and social sciences. These books and innumerable articles and essays include titles that focus on women and female perspectives, and yet it is safe to say that Holocaust studies have been reluctant to utilize the concept of gender as a tool to analyze relations between men and women and the manifest and hidden workings of ideas and imageries of masculinities and femininities.

Inquiries into women's suffering from, women's agency during, and women's complicity in the Holocaust have rendered obsolete initial worries of some Holocaust scholars in the 1980s and 1990s. A gendered approach, they suspected, might distract from the common suffering of Jewish men and women from Nazi persecution and obfuscate the priority of race over gender in the Nazi genocidal mind-set. But this is a misunderstanding of the concept of gender. As a category of social difference and social hierarchies—of power—gender operates in conjunction with other categories of difference and power, such as race. A gendered approach does not need to question the impact of racist ideologies, political institutions, great men (and women), military conquests, or economic exploitation. It rather supplements and often corrects them (Rittner and Roth 1993; Baumel 1998; Ofer and Weitzman 1998; Kaplan 2003).

Gender studies' initial and primary goal has been to unveil the obvious or clandestine marginalization of women in society. Subsequently, gender scholars have exposed specifically female experiences of victimization under the Holocaust such as the humiliation from head and body shavings, the loss of menstruation, and coerced abortions in the camps (Weitzman 2010). Gender scholars have drawn attention to previously neglected spaces of genocidal terror such as family life, intimacy, and sexuality. They have revealed how such terror challenged traditional gender roles, emasculated Jewish men, and enabled Jewish women to gain agency by assuming those traditionally male roles (Kaplan 1998; Tec 2003). More aggressive processes of female empowerment have been diagnosed for perpetrator society (Koonz 1987; Stibbe 2003). There, women pursued careers as camp guards, engaged in ethnic cleansing, served as military aides, or provided idyllic family retreats for male perpetrators (Schwarz 1997; Harvey 2003; Lower 2013; Mailänder 2015). Without these studies, our knowledge of the social fabric of the Nazi genocide and its broad social basis would be missing crucial pieces (Kühne 2010, 137–161).

Gender Dynamics and Male Perspectives

Only rarely have Holocaust scholars or genocide scholars more largely inquired into the male perspective of these gender dynamics or into men's gendered acting, enabling, or resisting genocide. Unwillingly, these scholars have thus confirmed the subtle power strategy of patriarchal gender regimes. These regimes "unmark" maleness and present it as the human normal, whereas the corresponding female category appears as derivation and thus less important or meaningful. Genocide studies have been, in the words of Elisa von Joeden-Forgey, "preoccupied with the lives of women, leaving men within the original framework of universal subjecthood and thereby unintentionally reaffirming the assumption of the gender-neutrality of men's lives" (2010, 67).

Adding men as gendered subjects removes the veil of invisibility of unmarked normative masculinity, as Björn Krondorfer in the programmatic essay (chapter 1) explains by putting unmarked masculinity in larger antisemitic and colonial contexts. Adding men and masculinity to Holocaust studies means to explore the gendered fabric of the agency, the suffering, the emotions, the actions, the thoughts of male perpetrators, victims, bystanders, enablers, resisters, rescuers, witnesses, interpreters, narrators, deniers, obfuscators during and after the Holocaust. Bringing men back into the history of the Holocaust—not as unmarked but as gendered beings—will be most successful if Holocaust scholars utilize the rich body of theoretically sophisticated and disciplinarily diverse research on the workings of different or even competing concepts of masculinity that has been done for a broad range of Western and non-Western societies, and for hegemonic as well as discriminated groups. Advocates of men's studies have since the 1980s shown that ideas and practices addressed as masculine or manly are not the result of biology but are socially and culturally constructed, changing over time and varying in different societies (Brod 1987; Kimmel and Messner 1989; Brod and Kaufman 1994; Gilmore 1990; Roper and Tosh 1991; Connell 1995; Kühne 1996; Kimmel, Hearn, and Connell 2004; Mosse 2008; Reeser 2010). Discarding vernacular concepts of manhood as a never-changing essence of the biological male fabric and inherent to all human cultures, gender scholars stress the social and historical contingency and changeability of what societies consider to be manly. In exploring these constructions, the relationality, multiplicity, and fluidity of masculinity, its intersection with other categories of social division, the hegemonic organization of competing concepts of masculinity, and not least the resilience of the patriarchal essence of most masculinities have been stressed. What do these categories mean to the study of the Holocaust?

Gender is a relational category. It is tied into binary pairings of the men-women dichotomy, of what is considered as manly and womanly, masculine and feminine (Scott 1986). This way, gender determines the relation between public and private spheres, home and workplace, production and reproduction, action and passivity, hardness and weakness, rationality and emotionality, aggression and peacefulness. Polarized sexual stereotypes present cultural constructs as biological givens. Men appear as energetic, powerful, brave, bold, aggressive, independent, rational, intellectual, and knowledgeable. Women embody the opposite. They are weak, yielding, modest, dependent, emotional, and intuitive.

How the polarization of gender stereotypes can shape experiences, coping strategies, and writings under the impression of genocidal terror is illustrated in this volume by Monika Rice's analysis of autobiographical writings of Jewish physicians about the Holocaust. Male doctors' memoirs and diaries are concerned with the public sphere, prefer abstract thinking, adhere to the ideal of the autonomous individual, and stress rational decision-making. Their female counterparts represent the respective opposites, the private sphere, the concrete, sociability, emotions, and compassion. And yet, the polarization is not rigid; the duress of events such as the Holocaust, or wars, economic crises, and social change challenged established gendered writing patterns.

Conventionally, masculinity is defined by the "repudiation of femininity." Being a man means "not being like a woman," and at the same time it means ruling over and controlling women, explains the sociologist Michael Kimmel (1994, 119–120, 126), a pioneer of men's studies in America. For men, however, "a terror remains," Kimmel continues, "the terror that the young man will be unmasked as a fraud" who has only superficially managed to rid himself of his mother's traits. The feminine coding of homosexuality and homoerotic desires causes an additional, yet related, threat. These desires must be suppressed. Masculinity means to repudiate the "homosexual within." Male homosociality—that is, all-male bonding—is, paradoxically, entrenched by homophobia, states Kimmel, which is "the fear that other men will unmask us, emasculate us, reveal to us and to the world that we don't measure up, that we are not real men." Masculinity is uncertain, "tenuous and fragile" (Kimmel 1994, 126–131).

A popular aggressive response to masculinity's fragility is examined in this volume by Edward Westermann: male drinking rituals. Controlling one's body despite intoxication made the man, and drinking rituals, Westermann shows, established the male bond. They radiated misogyny and transgression, facilitated inclusions, exclusions, and hierarchies among perpetrator groups (who holds most?), fueled social amalgamation and killing effectiveness of the all-male group. They reconfirmed the hypermasculine standard. But it did so only temporarily, in fact only for a moment, after which, as we know from many testimonies, doubts resurged, demanding new and more transgression and aggression.

The workings of the paradoxical web of fragility, homophobia, and patriarchy have been widely analyzed by scholars of different disciplines, most prominently by the German literature scholar Klaus Theweleit in his 1977–1978 inquiry into "male fantasies." Theweleit extracted these fantasies from the misogynist and militarist autobiographic writings of German post–World War I volunteer paramilitary (*Freikorps*) fighters. In Theweleit's view, *Freikorps* men radicalized common Western and German norms about male self-control, as well as about cold, tough, and hard masculinity, into a perpetual war against women and femininity, especially the latter when operative within men and experienced by them as a desire for domesticity, tenderness, and compassion. The men explored by Theweleit needed to fight the hybrid substances of the body and all flowing emotional conditions.

However, a plethora of research, not least on Nazi Germany, has shown that relations between men and women, between concepts of manliness and femininity, between different men, as well as between different women, were more complicated and complex than the polarizing models suggest. Often inspired by poststructuralism, anthropologists, philosophers, psychologists, and other students of male emotions, identities, and sociability have pointed to the "tensions and contradictions" of masculinity and to its fluidity and hybridity. They have cautioned against overemphasizing the antifeminine fabric of masculinity and suggested "explor[ing] the locus of expression of 'non-masculine' sentiments by men" (Vale de Almeida 1996, 116; classic: Sedgwick 1985). The "sign" masculinity, they say, is anything but stable. Instead, "masculinity always bleeds . . . over into its definitional others, despite efforts to the contrary." Gender is a "continuum." Human beings then "oscillate . . . between the two gender poles" (Reeser 2010, 38–39, 45). But how far does the inclusion of femininity go? What counts as femininity? And how is tied into masculinity?

Varied Masculinities among German Soldiers and Perpetrators

There is no generic, universal answer to this question. Instead, it depends on time and space, on which men are considered, and on the contexts in which they operate, think, and feel. My inquiries into ordinary German soldiers' experiences in the Nazi war of annihilation, and the memorialization of these experiences afterward, have illuminated the "protean" fabric of military masculinity (Kühne 2018). Already during and after the First World War, the traumatic experience of suffering—from facing death and mutilation, from constantly fearing either or both, from paralysis, powerlessness, and emasculation—shattered seemingly stable ideas about manliness being owned only by men and femininity only by women (Kühne 2017, 72). Subsequently, inclusive and fluid rather than exclusive and rigorous notions of martial masculinity emerged. Only the former gave meaning to the ambivalent, ambiguous, and complex desires, emotions, and experiences of soldier men and built bridges over diverging experiences, united disrupted identities, and could be adopted by different types of men as they fought together in modern conscripted mass armies.

Such concepts of military masculinity even demonstrated how femininity and masculinity could be on good terms within one person. The protean fabric of the concept of masculinity allowed soldiers to switch between different emotional and moral states without losing their male identity.

"O, what is man," lamented former *Wehrmacht* lieutenant Tim Gebhardt during a memorial service for his regiment's war dead in 1955. "What is virility, when death intervenes and obliterates everything?" Of course, being hurt, physically and mentally, had always been part and parcel of the construction of military masculinity. Initiation into the ranks of "real" men began with indignities and humiliations during the training period, and they did not end there but shaped the soldier's career till the end. The soldier man was never fully sure of his virility. Accepting this uncertainty, knowing about the risk of falling and how to get up again, was precisely what made a man. The cement of the male community was the shared knowledge of this uncertainty. If you felt it, you were not the only one: you knew that your comrades were with you. This is what Tim Gebhardt meant when he apodictically invoked the memory of soldiers' sacrifice in Russia: "The best thing in the life of a man is comradeship." As Gebhardt explained, comradeship meant empathizing with "the hardships and worries of others," and risking one's life "when it comes down to rescuing a wounded soldier, so that he won't fall into enemy hands. And when this wounded man, now a rescued comrade, feels his rescuer gently stroke his hair, just as a mother would, then he can die in peace." Tender manliness, even crying—otherwise the epitome of unmanliness—became respectable in the presence of death. The sphere of death ensured that the symbolic hierarchies—hardness containing weakness—were operative (Kühne 2017, 222–224).

By expressing feminine qualities, exclusively male societies did not simply refresh or remember their ties to the civilian world at home. Rather, they imagined themselves as independent from real women and real families—from the civilian society and civilian morality. The message was: being on our own, we men generate a sense of family, even if we fight cold-bloodedly shortly after; we are emotionally independent. We may miss the world at home, but now we create it ourselves. Paradoxically, the demonstration of the independence of male society from the world at home culminated in violating the very morality that the comradely community claimed to honor. An entire set of manly rituals, all of them violating domestic and civilian norms, served to conform the claim for autarky. Demonstrative excessive drinking, showing of sexual adventures, boasting misogynic rhetoric, staging rowdyism, even carrying out collective rape in extreme cases, all this gained its social momentum from being staged, practiced, reported, or applauded together (Elkins 1946). Abusing women in the occupied areas was the ultimate expression of performative masculinity, an assertion of the sovereignty of the male bond. Sexual violence during the Holocaust, as well as other genocides, is the ultimate expression of the patriarchal dynamic of masculinity (Mühlhäuser 2009; Morris 1996; Rittner and Roth 2012). Directed against women (in some cases also against men), it also organizes the informal hierarchy of all male society within: Who goes first, who is the most brutal, and who has the least restraints? (Kühne 2017, 169–176).

The language of womanhood, femininity, and patriarchal family used to address complex masculinity signaled the inclusion of diverse personalities and emotional conditions, but on a rigidly hierarchical basis. It was all about fitting in. Accepting the priority of the group's "We" over the individual "I" granted the latter some leeway. Not all men were equal when it came to assessing manliness, nor were the various emotional states considered equal. The Nazi machine of annihilation bore a surprisingly high degree of tolerance toward men who shied away from murder. When the German Police Battalion 101 was ordered to murder the Jews of Józefów in Poland in 1942, a minority eagerly agreed. They had internalized what in Nazi Germany counted as the ultimate proof of masculinity—the ability to overcome moral restraints and feelings of guilt about murdering Jews, including women and children. Most of the battalion was not able to simply discard those restraints but acted as ordered anyway, haunted with pangs of conscience. Another minority backed out, neither able nor willing to suppress the feelings of guilt. They had to swallow being labeled "weaklings" or "kids." They were placed at the bottom of an informal hierarchy that was led by those who demonstrated "hardness"—the alpha males. Importantly, however, the "weaklings" were not ousted. In fact, they avoided being ousted precisely by claiming to be "too weak" to commit murder. They could have claimed to be "too good," that is to say, to refuse on moral grounds, but they rarely did. Instead, they claimed to be too weak or at least accepted being seen that way. This is a crucial difference. It meant that they did not question the symbolic order of the male community, but that they interpreted their own constitution as deviant. They presented themselves as exceptions to the rule of hardness, thus confirming the rule and accepting the dominance of the alpha males. This way, they avoided being ousted, and were granted a spot within that community, although on the lowest level. In a culture of hard masculinity, the weaklings represented the other and thus helped to make the hegemonic virtues properly visible (Browning 1992; Kühne 2010, 83–87).

Christopher Browning has masterly explored how the social web of a murder unit such as Police Battalion 101 enabled genocide. To explain the choices these "ordinary men" took, Browning relied on the social psychology of obedience to authority and group conformity. The explanatory potential of these studies is enormous as Browning's application shows. But it is also limited, as has been argued in the debate on perpetrator behavior (Browning 2017). Psychological models of conformity and obedience tend to omit the historical factor—the specific cultural contexts that enforce or mitigate the way they work in concrete historical situations. It is here where a sociologically informed history of masculinities comes into play. In the case of Nazi Germany, the mythical inflation of the concept of comradeship in war, the ultimate experience of male solidarity, into a quasi-religious dogma that demands conformity and subjugation of the "I" under the "We" of the group lubricated the complicity of ordinary men in mass murder.

Religious Models of Stoic Masculinities

Hardness, toughness, aggressiveness, stoicism, endurance, self-control, and so forth, remained the vanishing point of all protean masculinity. Heinrich Böll, who after the war became an icon of West German pacifism, was drafted into the *Wehrmacht* (the regular army, not the SS and other police murder units) and served as private the entire war. He was a designated outsider, and he wanted to be one. What Böll found embarrassing was the military's demand that its members renounce their civilian self for the sake of group cohesion and dynamics. In a letter, he once called the community of comrades a "gathering of fishwives" (Böll 2001, 2: 899). In Böll's postwar novel *The Train Was on Time*, the soldier Andreas found it "terrible being among men only all the time. Men are so womanish" (1978, 108). But even individualists like Böll did not abandon heroic, hard masculinity altogether. Reading Ernst Jünger in early 1943 left Böll fascinated with the heroic warrior who fought ahead and above the mass of comrades; this man, in Böll's words, was "absolutely martially, truly the absolute soldier" (2001, 1: 592, 2: 1091). At the same time, Böll, like many other Christian believers, found solace by picturing himself as reenacting the sufferings and the sacrifice of Christ (Reid 2001; Kühne 2017, 184–190). Böll despised male camaraderie, but many of his fellow soldiers drew fighting spirit from the Christian interpretation of selfless comradeship by referencing the model offered in the Gospel of John (15: 13): "Greater love has no one than this: to lay down one's life for one's friends" (Kühne 2017, 19).

The polyvalent imagery of the imitation of Christ provided both Catholic and Protestant believers—in this volume, studied by Lauren Faulkner Rossi and Benedikt Brunner—also with another, more aggressive justification of engaging in the Nazi war on Europe and especially against Bolshevism in the East: the *miles Christi* (lit., soldiers of Christ). Such imageries of Christian masculinity that glorified stoic suffering and demanded the fight against bolshevist godlessness spurred Catholic and Protestant soldiers' combat motivation even in Hitler's war in the East. By reenacting the ideal of the *miles Christi*, Catholic and Protestant men claimed their belonging to the racial Nazi *Volksgemeinschaft*, the German nation that had cleansed itself of the Jews. And yet, Christian masculinity drew the line at the Nazi genocidal project. Rescuers of Jews in the German army were rare, and the number of soldiers who resisted orders or permission to murder Jews or other civilians was limited. Those who did either or both, however, were often motivated by a compassionate type of masculinity that was rooted in Christian belief systems (Wette 2002, 2003). This Christian manliness contrasted sharply with the Nazis' genocidal morality that demanded—as the ultimate proof of true manliness—merciless and remorseless brutality against alleged racial enemies, be they combatants or civilians; such morality feminized the virtue of compassion with the defenseless as weakness—as unmanly (Kühne 2017, 143–153).

Hegemonic, Complicit, and Subordinate Masculinities

R. W. Connell's theory of hegemonic masculinity (1995) provides the sociological framework to explore rivalry, overlaps, and entanglement of multiple conceptions of masculinity and, by extension, of diverse fabrics of complicity in the Holocaust. Not all men are equally able to match, and many do not even aim at matching, the bar of hard, rational, autonomous masculinity. Instead, they adhere to alternative masculinities, often depending on and intersecting with racial, class, professional, religious, and sexual identities. Different men—for example, generals versus the rank-and-file, war volunteers versus drafted soldiers, soldiers versus civilians, blue-collar workers versus white-collar workers, black men versus white men, Jewish versus Christian men—may honor different masculine norms (Hanisch 2005). Such plurality was operational still among Jewish camp prisoners, as Kim Wünschmann (2013) has shown in a pioneering article. Depending on their social upbringing, Jewish inmates of Nazi camps adhered to revolutionary, bourgeois, or soldierly concepts of masculinity.

The post-Holocaust masculinities in Austria analyzed by Carson Phillips in this volume represent another example of masculinity's plural condition. After 1945 in Austria, military masculinity did not entirely vanish, despite its disastrous consequences, but enjoyed some crude revival in the student fraternities. But at least three different civilian masculinities put them under pressure: the refined and charming one of the cultured gentleman, the physically strong and agile one of the soccer player, and eventually the deliberately pacifist one of the remembrance activist. Phillips juxtaposes these different masculinities but leaves open the question of their competition and rivalry. Connell (and, following Connell, many students of masculinity across the disciplines), by contrast, stresses the constant state of competition for broader social approval and power that fuels the dynamic of the construction of masculinities. They struggle for hegemony. Connell (1995) proposes to analyze the hierarchic order of multiple masculinities in a Gramscian fashion. While men's subordination of women constitutes hegemonic masculinity, the fabric of that masculinity also allows for a range of diverse yet hierarchically ordered male identities. Subordinate masculinities, represented paradigmatically by gay men in most of the twentieth century in Western societies, defy the hegemonic heterosexual hegemony and thus are considered illegitimate. Complicit masculinities, by contrast, also fail to embody the dominant standard, but they do so willingly. They confirm dominance to achieve assistant status and thus reap the "patriarchal dividend." Such masculinities are embodied, for instance, by unserviceable men in a militarized society or by unemployed men in civilian society. "Complicit" men still rule over women and rank above men of "illegitimate" male identities (Connell 1995, 77–80; Tosh 2004; Connell and Messerschmidt 2005).

The rigorousness and effectiveness of this hegemony and subordination, however, is historically and culturally contingent, and their fabric depends not least on their institutional and political context. Hegemonic masculinity, understood in a dynamic fashion, structured the social relations not only of the perpetrators, accomplices, and bystanders but also those of the victims of the Holocaust, as Michael Becker and Dennis Bock exemplarily show in this volume. The status of the *Muselmann*, Becker and Bock argue, was not a definite one but an assigned one that could be revoked. Eventually, most *Muselmänner* died. Assigning *Muselmann* status to certain prisoners allowed the other prisoners to preserve higher status, self-esteem, and agency. While the SS aimed at destroying the male honor and manly identity of all prisoners, the prisoners struggled competitively to save or regain at least some portions of that honor and identity. They did so, on the one hand, by labeling the SS guards as inhuman or non-human, thus denying them male honor and "feminizing" them. On the other hand, they distanced themselves from the physically and mentally weakened, emasculated *Muselmänner*. Eventually, they established a new social hierarchy that allowed them to secure remnants of agency, the resources for survival and resistance.

The complex and even paradoxical web of masculinity as a resource of Jewish agency, even resistance, on the one hand, and as a maelstrom of complicity on the other has been scrutinized also in other settings of Jewish struggle for survival. As Michael Geheran (2018) has shown, German Jewish World War I veterans fought their disempowerment and daily humiliation since 1933 by standing up against Nazi thugs publicly and in front of other men (and women). They displayed core features of martial masculinity such as bravery, strength, initiative, decisiveness, and perseverance. They retained their masculine honor and regained their self-esteem. In Connell's terms, these veterans deployed a "complicit" form of masculinity. By utilizing the hegemonic martial masculinity to secure their own status, agency, and identity, the veterans distanced themselves, although unwillingly, from nonmilitary Jews and thus confirmed Nazi stereotypes about these Jewish men's effeminacy. The analysis of Jewish veterans' struggle for male honor exemplifies how the hegemonic masculinity—including its unconscious workings—could eventually support or resist the Nazis' efforts of destroying Jewish solidarity structures.

Fragility, Fluidity, Reversals

Masculinity is fragile, fluid, and contested; many crises of masculinity have been observed in the past and in the present, which testify to that fragility. Yet the patriarchal fabric of hegemonic masculinity, which informs men's domination of women, and other characteristics such as notions of male autonomy, honor, control, strength, and decisiveness have proven extraordinarily stable and resilient. This resilience is at ease with arguments about the confusion of traditional gender stereotypes in Jewish families under Nazi terror and during the Holocaust. Most prominently, Marion Kaplan (1998) and Nechama Tec (2003) diagnosed a collapse of male gender identities and a role reversal under Nazi antisemitism in Germany and in the ghettos, camps, and resistance movements. Nazi persecution, they said, robbed Jewish men of their traditional roles of providers and protectors of their families, emasculated them, and left them apathetic, helpless, and passive. At the same time, these scholars argue, women took over; made decisions about emigration or staying in Germany or Europe; secured food and shelter for their families, including men, in the ghettos; and provided mental survival kits in the camps and elsewhere. Women performed roles and tasks that had been previously performed by men.

This role reversal did not last among those Jews who escaped and survived the Holocaust, immigrating to Palestine and Israel or other parts of the world. Instead, the polarization of sexual stereotypes remained intact or was restored, although with restrictions, as military service in Israel indicates. Similar paradoxical developments—temporary confusion, yet eventual reaffirmation of traditional gender roles—were common in all societies that engaged in and were targeted by the total wars of the twentieth century. Women volunteered and were mobilized for and targeted by war and genocide. But in the long run women's suffering from war and acting in war as factory workers, nurses, military aids, resistance fighters, or even regular soldiers (in the Soviet Union in World War II) did not overthrow the traditional gender order. Historians Margaret Higonnet and Patrice Higonnet (1987) deployed the metaphor of the double helix to explain this "paradoxical progress and regress" and the underlying constancy of a "gender-linked subordination." In the same spirit, literature scholar Susan Jeffords (1989) pointed to the "remasculinization" of America in the 1980s—the revival of patriarchal values and martial images of men and standards of masculinity that the Vietnam crisis and the defeat of the United States had undermined and weakened. The remasculinization reaffirmed the male-dominated gender order and even the public adoration of military values. Sarah Imhoff's inspiring inquiry in this volume into the reception of Zionist ideals of physically strong, muscular, fighter masculinity in post–World War II America points to older continuities of remasculinization. Her research suggests conceiving of remasculinization not as limited to certain time periods but rather as an ongoing dynamic process, as a cultural resource to be deployed by any society or groups whenever needed.

Inquiries into Jewish masculinities under Nazi terror by Kim Wünschmann (2013, 2015), Maddy Carey (2017), Michael Geheran (2016, 2018), and Sebastian Huebel (2017) raise more serious doubts of the gender role reversal. These scholars show that Jews could preserve or reassert male agency, male honor, male protector and provider roles and thus reverse or counter experiences of emasculation even in the ghettos, in resistance movements, or in the camps, thus inaugurating processes of "remasculinization" even during the Holocaust. Similar sequences of breakdown and recovery of masculinity are the subject of Patrick Farges's comparative argument in this volume about *Yekkes* (German-speaking refugee Jews) in Palestine and Canada. Although their environments were rather different, Jews in both countries countered experiences of disempowerment, humiliation, and emasculation by rebuilding traditional male identities—in the Canadian camps and postwar Jewish communities as providers and professionals, in the *Yishuv* by internalizing Zionist ideals such as pioneering farmer spirit and the appreciation of physical labor and of the muscular male body. Categorizing processes like these as "remasculinization" is not meant to distract from inherent changes: German Jews in Israel and in Canada did not simply reassert the same types of masculinity they or their fathers and grandfathers had adhered to before emigrating. Their masculine identities changed: they adopted softer traits in Canada, harder traits in Israel. As Farges points out, *Yekkes* in neither country followed one path of rebuilding masculinity but plural ones.

Moving Forward

This volume gathers first efforts to bring men back into Holocaust studies—men not as unmarked bearers of normality but as gendered beings whose choices, actions, mind-sets, feelings, capacities, and incapacities are motivated or impeded by cultural and social discourses on masculinity. Reflecting on masculinities during and after the Holocaust widens and deepens our understanding of the agency of victims, bystanders, and perpetrators, and it illuminates the complex and complicated mechanisms of complicity into and coping with the consequences of mass murder. Gender is the foremost category to study micro-politics, and as such gender comprises both femininity and masculinity. To gain momentum in Holocaust studies, further inquiries into the workings of masculinities will benefit from methodically 1) considering and distinguishing the rather different places, media, and practices of construction of masculinity; 2) historicizing and contextualizing the manifold ways masculinity operates; 3) utilizing the analytical potential of gender as a category that signifies, establishes, and fuels power structures.

Masculinity may be understood as ideology, and as such it is "created and propagated through various social forms, especially through images, myths, discourses, and practices" (Reeser 2010, 21). Consequently, masculinities have been studied—so also in this volume—from different disciplinary approaches and by using different types of sources. Analyzing the relation of two trajectories has been most successful: first, the representations of masculinity in laws, literature, and artifacts; and second, the subjective experience and appropriation of such representations. Neither exists independently from the other. It was the "crisscrossing of ideologies and experience, of discourses and material transformation" that propelled or barred change (Canning 2006, 15). To determine the causes, processes, and consequences of this change and to explore how masculinities are constructed, how they work, and what impact they have, students need to carefully reflect on the differences between those "social forms" and the specific knowledge they allow to be established. Nazi representations of martial, hard, and heroic masculinity contrast with the fluidity, flexibility, and ambiguousness of masculinity as practiced by ordinary men at home, on the battlefields, and anywhere in between.

Gender, as a category of social difference, works in conjunction with, and through distinction from, other categories of social differences. Constructions of masculinity intersect with, are shaped by, and themselves shape other constructions of social difference such as class, race, age, sexuality, religion, ethnicity, and nation (Collins and Bilge 2016). Masculinity operates in the mode of plurality. Multiple masculinities coexist or compete in any given society, at any given time. The full range of this plurality has barely been fathomed yet. Instead, martial masculinity, often in its superhuman representations of Nazi art and propaganda (Mangan 1999), is usually considered as the idiosyncrasy of male perpetrators and bystanders, as if they all were enthused about war or even genocide. However, the social cleavages of German as well as other European societies, the division between Christian believers and Nazis, between working- and middle-class men, between entrepreneurs and soldiers, between older and younger men did not simply disappear after Hitler's ascent to power in 1933 or the beginning of World War II in 1939, nor did the different codes and norms of masculinity they had honored before the Nazis tried (but never succeeded) to establish a totalitarian society. And when it comes to assessing masculinities of the victimized people, generic ideas about provider and protector roles of men in modern societies are taken as the standard of Jewish and non-Jewish societies. But the Jews that were thrown together in the ghettos and camps or escaped or resisted the Nazis came from rather diverse Jewish communities in Europe, highly assimilated and secular ones on the one hand, orthodox and ultraorthodox ones on the other. This diversity was reflected in an equally wide range of masculinities. In this range, assimilated masculinities revolving around military honor, national pride, and economic success contrasted sharply with religious alternatives, such as effeminate, gentle, and delicate maleness of *Edelkayt*, whose ideal subject was the *Yeshiva-Bokhur* who devoted his life to the study of the Torah (Boyarin 1997, 23; Carey 2017, 21–48; Brod 1988; Brod and Zevit 2010; Baader, Gillerman, and Lerner 2012). How did this diversity affect discourses and experiences of masculinity during the Holocaust?

Codes and norms of masculinity have influenced, and have been created or challenged by, men and by women. Masculinity is a concept that defines power relations between men, but foremost they define power relations between men and women. In response to popular dichotomist conceptions of patriarchy as a system of male domination over women—as if all men oppressed all women—men's studies have highlighted gendered hierarchies between men. Too often, inquiries into masculinities in general and especially those that mattered during and after the Holocaust are restricted to men's perspectives, thus reasserting inadvertently the ideology of the unmarked male universal. Typically, and so mostly in this volume, masculinities are examined through the lens of those men who enact them—perpetrators, Christians, Jewish and non-Jewish camp prisoners, Jewish refugees, Jewish settlers. While codes and norms of masculinity need the approval of men to exert power, they are also negotiated in interaction with women, who may applaud, doubt, or challenge the performance of masculinity. The construction of gender is a societal concert that includes women as well, and men who did not or did not want to "match the bar." How did they perceive, confirm, or question martial or other masculinities? Neither the hypermasculinity of merciless genocidaires, nor the emasculation and possible remasculinization of their victims, nor the adherence of bystanders and onlookers to the moral inflation of men's solidarity and conformity operate in a world without women. The female perspective on masculinity cannot be omitted when it comes to bringing men back into a gendered research agenda of the Holocaust.

References

Baader, Benjamin Maria, Sharon Gillerman, and Paul Lerner, eds. 2014. *Jewish Masculinities: German Jews, Gender, and History*. Bloomington: Indiana University Press.

Baumel, Judith Tydor. 1998. *Double Jeopardy: Gender and the Holocaust*. London: Valentine Mitchell.

Böll, Heinrich. 1978. "Der Zug war pünktlich (1949)." In *Werke: Romane und Erzählungen*, vol. 1: 1947–1951, edited by Bernd Balzer, 66–168. Cologne: Kiepenheuer & Witsch.

———. 2001. *Briefe aus dem Krieg 1939–1945*, 2 vols. Edited by Jochen Schubert. Cologne: Kiepenheuer & Witsch.

Boyarin, Daniel. 1997. *Unheroic Conduct: The Rise of Heterosexuality and the Invention of the Jewish Man*. Berkeley: University of California Press.

Brod, Harry, ed. 1987. *The Making of Masculinities: The New Men's Studies*. Boston: Allen & Unwin.

———, ed. 1988. *A Mensch among Men: Explorations in Jewish Masculinity*. Freedom, CA: Crossing Press.

Brod, Harry, and Michael Kaufman, eds. 1994. *Theorizing Masculinities*. Thousand Oaks: Sage.

Brod, Harry, and Shawn Israel Zevit, eds. 2010. *Brother Keepers: New Perspectives on Jewish Masculinity*. Harriman, TN: Men's Studies Press.

Browning, Christopher. 1992. *Ordinary Men: Reserve Police Battalion 101 and the Final Solution in Poland*. New York: HarperCollins.

———. 2017. "Twenty-Five Years Later." In *Ordinary Men: Reserve Police Battalion 101 and the Final Solution in Poland*, rev. ed., 225–291. New York: Harper Perennial.

Canning, Kathleen. 2006. *Gender History in Practice: Historical Perspectives on Bodies, Class, and Citizenship*. Ithaca: Cornell University Press.

Carey, Maddy. 2017. *Jewish Masculinity in the Holocaust: Between Destruction and Construction*. London: Bloomsbury.

Collins, Patricia Hill, and Sirma Bilge, eds. 2016. *Intersectionality*. Cambridge: Polity.

Connell, R. W. 1995. *Masculinities*. Berkeley: University of California Press.

Connell, R. W., and James W. Messerschmidt. 2005. "Hegemonic Masculinity: Rethinking the Concept." *Gender & Society* 19, no. 2: 829–859.

Dietrich, Anette, and Ljiljana Heise, eds. 2013. *Männlichkeitskonstruktionen im Nationalsozialismus: Formen, Funktionen und Wirkungsmacht von Geschlechterkonstruktionen im Nationalsozialismus und ihre Reflektion in der pädagogischen Praxis*. Frankfurt: Lang.

Elkins, Henry. 1946. "Aggressive and Erotic Tendencies in Army Life." *American Journal of Sociology* 51: 408–413.

Geheran, Michael J. 2016. "Betrayed Comradeship: German-Jewish World War I Veterans under Hitler." PhD dissertation. Clark University.

———. 2018. "Remasculinizing the Shirker: The Jewish *Frontkämpfer* under Hitler." *Central European History* 51, no. 3: 440–465.

Gilmore, David D. 1990. *Manhood in the Making: Cultural Concepts of Masculinity*. New Haven: Yale University Press.

Hagemann, Karen, and Jean H. Quataert, eds. 2007. *Gendering Modern German Historiography*. New York: Berghahn.

Hanisch, Ernst. 2005. *Männlichkeiten: Eine andere Geschichte des 20. Jahrhunderts*. Cologne: Böhlau.

Harvey, Elizabeth. 2003. *Women and the Nazi East: Agents and Witnesses of Germanization*. New Haven: Yale University Press.

Higonnet, Margaret, and Patrice Higonnet. 1987. "The Double Helix." In *Behind the Lines: Gender and the Two World Wars*, edited by Margaret Higonnet et al., 31–47. New Haven: Yale University Press.

Huebel, Sebastian. 2017. "Stolen Manhood: German-Jewish Masculinities in the Third Reich, 1933–1945." PhD dissertation. University of British Columbia.

Jeffords, Susan. 1989. *The Remasculinization of America: Gender and the Vietnam War*. Bloomington: Indiana University Press.

Joeden-Forgey, Elisa von. 2010. "Gender and Genocide." In *The Oxford Handbook of Genocide Studies*, edited by Donald Bloxham and Dirk Moses, 61–80. Oxford: Oxford University Press.

Kaplan, Marion. 1998. *Between Dignity and Despair: Jewish Life in Nazi Germany*. New York: Oxford University Press.

———. 2003. "Gender: A Crucial Tool in Holocaust Research." In *Lessons and Legacies IV*, edited by Larry V. Thompson, 163–170. Evanston: Northwestern University Press.

Kimmel, Michael S. 1994. "Masculinity as Homophobia: Fear, Shame, and Silence in the Construction of Gender Identity." In *Theorizing Masculinities*, edited by Harry Brod and Michael Kaufman, 119–141.Thousand Oaks: Sage.

Kimmel, Michael S., Jeff Hearn, and R. W. Connell., eds. 2004. *Handbook of Studies on Men and Masculinities*. Thousand Oaks: Sage.

Kimmel, Michael, and Michael A. Messner. 1989. *Men's Lives*. New York: Macmillan.

Koonz, Claudia. 1987. *Mothers in the Fatherland: Women, the Family, and Nazi Politics*. New York: St. Martin's Press.

Kühl, Stefan. 2016. *Ordinary Organizations: Why Normal Men Carried Out the Holocaust*. Cambridge: Polity.

Kühne, Thomas. 1996. "'Kameradschaft—das Beste im Leben des Mannes': Die deutschen Soldaten des Zweiten Weltkrieges in erfahrungs- und geschlechtergeschichtlicher Perspektive." *Geschichte und Gesellschaft* 22: 504–529.

———, ed. 1996. *Männergeschichte—Geschlechtergeschichte: Männlichkeit im Wandel der Moderne*. Frankfurt: Campus.

———. 2006. *Kameradschaft: Die Soldaten des nationalsozialistischen Krieges und das 20. Jahrhundert*. Göttingen: Vandenhoeck & Ruprecht.

———. 2010. *Belonging and Genocide: Hitler's Community, 1918–1945*. New Haven: Yale University Press.

———. 2017. *The Rise and Fall of Comradeship: Hitler's Soldiers, Male Bonding and Mass Violence in the Twentieth Century*. Cambridge: Cambridge University Press.

———. 2018. "Protean Masculinity, Hegemonic Masculinity: Soldiers in the Third Reich." *Central European History* 51, no. 3: 390–418.

Lower, Wendy. 2013. *Hitler's Furies: German Women in the Nazi Killing Fields*. Boston: Houghton Mifflin.

Mailänder, Elissa. 2015. *Female SS Guards and Workaday Violence: The Majdanek Concentration Camp, 1942–1944*. East Lansing: Michigan State University Press.

Mangan, J. A., ed. 1999. *Shaping the Superman: Fascist Body as Political Icon—Aryan Fascism*. London: Frank Cass.

Martschukat, Jürgen, and Olaf Stieglitz. 2008. *Geschichte der Männlichkeiten*. Frankfurt: Campus.

Morris, Madeline. 1996. "Rape, War, and Military Culture." *Duke Law Journal* 45: 651–781.

Mosse, George L. 2008. *The Image of Man: The Creation of Modern Masculinity*. Oxford: Oxford University Press.

Mühlhäuser, Regina. 2009. "Between 'Racial Awareness' and Fantasies of Potency: Nazi Sexual Politics in the Occupied Territories of the Soviet Union, 1942–1945." In *Brutality and Desire: War and Sexuality in Europe's Twentieth Century*, edited by Dagmar Herzog. 197–220. Houndmills: Palgrave.

Ofer, Dalia, and Lenore Weitzman, eds. 1998. *Women in the Holocaust*. New Haven: Yale University Press.

Reid, James. 2001. "Nachwort." In Heinrich Böll, *Briefe aus dem Krieg 1939–1945*, volume 2, edited by Jochen Schubert, 1509–1621. Cologne: Kiepenheuer & Witsch.

Reeser, Todd W. 2010. *Masculinities in Theory: An Introduction*. Malden: Wiley-Blackwell.

Rittner, Carol, and John K. Roth, eds. 1993. *Different Voices: Women and the Holocaust*. New York: Paragon.

———, eds. 2012. *Rape: Weapon of War and Genocide*. New York: Paragon.
Roper, Michael, and John Tosh, eds. 1991. *Manful Assertions: Masculinities in Britain since 1800*. London: Routledge.
Schwarz, Gudrun. 1997. *Eine Frau an seiner Seite: Ehefrauen in der "SS-Sippengemeinschaft."* Hamburg: Hamburger Edition.
Scott, Joan W. 1986. "Gender: A Useful Category of Historical Analysis." *American Historical Review* 91: 1053–1075.
Sedgwick, Eve Kosofsky. 1985. *Between Men: English Literature and Male Homosocial Desire*. New York: Columbia University Press.
Stibbe, Matthew. 2003. *Women in the Third Reich*. New York: Oxford University Press.
Tec, Nechama. 2003. *Resilience and Courage: Women, Men, and the Holocaust*. New Haven: Yale University Press.
Theweleit, Klaus. 1989. *Male Fantasies, Vol. I: Women, Floods, Bodies, History; Vol. II: Male Bodies: Psychoanalyzing the White Terror*. Minneapolis: University of Minnesota Press. (German original 1977–1978.)
Tosh, John. 2004. "Hegemonic Masculinity and the History of Gender." In *Masculinities in Politics and War: Gendering Modern History*, edited by Stefan Dudink, Karen Hagemann, and John Tosh, 41–58. Manchester: Manchester University Press.
Vale de Almeida, Miguel. 1996. *The Hegemonic Male: Masculinity in a Portuguese Town*. Providence: Berghahn.
Weitzman, Lenore J. 2010. "Women." In *The Oxford Handbook of Holocaust Studies*, edited by Peter Hayes and John K. Roth, 203–217. Oxford: Oxford University Press.
Wette, Wolfram. 2002. *Retter in Uniform: Handlungsspielräume im Vernichtungskrieg der Wehrmacht*. Frankfurt a. M.: Fischer Taschenbuch Verlag.
———. 2003. *Zivilcourage: Empörte, Helfer und Retter aus Wehrmacht, Polizei und SS*. Frankfurt a. M.: Fischer Taschenbuch Verlag.
Wünschmann, Kim. 2013. "Männlichkeitskonstruktionen jüdischer Häftlinge in NS-Konzentrationslagern." In *Männlichkeitskonstruktionen im Nationalsozialismus: Formen, Funktionen und Wirkungsmacht von Geschlechterkonstruktionen im Nationalsozialismus und ihre Reflektion in der pädagogischen Praxis*, edited by Anette Dietrich and Ljiljana Heise, 201–219. Frankfurt: Lang.
———. 2015. *Before Auschwitz: Jewish Prisoners in the Prewar Concentration Camps*. Cambridge: Harvard University Press.

Contributors

MICHAEL BECKER is a PhD candidate in sociology in the Faculty of Social and Behavioral Sciences at the Friedrich Schiller University Jena. He holds a degree in social sciences from the University of Mannheim. His research interests are the history of sociology, historical sociology, social theory, history and memory of National Socialism, and Holocaust studies. He coorganized the eighteenth Workshop on History and Memory of NS Concentrations Camps in 2012 and is coeditor of and contributor to the anthology *Orte und Akteure im System der NS-Zwangslager*.

DENNIS BOCK is a sociologist and literary scholar. He received his PhD from the University of Hamburg in 2016. His research interests are representations of violence and persecution, Holocaust and gender studies, and history and memory of NS concentration camps. He currently works on knowledge transfer in comic books. Dennis has coorganized the eighteenth Workshop on History and Memory of NS Concentrations Camps in 2012 and is coeditor of and contributor to the anthology *Orte und Akteure im System der NS-Zwangslager*. He has collaborated actively with researchers from several other disciplines, including history, sociology, comparative literature, and cultural studies.

BENEDIKT BRUNNER is a Research Fellow at the Leibniz-Institute for European History in Mainz, Germany. He holds a PhD in history at the University of Münster. In 2015, he published a chapter on "Geschlechterordnung im Kirchenkampf: Konstruktionen von Gender in der autobiographischen Verarbeitung der Zeit des Nationalsozialismus." His research interests are contemporary church history in West and East Germany, religious history of North America, and the history of grief and consolation in sixteenth- and seventeenth-century Europe.

OVIDIU CREANGĂ is a historian with the Conference on Jewish Material Claims against Germany. From 2011 to 2015, he was a researcher in the Jack, Joseph and Morton Mandel Center for Advanced Holocaust Studies at the United States Holocaust Memorial Museum in Washington, DC. His area of research and writing for the USHMM's *Encyclopedia of Camps and Ghettos* concerns the fate of Jews, Roma, Soviet and Allied prisoners of war, and religious minorities during the Holocaust in Romania. Within that spectrum, he maintains an interest in the intersection of religion and gender. He holds a doctorate in theology and religious studies from King's College London (UK). His three edited volumes, *Men and Masculinity in the Hebrew Bible and Beyond* (2010), *Biblical Masculinities Foregrounded* (with Peter-Ben Smith, 2014), and *Hebrew Masculinities Anew* (2019) established "biblical masculinities" as a research area in biblical studies.

PATRICK FARGES is Professor of German and Gender History at the University Paris Diderot (France). He studied social sciences and German history and literatures in Paris, Berlin, Toronto, and Berkeley. He holds a PhD in German studies (2006). His research interests include oral history of migration, migrant memories, and gender history. He is currently working on a book on the history of German Jewish masculinities in Palestine/Israel. Recent publications include *Bindestrich-Identitäten? Sudetendeutsche Sozialdemokraten und deutsche Juden als Exilanten in Kanada* (2015), "Forum: Holocaust and the History of Gender and Sexuality" (with Hájková, Mailänder, Bergen, and Grossmann, 2018), "Pioneers, Losers, White Collars: Narratives of Masculinity among German-Speaking Jews in Palestine/Israel" (2018).

LAUREN FAULKNER ROSSI currently teaches German history, the world wars, and genocide studies at Simon Fraser University in Vancouver, Canada. She completed her PhD at Brown University in 2009. She is the author of *Wehrmacht Priests: Catholicism and the Nazi War of Annihilation* (2015) and coeditor of *Lessons and Legacies XII: New Directions in Holocaust Research* (2017). She is currently completing a chapter about the causes of genocide in the nineteenth century for a forthcoming work on the cultural history of genocide.

SARAH IMHOFF is Associate Professor in the Department of Religious Studies and the Borns Jewish Studies Program at Indiana University. She writes about gender, sexuality, and American Judaism both historically and in the present. She is the author of *Masculinity and the Making of American Judaism* (2017). She also has interests in the role of DNA and genetic discourse in constructions of Jewishness, race, and Jewishness in the American context, and the history of the field of religious studies, especially in its relation to U.S. law.

BJÖRN KRONDORFER, PhD, is Director of the Martin-Springer Institute at Northern Arizona University and Endowed Professor of Comparative Religious Studies. His field of expertise is religion, gender, culture, (post-) Holocaust studies, and reconciliation studies. Publications include, among others, *Unsettling Empathy: Working with Groups in Conflict* (2020), *Reconciliation in Global Context* (2018), *Male Confessions* (2010), *Men and Masculinities in Christianity and Judaism* (2009), *Remembrance and Reconciliation* (1995), and three volumes in German on the cultural and theological legacy of the Holocaust. His scholarship helped to define the field of critical men's studies in religion. He has been Visiting Faculty at the Freie Universität, Berlin, and held Affiliate Visiting Faculty status at the University of the Free State, South Africa. He facilitates intercultural encounters on issues of conflict, memory, and reconciliation. He has presented his research and facilitated workshops and seminars in Armenia, Australia, Austria, Belgium, Bosnia and Herzegovina, Canada, Finland, Germany, Italy, Israel and Palestine, Poland, South Africa, South Korea, Switzerland, the Netherlands, the United Kingdom, and the United States.

THOMAS KÜHNE is Director of the Strassler Center for Holocaust and Genocide Studies at Clark University, where he holds the Strassler Chair in Holocaust History. He received his PhD at the University of Tübingen in 1992. He studies the cultural history of war and genocide, with a focus on Holocaust perpetrators and bystanders, on masculinities, and on the construction of collective identity through mass violence. His essay collection on the history of masculinities in modern Germany, *Männergeschichte-Geschlechtergeschichte* (Men's history—gender history, 1996) established this field in Central Europe. He has been awarded fellowships from the John Simon Guggenheim Memorial Foundation, the Institute for Advanced Study at Princeton, the Center for Contemporary History in Germany, and the German Research Foundation. He won the German Bundestag Research Prize for his dissertation on electoral cultures and suffrage reform in Pre-1914 Prussia. His most recent book publications include the monographs *The Rise and Fall of Comradeship: Hitler's Soldiers,*

Male Bonding and Mass Violence in the 20th Century (2017) and *Belonging and Genocide: Hitler's Community, 1918–1945* (2010).

CARSON PHILLIPS, PhD, is Managing Director of the Neuberger Holocaust Education Centre in Toronto, Canada. He is the recipient of numerous scholarly awards, most recently a research fellowship with the Wiener Wiesenthal Institut für Holocaust-Studien. An editorial board member of *PRISM: An Interdisciplinary Journal for Holocaust Educators* and an expert on Holocaust education and pedagogy, his research interests focus on post-Holocaust conceptualizations of masculinity and gender. He is also adjunct faculty at Gratz College, where he teaches courses in the Holocaust and Genocide Studies program. He has recently published book chapters on "Using Recorded Testimonies of Holocaust Survivors with English Language Learners" (2018) and "Väterliteratur: Remembering, Writing, and Reconciling the Familial Past" (2018).

LISA PINE is Associate Professor of History at London South Bank University. She received her PhD from the University of London in 1996. Her publications include *Debating Genocide* (2019), *Life and Times in Nazi Germany* (2016), *Education in Nazi Germany* (2010), *Hitler's "National Community": Society and Culture in Nazi Germany* (2007 and 2017), and *Nazi Family Policy, 1933–1945* (1997). She has published a chapter on "Gender and the Holocaust: Male and Female Experiences of Auschwitz" (2015) and contributed chapters on "Germany" (2016) and "The Family and Private Life" (2018). An edited volume on *The Family in Modern Germany* is forthcoming.

MONIKA RICE is Director of the Holocaust and Genocide Studies Program at Gratz College. She received her PhD from Brandeis University in 2014. Her first book, *What! Still Alive?! Jewish Survivors in Poland and Israel Remember Homecoming* (2017), chronicles the evolution of Holocaust survivors' memories of their first encounters with Polish neighbors after the war, recorded in immediate postwar testimonies, as compared to similar accounts collected years later in Israel. Her articles, book chapters, and reviews have been published in edited volumes and academic journals. She has taught courses on the Holocaust, Jewish-Christian relations, and women's spirituality, and has been a recipient of several prestigious fellowships and grants, among them: The Claims Conference Fellowship in Advanced Shoah Studies, Albert Abramson Fellowship in Holocaust Studies, and the Hadassah-Brandeis Institute. Currently, her larger research project investigates postwar mixed identities of Polish Jewish doctors.

ROBERT SOMMER is a historian and scholar in cultural studies. He received his PhD in 2009 from Humboldt University of Berlin, Germany. His research focuses on sexuality and sexual exploitation in Nazi concentration camps as well as prostitution politics in the Third Reich. For his dissertation on camp brothels, he conducted numerous interviews with survivors and extensive research in archives in Germany, Poland, and the Unites States. He worked as research associate for the concentration camp memorials of Ravensbrück and Flossenbürg and for the BBC documentary *Auschwitz: The Nazis and the "Final Solution."* He is the author of *Das KZ Bordel* (The camp brothel: Forced sexual labor in National Socialist concentration camps; 2009).

EDWARD B. WESTERMANN is Professor of History at Texas A&M University–San Antonio. He received his PhD from the University of North Carolina, Chapel Hill. He has published extensively on the Holocaust and military history and is the author of *Hitler's Ostkrieg and the Indian Wars: Comparing Genocide and Conquest* (2016), *Hitler's Police Battalions: Enforcing Racial War in the East* (2005), and *Flak: German Anti-Aircraft Defenses, 1914–1945* (2001). He is a former Fulbright Fellow at the Free University of Berlin, a J. B. and Maurice C. Shapiro Fellow at the United States Holocaust Memorial Museum, and a three-time fellow of the German Academic Exchange Service. His current book project, *Drunk on Genocide? Drinking Ritual, Masculinity, and Mass Murder*, focuses on the relationship of alcohol and atrocity in the Holocaust.

Author Index

Abbey, Antonia, 159, 164
Abella, Irving, 249, 263
Agamben, Giorgio, 143, 144
Aghacy, Samira, 263
Aleksandrowicz, Juliun, 105, 114, 116, 125
Aleksiun, Natalia, 25, 45
Alheit, Peter, 206, 215
Almog, Oz, 281, 282
Altinay, Ayşe Gul, 38, 45
Amesberger, Helga, 141, 144
Andersen, Pablo Dominguez, 43, 45, 50
Anderson, Margaret L., 193, 197
Angrick, Andrej, 153, 154, 164
Anonymous, 163, 164
Arendt, Hannah, 271, 272, 280, 282
Auer, Katrin, 141, 144
Auga, Ulrike, 206, 215
Auslander, Fietje, 184, 197

Baader, Benjamin Maria, 5, 11, 47, 51, 245, 263, 273, 282, 299, 300
Baer, Elisabeth, 2, 11, 42, 45, 46, 77, 95, 96, 125
Balińska, Marta A., 99, 100, 104, 106, 107, 108, 125, 126
Banauch, Eugen, 249, 263
Barnett, Victoria J., 187, 197
Bartov, Omer, 172, 191, 194, 197

Bartrop, Paul, 79, 95
Barwich, Beate, 212, 216
Bauer, Yehuda, 21, 42, 45
Baumel, Judith Tydor, 127, 285, 300
Beck, Birgit, 154, 164
Becker, George, 278, 282
Becker, Michael, 8, 39, 45, 129, 139, 142, 143, 144, 295
Ben Rafael, Eliezer, 257, 263
Ben-Ari, Eyal, 258, 264
Benz, Angelika, 151, 154, 160, 164
Benz, Wolfgang, 211, 216
Beorn, Waitman, 153, 162, 164
Bergen, Doris L., 6, 10, 11, 12, 44, 210, 214, 216, 264
Berger, Maurice, 81, 95
Bessel, Richard, 147, 164
Betlen, Oszkar, 54, 55, 73
Bettelheim, Bruno, 82, 95
Biale, David, 5, 12
Bilge, Sirma, 298, 300
Birnbaum, Walter, 211, 214, 216
Black, Peter, 161, 162, 164
Blackburn, Gilmer W., 150, 165
Blady-Szwajgier, Adina, 125, 120
Blankfort, Michael, 272, 275, 277, 278
Blaschke, Olaf, 214, 216
Bock, Dennis, 39, 45, 129, 139, 142, 143, 144, 145, 295
Bock, Gisela, 4, 12

311

Boer, Roland, 45
Bohler, Jochen, 162, 167
Böll, Heinrich, 292, 293, 300, 302
Borowski, Tadeusz, 56, 58, 73
Bos, Pascale, 43, 46
Bourdieu, Pierre, 140, 141, 145, 205, 216, 218
Boyarin, Daniel, 4, 12, 45, 46, 77, 95, 251, 256, 263, 299, 300
Boyer, John W., 196, 198
Brandt, Hans Jürgen, 196, 197
Brehm, Hollie Nyseth, 24, 47
Breines, Paul, 4, 12, 281, 282
Breuer, Thomas, 195, 196, 197
Bridenthal, Renate, 11, 12
Brod, Harry, 4, 12, 48, 221, 287, 299, 300, 301
Broszat, Martin, 74, 172, 185, 186, 187, 196, 197
Browning, Christopher, 29, 46, 161, 165, 292, 300
Brunner, Benedikt, 9, 11, 203, 216, 293
Buchbender, Ortwin, 195, 197
Buckley-Zistel, Susanne, 43, 51
Bukey, Evan Burr, 222, 223, 242
Burke, James Henry, 276, 282
Byrne, Rachel, 44, 46

Canning, Kathleen, 298, 300
Caplan, Gregory A., 11, 12, 44, 46
Caplan, Jane, 3, 12, 30, 148, 165
Card, Claudia, 43, 46
Carey, Maddy, 2, 5, 12, 18, 22–26, 29, 36–38, 46, 297, 299, 300
Carney, Amy, 4, 12
Carrigan, Tim, 140, 145
Cesarani, David, 78, 95, 249, 264, 268, 282
Chapoutot, Johann, 44, 46
Chappel, James, 207, 216
Chiari, Bernhard, 162, 165

Cocks, Geoffrey, 148, 165
Cohen, Sharon Kangisser, 272, 282
Collins, Patricia Hill, 298, 300
Collinson, David, 21, 48
Connell, R. W., 21, 44, 46, 139, 145, 163, 165, 239, 242, 247, 263, 287, 293–295, 300, 301
Conway, John, 185, 197
Crawford, Michael T., 159, 165

Dausien, Bettina, 206, 215
De Visser, Richard O., 163, 165
Dean, Carolyn, 96, 127
Dearn, Alan, 231, 242
Dehn, Günther, 208, 212, 216
Demianova, Genia, 155, 165
Denzler, Georg, 185, 197
Depkat, Volker, 206, 215, 216
Des Pres, Terrence, 79, 96
Desbois, Patrick, 153, 165
Deselaers, Manfred, 44, 46
Dibelius, Otto, 204, 209, 214, 216
Diehl, Guida, 210, 211, 216
Diem, Hermann, 209, 210, 217
Diestel, Barbara, 211, 216
Dietrich, Anette, 214, 217, 301, 303
Dietrich, Donald J., 185, 197
Dillon, Christopher, 149, 165
Dilthey, Wilhelm, 205, 217
Diner, Dan, 260, 263
Diner, Hasia R., 268, 269, 281, 282
Dirks, Walter, 207, 217
Draper, Paula Jean, 249, 252, 263
Dupont, Marc, 72, 73
Dürr, Renate, 205, 206, 217

Eakin, Paul John, 100, 101, 103, 107, 125, 126
Edelman, Marek, 117, 118, 119, 124, 126
Eichler, Maya, 194, 198
Elkins, Henry, 291, 301

Ephgrave, Nicole, 42, 47
Ericksen, Robert P., 187, 198, 215, 217

Farges, Patrick, 9, 10, 11, 12, 249, 263, 264, 297
Faulkner Rossi, Lauren, 8, 195, 198, 293
Federn, Ernst, 56, 61, 67, 73
Fehrenbach, Heide, 225, 242
Fein, Helen, 77, 96
Felman, Shoshana, 80, 96
Ferme, Valerio, 23, 47
Ferrales, Gabrielle, 24, 47
Fischer-Hupe, Kristine, 204, 217
Förster, Jürgen, 172, 194, 198
Foucault, Michel, 53, 70, 73
Frankenberg, Ruth, 44, 47
Frankl, Viktor, 54, 55, 56, 57, 64, 74, 81, 91, 95, 96
Freudenthal, Herbert, 149, 165
Frevert, Ute, 150, 165
Friedländer, Saul, 78, 96, 265
Friedler, Eric, 85, 96
Friedman, Paul, 56, 74
Frister, Roman, 61–63, 74
Fritsche, Maria, 222, 223, 242
Fuchs, Emil, 127, 208, 212
Fulda, Daniel, 206, 217

Ganzevoort, Ruard, 45, 47
Garbarini, Alexandra, 126
Gastfriend, Edward, 39, 47
Gawalewicz, Adolf, 139–142, 145
Geheran, Michael J., 295, 297, 301
Gellately, Robert, 187, 198
Geller, Jay, 5, 12
Geyer, Michael, 44, 47, 196, 198
Giancola, Peter R., 159, 165
Gilbert, Shirli, 11, 12
Gillerman, Sharon, 5, 11, 44, 47, 51, 245, 263, 273, 282, 299, 300

Gilman, Sander, 5, 12, 38, 44, 47
Gilmore, David D., 287, 301
Goldenberg, Myrna, 2, 11, 23, 42, 43, 45, 46, 47, 77, 81, 95, 96, 125
Goldhagen, Daniel Jonah, 29, 47
Gorn, Lester, 272, 275, 282
Grabowski, Jan, 156, 165
Graf, Margret, 142, 145
Grau, Gunter, 47
Greenspan, Henry, 78, 96, 97
Gregory, Jeanne, 159, 165
Greif, Gideon, 254, 263, 264
Grenz, Sabine, 73, 74
Gross, Jan Tomasz, 160, 165
Gross, Michael B., 193, 198
Grossmann, Atina, 2, 11, 12, 246, 264
Grüber, Heinrich, 211–214, 217
Grunberger, Richard, 152, 166
Günther, Dagmar, 215, 217
Gurewitsch, Brana, 80, 96
Gusdorf, Georges, 101, 102, 103, 108, 124, 126
Gutman, Israel, 133, 145

Hackett, Alice Payne, 276, 282
Hagemann, Karen, 164, 301, 303
Hájková, Anna, 10, 12, 23, 47, 59, 74, 141, 145, 247, 264
Hakak, Yohai, 4, 12, 45, 47
Halbmayr, Brigitte, 141, 144, 155, 166
Hanisch, Ernst, 294, 301
Haraway, Donna, 30, 48
Hardman, Anna, 80, 96
Harvey, Elizabeth, 4, 12, 286, 301
Hastings, Derek, 179, 198
Haynes, Stephen R., 3, 12, 20, 27–30, 44, 48, 77, 96, 147, 166
Hearn, Jeff, 21, 48, 287, 301
Hedgepeth, Sonja, 11, 13, 43, 48, 163, 166, 168
Heineman, Elizabeth, 30, 48
Heinemann, Marlene E., 2, 11, 13

Heinze, Carsten, 206, 217
Heise, Ljiljana, 214, 217, 301, 303
Herzog, Dagmar, 4, 13, 43, 48, 75, 159, 162, 166, 167, 168, 302
Herzstein, Robert Edwin, 236, 242
Higonnet, Margaret, 296, 301
Higonnet, Patrice, 296, 301
Hilberg, Raul, 21, 42, 48
Hildenbrand, Bruno, 205, 218
Hillenbrand, Karl, 196, 198
Hinojosa, Ramon, 44, 48, 196, 198
Hirszfeld, Ludwik, 100, 103, 104, 105–108, 114, 116, 125, 126
Hoffmann, Peter, 184, 196, 198
Holdenried, Michaela, 205, 218
Horak, Roman, 233, 242
Horowitz, Sara R., 42, 48
Höss, Rudolph, 27, 31–34, 42, 44, 48, 64, 65, 74
Hotam, Yotam, 254, 256, 264, 265
Huebel, Sebastian, 297, 301
Hummel, Karl-Joseph, 196, 198
Hunt, Geoffrey P., 149, 166
Hutner, Gordon, 273, 282

Imhoff, Sarah, 10, 31, 45, 48, 273, 282, 296
Ingrao, Christian, 155, 162, 166

Jarusch, Konrad, 44, 47
Jarvis, Christina, 27, 48
Jeffords, Susan, 296, 301
Jelinek, Estelle C., 102, 126
Jerome, Roy, 4, 13, 242
Jockusch, Laura, 125, 126
Joeden-Forgey, Elisa von, 286, 301
Jones, Adam, 77, 96
Joshi, Vandana, 152, 166

Kahn, Leo, 156, 166
Kaplan, Danny, 258, 264

Kaplan, Marian, 2, 11, 12, 285, 286, 296, 301
Ka-Tzetnik 135633, 51, 61, 74
Kaufman, Michael, 48, 287, 300, 301
Kautsky, Benedict, 56, 139, 145
Kellenbach, Katharina von, 4, 13, 44, 48, 49, 218
Kershaw, Ian, 187, 196, 198
Kielar, Wiesław, 58–60, 74
Kilian, Andreas, 85, 96
Kimmel, Michael, 42, 48, 250, 264, 287, 288, 301
Kislinger, Florian, 195, 198
Klee, Ernst, 27, 48
Klein, L. Ruth, 249, 264
Kleinberg, Ethan, 206, 218
Klemp, Stefan, 157, 166
Klemperer, Victor, 158, 166
Kłodziński, Stanisław, 129, 130, 136, 137, 139, 143, 144, 145
Koch, Eric, 252, 254, 258, 264
Koch, H. W., 150, 166
Koch, Peter-Ferdinand, 34, 48
Koenen, Gerd, 188, 198
Kogon, Eugen, 151, 166
Kolinsky, Eva, 85, 96
Konner, Melvin, 38, 49
Koonz, Claudia, 2, 11, 12, 286, 301
Kosta, Barbara, 237, 242
Krall, Hanna, 117, 118, 119, 126
Kranz, Dani, 261, 264
Kremer, Lillian S., 2, 11, 13, 23, 49
Krondorfer, Björn, 6, 21, 31, 39, 44, 45, 47, 49, 203, 204, 211, 218, 286
Kühl, Stefan, 215, 218, 302
Kühne, Thomas, 3, 10, 11, 13, 27, 28, 43, 49, 148, 150, 159, 166, 188, 192, 196, 199, 215, 218, 262, 286, 287, 289–293, 302
Kulisiewicz, Aleksander, 55, 74
Kundrus, Birthe, 211, 218

Author Index

Künneth, Walter, 218
Kunze, Regina, 53, 74
Kushner, Tony, 249, 264

Lacan, Jacques, 73, 74
Laclau, Ernesto, 206, 219
Lagerwey, Mary, 81, 96
Laidler, Karen Joe, 149, 166
Lambert, Joshua, 281, 282
Landwehr, Achim, 206, 218
Langbein, Hermann, 56, 59, 61, 62, 74, 137, 145
Langer, Lawrence L., 21, 49, 78, 96, 121, 126
Latzel, Klaus, 188, 199
Laub, Dori, 80, 96
Lee, John, 139, 145
Lees, Sue, 159, 165
Lehmann, Jürgen, 58, 75, 206, 218
Lejeune, Philippe, 100, 101, 126, 205, 218
Lemle, Russell, 149, 166
Lensky, Mordechai, 108–114, 116, 117, 124, 126
Lerner, Paul, 5, 11, 47, 51, 245, 263, 273, 282, 299, 300
Lesniak, Roman, 57, 74
Lessing, Hans-Ulrich, 205, 218
Levenkron, Nomi, 160, 166
Levi, Primo, 23, 47, 49, 83, 85, 96, 130, 131, 132, 133, 136, 139, 140, 143, 145, 172, 199
Levin, Meyer, 272, 275, 277, 279, 282, 283
Levitt, Laura, 4, 13
Lewy, Guenter, 185, 199
Lifton, Betty Jean, 107, 126
Lilje, Hanns, 209, 218
Linke, Uli, 4, 13
Loewenich, Walther von, 219
Loewy, Ernst, 255, 264

Lomsky-Feder, Edna, 258, 264
Longerich, Peter, 151, 167
Lothe, Jakob, 78, 97
Lower, Wendy, 4, 13, 156, 167, 286, 302

Machtan, Lother, 204, 218
Mailänder, Elissa, 4, 10–13, 264, 286, 302
Makower, Henryk, 114 126
Makower, Noemi, 115, 126
Mallmann, Klaus-Michael, 153, 154, 157, 158, 162, 167
Maman, Daniel, 258, 264
Mangan, J. A., 156, 167, 298, 302
Mann, Michael, 43, 49
Margolis-Edelman, Alina, 118, 126
Martschukat, Jürgen, 206, 218, 302
Marwick, Arthur, 206, 219
Mason, Mary G., 101, 102, 126
Matthäus, Jürgen, 78, 97, 162, 167
Matussek, Paul, 56, 74
Mcelrath, Suzy, 24, 47
Mckenzie, Callum, 156, 167
McLeod, Hugh, 207, 219
McNay, Lois, 213, 219
Meier, Kurt, 215, 219
Mermelstein, Mel, 160, 167
Messerschmidt, James W., 21, 44, 46, 163, 165, 294, 300
Messerschmidt, Manfred, 191, 199
Messner, Michael A., 287, 301
Meune, Manuel, 248, 264
Meuser, Michael, 139, 145
Michel, Jean, 69, 70, 74
Michener, James, 272, 275, 276, 277, 279, 281, 283
Mielke, Fred, 125, 126
Milch, Baruch, 120, 125, 126
Milch-Avigal, Shosh, 125, 126
Misch, Georg, 205, 219

Mishkind, Marc, 149, 166
Mitscherlich, Alexander, 125, 126
Moltke, Johannes von, 225, 242
Moore, Jacqueline M., 148, 163, 167
Morris, Madeline, 291, 302
Mosse, George L., 3, 13, 43, 49, 183, 199, 206, 219, 231, 232, 242, 255, 264, 287, 302
Mostowicz, Arnold, 119, 120–124, 126
Mouffe, Chantal, 206, 219
Muhlhauser, Regina, 43, 49, 152, 154, 155, 158, 167, 291, 302
Müller, Filip, 91, 92, 97, 160, 161, 167
Muller-Hildebrand, Burkhart, 196, 199
Mushaben, Joyce Marie, 42, 50

Naor, Simha, 59, 74
Naujoks, Harry, 62, 74, 75
Niemöller, Wilhelm, 208, 210, 215, 219
Niethammer, Lutz, 69, 74
Nomberg-Przytyk, Sara, 59, 75
Nordau, Max, 4, 36, 44, 273, 283
Novick, Peter, 270, 281, 283
Nowak, Kurt, 203, 219
Nur, Ofer Nordheimer, 4, 13, 44, 50, 256, 264, 273, 283
Nyiszli, Miklos, 86–89, 92–94, 97

Ofer, Dalia, 2, 11, 13, 21, 42, 49, 77, 97, 127, 285, 302
Oster, Sharon, 130, 133, 145
Ouzan, Françoise, 271, 283

Palshikar, Sanjay, 160, 167
Paul, Christa, 69, 75
Paul, Gerhard, 167, 184, 197, 199
Pawełczyńska, Anna, 137, 138, 145
Peer, Yvonne, 56, 75
Peralta, Robert L., 152, 167
Perechodnik, Calel, 39–42, 45, 50

Pergher, Roberta, 10, 13
Peskowitz, Miriam, 4, 13
Pető, Andrea, 38, 45, 49, 50
Petropoulos, Jonathan, 97
Peukert, Detlev, 147, 167, 187, 199
Pfeiffer, Julius, 247–249, 264
Phelan, James, 78, 97
Pilarczyk, Ulrike, 256, 262, 264
Pine, Lisa, 3, 7, 13, 23, 24, 42, 50, 87, 97
Pisar, Samuel, 58, 60, 72, 73, 75
Plattner, Karl, 61, 75
Pohl, Oswald, 33, 34, 44, 50, 66, 76
Ponzio, Alessio, 27, 50
Popkin, Zelda, 272–275, 283
Presner, Todd S., 255, 264, 273, 283
Puckhaber, Annette, 249, 264
Pyta, Wolfram, 153, 157, 158, 167

Rahden, Till van, 207, 219
Randall, Amy, 13, 44, 48, 77, 96, 97, 166
Rathkolb, Oliver, 223–225, 242
Reading, Anna, 23, 50
Reese, Willy Peter, 154, 167
Reeser, Todd W., 30, 50, 287, 289, 298, 302
Reeves Sanday, Peggy, 155, 167
Reichardt, Sven, 147, 149, 150, 168
Reid, James, 293, 302
Rice, Monika, 7, 8, 125, 126, 127, 287
Rieß, Volker, 153, 157, 158, 167
Ringelheim, Joan, 2, 11, 13, 19, 20, 50
Rittner, Carol, 2, 11, 13, 43, 50, 77, 97, 125, 127, 285, 291, 302
Roberts, James, 149, 168
Robinson, Sally, 31, 44, 50
Rödder, Andreas, 204, 219
Roediger, David, 44, 50
Roper, Michael, 287, 303
Roseman, Mark, 10, 13
Ross, Ronald J., 193, 199

Author Index

Roth, John K., 11, 13, 43, 77, 97, 125, 127, 285, 291, 302, 303
Rubin, Agi, 78, 97, 232
Ryback, Timothy W
Ryn, Zdzisław, 161, 168

Saidel, Rochelle G., 2, 11, 13, 43, 48, 152, 163, 166, 168
Salton, George L., 161, 168
Salvante, Martina, 27, 50
Saraga, Esther, 11, 14
Schafer, Silke, 55, 75
Schelvis, Jules, 162, 168
Schild, Erwin, 253, 262, 265
Schissler, Hanna, 204, 219
Schneider, Karl, 157, 168
Schneider, William H., 100, 104, 106–108, 125, 126
Schoenfeld, Gabriel, 19, 42, 50
Scholder, Klaus, 185, 199
Schönstedt, Walter, 149, 164, 168
Schoppmann, Claudia, 61, 75
Schüler-Springorum, Stefanie, 4, 14, 164
Schwaiger, Georg, 173, 196, 199
Schwarz, Gudrun, 4, 14, 286, 303
Schweitzer, Petra, 78, 97
Scott, Joan W., 287, 303
Sedgwick, Eve Kosofsky, 289, 303
Segev, Tom, 246, 265
Seibel, Paul, 193, 199
Seibel, Wolfgang, 43, 50
Seidel, Thomas A., 207, 208, 214, 219
Seidler, Victor, 77, 97
Shapira, Anita, 259, 265, 271, 283
Shapiro, Amy, 42, 47, 95, 96
Sharot, Stephen, 257, 263
Shepherd, Ben H., 154, 164, 168
Shik, Na'ama, 54, 59, 75
Shohat, Ella, 257, 265
Siebert, Barbara, 85, 96
Siegemund, Anja, 254, 265

Sierakowiak, Dawid, 25, 50
Silver, M. M., 274, 283
Simon, Marie, 134, 135, 145
Sinnreich, Helene, 153, 168
Smith, Jonathan, 163, 165
Smith, Roger, 77, 97
Smith, Sidonie, 100, 110, 127
Smolinsky, Heribert, 177, 195, 199
Sofsky, Wolfgang, 56, 68, 75, 138, 143, 145
Sommer, Robert, 7, 39, 51, 62, 66–69, 72, 73, 75
Sontag, Susan, 233, 242
Spicer, Kevin P., 196, 200
Spode, Hasso, 149, 168
Sremac, Srdjan, 45, 47
Staats, Reinhart, 203, 219
Stahel, David, 154, 168
Sterz, Reinhold, 195, 197
Stibbe, Matthew, 286, 303
Stieglitz, Olaf, 206, 218, 302
Strohm, Christoph, 215, 219
Strutz, Andrea, 249, 265
Suderland, Maja, 140, 141, 142, 145
Suleiman, Susan, 78, 97
Swartout, Lisa, 11, 14

Tanenbaum, Roy, 72, 75
Tec, Nechama, 158, 168, 286, 296, 303
Thamer, Hans-Ulrich, 215, 219
Theweleit, Klaus, 3, 14, 26–28, 43, 51, 161, 168, 288, 289, 303
Thum, Gregor, 188, 200
Thygesen, Paul, 58, 75
Timm, Annette F., 20, 43, 51, 154, 159, 168
Tongue, Samuel, 45, 51
Tory, Avraham, 161, 168
Tosh, John, 287, 294, 303
Touquet, Helen, 45, 51
Trillhaas, Wolfgang, 208, 212, 220
Troper, Harold, 249, 263

Turda, Marius, 78, 88, 97

Uris, Leon, 272–275, 277, 279, 281, 283
Usborne, Cornelie, 3, 14

Vale de Almeida, Miguel, 289, 303
Van Alphen, Ernst, 23, 51
Vansant, Jacqueline, 226, 242
Venezia, Shlomo, 86, 87, 89–94, 97
Vettel-Becker, Patricia, 232, 234, 242
Vogt-Moykopf, Chaim, 249, 265
Volk, Ludwig, 195, 200
Volkmann, Hans-Erich, 188, 199, 200
Volkov, Shulamit, 246, 265

Wachsmann, Nikolaus, 12, 46, 165, 211, 220
Wackerfuss, Andrew, 4, 14
Wagner-Egelhaaf, Michaela, 205, 220
Wakefield, Dan, 274, 283
Wallen, Jeffrey, 39, 51, 73
Wallis, Brian, 81, 95
Walser-Smith, Helmut, 193, 200
Walter, Dirk, 149, 168
Walter, Verena, 39, 51
Warmbold, Nicole, 135, 138, 146
Warren, Mary Anne, 77, 97
Watson, Julia, 100, 107, 127
Watson, Simon, 81, 95
Waxman, Zoë, 2, 11, 14, 97, 127, 247, 261, 265

Weidinger, Bernhard, 228, 241, 242
Weigand, Rudolf, 196, 198
Weitzman, Lenore J., 2, 11, 13, 21, 42, 49, 51, 77, 97, 127, 285, 286, 302, 303
Wendland, Heinz-Dietrich, 208, 212, 215, 220
Wendt, Simonen, 43, 45, 50
Wermuth, Henry, 83, 97
Werner, Frank, 27, 51, 162, 163, 168
Wesołowska, Danuta, 135, 146
Westermann, Edward B., 8, 21, 28, 49, 51, 92, 97, 147, 164, 168, 288
Wette, Wolfram, 191, 199, 293, 303
White, Theodore H., 282, 283
Whitehouse, Christine, 249, 262, 265
Wieland, Christina, 148, 152, 169
Wiesel, Elie, 79–84, 97, 135, 146
Wieviorka, Annette, 78, 97
Wijze, Louis de, 82, 97
Williams, Timothy, 43, 51
Wittler, Kathrin, 134, 135, 146
Wu, Albert, 215, 220
Wünschmann, Kim, 294, 297, 303

Zahn, Gordon C., 195, 200
Zevit, Shawn Israel, 4, 12, 299, 300
Zimmerman, Stefan, 226, 243
Zimmermann, Moshe, 254, 265
Zinke, Peter, 258, 265
Zwicker, Lisa Fetheringill, 11, 14, 44, 51

Subject Index

abuse, 24, 114, 153; alcohol, 148, 161–62; physical, 152; sexual, 63, 65, 71, 162. *See also* assault; violence
accomplice, 1, 21, 29, 35, 40–41, 156, 295
accountability, 1, 233
agency, 30, 40, 95, 130, 136, 143, 213, 250, 286, 295, 297; male, 1, 3, 6, 21, 29, 31, 34–35, 37–39, 41, 214, 297; moral, 39, 204; women's, 285–86
aggression, 19, 159, 231, 234, 238–40, 287–88; sexual, 152, 154, 159, 161-62. *See also* violence
aggressive, 62, 159, 162, 178, 271, 286–88, 293; -ness, 292; non-, 227
alcohol, 8, 27–28, 86, 92, 147–55, 157–59, 161–63. *See also* intoxication
America(n), 4, 5, 10, 20, 33–34, 222, 226, 232, 267–74, 278–81, 288, 296; Jewish masculinity, 268, 279–80; (norms of) masculinity, 270, 272, 268; Zionism, 273, 275. *See also* United States
anger, 87, 113, 138
annihilation, 19, 35, 37, 39, 107, 116, 268, 291; war of, 163, 289
anti-Jewish, 5, 191, 230

antisemitic/antisemitism, 4–5, 19, 34, 36, 38, 45, 179–80, 182, 187, 191–92, 254–55, 286, 296
apathy, 54–55, 64, 174, 186
Arab, 135, 257–60, 277, 280–81
Aryan, 8, 58, 108, 115, 152, 186, 231–33, 253; non-, 8, 211
assault(ed), 37, 141, 161, 211; physical, 37–38; sexual, 8, 26, 38, 152, 154, 159, 162–63; testicular 38. *See also* violence
assimilate(d), 24, 38, 103, 239, 246, 269, 299
assimilation, 45, 104, 246
atrocity, 28–29, 61, 142, 180, 188, 192, 268–71
Auschwitz, 6, 7, 27, 31–32, 54–60, 62–64, 66, 68–69, 71, 77–95, 117, 120, 135, 137, 140, 142, 160, 221, 236. *See also* camps
Austria, 6, 54, 65, 221–40, 245–46, 249–50, 257–58, 294; maleness/masculinity/ men, 9, 222–40; soldier, 222–23, 232
authority, 1, 32, 36, 41, 186, 239; camp, 53, 64; crisis, 207; figure, 1; moral, 34; obedience, 292; SS, 69
autobiographical, 32, 99–103, 116, 130, 205–207, 213–14, 236, 287

Subject Index

autobiography, 54, 62, 100–103, 107–108, 124, 205–206, 208, 210–12, 253; studies, 7
autonomy, 65, 77, 82–83, 95, 172, 185, 190, 296

barter(ing), 39, 71
battle, 2, 66, 85, 101, 150, 171–72, 175–76, 179–83, 190–91; -field, 163, 298; -front, 162, 180, 187; inner, 175
Belorussia/Belarus, 157, 162
beneficiay, 1, 21, 35, 41
Bergen-Belsen, 57, 59, 71, 248. *See also* camps
binary, 186, 287; construction, 26–27; language, 27; model, 28, 36, 103; theory, 33
Birkenau. *See* Auschwitz
bodily, 247, 260; ailment, 106; characteristics, 36; markers, 24; perfection, 232; training, 256; wounds, 115
body, 7, 24, 31, 38–41, 53, 55, 70–71, 83, 89, 142, 161, 232, 234–35, 287–89; corpulent, 71; culture, 232, 255; desexualized, 269; fatherly, 40; hard, 231; image, 232; inmate, 54; Jewish male, 4, 5, 37–39, 268, 273, 279; male, 5, 31, 37–39, 231–32, 235, 258, 268–70, 273, 279, 297; material, 114; prisoner's, 136; sexual/ized, 55, 71; shaving, 286; women's, 20. *See also* Jewish; male
Bolshevism, 8, 171, 173–74, 176–82, 189–92, 293
bonding; comradely/of comradeship, 28, 208; homosexual, 4; homosocial, 4, 27; male, 3, 6, 23, 39, 92, 151, 155, 159, 254, 288, 291; social, 23, 28, 78, 83, 150
Bonhoeffer (Dietrich), 184, 186, 209

boy, 39, 61–63, 65, 67, 71, 107, 150, 155, 182–83, 213, 231, 233, 254, 257, 259, 277; "Camp," 249–54; "toy," 39. *See also* children; *Pipel*
brothel, 7, 53, 57, 60, 65–72, 154, 213
brother, 83, 86–88, 109, 189, 256–57, 280; warm (*warmer Bruder*), 251
brotherhood, 187–88, 191
Buchenwald, 56, 61, 66–67, 69, 84, 140, 151, 267. *See also* camps
Burschenschaften, 6, 9, 149, 227–30. *See also* fraternity
bystander, 1, 4, 29, 35, 41, 286, 295, 297–99

camaraderie, 8, 28, 83, 92, 149, 211, 234, 293. *See also* comradeship
camps, 6, 7, 20–22, 39, 53, 61–62, 64–65, 67, 70, 72, 79, 82, 85, 116, 130, 132, 134–35, 139, 143, 159–61, 213, 275, 279, 286, 294, 296–97, 299; concentration, 8, 30, 53–54, 56–57, 59, 61, 65–68, 70–71, 73, 79, 129–30, 132–35, 138–40, 142–43, 153, 211, 275; death, 6, 23, 147; extermination, 160, 172; internment, 249–52; labor, 6, 23, 78; Nazi, 7, 8, 20, 30, 33, 53–54, 57, 65, 70–71, 73, 79, 85, 129, 132, 135, 213 294; paramilitary, 209; sports, 212; women's, 61, 66, 71. *See also* Auschwitz; Bergen-Belsen; Buchenwald; Dachau; Flossenbürg; Mauthausen; Mittelbau-Dora; Neuengamme; Ravensbrück; Sachsenhausen
Canada, 9, 245–50, 252–54, 261, 297
career, 188–89, 256, 286; military, 189, 259; Nazi, 32–33; political, 236; soldier's, 290
Catholic, 32, 57, 104, 177–78, 182, 186, 191–93, 207, 239, 248, 293;

Church, 33, 172–73, 175, 178, 184–87, 190, 192; faith, 8, 172–73, 189–90, 193; Field Bishop, 182; fraternities, 228–29; men, 172–73; priests, 6, 182–83; resistance, 185; seminarians, 8, 171–74, 179, 182, 188–90; soldier, 293. *See also* clergy
Catholicism, 32, 192–93
child/children, 19–20, 25, 32, 35, 40–41, 86, 96, 102, 104, 106–107, 109–10, 113, 115–17, 119–20, 160, 163, 261, 271, 291. *See also* boy
childhood, 107, 189, 226
choice, 1, 21, 23, 30, 40, 78, 85–86, 90, 120, 184 187, 259, 279, 292, 297
choiceless choice, 90, 120
Christianity, 33, 104, 176–77, 181, 189. *See also* Catholic; Catholicism; church; Protestant; religion; Russian Orthodox Church
church, 9, 33, 172–73, 175–78, 182, 184–87, 190, 192, 203–204, 207–11, 214. *See also* Christianity
Church Struggle (*Kirchenkampf*), 204, 207, 209–10
circumcision, 24, 38
clergy/clergymen, 4, 173–74, 182–83, 208. *See also* Catholic; Rabbi; theologians
coercive, 60–61, 72, 183, 185; -iveness, 36–37
collaboration, 107, 172, 186, 192
collaborator, 36
combat, 176, 293
combatant, 3, 293, 258–59
companion, 275, 279
companionship, 7, 23
competition/competitive, 81, 93, 189, 232–34, 251, 294–95
complicit, 9, 34, 90, 116, 182, 192–93, 236, 275, 293–94; masculinity, 35, 294–95

complicity, 1, 4, 21–22, 72, 172, 182, 186–88, 192, 211, 224, 235–36, 240, 272, 285, 292–93, 295, 297
comrade, 62, 148, 150, 171, 176, 179, 184, 188–89, 260, 290, 292
comradeship, 3, 27–28, 150, 187–88, 208–209, 211, 214, 258, 290, 292–93. *See also* camaraderie
conditions of extremity, 2, 25. *See also* extreme
conscription, 182–83, 191
control, 53, 72, 95, 150, 162, 186, 226–27, 231–34, 250, 296; controlling women's bodies, 20, 288; controlled masculinity, 226, 234; self-, 87, 151, 209, 288, 292; uncontrollable, 111
courage, 19, 33, 77, 82, 95, 113, 175–76, 208, 210, 214, 232, 271, 275–76; moral, 109
crime, 26, 34, 116, 152, 188, 224, 235–36, 239–40; war, 223, 236
criminal, 4, 9, 62, 172, 184, 193, 235; -ity, 173
critical masculinity/men's studies, 2, 3, 5, 10, 17–19, 20–28, 33, 287–88, 299
culpability, 1, 4, 32–33, 204
culpable wrongdoing, 21, 31
Czechoslovakia, 83, 245

Dachau, 56, 64, 66, 140, 161, 211, 213, 253. *See also* camps
danger, 71, 109, 134, 139, 179, 213, 229, 234, 248, 260
death, 5, 7, 24, 33, 40–41, 54–55, 60, 63–64, 66, 68, 72, 82, 88–95, 99, 104, 106, 110, 112, 115, 119–23, 129, 132–33, 136–38, 141–43, 152, 173, 181, 184–85, 192, 212–13, 223, 233, 248, 271, 289–90; -bed, 39; march, 63, 83–85, 93; sentence, 23;

death *(continued)*
  squad, 180; threat, 60, 71, 120. *See also* camps
death camp. *See* Auschwitz; camps
defensive, 36–37, 121, 149, 207, 259; war, 178, 182, 186, 188
dehumanization, 7, 54–55, 69–70, 117, 151
dehumanize, 143, 156
denazification, 222–23. *See also* Nazi
deportation, 40, 57, 86, 100, 109, 112–13, 115–16, 120–21, 160, 186–87, 236, 250
desexualized, 256, 268–70. *See also* sexual
desexualization, 54, 70
deviant, 291; behavior, 257; group, 239; masculinity, 252
dignity, 37, 85, 92, 106, 121, 251. *See also* indignity
disability, 3, 35
discrimination, 37, 187, 223, 257
disempowerment, 250, 295, 297. *See also* powerless
dishonor, 8. *See also* honor
doctors (physicians), 61, 99–100, 106, 112, 114, 117–24, 274, 277; female, 7, 117, 124–25; camp inmates, 58–59, 87–89; Jewish (male), 6–7, 99–101, 103, 109, 120, 124, 287
domestic, 225–26, 290
domesticity, 27, 227, 288
dominance, 30–32, 34, 139, 155, 159, 161–62, 229, 233, 250, 270, 291, 294
dominant, 35–36, 56, 72, 77, 138, 148, 159, 177, 206, 224, 231, 248, 257, 270, 294; masculinity, 30–31, 35–38, 238–39
domination, 155, 222, 251, 261; Jewish world, 34; over men, 252;
of/over women, 152, 296, 299; sexual, 152, 154, 160, 250, 252

East(ern); Europe, 58, 67, 256; Front, 174, 177, 191, 208; Galicia, 25; occupied territories, 147, 152, 154
education, 18, 39, 57, 107, 233, 247, 252; Holocaust, 9, 17, 237–38; in ghetto, 233; Nazi, 150; of priests, 173–74
effeminacy, 295
effeminate, 299; Jew, 273, 277
Eichmann trial, 270–72
Einsatzgruppen (mobile killing units), 27–28, 92, 180, 192
emasculate(d), 72, 273, 286, 288, 295–96. *See also* effeminate
emasculation, 6–8, 72, 151, 273, 286, 288–89, 295–97, 299. *See also* remasculinization
emigration. *See* migration
empathy, 28, 143, 270
enabler, 1, 4, 29, 36, 41, 286
enemy, 38, 71, 134, 163, 171–72, 176, 179–80, 182, 184, 189, 191, 258, 290; arch-, 179; alien, 245, 248–50, 261; primal, 174
England. *See* United Kingdom
exhausted, 58, 84, 108, 213, 224, 260
exhaustion, 70, 81, 89, 130, 132–33. *See also* fatigue
exploitation, 35, 59, 62, 72, 154, 285
extermination, 32, 116, 187; camps, 160, 172; war of (*Vernichtungskrieg*), 174, 187
extreme; alcohol consumption, 158; case, 291; circumstances, 38–39, 77, 96, 142; conditions, 78, 143; embodiment, 142; gruesome, 85; harsh, 111; hierarchies, 136; painful,

Subject Index 323

87; temperatures, 81. *See also* conditions of extremity

faith, 32, 81–82, 91, 113, 172–73, 177–80, 183, 189–91, 212; Catholic, 8, 172–73, 189–90, 193; in God, 32, 178; loss of, 81, 104, 175. *See also* God; prayer; religion; spiritual
family, 4, 26–27, 38–39, 54, 82, 86–87, 94–95, 103, 116, 121, 141, 154, 173–74, 182, 189, 227, 238, 246–48, 250, 253, 268, 286, 290–91, 296
fascism, 4, 231
fascist, 26, 233; aesthetics, 232–33; masculinity/manliness, 27, 221, 223, 230–31; warrior, 233
father, 1, 25–26, 34, 40–41, 82–84, 91–92, 104, 120, 208, 212, 227, 229, 232, 235, 270, 275, 278, 297; -son relation, 26, 83, 212
fatherhood, 4
Fatherland, 176, 179, 189
fatigue, 68, 109, 111. *See also* exhaustion
fear, 7, 8, 80, 87, 111, 113, 115, 132, 138, 178–79; -ful, 24, 110; -less fighter, 271; of becoming a victim, 152; of being shamed, 8; of conscription, 191; of exclusion, 27; of execution, 183; of homosexuality, 235; of loss of privilege, 139; of retribution, 32; of selection, 81
fellowship, 150–51, 162, 185
female, 53, 61, 80–81, 83, 86–88, 91–92, 99, 101, 103, 141, 150, 152, 156, 160, 270, 285–87; autobiography, 101–102, 124; beauty, 55; behavior, 80; camps, 71; companion, 275; doctors, 7, 117, 124–25; genitalia, 270; in brothels, 65; narratives, 91, 93,

119; perpetrator, 4; perspective, 285, 300; pioneer, 256; presence, 175; prisoner (inmate), 58–61, 66, 71, 95, 129, 141, 154; sexuality, 72; survivors, 55, 57, 81, 87; writings, 94. *See also* women
femininity, 26, 55, 135, 141–42, 148, 161, 176, 270, 288–91, 298
feminist; critics, 101; historians, 3; Holocaust scholarship, 19–22; scholars, 4, 103; theorizing, 38
fight/fighting, 28, 54 82, 84, 119, 136, 147, 150–51, 163, 172–74, 176, 178–82, 188, 191–92, 204, 208–10, 223, 229, 250, 252, 254, 258, 270, 272–74, 277, 279–80, 289–90, 293
fighter, 22, 35, 123, 210, 260, 268, 271, 273–80, 288, 296. *See also* warrior
filth, 121, 177, 188. *See also* hygiene
filthy, 90–91, 111, 113
Flossenbürg, 62–63, 66. *See also* camps
fluid, 59; gender, 8; masculinity, 34, 289, 295; memories, 8; notions of identity, 2
fluidity, 101, 251, 289; of masculinity, 287, 298
fraternity, 9, 37, 149, 224, 228, 229, 294. *See also Burschenschaften*
Freikorps, 26–27, 288
friend, 34, 69, 93, 102, 111, 118, 172, 213, 257, 278
friendship, 23, 257

Galicia, 25, 153
gay, 62, 158, 239, 294. *See also* homosexual; queer
gender, 1, 2, 8, 17, 19, 22, 24, 27–31, 35–39, 72, 77, 80–81, 86, 94–95, 99, 114, 135, 141–43, 148, 151–52, 162,

gender *(continued)*
173, 183, 204, 206, 214, 239–40, 247–48, 256–58, 273, 285–87, 296–300; analysis, 25, 28, 36, 203; consciousness, 29; differences, 21, 25–26, 100, 102, 116, 124; discourse, 77; dynamics, 10, 41, 247, 254, 286; fluid, 8; genocide, 20. 77; hierarchy, 81, 299; historians, 2; ideal, 148; identity, 7, 8, 23, 39, 140, 247–48, 256, 296; implications, 17, 26, 39, 206, 261; neutral/ity, 29, 286; norms, 7, 9, 78, 80–81, 83, 93, 95, 270; order, 25, 39, 129, 296; performance, 245; performativity, 224–25; relations, 3, 4, 35–36, 203, 214, 287; roles, 9, 25, 86, 214, 245, 250, 274, 286, 296; scholars, 19, 286–87; studies, 19–21; theory, 4, 29, 41

gendered; beings, 1, 22, 287, 297; blind spots, 26; experiences, 30–31, 78, 94, 129, 142–43; expressions, 6, 7, 204; interaction, 252; male, 2, 6, 7, 9, 18–19, 29, 31, 39, 83, 86, 93, 148, 204, 296; perspective, 2; reading, 7; sexuality, 54, 73; space, 162; testimony, 78; wounding, 21; writing patterns, 288; violence, 257

genocidal, 2, 6, 18, 20, 25, 38, 92, 147, 193, 293; antisemitism, 19; culpability, 4; destructiveness, 5; impulse, 192; machinery, 8, 27; mind-set, 285; mission, 285; terror, 286–87; violence, 77

genocide, 4, 19, 38, 42, 77, 154, 192, 279, 286, 291–92, 296, 298; feminist theorizing, 38; gender, 20, 77; mechanism of, 10; studies, 77

German, 3, 26, 41, 56, 59, 106–107, 109, 121, 133–34, 149, 152–55, 157, 159, 162, 173, 176–92, 204, 210, 222, 224–31, 288; army, 8, 178, 222, 293; Christians, 209–11, 214; civilization, 171, 177–80; criminal prisoners, 62; Fatherland, 176; identity, 228; Jews/Jewish-, 5, 9, 10, 37, 226, 245–61, 295, 297; language, 158; masculinity/men, 4, 8, 160, 172, 191, 222; memory, 203; military, 171, 182, 187, 191, 208; nation, 179, 293; nationalism, 8, 172, 189, 228; occupation, 161; oppression, 99; ordinary, 3, 29; pacificism, 292; perpetrators, 3, 17–18, 28–29, 155; police (gendarmes), 38, 40–41, 157–58, 163; political prisoners, 62; postwar, 4, 9, 32, 159, 208; prisoners-of-war, 249; race, 183; society, 34, 149, 183, 186–87, 207; soldier, 3, 5, 10, 28, 155, 163, 176, 178, 187–89, 192, 289; theologians, 6, 9, 203, 208, 214; war effort, 22; women, 20, 66, 148, 156, 163.

German Protestant theologians. *See* theologians

Germany, 6, 9, 27, 107, 134, 149, 152, 154, 172, 176–77, 180–82, 186, 189, 191–92, 203, 205, 210–11, 222–26, 229, 237, 240, 245–46, 248, 251–58, 296; Imperial, 149; medieval, 173; Nazi, 3, 152, 159, 181, 190, 222, 248, 253, 289, 291–92; postwar, 4, 9, 208; West, 207, 256

Gestapo, 152, 156–58, 208, 211

ghetto, 5, 6, 7, 21, 24–25, 38–41, 59, 100, 104–10, 113, 116–17, 119–23, 153, 157, 160, 181, 276, 279, 296–97, 299; ghettoization, 5; policeman, 17–18, 39–41. *See also* Lodz Ghetto; Warsaw Ghetto

God, 32–34, 40–41, 60, 84, 91–92, 102, 113, 122–23, 171, 177–78,

180–81, 188, 208, 239; -less(ness), 176–77, 190, 293. *See also* faith; prayer; religion
gray zone, 21, 35, 172
Great Britain. *See* United Kingdom
Gypsy. *See* Sinti and Roma

hair, 24, 54, 60, 115, 141, 235, 248, 290; -cut, 66, 235; -dresser, 67; -less, 232; -style, 235
hard, 26–27, 90, 150, 234, 277, 293; body, 231; labor, 64; like Krupp, 150, 231; masculinity, 288, 292, 298; work(ing), 10, 53, 65–66, 72, 86
hardness, 17, 27, 22, 81, 147, 150, 287, 290–93
hardship, 25, 175–76, 179, 189, 255–56, 290
hate, 34, 85, 105, 107, 181; -ful, 36
hegemonic, 31, 72, 135, 139, 141, 144, 206, 287, 292–95; heterosexuality, 159; non-, 138–39, 254
hegemonic masculinity, 4, 7, 8. 9, 34–35, 136, 141, 143, 148, 224, 239–40, 252, 255–58, 268, 293–95; counter-, 256; non-, 254. *See also* masculinity
hegemony, 35, 130, 139, 260, 294
Heimat, 162, 176, 178, 191, 226; *-film*, 225–27. *See also* home
hero, 117, 181, 185, 229, 259, 275–77
heroic, 102, 119, 253, 271, 278; anti-, 25; male life writing, 108; masculinity, 280, 292, 298; warrior, 292
heroism, 113, 117, 271–72
heteronormative, 234, 252. *See also* normative
heterosexual, 53, 55, 57, 61, 65, 72, 227, 234–36, 239, 294. *See also* sexual

heterosexuality, 7, 58–59, 159, 236, 239; situational, 7, 53. *See also* sexuality
hiding, 18, 21, 24–25, 39, 110, 114–16, 120, 248; Jews in, 115, 120, 160
hierarchy, 8, 58, 68, 72, 136, 139, 148, 150, 188–89, 209, 247, 250, 261, 285, 288–91, 294–95, 299; camp, 39, 61, 140
Himmler (Heinrich), 28, 65, 67, 210
historiography, 18, 25, 78, 185, 254, 261
Hitler (Adolf), 150, 171–74, 184, 186, 222, 231, 238, 250, 280, 293, 299; army, 172, 193; regime, 105, 192
Hitler Youth, 150, 182–83, 189, 231
Höss (Rudolf), 27, 31–34, 64–65
Holocaust, 1, 4–10, 17–31, 35–42, 77–79, 94, 99, 101, 117, 129, 211, 236–38, 245, 247–48, 253, 261, 268–74, 277–81, 285–88, 291, 293, 296–97, 299; Americanization, 270; autobiography (life writing), 99, 103, 109, 114, 124; awareness, 237–38; denier, 228; education/educators, 9, 17, 237–38; gender analysis, 28; gendered experiences, 94–95; gendered perspective, 2; gendered research, 300; historiography, 78, 261; history, 2, 22, 29, 54, 278, 287; images, 268–70; legacy, 2; literature, 130–32; memorial, 237; metaphor, 130; moral challenge, 124; perpetrator, 3, 26, 29–30; post-, 9, 246, 248, 253, 256, 268, 281, 294; pre-, 4, 133; Remembrance Day, 230; studies/scholarship, 3, 4, 5, 10, 18–19, 28–29, 99, 161, 247, 261, 285–87, 297–98; survivor, 9, 22, 78–80, 117, 238, 246, 253, 272–75, 277–78; testimony, 17, 78–80, 129, 133, 142;

Holocaust *(continued)*
  unifying experience, 20; victim, 7, 10, 77–80, 84, 95, 116, 269–72, 275, 295; women, 2, 17, 19–21, 94–95. *See also* Shoah
home, 81, 95, 11, 131, 150, 163, 173–74, 177, 185–86, 191, 208, 225, 237, 248, 287, 290, 298; -front, 162, 172, 187; -land, 176, 223, 272, 274. See also *Heimat*
homoerotic, 234, 239, 288
homogeneous, 94, 141, 246
homophobia, 288
homosexual, 4, 7, 53, 61, 63–65, 69, 159, 238–39, 251, 288; gazing, 235. *See also* gay; same-sex; sexual
homosexuality, 53, 61, 64–66, 68, 80, 235, 239, 251, 288; situational, 7, 53, 61, 64. *See also* sexuality
homosocial, 4, 61, 229, 235–36; bonding, 4, 27–28; dynamic, 228; environment, 23, 135, 140, 176; relations, 8; settings, 129, 143
homosocialty, 288
honor, 37, 139–41, 144, 150, 158, 223, 229, 257, 290, 294–97, 299. *See also* dishonor; respectability
hope, 105, 107, 109, 115, 124, 136, 227; rechristianization, 207; religious, 113
hopelessness, 33, 41, 89, 278
household, 25, 235
humiliate(d), 109, 111, 140, 153
humiliating, 36, 54, 64, 112, 140, 153, 248
humiliation, 37, 70, 87, 152, 155, 159–61
Hungarian, 60, 86, 240
hunger, 10, 54, 57, 62, 68, 71, 80–81, 90–91, 106, 111. *See also* malnutrition; starvation

hunt(ing), 115, 155–56, 278; man-, 139, 180
husband, 102, 114–16, 213
hybrid/hybridity, 19, 101, 289
hygiene, 24–25, 65. *See also* filth
hypermasculine, 152, 288. *See also* masculine
hypermasculinity, 3, 148, 159, 161, 163, 299. *See also* masculinity

identity, 2, 53, 70, 78, 87, 102–103, 107, 114, 141, 147, 149, 206, 233, 251–52, 295; American, 269; collective, 136, 255; formation, 102, 247, 258; gender(ed), 8, 23, 25, 140, 248, 256; German, 228; heterosexual, 235; Jewish, 24, 250; male/masculine, 1, 5, 8, 9, 25, 38, 55, 141–43, 234, 250, 253, 256, 290, 295; national, 9, 176, 207, 222–25, 227; paradoxical, 254; Protestant, 204; self-, 172; sexual, 53, 59, 69–70; social, 38
ideology, 32, 178, 185, 233, 273, 298–99; antisemitic, 5; Nazi, 8, 20, 22, 56, 172–74, 176, 182–84, 186, 188–90, 192; racial, 188, 193
immoral, 183, 239, 290, 293. *See also* moral
indignity, 188. *See also* dignity
inferior; culture, 171; race, 154–55
intercourse, 72; sexual, 53, 72, 154; social, 138; undesirable, 154. *See also* sex; sexual
internment, 61, 65, 81–82, 250–51, 253; camp, 248–49; center, 6; experience, 252
intersection/ality, 2, 3, 22, 190, 238, 287
intoxication, 28, 150, 153, 288. *See also* alcohol

Subject Index

Israel, 4, 6, 9–10, 62, 113, 238, 245–46, 254, 257–61, 267–69, 271–80, 296–97
Israeli, 258, 260, 268, 273, 275–80; courage, 271; gender roles, 274; heroism, 271; independence, 272; Jews, 269, 274, 280; masculinity, 272; men, 277; nation-building, 257; society, 254, 257, 272; soldier, 267, 280; supermen, 273

Jew(s), 5, 6, 32, 35, 37, 39, 67, 104, 106, 108–16, 119–20, 124, 153, 155–58, 160, 179–81, 186–88, 192, 211, 238, 245, 257, 259, 267–71, 276, 280, 291–93, 296–97, 299; American, 268, 272–73, 290; assimilated, 24, 38, 103, 246, 299; Austrian, 250; effeminate, 273, 277; German (speaking), 5, 245–46, 253–56, 258, 260–61, 297; in hiding, 115, 120; Israeli, 269; masculinity, 3; new, 230; 160; non-military, 295; orthodox, 24, 38, 246–47, 250, 299
Jewish; *Bildungsbürger*, 10, 251; boys, 39, 63; captives, 156; character, 272–76, 278–79, 281; combatant, 259; communities, 35–37, 39, 124, 253, 268, 279, 297, 299; conscripts, 37; converts, 104; corpses, 158; counterdiscourse, 5; diaspora, 246; doctors/physicians, 6–7, 101, 103, 109, 120, 124, 287; Enlightenment, 4, 37; families, 246, 296; father, 26; fraternity, 37; gender relations, 36; ghetto police, 17–18, 38–39, 113, 116; girls, 153; historians, 110; identity, 24, 250; imagination, 273; immigration/immigrants/migration, 249, 254, 259, 276; influence, 180; internees, 251–52; male agency, 37–38, 295; (male) body, 4, 5, 37–39, 60, 158, 268–69, 273, 279; male youth, 259; masculinity, 2, 4, 5–6, 9–10, 22, 35–36, 39, 245, 247, 249, 254, 256–57, 261, 268–72, 274–75, 278–81, 297; men, 5, 7, 9–10, 20, 22, 24–26, 35–39, 41, 251, 255–56, 260–61, 268, 272–73, 281, 285–86, 295–96; nation, 256; passivity, 271; population, 116, 236; prisoner (inmate), 7, 63, 160, 294, 299; redemptive masculinity, 279–80; refugees, 6, 9, 245–47, 253–54, 261, 299; self-defense, 258–59; settlement, 254, 259; soul, 106; strongman, 5; suffering, 112, 271; survivor, 155, 157; tragic masculinity, 10, 280; veterans, 295; victims, 6, 10, 104, 270, 274; women, 20, 25, 60, 80, 152–54, 285–86; world domination, 34. *See also* ghetto; Judaism
Jewish Councils (*Judenrat/räte*), 24, 35, 110–11, 272
Judaism, 36–37, 179, 186, 276. *See also* Rabbi; religion

kapo, 55, 58, 60, 62, 67–68, 72, 212
kibbutz, 6, 255–56, 273, 275–79
killing fields, 1, 6, 147, 153, 159–60
kindness, 23, 105

labor camp. *See* camps
labor(er), 3, 64–65, 68, 81, 212, 255–56, 267, 278–79, 297; camps, 6, 23, 78; division of, 25; in labor (childbirth), 118; slave, 37, 65
Latvia, 161
Lithuania, 110, 161
Lodz Ghetto, 119–20. *See also* ghetto

Lutheran. *See* theologian

male, 3, 4, 7, 9, 20, 22–25, 29–30, 38, 41, 55, 61, 80, 90, 92, 101, 148–52, 156, 159, 161, 176, 213, 227–28, 121–35, 237, 247, 256, 259, 273, 275, 286–93; agency, 1, 3, 6, 21, 29, 31, 34–35, 37–39, 41, 214, 297; Aryan, 231; authority, 32, 41; autobiography (life writings), 101–103, 108, 116, 124; behavior, 19, 26, 78, 80, 85, 87, 92–94; body, 5, 31, 37–39, 231–32, 235, 258, 268–70, 273, 279, 297; bond(ing), 3, 6, 23, 39, 92, 151, 155, 159, 254, 288, 291; camps, 64, 66, 71; companionship, 23; comradeship, 150; doctor/physician, 99, 103, 109, 124, 287; domination/dominance, 31, 160–62, 175, 296, 299; eros, 3; experience, 1, 21–22, 29, 77, 83; fellowship, 162; friendship, 23; gender(ed), 2, 6, 7, 9, 18–19, 29, 31, 39, 83, 86, 93, 148, 204, 296; hardness, 33; honor, 140–41, 144, 295, 297; identity, 1, 7, 9, 141–43, 289–90, 294, 297; Jewish body, 4, 5, 37–39, 268, 273, 279; kapo, 60; marker, 17–18; memoirs (survivor accounts), 78, 81–83, 87–88, 94; narratives, 83, 87–88, 93; norms, 18, 80, 83; perpetrator, 3, 21, 26–30, 33, 286, 298; politics, 147, 149; power, 53, 152, 155, 160; prisoners (inmates), 8, 53, 56, 58–59, 70–71, 86, 95, 129, 140–42, 161, 214; privilege, 35; respectability, 3; sexuality, 7, 54, 68, 72–73; solidarity, 292; subjectivity, 204; survivor, 23, 54, 56–57, 78, 80, 83, 87, 91, 93, 273; testimony, 17, 22–24, 80, 87; unmarked, 299; victim, 38, 78, 94–95, 254, 268, 270, 273, 281; virility, 72; warrior, 231; weakness, 33. *See also* maleness; masculine; unmanly

maleness, 6, 18, 36, 224, 229, 237, 299; Austrian, 224–25; 232–37; conceptions of, 77, 150; presence of, 18; unmarked, 10, 286. *See also* manliness; masculinity

malnutrition, 56, 132, 135, 267. *See also* hunger; starvation

manhood, 23, 38, 160, 163, 173, 204, 234, 250, 256, 275, 287. *See also* maleness; manliness; masculinity

manhunt, 139, 180. *See also* hunt(ing)

manliness, 8, 35, 56, 134, 140–41, 144, 147–48, 150, 183, 188, 210, 251–52, 258, 289–91, 293; fascist, 231. *See also* maleness; manhood; masculinity; unmanliness

manly, 22, 162, 208–209, 211, 214, 231, 251, 253, 256, 271, 273, 278, 287, 290, 295; church, 210. *See also* unmanly

marginal, 3, 7, 20–21, 35, 132, 247, 261; -ity, 36; -ization, 104, 135, 138–39, 143, 210, 286; -ized, 9, 20–21, 152, 173, 210, 226, 231, 247, 253; masculinity 7, 35

marked; male body/masculinity, 36, 147, 150, 258; whiteness, 257. *See also* unmarked

martial, 9, 21, 33, 151, 204, 211, 292, 296, 298; ideal, 156; Jewish masculinity, 274; language, 33; masculinity, 8, 150, 289, 295, 298–99

martyr, 185; -dom, 183, 213; -ed, 111, 113; -ium, 213

masculine, 6, 17, 61, 71, 105, 114, 149–50, 154, 173–75, 227, 239, 257, 287; behavior, 152, 227; discourse, 100; fascist, 223; identification,

233; identity, 5, 8, 9, 25, 38, 55, 234, 250–53, 256, 297; honor, 295; hyper-, 152, 288; ideal, 148, 150, 156, 223; non-, 289; norms, 10, 294; power, 154, 156; sexuality, 61, 72; sociability, 149; virtue, 162. *See also* male; manly

masculinity, 1–10, 17–31, 33–39, 42, 55, 72, 77, 80, 129–30, 135, 140–43, 147–55, 158–60, 162, 172, 176, 191, 203–204, 207, 211, 213–14, 221–38, 240, 245, 247, 250, 255–57, 261, 268–70, 277, 285–300; American, 268, 270, 272; Aryan, 152, 231; Austrian, 9, 222–40; compassionate, 293; complicit, 35, 294–95; controlled, 226, 234; deviant, 252; dominant, 30–31, 33, 35–38, 238–39; fascist, 27, 221, 230; fluid/ity, 34, 289, 295; German, 8, 222; hard, 26 288, 292–93; Hebrew, 255–56; heroic, 280, 292, 298; heteronormative, 252; imperial, 103; Israeli, 272, 277; Jewish, 2, 4, 5, 6, 9–10, 22, 35–36, 39, 245, 247, 249, 254, 256–57, 261, 268–72, 274–75, 278–81, 297; loss of, 70; marginal, 7, 35; marked, 147, 150, 258; martial, 8, 150, 289, 295, 298–99; military, 235, 271, 289–90, 294; militarized, 21, 27, 175–76, 191, 237–38; multiple, 245, 254, 260, 298; muscular, 10, 232, 296; Nazi, 3, 148, 154; nonaggressive, 227; normative, 23, 30, 34–37, 286; ordinary, 3, 27–28, 77; performative, 156, 159, 235, 291, 299; post-Holocaust, 2, 294; redemptive, 10, 279–81; resistant, 35; soft, 237; soldierly, 33, 147, 294; stoic, 292; strong, 33; subordinate, 7, 34–35, 39, 136, 141, 143, 260; tough, 26, 288; tragic, 10, 270–72, 278, 280; unmarked, 286; warrior, 232; white, 30; *Yekke*, 259; Zionist, 256. *See also* critical masculinity studies; hegemonic masculinity; hypermasculinity

massacre, 110, 156–57

masturbation, 55–57, 64, 68

Mauthausen, 65–69, 93. *See also* camps

memory, 9, 101, 132, 203, 205, 252, 254, 259, 261, 290

men. *See* maleness; manliness; masculinity

men's studies. *See* critical masculinity studies

migration, 245–47, 249, 254–55, 261, 296. *See also* refugee

militarism, 207, 260; *Gesinnungsmilitarismus*, 207, 214; Prussian, 148, 150

military, 9, 66, 162, 171–75, 181–85, 187–91, 208, 223, 229, 235–36, 255, 258, 260, 285–86, 292, 296; campaign, 162; career, 189, 259; conscription, 173, 191; defeat, 155, 193; ethos, 299; formation, 151, 258; honor, 299; institution, 21; leadership, 184; masculinity, 235, 271, 289–90, 294; para-, 4, 147, 149, 209, 259, 288; service, 175–76, 183, 191, 209, 234–37, 296; training, 183, 255. *See also* soldier *Wehrmacht*

misogyny/misogynist, 20, 27, 288, 291

Mittelbau-Dora, 66, 69. *See also* camps

mobile killing units. See *Einsatzgruppen*

moral, 54, 71, 100, 105, 108, 117, 119–21, 123–24, 181, 186–87, 213, 255, 290–91, 299; agency, 39, 204; ambiguity/ambivalence,

moral *(continued)*
41, 85, 172; authority, 34; code, 162; courage, 109; cowardice, 187; decision-making, 29; discourse, 100; framework, 192; grammar, 28; judgment, 124, 214; loophole, 122; reasoning, 120, 125; refusal, 121; repair, 26; repugnance, 87; responsibility, 28, 32; restraint, 29; wrong question, 20. *See also* immoral
morality, 117, 119–20, 122–23, 279
mother, 25, 32, 40–41, 80, 82, 86, 118–21, 210, 232–33, 235, 248, 278, 288
motherhood, 21
Muselmänner, 6, 8, 35, 129–44, 295
Muslim, 133–35, 257
muscular, 275–76; Jewish men, 273; masculinity, 10, 232, 296; male body, 297
Muskeljudentum, 4, 36, 273. *See also* muscular

naked, 54, 153–55, 160–61, 267, 270; -ness, 161
narrative, 1, 7, 18, 40–41, 62, 78–81, 83, 87–88, 92, 94–95, 99–100, 108–109, 111, 114–19, 124, 133, 136, 142, 205, 207, 254, 260, 268–69, 271–72, 277, 279–81; autobiographical, 102–103; erasure, 6, 23; female/women, 91, 93, 102, 119; flow, 20; frame, 81, 269; historical, 80, 115, 273; judgment, 133; life, 101–102, 107, 114, 120, 124, 245; master, 21, 207, 257; male, 83, 87–88, 93; *Muselman*, 130–32; redemptive, 268; self-, 246, 252–53, 257; strategy, 17, 23, 33; tropes, 257

nation, 9, 27, 102, 105, 108, 111, 113, 179, 189, 224, 227, 234, 240, 256–57, 280, 293, 298
national, 179, 209, 256, 279; belonging, 176; ethos, 254; ideology, 3; identity, 9, 176, 207, 222–25, 227; obligation, 183; pride, 234, 299; propaganda, 176; self-fashioning, 279; trans-, 45–46; unity, 208
nationalism, 37, 180, 228, 231, 237; German, 8, 172, 189, 228; modern, 37
nationalist, 33, 179, 193, 232, 255–56, 259–60, 273
nationality, 132, 240
nationhood, 229, 231, 240
National Socialism/Socialist, 6, 27, 134, 142, 147–51, 154, 158–59, 163, 207–208, 212, 222–28, 231, 233, 235–37, 239–40, 249. *See also* Nazi Party
nation-state, 22
Nazi, 3, 4, 5, 7, 19, 21, 24, 32–38, 53, 72, 78, 100, 107–10, 112–13, 116–20, 124, 142, 148, 150, 156, 173, 178, 189–81, 185–93, 204, 207, 209–10, 212, 222, 225, 230, 236, 238, 245, 247–49, 252, 254, 260, 267–68, 277, 285–86, 291, 293, 295–99; camps (concentration), 7, 8, 20, 30, 33, 53–54, 57, 65, 70–71, 73, 79, 85, 129, 132, 135, 213, 294; career, 32–33; Germany, 3, 152, 159, 181, 190, 222, 248, 253, 289, 291–92; ideology, 8, 20, 22, 56, 172–74, 176, 178, 181–84, 186, 188–90, 192–93; masculinity, 3, 148, 154; perpetrator, 8, 17, 31; persecution, 80, 132, 285, 296; propaganda, 8, 36, 172, 174, 176, 179, 188–89, 298; regime, 9, 34,

Subject Index

147, 152, 182–83, 187, 192, 207, 271; soldier, 6, 8; state, 27, 65. *See also* denazification

Nazi Party (NSDAP), 147, 186–87, 209–10, 225, 236. *See also* National Socialism

Nazism, 2, 4, 9, 22, 36–37, 158, 171–73, 177, 179–81, 183–87, 190–92, 208, 211, 253

Neuengamme, 58, 66. *See also* camps

non-absence, 7, 29–31, 33, 35–37, 41; double, 7, 34, 37, 39, 41

normative, 29–31, 36, 81; assumption, 22, 40; behavior, 86, 92–93; discourse, 31; masculinity, 23, 30, 34–37, 286; operation, 18; presence, 5; voice, 41. *See also* heteronormative

normativity, 34

nudity. *See* naked

NSDAP. *See* Nazi Party

obedience, 184, 292; dis-, 53

ordinary, 29, 54, 109; German soldiers, 289; German women, 3; masculinity, 3, 27–28, 77; men, 21, 292, 298

Ordinary Men, 29

orthodox. *See* Jews; Russian Orthodox Church

Palestine, 9, 83, 245–46, 254–59, 272–73, 276, 279, 296–97

paramilitary. *See* military

passive, 72, 187, 268–69, 273–75, 281, 296; *Muselmänner*, 140 ; victim, 130, 268, 277; voice, 31, 34, 40

passivity, 271–72, 277, 287

patriarch, 275, 278

patriarchal, 20, 22, 72, 140, 286–87, 291, 294–96

patriarchy, 237, 288, 299

performance, 8, 66, 138, 153, 225, 245, 252, 299

performativity, 224–25, 235, 242

persecution, 25, 38, 80, 132, 187, 255, 285, 296

perpetrator, 1–10, 26–29, 31–32, 33, 35, 41, 64, 70–71, 77, 92, 148, 151, 153–58, 161–62, 286, 288, 292, 295, 207, 299; female, 4; German, 17–18, 28–29, 155; male, 3, 21, 26–30, 33, 286, 298; Nazi, 8, 17, 31; ordinary, 29. *See also Einsatzgruppen*; Gestapo; SA; SS

physician. *See* doctors

Pipel, 39, 61–63, 65, 65–69. *See also* boy

plundered/ing, 152–53, 162

Pohl (Oswald), 33–34, 66

Poland, 5, 29, 99, 101, 103, 107–108, 117, 237, 291

police, 27, 154, 277–78; auxiliary, 157; Battalion, 28–29, 157, 291–92; camp-, 67; (Jewish) ghetto, 1, 18, 39–41, 113, 116, 123, 163; Jewish Settlement, 259; German, 38, 41, 156, 158; officer, 277; Security, 153; SS and, 147–48, 152–54, 158–59, 163, 222

Polish, 56–57, 59, 62–63, 103, 105, 109–10, 136, 156, 182; block supervisor, 83; patriotism, 103; political prisoner, 59, 63; prison, 32; survivor, 55, 59

postwar, 6, 34, 204, 207, 225–27, 292; Austria, 224, 226–27, 231–34, 238; autobiography, 9, 207, 211, 214; Germans/Germany, 4, 9, 32, 159, 208; German memory, 203; historiography, 185; Holocaust survivors, 246; Jewish community,

postwar *(continued)*
  253, 297; refugees, 5; trials, 27; writings, 27, 34
POW/prisoner of war, 177, 192, 208, 249
power, 1, 3, 5, 10, 22, 34–35, 38, 53, 56, 63–65, 68, 70–73, 104, 138–39, 142, 148, 152, 154–55, 159–60, 172, 177–78, 234, 245, 247, 250–54, 271, 285–86, 294, 298–99; absolute, 3, 53, 57, 69–70, 148; asymmetrical, 3, 64; bonding, 3, 27; imperial, 230; male, 53, 152, 155, 160; position, 31; relations, 3, 6, 237; structure, 5, 35, 63–64, 73, 261, 298; total, 185; women, 3
powerless, 86, 138, 268; -ness, 89, 112, 130, 268, 289. *See also* disempowerment
prayer, 81–82, 91–92, 94, 113, 189; shawl, 112. *See also* faith; God
preservation, 70; self-, 136, 138, 140–41. *See also* resilience; survival
privilege, 1, 3, 30, 35, 53, 60, 65–67, 71–72, 85, 88–89, 82, 99, 131, 139; in camp hierarchy, 39; kapo, 60; non-, 138; men, 22; prisoners, 8, 58, 62–63, 70, 72, 138, 212; *Sonderkommando*, 89; under-, 233; white masculinity/males, 30, 101
priest. *See* Catholic; clergy
prisoner (inmate), 1, 7, 8, 23, 53–54, 56–59, 61–72, 81, 83–89, 93–94, 129–44, 151, 160–61, 177, 208, 211–14, 267, 294–95, 299; criminal, 62; elite, 60; female/women, 58–61, 66, 71, 95, 129, 135, 153–54; functionary, 62, 67–69, 138–39; hierarchy, 58; political, 59, 61–63, 66; privileged, 58, 63, 67, 72, 138, 212

propaganda, 181, 232; anti-Bolshevik, 191; Bolshevik, 182; Nazi, 8, 36, 172, 174, 176, 179, 188–89, 298
prostitute/prostitution, 65–66, 154
protection, 55, 59, 62, 64, 71–72, 129, 152, 163, 182, 211
Protestant, 204, 209–11, 293; church, 9, 177, 184, 207, 209; -ism, 207; theologians, 6, 9, 203, 207–208, 211
Prussia. *See* militarism
punish(ed), 53, 60, 64, 212–13; -able, 152, 184
punishment, 62, 161, 213, 152

queer, 3. *See also* gay; homosexual

Rabbi, 38, 112, 250–51, 253, 256. *See also* Judaism
race, 3, 4, 38, 88, 148, 162, 183, 188, 285, 298; defilement (*Rassenschande*), 152; inferior, 154
racial, 30, 162, 179, 247, 257, 293; antisemitism, 179, 182; bio-, 36; idea, 56; ideal, 149; ideology, 188, 193; inferior, 155; -ized, 22, 39; purity, 232; state, 154; superiority, 178, 183; war, 163; worldview, 173
racist, 130, 134, 190; agenda, 209; discrimination, 257; ideology, 285; language, 187; sentiment, 192
rape(d), 20, 53, 59, 61–64, 71, 117, 152–55, 158, 160, 162–63, 291. *See also* abuse; assault; violence
Ravensbrück, 65–66. *See also* camps
refugee, 5, 111, 249–50, 252, 260, 275, 277–78; Jewish, 6, 9, 245–47, 253–54, 261, 297, 299. *See also* migration
religion, 57, 105, 134, 171, 174, 176–77, 179, 181, 191, 206, 214, 298. *See also* Catholicism; Christianity; faith; God; Judaism; prayer; Rabbi; spiritual

Subject Index

remasculinization, 69, 296–97, 299.
  See also emasculation
resilience, 10, 38, 287, 296. *See also*
  preservation
resistance, 35, 37–38, 63, 69–70, 106,
  113, 117, 120, 172, 182–88, 190–91,
  213, 256, 272, 295–97
respect, 148, 207, 230; -able, 290;
  self-, 251
respectability, 3, 35, 141, 148. *See also*
  honor
responsibility, 31, 33, 84, 86, 95, 121,
  123, 192, 222, 237–40, 278; moral,
  28, 32
revenge, 23, 163, 180–81, 258
ritual, 82, 87, 151, 155–56, 161, 229;
  drinking, 149, 151, 158, 288; festive,
  161; humiliation, 160; manly, 200;
  martial, 151, purity laws, 38
Russia, 171, 177–79, 182, 186, 192, 290.
  See also Belorussia; Soviet Union
Russian, 62, 155, 161, 163, 174,
  177–78, 181–82, 188; civilian, 190;
  hordes, 163; prisoners-of-war, 208;
  village, 154; women, 153

SA (Stormtrooper), 4, 149–51, 209.
  See also perpetrator; SS
Sachsenhausen, 52, 62, 66, 211–12,
  253. *See also* camps
sacrifice, 10, 176, 191, 290, 293
same-sex. *See* sex
Schmuckstück, 141–42
selection, 70, 78, 80–81, 87, 95, 100,
  120, 123–24
seminarian. *See* Catholic; theologian
sex, 7, 8, 19, 30, 38, 53, 57–58, 60–61,
  64, 71–72, 153–54, 232; same-, 143,
  234, 239. *See also* intercourse
sexual, 39, 55–62, 64–66, 68–72,
  151–54, 156, 158, 160–62, 214,
  233, 250–52, 287, 290–91, 294,
296; abuse, 63, 65, 71, 162; assault,
  8, 26, 38, 152, 154, 159, 162–63;
  barter, 71; body, 55, 71; desire,
  55–58, 278; domination, 152, 154,
  160, 250, 252; exploitation, 59, 62,
  72; humiliation, 152–53, 159–61;
  hyper-, 159; identity, 53, 59, 69–70;
  relation(ship), 7, 38, 53, 57–62,
  66, 69, 71, 213, 239; slave(ry), 53,
  64, 69–72; study of, 2; torture,
  161; violation, 38; violence, 19,
  26, 28, 64, 70–72, 148, 152–59,
  161–62, 291. *See also* desexualized;
  heterosexual; homosexual; rape;
  sex
sexuality, 7, 21–22, 30, 35, 53–54,
  56–58, 61, 64, 70–73, 162, 206–207,
  231, 237–39, 270, 278, 286, 298. *See
  also* heterosexuality; homosexuality;
  male
shamed/ashamed, 8, 54, 84
Shoah, 18, 271. *See also* Holocaust
silence, 31, 87–88, 132, 183, 192, 206,
  252, 268; relegated to, 104; within
  silence, 38
silenced, 38, 224, 239; voice, 20
Sinti and Roma, 60, 67, 120
Six-Day War, 10, 268, 272–73, 280.
  See also war
slave labor, 37, 65. *See also* labor
slavery. *See* sexual
soldier, 1, 6, 8, 26, 41, 154–55,
  173–76, 182, 184, 191–92, 208, 212,
  292–94, 296, 298; Austrian, 222–23,
  232; Catholic, 293; German, 3, 5,
  10, 28, 155, 163, 176, 178, 187–89,
  192, 289; Israeli, 267, 272, 277, 280;
  of Christ, 293; Nazi, 6, 8; political,
  162; Soviet, 20, 163; *Wehrmacht*,
  153–54, 159, 163, 171. *See also* war;
  Wehrmacht
soldiering, 21

solidarity, 28, 93, 101, 143, 149–50, 179, 184, 202, 295, 300
son, 61, 82–83, 119, 156, 208, 248, 259–60; father- relations, 26, 83, 212
Sonderkommando, 6, 7, 39, 85–94, 160
Soviet, 161, 171, 178, 182, 186, 192; POWs, 67; soldier, 20, 163
Soviet Union, 176, 178, 180–81, 222, 296. *See also* Russia
spiritual, 82, 113, 171, 175–77, 180, 182, 184–85, 189, 191, 212, 233; brother, 189; healing, 106; health, 174; homeland, 176; injury, 38; manhood, 38; values, 183; weapons, 208, 212. *See also* faith; religion
SS (*Schutzstaffel*), 27, 53, 55–56, 58–61, 64–70, 72, 84, 88, 91–93, 134–35, 138, 140–41, 143, 148, 151, 153–54, 159–60, 162, 180, 212–13, 292, 296. *See also* perpetrator; SA
starvation, 91, 100, 115, 130, 133. *See also* hunger; malnutrition
starved/starving, 25, 56, 68, 84, 116, 129
status, 35, 71, 249, 294–95; brothel visitor, 68; Holocaust survivor, 253; *Muselmänner*, 295; victim, 253
sterilization, 59, 187
stoic(ism), 1, 292; masculinity, 292; suffering, 293
subhuman, 178–79, 188
subjugation, 154–55, 292
submission, 53, 60, 70, 183
suicide, 5, 59, 121
superiority, 152, 162, 178, 183, 223, 229, 233
survival, 7, 21–22, 25, 39, 54–55, 57, 59–60, 63, 70–71, 78, 87, 90–91, 94–95, 116, 119–20, 133, 135–36, 140–41, 143, 185, 189, 213, 295–96;

strategy, 59, 65, 71, 81, 94. *See also* preservation; resilience
survivor, 1, 9, 22, 29, 32, 54–56, 58–59, 61–62, 69, 78–79, 85, 92, 133, 137, 151, 155, 157, 160–61, 238, 246, 253, 271–72, 275, 277–79; account, 79, 81, 87, 94, 129, 132, 140, 140–43; child, 117; female, 55, 57, 81, 87; male, 23, 54, 56–57, 78, 80, 83, 87, 91, 93, 273; women, 7, 141; testimony, 38, 78–81

taboo, 38, 56, 80, 236
tattoo(ing), 87, 235
terror, 89, 116, 119, 147, 173, 178, 286–88, 296–97
testicular assault, 38. *See also* assault
testimony, 17–18, 23–25, 29, 31, 38, 58, 61, 63–64, 78–80, 83–84, 86–87, 94, 104–105, 110, 119, 129–30, 133, 136, 142–43, 213, 252, 288; male/men, 22–24, 80, 87, 94; male-authored, 17; oral, 6; survivor, 38, 78–81; unpublished, 63; written, 8, 79, 94. *See also* witness
theologian, 6, 9, 203–204, 206–11, 213–14; Lutheran, 209. *See also* clergy; Protestant
threat, 20–21, 24–25, 35, 60, 71, 120, 149, 151, 177, 183, 185, 210, 213, 235, 288. *See also* death
tough, 27, 276–77, 280; masculinity, 26, 288; Jewish man, 281; like leather, 150, 231; men, 82, 147
toughness, 27, 77, 81, 147, 150–51, 292
torture, 45, 59, 64, 93, 104, 155, 161–62, 275; sexual, 161
training, 100, 151, 173, 175–76, 183, 189, 233, 255, 259, 290. *See also* military

trauma, 39; -tic, 289

Ukraine, 156
Ukrainian, 161–62, 180; guards, 117; women, 153
Umschlagplatz, 113, 117
United Kingdom (England/Great Britain), 222, 248–49, 252, 254
United States, 6, 27, 222, 236, 252, 269, 279, 296. *See also* America(n)
unmanliness, 130, 135, 139, 290. *See also* manliness
unmanly, 8, 134, 140, 142, 144, 223, 256, 272, 293. *See also* manly
unmarked (men/masculinity), 11, 30–31, 36, 286–87, 297, 299. *See also* marked

victim, 1, 4, 20, 23, 26, 29, 35, 41, 62, 64–65, 70, 78, 85, 89, 93–94, 104, 106 113, 119–20, 130, 143, 152–57, 160–63, 182, 230, 250, 268, 272, 277–78, 280, 286, 297, 299; first of Nazism, 9, 222–23, 225, 237–40; Holocaust, 7, 77–78, 80, 84, 94–95, 116, 269–72, 274–75, 295; male, 24, 38, 78, 254, 268, 270; sexual abuse/violence, 65, 71, 153
victimhood, 230
victimization, 1, 78, 272, 286
victimized, 25, 230, 281, 299
victimology, 19
violence, 8, 20, 28, 54, 63, 65, 90, 105, 130, 136, 138–39, 147–54, 159–62, 211–12, 227, 271–78; cultural, 188; gendered, 257; genocidal, 77; political, 149–50; sexual, 19, 26, 28, 64, 70–72, 148, 152–59, 161–62, 291. *See also* abuse; assault; rape
virile/virility, 72, 141, 148, 158, 161, 290

virtue, 293; hegemonic, 292; manly, 22; masculine, 162
völkisch, 3, 228
Volk, 27, 179
volksfremd, 228
Volksgemeinschaft, 208, 231, 228, 293

vulnerability, 141; feminine, 270; narrative, 272
vulnerable, 24, 270; *Muselmänner*, 8

Waldheim (Kurt), 235–36, 240
war, 4, 8, 9, 22, 27, 61, 63, 66, 72, 93, 101, 105, 107–108, 114–15, 117, 147, 172, 174–75, 177–82, 184, 188–93, 207–11, 222–23, 225, 232–34, 236, 238, 249, 253, 257–59, 271, 276, 279, 288–90, 292–94, 296, 298; annihilation, 163, 289; defensive, 178, 182, 186, 188; extermination, 174, 181. *See also* Six-Day War; World War I; World War II
warrior, 184, 190, 231–32; fascist, 233; heroic, 292; masculinity, 232. *See also* fighter
Warsaw Ghetto, 104, 108–12, 114, 116–17, 160, 237; Uprising, 114, 271; Ghetto Fighters' Memorial, 237. *See also* ghetto
weak, 8, 81, 135, 140, 152, 183, 255, 267–70, 273–74, 277, 287, 291
weakened, 131, 134–35, 138, 142, 144, 295–96
weakling, 291–92
weakness, 28, 33, 81, 130, 134–35, 151–52, 287, 290, 293
Wehrmacht, 3, 6, 8, 153–54, 159, 162–63, 171–74, 180–81, 183–84, 188, 190, 192, 208, 222–23, 236, 290, 292. *See also* military; soldier

white; European, 270; masculinity 30; men/males, 101, 294; men's burden, 178
whiteness; marked, 257; studies, 30
witness(ing), 60, 62, 78–79, 85, 88, 92, 94, 104, 107, 109, 111, 114, 142–43, 152, 157, 160–61, 177, 180–81, 192, 203–204, 209, 212, 260, 271, 286; eye-, 87. *See also* testimony
women, 2, 3, 9, 18–30, 35, 37–38, 54–60, 65–67, 69–71, 77, 94–95, 102, 110, 112, 124, 148, 150, 152–53, 156, 160–63, 173, 175–76, 209–10, 213–14, 239, 247, 259, 276, 285–91, 294–96, 299–300; as mothers, 80; Auschwitz, 81, 93–95; autobiographical writing, 101; German, 20, 66, 148, 156, 163; -hating, 20; hiding, 24; Holocaust, 2, 17, 19–20, 95; Jewish, 20, 25, 60, 80, 152–54, 285–86; movement, 210, 237; naked, 160; non-Aryan, 8; prisoner, 129, 135; prostitution/brothel, 65–66; sexual behavior, 57; sexual violence, 26, 152–54, 159, 162, 291; survivor, 7, 141. *See also* doctors; female; feminist
wound, 115, 155, 225
wounded, 109–10, 229; children, 109; civilization, 103; gendered, 21; man, 290; soldier, 290
World War I (First World War), 4, 26, 37, 103, 107, 288–89, 295. *See also* war
World War II (Second World War), 3, 22, 28, 174, 176, 203, 207–208, 210, 221–24, 236–38, 270, 272, 279, 296, 299. *See also* war

Yekke, 9, 246, 248, 255, 257, 259, 261, 297; masculinity, 259
Yiddish, 61, 110
Yishuv, 254, 257, 259, 297

Zionism, 5, 37, 254–55, 273
Zionist, 245–46, 255–58, 260–61, 275; discourse, 256; ideals, 4, 10, 257, 296–97; imagination, 274; masculinity, 256; master narrative, 257; pioneer, 255; struggle, 258

www.ingramcontent.com/pod-product-compliance
Lightning Source LLC
Chambersburg PA
CBHW020330240426
43665CB00043B/200